Management Communication

Principles and Practice

Management Communication

PRINCIPLES AND PRACTICE

THIRD EDITION

Michael E. Hattersley
Former Course Head,
Management Communication,
Harvard Business School

Linda McJannet
Bentley College

Boston Burr Ridge, IL Dubuque, IA New York San Francisco St. Louis
Bangkok Bogotá Caracas Kuala Lumpur Lisbon London Madrid Mexico City
Milan Montreal New Delhi Santiago Seoul Singapore Sydney Taipei Toronto

The McGraw-Hill Companies

MANAGEMENT COMMUNICATION: PRINCIPLES AND PRACTICE
International Edition 2008

Published by McGraw-Hill/Irwin, a business unit of The McGraw-Hill Companies, Inc. 1221 Avenue of the Americas, New York, NY 10020.

10 09 08 07 06 05 04 03
20 09 08
CTF BJE

When ordering this title, use ISBN: 978-007-125926-2 or MHID: 007-125926-0

Printed in Singapore

www.mhhe.com

About the Authors

MICHAEL ELKINS HATTERSLEY graduated from Swarthmore College and received his Ph.D from Yale University in 1976. He has worked as communication director or consultant for major companies, governments, academic institutions, and nonprofit organizations. From 1985 to 1993 he taught in and headed the Management Communication course at Harvard Business School.

LINDA McJANNET (formerly LINDA McJ. MICHELI) graduated from Wellesley College and received her Ph.D. from Harvard University. She has taught at Harvard Business School, and she is currently Professor of English at Bentley College in Waltham, MA. She is the coauthor of *Managerial Communication* (Scott, Foresman, 1984).

This book is dedicated to our parents (in memoriam)
Enid Valerie Elkins Hattersley,
E. Vanness Hattersley,
Antoinette D. McJennett, and
John F. McJennett.

Contents

Preface

To the Student

This book covers the range of communication issues a manager will face in the coming decade. It addresses enduring issues—how to write well, how to speak well, how to devise a successful communication strategy—as well as evolving issues, such as how to make the best use of telecommunications technology.

We have subtitled the book *Principles and Practice* for two reasons. Most of the *principles* of effective communication have been well researched and documented in work going back to the ancient Greeks. These include defining a clear *goal*, analyzing the *context* in which you're operating, understanding the needs and interests of your *audience*, defining an appropriate *message*, choosing the right *media*, and providing ample opportunity for *feedback*. The *practice* in the text consists of a collection of classic and contemporary cases which address a representative range of organizational communication challenges. These invite you to move from the abstract to the concrete: Given my analysis of this real situation, what should I do, write, or say?

Communication is a tricky subject both to teach and to learn. In one way or another, all of us have been communicating for our whole lives. While the principles of effective communication have been well established and documented, the practice is the hard part. Every student has his or her own background, personality, values, strengths, weaknesses, and personal goals. Consequently, when reading each chapter or preparing each case, you must constantly weigh two factors: What do I believe, and what can I learn from how my audiences react to me?

This text offers a wide variety of opportunities to look at yourself as a credible source, a writer, a speaker, a meeting participant, a strategist—in short, a manager. Learn from the principles we teach, but learn more from the reactions you get—from your teacher, your classmates, and yourself. A course in management communication may be the last opportunity you have to get unbiased feedback in a supportive learning environment. Being praised is easy. Taking constructive criticism is hard, but you'll learn more if you let yourself hear it.

No book can include everything every manager should know about communication; consequently, we regularly refer the reader to additional resources on writing, speaking, the use of graphics, how to work in meetings or groups, managing crisis communication, bringing about change, maximizing effective use of the Internet, negotiations and conflict resolution, and how to communicate well both internally and externally. We do not pretend to tell you all you should know about interpersonal relationships, organizational behavior, marketing, or public relations, although each of these topics come into play in the following pages.

Some would argue that good writing and good speaking are out of date on the information highway. Nothing could be further from the truth. The same principles that applied to delivering a good speech in the Roman Senate apply to sending an effective E-mail message. People must trust you, you must get their attention, you need to be in command of your material, and you must have a clear road map to get where you're going. You also need to demonstrate that your idea is superior to the alternatives in the marketplace. This text will help you master the full range of skills required by a successful manager.

To the Instructor

This text, aimed at advanced undergraduates and MBA candidates, is evenly divided between *principles* (how to communicate based on best current research) and *practice* (cases that put students in the roles of decision-makers and communicators in real business situations). We also include guides on writing and speaking, which students can refer to both during the course and for the rest of their careers. Given the increasing pervasiveness of electronic communications, consider encouraging students to read and discuss Chapter 15 early in the course.

Management communication courses (by whatever name) range from electives on writing and speaking to required courses covering all aspects of communication strategy. Often, the courses face constraints of time, scheduling, and resources. We have tried to provide a flexible package, adaptable to these varying circumstances. The *Teacher's Manual*, written by the authors, includes scheduling advice, an overview of best-practice case teaching, suggested assignments, and detailed teaching notes on each case.

Pieces of these materials are available elsewhere; many instructors, for example, use a good style guide, articles on particular types of communication such as speaking and graphics, and cases ordered from Harvard Business School Press or elsewhere. Here, we pull all these materials together. We also address a number of current (and future) issues hardly touched on by other pedagogical materials, such as personal and organizational ethics, multicultural and electronic communication, and managing diversity.

Some schools offer only limited communication training because they don't believe that the field has been sufficiently defined or that good teaching materials are available. This text aims to fill that gap. In considering whether to adopt *Management Communication*, we suggest that the instructor alternate reading the text chapter and case and the matching chapter in the *Teacher's Manual*. This will suggest how theory, experience, and practice can be joined in each class or module.

Acknowledgments

The authors would like to thank all their colleagues, especially those with whom they taught at Harvard Business School, among them Robert W. Kent, Linda Doyle, Frank V. Cespedes, Thomas J. Raymond, Donald Byker, Gwen L. Nagel, Mary Gentile, Susan Kelly, Sally Seymour, Thomas Piper, Ellen D. Herman, J. Janelle Shubert, S. Lindsay Craig, and Sharon M. Livesey. We learned a great deal from each of them.

We especially thank David T. Harkins and Michael O'Shea for their personal and technical support, and Harvard Business School Press for permission to use some of the following material.

We also thank the reviewers for their valuable insights and suggestions in refining the manuscript. These include Robert W. Kent, Harvard Business School (retired); Charlotte Rosen, Cornell University; J. Douglas Andrews, University of Southern California; John D. Stegman, Ohio State University; Joanne Yates, Massachusetts Institute of Technology; Sherron Kenton, Emory University; Christine Kelley, New York University; Dr. Billy F. Broun, William Carey College on the Coast; Kathleen A. Fitzgerald, University of Maryland, College Park; Lon Addams, Weber State University; Sandra Stark, University of Wisconsin, Madison; Donna Luse, University of Louisiana at Monroe; Beverly Y. Langford, Georgia State University; Robert H. Stowers, College of William & Mary; Anne Orinals, University of Illinois, Champaign; Brian Polk, Penn State Abington; Kristen DeTienne, Brigham Young University; Mary J. Faure, The Ohio State University; Cynthia C. Barnes, Lamar University; Gary F. Kohut, The University of North Carolina at Charlotte; Richard L. Jines, Oakland City University; Henrietta Shirk, Montana Tech of the University of Montana.

Management Communication

Principles and Practice

PART ONE

Principles of Effective Communication

CHAPTER 1

Foundations of Management Communication

In business, as in most other areas of life, the best idea in the world can fail if it's not communicated effectively. How clearly and persuasively you present your information and recommendation matters as much as how well you've analyzed your data or how sensibly you've outlined a course of action. This book offers exercises to strengthen yourself as a business communicator.

Two schools of thought have dominated the teaching of business communication. One, derived from behavioral science, emphasizes that an organization, like an organism, has very complex communication pathways. This school has developed important concepts, such as an emphasis on the need to shape your communication to the situation of your audience. At the same time, it tends to downplay the importance—and opportunity—of the individual.

The other dominant school argues that effective business communication entails mastering proven techniques of writing and speaking. Many fine books explain how to avoid convoluted language, grammatical errors, passive expression, or technical jargon. This approach draws on a rhetorical tradition going back at least to the ancient Greeks, and it emphasizes the connection between clear thinking and clear communication. It also encourages the writer or speaker to take advantage of the vast resources of logic, evidence, persuasion, and imagery inherent in our language. At the same time, it tends to give too much attention to the communicator and too little attention to the context in which he or she is communicating.

Both the behavioral and rhetorical schools are right, and neither, alone, meets the full needs of the manager. Every communication is both situational (organizational) and personal (stylistic). Successful business communication depends on answering a few crucial questions: Have you mastered and organized all the relevant information? Have you taken into account the personal and organizational context? Have you defined a clear, achievable goal? Have you considered the needs of your audiences? Have you expressed yourself as clearly, vividly, and forcefully as possible? Have you chosen the right communication channels?

Managers send messages through writing, speaking, actions, gestures, electronic media, graphics, the grapevine, and force of personality. Good business people devote tremendous attention to shaping their message and deciding how to deliver it. Experienced managers insist that success depends largely on effective communication.

MANAGERS AND COMMUNICATION

As early as 1916, Henri Fayol defined the central functions of management as *planning* (developing an outline of things that need to be done), *organizing* (establishing a formal structure within which tasks are arranged and defined), *coordinating* (relating one aspect of the organization's work to other aspects), *commanding* (indicating what needs to be done, including rewards and penalties), and *controlling* (establishing a system capable of measuring how well the organization is doing). Researchers who have studied management empirically have found these categories to be useful but too rigid. In the 1970s, Henry Mintzberg identified 10 "working roles" that, in varying proportions, make up the manager's job: figurehead, leader, liaison, monitor, disseminator, spokesperson, entrepreneur, disturbance handler, resource allocator, and negotiator. Today, some of these terms might be translated as image-maker, motivator, or facilitator. Every one of these tasks requires effective communication to succeed.

As Mintzberg notes, "Verbal and written contacts *are* the manager's work." He goes on:

> Managers must be able to communicate easily and efficiently, and they must share a vision of the direction in which they wish to take their organization. If they cannot agree with reasonable precision on these "plans," then they will pull in different directions and the team (or organization) will break down.[1]

Mintzberg hits on a key point here: Effective communication, whether in response to a crisis or in service of a long-term plan, flows from a vision of success that includes, and motivates, your audience. This means that by the time you call the meeting, write the memo, initiate the conversation, send the E-mail, or give the speech, 90 percent of your communication work should already be done.

ELEMENTS OF COMMUNICATION

A communicator, or source, sends a message to a receiver, or audience, through chosen media, provoking a response. This feedback, in turn, often creates an ongoing dialogue. Building on this model, which originates early in the history of communication research, we suggest seven categories that will help you define and analyze any business communication situation:

SOURCE. This theme pervades the book. Who is initiating action, and why should she or he be believed? How can you become a credible and effective source?

[1]Henry Mintzberg, *The Nature of Managerial Work* (New York: Harper and Row, 1973), p. 180.

GOAL. What result do you seek? This will seem obvious at first, when you've received an assignment or gotten a good idea. Write it down as a reality check. Then weigh it against the costs of achieving it. Can it stand on its own merits? Does it conflict with other goals of equal or greater importance? How are you or others going to gauge the risks and reap the benefits? How, in short, will you measure success?

AUDIENCE. Define your audience. What will move them to support you? Is their attitude toward your proposal positive, neutral, or negative? How are they likely to perceive you? Do you face one key audience or several? Are there secondary audiences who will be affected by the success or failure of your plan? Are there hidden audiences you haven't considered?

CONTEXT. Communication occurs in a specific environment. It can involve an effort to reach one person or to reach millions. It can mean working within the norms of a particular corporate culture, its history, and its competitive situation or challenging those norms. It can involve external communications: clients, potential customers, local or national media. When designing your communication strategy, keep in mind the big picture: in an increasingly polarized political culture, people increasingly get their opinions from Rush Limbaugh, John Stewart, Howard Stern, their favorite cable news channel, or the blogosphere. If your organization is involved in an effort to reach the general public, be aware of the opportunities and perils posed by our increasingly polarized and diversified media culture. Before you plan your communication strategy, be sure you know the territory.

MESSAGE. What message will achieve your goal with these particular audiences? Consider how much information they need, what doubts they're likely to have, how your proposal will benefit them, how to make your message convincing and memorable, and how your points can be organized most persuasively.

MEDIA. Which medium will convey your message most effectively to each significant audience? Should you speak, write, call, send E-mail, meet, fax, produce a videotape, or hold a press conference? We all know that "the medium is the message." What message will your choice of medium convey? Sending a memo to an office mate, for example, may express an unwillingness to talk face to face.

FEEDBACK. Communication is not an act but a process. A message provokes a response, which requires another message. The business communicator doesn't shoot an arrow at a target but sets in motion a process designed to achieve a considered result. This means polling your audience at every stage of the communication and, more importantly, giving them an opportunity to respond. That way, you know what they think and can tailor your message accordingly. They are more likely to feel involved in the process and committed to your goal.

(See *Exhibit 1.1*, Sample Communication Analysis.)

Even a brief consideration of these seven analytical tools will reveal that any business communication task is really a management task. Many communication situations *happen to* a manager rather than occur as planned events. Some of your key topics and goals may not be listed on any overt agenda. How can these realities be turned to advantage? Considering the source, goal, audience, context, message,

EXHIBIT 1.1 Sample Communication Analysis

You're going to ask your boss if you can take a vacation during a busy period.

Source	You're a star/good/mediocre subordinate asking a favor. You're a senior/junior.	
Goal	Get the time off when you want it.	
Audiences	*Primary*	Your boss, who is close or remote, friendly or unfriendly, flexible or rigid.
	Secondary	Your colleagues, subordinates, customers; and others who may be affected by the outcome.
Context	Workload is heavy. You're marginal/critical to the department's operation. You have/haven't asked for special consideration before. There are/aren't fixed precedents and procedures. Others are/aren't asking for the same consideration.	
Messages	Personal considerations make it crucial that I go at this time. I've arranged for my work to be covered by colleagues. Others have been given similar consideration. I can keep on top of the job by putting in longer hours before and after the vacation. Schedules and deadlines can be rearranged to make this possible. I'll repay the favor. Because the vacation will be good for me, it will be good for the company.	
Media	One-on-one conversation Phone call Memo Meeting Electronic communication Some of or all the above	
Feedback	Various audiences are supportive, receptive, indifferent, or hostile. Perhaps they remind you of possible consequences you haven't considered.	

Analyzing even this apparently simple situation demonstrates how many factors we consider—often half-consciously—before communicating. Variables in source, context, and likely audience attitude will shape our choice of message and media. We may decide to send different messages to different audiences (as long as they're not in direct conflict). Having weighed the costs and benefits carefully, we may decide not to make the request.

media, and feedback provides you with an economical framework for introspection in any business situation, whether you're planning a broad strategy or devising a particular communication effort. Using this checklist will ensure that by the time you actually engage in the communication process, you are executing a particular task in service of a larger vision and are therefore more likely to succeed.

Each of the chapters in Part One will focus on one of these key communication tools. The remainder of this chapter will concentrate on exploring the characteristics unique to business communication and the importance of "knowing yourself," that is, analyzing your strengths and weaknesses as a *source*.

Communication is something we're doing most of our waking life, and it's hard work. Human beings have been communicating in some form or another since they cried at being forced out of the womb, and most human communication is instinctive, experiential, or personality-based. The job of a successful manager is to become more analytical about planning communication and more objective about how it likely will be received. This section covers the basic tools that should be a conscious part of every manager's communications planning and execution.

Communicating effectively in business is at least as challenging as communicating well in a personal relationship. In his examination of how hard it is to communicate in a business situation, Peter Drucker,[1] an astute observer of management, any of whose books or articles is worth reading, has identified four fundamental communication principles:

1. *Communication is perception.* "In communicating, whatever the medium, the first question has to be 'Is this communication within the recipient's range of perception? Can he receive it?' "[2] Only what has actually been understood will have been communicated. Consider the situation of employees receiving bad performance evaluations. Are they likely to rationalize away the criticism? Do they have the capacity and resources to change?
2. *Communication is expectation.* Seventy years of research find agreement on one fundamental conclusion: People tend to hear what they want to hear, and they block out the unfamiliar or threatening. "A gradual change in which the mind is supposedly led by small, incremental steps to realize that what is perceived is not what it expects to perceive will not work."[3] Only by understanding your audience members' interests and expectations can you jolt them into seeing something in a new light.
3. *Communication makes demands.* "[Communication] always demands that the recipient become somebody, do something, believe something."[4] Communication, in other words, usually invites the recipient to give—attention, understanding, insight, support, information, and/or money. Perhaps most important, communication demands *time,* a business person's most valuable commodity. Before engaging in any business communication situation, you should ask yourself,Why should I spend time on this? What will motivate someone to give me their valuable time, and will they be convinced at the end that it has been well spent?
4. *Communication and information are different and indeed largely opposite, yet interdependent.* For most of human history, plenty of communication happened, but facts were at a premium. Now, due to an explosion of media in the last century, the sheer data overwhelm us and our audiences. High school

[1]Peter Drucker lays out his basic principles in *Management: Tasks, Responsibilities, and Practices* (New York: Harper and Row, 1974).
[2]Ibid., p. 484.
[3]Ibid., p. 486.
[4]Ibid., p. 487.

students can reach Bill Gates via E-mail and access vast databases. Plenty of pieces of information—that is, facts—are available, but how do we identify them and sort the important from the unimportant? This situation poses new questions: When do you want to communicate, when do you want to impart information, and under what circumstances are the two compatible? Why should your audience pick your communication out of the constant barrage and pay attention?

Given that people resist change and that their attention is a valuable commodity, how can you reach them with maximum effect? Start your planning by considering who you are as a *source.*

SOURCE: WHO ARE YOU AS A COMMUNICATOR?

While it's crucial to master the tools of communication analysis and the techniques of effective delivery, ultimately your success as a communicator will depend heavily on how you are perceived as a person. Aristotle spoke directly and often to this issue in the first, and still the best, general study of communication, his *Rhetoric*. He defined three essential qualities of successful communication: *logos, pathos*, and *ethos*.

Logos, essentially, means command of the language. Have you chosen the right words? Have you built them into clear, coherent sentences? Does each paragraph convey a succinct unit of thought? Have you identified all the relevant data and constructed a convincing argument? Do you, in short, have the fundamental skills to be an effective communicator? This Aristotelian category includes many crucial qualities, such as a command of structure and style, that will be addressed often in the following pages.

Pathos means command of your own, and the audience's, emotions. Emotion may seem out of place in a business setting, but in fact it plays a major role in every interaction. You're more likely to help out a colleague you like; you work harder for a boss who, you feel, respects and counts on you; you'll probably promote a competent friend instead of a talented competitor whom you vaguely distrust. Pathos also contains the idea of empathy—individuals and mass audiences alike will be more prone to support someone who understands their point of view, even if they disagree. Most important, the ability to appeal to an audience's sense of justice, fair play, and human dignity matters as much in a business situation as in other communications, and it can sometimes override a call to narrow personal advantage.

Ethos, essentially, means who you are as a person. Do your employees, your colleagues, your bosses have reason to trust you? Have you subordinated your needs to theirs when their goals were paramount? Have you kept your word and delivered what you said you would? Perhaps the best modern translation of *ethos,* at least in a business context, is *credibility*.

Pathos and ethos, especially, raise ethical considerations for the business communicator. Leaders, like other human beings, will have unpleasant qualities and make mistakes. The immensely successful bond trader, widely known to be driven and tyrannical, probably makes sure that her useful subordinates share in the profits. Constituents will forgive the congressman his extracurricular dalliances with pages if they like and believe him, and if he has delivered extended fishing rights for his coastal district. But audiences are always making judgments about whether their leaders are, on balance, decent people, worthy of support and respect. All the analysis and technique in the world won't move them to support you if, at all times, that balance isn't working in your favor. Whether you are credible depends largely on whether you're perceived to be working for a larger purpose than your own short-term interest.

Aristotle's categories suggest another important point, widely validated by current experience in teaching and practicing business communication. Command of communication theory or public relations tricks will get the manager nowhere without an understanding of human nature, which can come only from a broad base of knowledge and experience. Communication is not a body of knowledge to be mastered, like biology or literature. Communication is always about something else.

The newly hired manager may be able to make a great success for a time out of her command of a narrow specialty or technical area. But as that manager's responsibilities increase, she will be dealing with other departments, external constituencies, and leaders in business, culture, and government.

While it's unarguable that some business people have made brilliant careers out of a narrow specialty or one great idea, in general, successful managers are also cultivated people. This means they write well, speak well, and maintain a broad range of interests both within and outside their fields. Good writers, for example, are also good readers: they regularly read good journalism, novels, and poetry as well as keep up with developments in their personal area of expertise. Good speakers listen to, and learn from, good speeches, whether given by politicians on television or visiting experts at the local university. A broad range of interests—in national and international affairs, history, science, and the arts—not only gives you something to talk about at the next office party, but also helps you grow as a whole person. The ability to engage in informed conversation about someone else's interests both establishes rapport and increases willingness to grant you credibility on your own turf.

Listening

It's very important to remember that *good communicators are good listeners.* By the time you've identified your goal and chosen a plan of action to achieve it, you'll likely be so convinced you're right (or under so much pressure from your boss to succeed) that you'll be tempted to become a good promoter but a bad listener. Remember that all business goals require teamwork to achieve.

Several techniques can ensure that you become a better listener.

1. **Practice empathy.** Whether you're interacting with an individual or a large audience, whether you agree or disagree with the point of view being expressed, *show you understand it.* If you're paying close attention to what's being said, you'll find opportunities to cite analogous examples from your own experience that demonstrate you share your audience's concerns. This can often create common ground, which is the necessary condition for reaching agreement.
2. **Bring areas of disagreement into the open.** Opposition to your point of view won't go away just because you ignore it. Often, only patient listening can bring the real causes of disagreement to the surface.

3. **Paraphrase.** Restate your audience's concerns succinctly before you respond to them. If you haven't understood them correctly, this is the time to find that out.
4. **Ask the right questions.** If an employee complains about being overworked and you think the issues he raises are legitimate, ask: "What are your most important tasks, and what aspects of your job are distracting you from them?" This prepares for a resolution of the problem.
5. **Listen actively.** Try to understand the emotions or interests that may lurk hidden beneath a given complaint or statement. Often the person you're talking with won't be fully aware of them themselves.
6. **Provide immediate feedback.** While it's often true that you can't offer an instant solution to a request or concern, you should at least tell the person how you intend to address it. Except in very special situations, leaving your interlocutor in suspense about how you intend to proceed will just create frustration and paralysis.

To summarize: Be very careful to understand the motives and interests of those whose cooperation you need to succeed. Try not to send overt or covert messages that you don't want to hear suggestions or opposing points of view. Even someone who disagrees with your goal, or your plan to achieve it, will be more likely to go along if she feels she's had a fair hearing and that her concerns have been understood.

Someone who shows informed interest in what others have to say will inevitably develop a reputation as a good conversationalist and communicator. In the following pages we will repeatedly stress the importance of understanding the needs and interests of your audience. Some of these points are addressed in more detail in "Handling Q&A: The Five Kinds of Listening" (*Harvard Communications Update,* February 1999).

Authority

Your credibility as a source will also be intangibly affected by what the ancient philosophers called *auctoritas,* best translated as "authority." Authority can derive from several different sources and can arise at any level within an organization. The person who runs the janitorial staff well can be a real authority within his sphere of operations and perhaps be more valued by a major corporation than a senior executive.

Factors that determine your authority include:

- How much you know about your field
- How well you perform your job
- How much others have learned to trust you
- Whether your ideas break new ground
- Your past accomplishments
- Raw intelligence
- Understanding of human nature
- How right your judgments have proven in previous situations
- How you come across in person

While authority certainly depends in part upon how much raw power you have to tell others what to do, in many business situations the decisions are really driven by the person who has the most authority, not necessarily the one who has the highest position in the organizational hierarchy. Try to manage your communications so that you become an authoritative source.

QUALITIES OF EFFECTIVE COMMUNICATION

Once you've examined your position as the source of a communication, you want to ensure that each conversation, memo, phone call, Internet message, presentation, proposal, or report carries the maximum impact possible. Here we want to address the fundamental qualities shared by any effective source of business communication. We also encourage you to refer throughout the course to the technical manuals on writing and speaking in Part Three of this book.

It's important to understand that these chapters are not addenda but are crucial to success in the course. The authors recommend that you consult them regularly in conjunction with writing or speaking assignments and bring up the points they address in class discussions. Qualities to aim for, whenever you write or speak, include:

Accuracy

When you approach an audience, you are implicitly seeking trust. If even one member of your audience recognizes a factual error, you are in trouble. Inaccuracy, in business, takes several typical forms: insufficient data, misinterpretation of the data, ignorance of key factors, unconscious bias, and exaggeration. Guard against them all to preserve and enhance your credibility.

Clarity

Clarity is hard won. To function efficiently, an organization depends on accurate and complete information, intelligible instructions, and policies capable of guiding the decision-makers in both routine and unexpected situations. Misunderstandings, ambiguity, and confusion cost money and cause frustration.

Some teachers and managers adhere to the slogan KISS—Keep It Simple, Stupid. But most business situations don't lend themselves to simple or stupid solutions; clarity results from careful preparation. To achieve it, you must include, interpret, and organize. Achieving clarity in business writing and speaking requires clear thinking and expression.

Clarity of Thinking

If you haven't thought through the rationale for your proposal, the plan of action to achieve it, and the possible consequences, then you can't expect your audience to follow you. Most bad writing or speaking is the result of shoddy thinking or slapdash preparation.

Clarity of Expression

Over the last 15 years or so, many corporations, including General Motors, have instituted large and expensive programs to train their managers to write and speak in clear English. Correctness, conforming to standard grammar and usage, is the baseline for effective communication; errors in spelling or sentence structure will call into question your ability to manage information. But for many communications, correctness is not enough. While it may ensure clarity in instructions for routine procedures, in policy statements, reports, persuasive presentations, and memos, you may have to discard many "correct" sentences before your language clearly conveys your meaning. If you find that you can't write or speak your communication clearly, you need to reexamine the thinking that has led you to your conclusion.

Brevity

Good managerial communications should be brief, to accomplish much in few words. Brevity is a cardinal virtue whether your communication is going to the president, to a junior executive, or to hourly employees. Everyone's time is valuable; no one enjoys sitting through needlessly long communications when there's work to be done. Some companies, such as Procter & Gamble, legislate brevity; executives won't read a memo than runs over one or two pages. Such limits cut down on the flow of paper, although they can't guarantee that the memo says what needs to be said. Concision does not mean writing exclusively in short sentences or omitting necessary detail. It means making every word count.

Vigor

Vigor means vividness and memorability. People in organizations have multiple responsibilities and receive communications from many sources each day. Mintzberg has shown that managers usually can give ideas and information their attention for only short periods. Interruptions, distractions, and competing responsibilities all characterize managerial work. A vigorous style helps your communication stand out from the clutter.

Vigor results partly from accuracy, clarity, and brevity and partly from your choice of words, images, and sentence patterns. Vigorous sentences boast active verbs, concrete nouns, and a minimum of well chosen modifiers (see Chap. 16, Effective Writing, and Chap. 17, Effective Speaking, in Part Three for examples). Vigorous language aids understanding and makes your message more memorable. It also conveys confidence and conviction.

No one will be fooled by typical organizational doublespeak such as "We plan to devote considerable effort to the study of developing requirements and will seek to develop proposed solutions to the various possible needs we can foresee well in advance of the time that a decision will be needed." This sentence violates all the criteria for good business writing. "We plan to" should be "We're acting now." Repeated words, such as *develop* and *developing,* and repeated meanings, such as *considerable* and *well,* are padding. Useless modifiers such as *proposed* and *possible* weaken the impact of key nouns. "Will be needed," a passive construction, begs the questions *by whom* and *when?* "We will present our recommendations for expanding your product line on November 1" takes one-third the space, sticks in the mind, and conveys much more useful information.

Effective use of language will be the subject of exercises throughout the following course. You can hone your writing, speaking, and general communication skills only by practicing them. This means attuning them to a variety of audiences. The more successful you are as a manager, the more likely it is that these audiences will be multicultural. Therefore, as a general rule, the practical cases we ask you to consider building from typical middle-management situations to major organizational, external, and even international communication challenges.

WHY BUSINESS COMMUNICATION IS UNIQUE

Lamar N. Reinsch Jr. surveyed "Business Communication as a Field of Study" (*Management Communication Quarterly,* Thousand Oaks, 1996). He examined the field from Aristotle's teaching on rhetoric in ancient Athens to modern practitioners of management communication training and reached several conclusions worth noting by contemporary students of communication. He concluded that effective business communication must embrace both *knowing what* and *knowing how.*

This insight, simple as it may seem, captures the essence of business communication. Knowing what, as we'll describe in the next chapter, means defining your goal clearly. Knowing how takes up the rest of the book: how to understand yourself, understand your audience, design your message, develop a logical argument, choose the right media to send it, remain sensitive to style and tone. Citing Mary Munter's classic text and other research, he emphasizes the uniqueness of business communication. Because it's designed to produce results, unlike, say, a novel, which is intended to produce contemplation and enjoyment, business communication should:

1. Focus on your conclusions rather than the thought process that led you to them.
2. Be direct and emphasize your purpose at the beginning.
3. Highlight your main points by using headings, bolding, italics, and numbered or bullet-points. In the case of presentations, achieve emphasis by repetition, tone, and the support of clear graphics. The ultimate recipient of your document or statement—someone you may never talk to directly—may be so busy she or he will only skim it.
4. Emphasize the positive impact of your proposal on its immediate audience, your organization, and the larger community.
5. Be sensitive to the fact that in a country—and a world—where there are many varieties of English, you should make sure your message gets through to all your key constituencies.

EVOLVING COMMUNICATION CHANNELS

This book focuses on the principles and practices that produce effective communication in any medium. But while we will explore all the traditional channels of management communication—writing, speaking, graphics, meetings, actions—much if not most business communication today is electronic. E-mail, websites, blogs, text-messaging, and the Internet as a whole are rapidly reshaping both the structures of organizations and how they communicate both internally and externally. Many shrewd observers believe this trend will expand exponentially over the next couple of decades. Ray Kurzweil, a futurologist with a strong record of invention and accurate prediction in the field of electronic communication and artificial intelligence, argues in *The Singularity is Near*[1] that the exponential growth of information technologies will soon produce a transformational melding of mind and machine.

The recent explosion of the Internet supports this point. Discounting the financial collapse of many e-companies in the late 1990s as a necessary correction, Kurtzweil argues: "New models based on direct personalized communication with the customer will transform every industry, resulting is massive disintermediation of the middle layers that have traditionally separated the customer from the ultimate source of products and services . . . The boom and bust cycle in these information technologies was strictly a capital-markets (stock value) phenomenon . . . actual business-to-consumer revenues grew smoothly from $1.8 billion in 1997 to $70 billion in 2002. Business to business had a similarly smooth growth from $56 billion in 1999 to $482 billion in 2002. In 2004 it is approaching $1 trillion."[2] (103)

If one believes that the primary product of the future will be information, these trends have enormous implications for the future of management communication, including:

1. Relatively soon, organizations will be contacting their customers and constituencies, and shaping opinions of their products and services, primarily through websites, blogs, online advertising, and other modes of electronic communication we haven't even imagined yet.
2. Information technologies will provide ever more sophisticated tools to shape organizations' response to consumer demand, radically increasing their efficiency. Kurzweil writes, "Companies in every industry are using AI (Artificial Intelligence) systems to control and optimize logistics, detect fraud and money laundering, and perform intelligent data mining on the hoard of information they gather each day. Wal-Mart, for example, gathers vast amounts of information from its transactions with shoppers. AI-based tools using neural nets and expert systems review this data to provide marketing reports to managers. This intelligent data mining allows them to make remarkably accurate predictions of the inventory required for each product in each store for each day."[3] (283) This sort of software is already incorporating automatic capabilities to repair and optimize its functions without the intervention of the human user.
3. Odds are that the companies of the future, in order to maximize these technological advantages, will increasingly resemble the relatively egalitarian model of high-tech companies such as Apple or Microsoft rather than the hierarchical models of 20th-century manufacturing corporations. This has profound implications not only for how an organization communicates with its customers or constituents, but also how it communicates internally, and suggests the gradual elimination or transformation of traditional middle management. In an increasingly egalitarian work environment, more and more electronic options are available to circumvent executives who horde information to retain power.

In this environment, many of your closest colleagues and important customers may be people you never meet. Two cautions here. First, the fact that one can conduct a successful international business with a desk and a computer doesn't

[1](New York: Viking, 2005).
[2]Ibid., p. 103.
[3]Ibid., p. 283

obviate the need for human contact and personal social skills. Second, while rapid technological advances can do more and more internal and external management communication mechanically, human beings, as everyone who has tried to get a mortgage from a recently globalized local bank or advice on a faulty product over the telephone will testify, have a resistence to communicating with machines, although it's perfectly possible that we'll live to see machines that can express sympathy and sense frustration, or come up with a creative solution to a unique personal situation. To a frustrated consumer, a human voice can make a lot of difference, even if it's coming from another continent. In a more profound sense, having a "voice"—that is, a set of values, an appropriate tone, and a message shaped to the needs of your audience—will never become obsolete even if it is being expressed electronically or through machines you have programmed.

The impact of these trends pervades this text, but we have also included classic cases, written before the advent of E-mail, that emphasize the fundamental elements of successful communication. We urge the student to review Chapter 15, Electronic Communication, early in the course, and discuss how these enduring principles and practices apply in the age of the Internet.

ORGANIZATION OF THIS BOOK

This book has three major purposes. First, it presents the tools that can help you define and master business communication situations. Second, it encourages you to exercise the skills needed for clear, persuasive writing and speaking. Third, it invites you to test yourself against a representative range of managerial challenges. In each instance someone must produce written, oral, or electronic communication that addresses the demands of a specific managerial situation, such as motivating employees, persuading a superior, building consensus, introducing change, explaining a financial position, providing feedback to a colleague, getting a proposal adopted, making a sale, interacting with the media, or coordinating a strategy.

Part One of this book focuses on how to use the basic elements of communication analysis—source, audience, goal, context, message, media, and feedback—to achieve your desired result. Part Two invites you to apply these tools to a representative variety of business situations. Part Three consists of brief guides to effective writing and speaking which we recommend that you review early and use as references throughout the course.

HOW TO PREPARE A CASE

A word about the use of case studies in this text. Every manager brings certain strengths, weaknesses, biases, ideas, and assumptions to any communication situation. An effective manager understands his or her own and others' points of view—how to respond to disagreement, willingness to modify a plan in the face of audience analysis or new information, the ability to get diverse constituencies committed to a single goal. In our experience, cases and actual practice—writing, speaking, role playing—provide the best way to develop communication understanding and skills in the classroom.

Cases also enable us to bring together the various techniques and topics covered in the previous paragraphs. In real business situations, tasks and opportunities don't usually arrive in packages labeled *finance situation, marketing opportunity,* or *public relations crisis.* Defining the challenge is often the hardest task facing a manager. Only effective analysis can help you reach this point. We believe these cases will help you develop the knowledge, tool kit, skills, sense of style, flexibility, and leadership needed to succeed in a business communication situation. It's a reasonable assumption that preparing a case means reading it, but nothing could be further from the truth. Preparing a case means deciding how to resolve the problems it raises, comparing the data in the exhibits to the case narrative, and developing a plan of action you're willing to defend in class discussion. Most of the value of a good case discussion comes from a clash of perspectives on basic situation analysis and on what to do next. Come to class prepared with specific recommendations and justifications for them. Often it's wise to look over the Study Questions first and make marginal notes to address while you're reading the case and examining the exhibits.

CONCLUSION

Business students rank communication skills as among the most important they have to master. Executives say they spend more time communicating than doing anything else. However, unlike production, marketing, managerial economics, or accounting, communication doesn't have a number at the bottom. Consequently, its results are hard to measure. Moreover, as technology provides faster and more various means of communication, managers must develop better communication *instincts.* You are likely to respond more impulsively in an E-mail than in a letter that you would review and edit before sending.

This means that to improve as a communicator, you must listen to your only real judge—your audience. This can be a classmate, instructor, informal or social group, client, boss, employee, colleague, meeting, department, division, workforce, top management, government, interest groups, stockholders, the media, or the public. Every successful manager, at one time or another, is likely to address these audiences.

This analytical model begs an obvious and important question: Who is my appropriate audience? This usually means: Who can make the decision I want? Sometimes, to accomplish your goal, you just need one person's signature. In such cases, a broader communication strategy that might alert opponents isn't wise. Try to identify the decision-makers and approach them through the strategies suggested in this book. Don't struggle your way up through the bureaucracy if you can get your proposal directly to the person or audience that will decide the issue. Technologies such as websites and E-mail offer more opportunities for this approach than were available in the more hierarchically structured organizations of the 20th century.

While trenchant analysis provides the crucial underpinnings for a successful communication process, only practice can ensure that effective communication becomes second nature to you as a manager. The following discussions, cases, and exercises ask you to test yourself against a representative range of business communication challenges.

CHAPTER 2

Setting Goals

Management communication differs from some other types of communication in that it's designed to get a specific result. It's more like walking into a store and placing an order than like telling a friend about your day. This chapter focuses on establishing achievable goals within a particular *context.* Of course, the business context in which you are pursuing your goals is shaped importantly by less formal communications including social interactions with subordinates, peers, superiors, customers, and many others.

It's relatively easy to execute most communication tasks. Unfortunately, managers invariably face many communication decisions simultaneously. The right decision on one task often involves the wrong decision on another. Superiors have conflicting, hidden, or counterproductive demands. Subordinates' requests are sometimes unreasonable or incompatible. Before communication happens, the manager must define priorities. This means developing a strategy, setting clear goals, assessing the context, designing a course of action, and communicating in a way that will achieve the desired results. Doing this well usually involves considering other people's feelings, interests, and values. It always involves sorting out your own priorities.

GOALS

In many management situations, your goals seem self-evident: You want to fix a problem; get your proposal adopted; earn the respect of your subordinates, colleagues, and superiors. Often, however, focusing on specific short-term goals can blind you to the bigger picture. An old parable holds that leaders are either hedgehogs or foxes. Hedgehogs know one thing very well. Foxes know many things in some detail. In politics, for example, Ronald Reagan was a hedgehog and Bill

Clinton a fox. The good manager knows how to be both a hedgehog and a fox, holding to a principled vision while making informed choices among a number of specific options. Translated to action, this means being a hedgehog on strategy and a fox on implementation.

When you are facing a complex managerial context, list the full range of goals you'd like to achieve. Then play the hedgehog: Identify the one or two most important long-range accomplishments on your agenda. Now you can play the fox and measure your subordinate goals against these. Which are urgent, which are incompatible? Which are your responsibility, and which can be delegated or reassigned? Which, however important, can be delayed until time is available or more information comes in? Having answered these questions, you're well on your way toward a sensible plan of action.

You can best sort your goals according to whether they are purposes, strategies, tactics, or tasks. For example:

Purpose	Increase the sales of my product.
Strategy	Attain higher availability and visibility.
Tactics	Acquire new outlets.
	Increase advertising budget.
	Gain greater corporate support.
Tasks	Develop budget proposal for top management.
	Hire more representatives to contact potential outlets.
	Present proposal at corporate planning meeting.
	Develop advertising and public relations programs.

In this model, only the *purpose* represents your real *business goal.* But achieving that purpose requires you to define and accomplish a set of subsidiary goals, or tasks, all of which become *communication goals:* writing up your budget proposal with justifications and projections, conducting interviews, making a successful presentation at the meeting, designing advertising, attracting media attention.

You may find that a *process approach* is most helpful in separating out your primary, secondary, and tertiary goals. Try using the following analytical tools:

1. Determine your primary, or business goal. Often it's helpful to write this down and keep it in front of you during your planning.
2. Consider the various reasonable strategies for achieving your primary goal, and choose the one most appropriate to the context and your position within the organization.
3. Define your secondary goals—those actions necessary to achieve your business goal. In short, what do you need others to do?
4. Plan the tasks most likely to achieve your secondary goals. While these may involve managerial activities like gathering more information, they will generally be communications like persuading an individual, holding a meeting, writing a proposal, sending E-mails, or even choosing whether or not to show up at an event. These are your tertiary, or communication, goals.

Keep in mind this distinction among business (strategic) goals, secondary (tactical) goals, and tertiary (communication) goals throughout your planning. Keep your eye on the ball and don't let your means become your ends.

REALITY TESTING: CONTEXT

Goals must be tested immediately against the context in which you're trying to achieve them. That context includes your personal position within the organization, the available resources, the organization's traditions and values, networks of personal relationships, the interests and biases of superiors, communication channels, the situation of your business vis-à-vis that of competitors, how your area fits into the larger organization, and even the general cultural climate.

Test each of your goals against the context by asking a few key questions:

1. Are my goals ethically sound?
2. Am I a credible source for this direction or proposal?
3. Are adequate resources available to achieve my purpose?
4. Will my goals enlist the support of others whose cooperation I need?
5. Do they conflict with other goals of equal or greater importance?
6. Do they stand a reasonable chance, given the internal and external competitive environment?
7. What will be the *consequences* of success? Overall, will I and my organization be better off after achieving these goals?

These tests may cause you to conclude that either your goals need to be modified or other goals that you hadn't considered at first may be more important than those you had identified initially.

Two major considerations will help managers rank their goals:

Urgency

This goes back to a point we stressed in the introduction: the value and management of *time*. Managers are constantly confronted with requests for decisions on matters that are very important to those making the request but less important in the overall picture. Ask yourself: What will happen if I don't resolve this now? Will a minor problem turn into a major one, or could the matter benefit from more consideration? If I need more evidence to make a wise decision, can I delegate the task of gathering it? Is someone else in a better position to make this decision? What are the time constraints on me, my audience, and those who will be involved in implementing this project?

Quick, accurate decisions on urgency define the successful manager. While it's a hard thing to do, managers regularly have to ask people to wait; superiors may demand action before the right course of action is clear, or subordinates may be champing at the bit to get on with something that doesn't matter much in the overall scheme of things. Often, they will respond to evidence that the time isn't ripe for this particular decision.

Importance

Once you've sorted out your goals, you'll typically find that several are of high priority and that some of these are in direct conflict. The urgency test may help here. Some very important situations can wait a day, a week, or a month to resolve, while others can present a now-or-never opportunity. Sometimes less immediately obvious goals, such as establishing your credibility with coworkers, can be more important in the long run than getting a specific proposal approved.

To summarize: The very definition of management turns on determining long-term goals and setting the processes in motion to achieve them. Time constraints require that you do some things and postpone others. Any successful manager will be deluged with requests to do more than is humanly possible. Often, you'll have to say "no," or "later." If you can explain these responses in understandable terms, you'll gain credit from your various audiences and earn the time to make informed decisions.

Put yourself in the position of the protagonist in the following case, define your business goals, derive your key communication goals, and then ask yourself, What would I write? What would I say? While this case predates the age of the Internet, consider whether the protagonist's communication choices might be different if E-mail existed.

CASE 2.1

Yellowtail Marine, Inc.

"I wouldn't offer you a job like this unless I thought you had the ability to run the company and the guts to buy me out within seven years. You know how I've always made my money: turning rundown companies around by providing an opportunity to a talented manager who's wasting away inside some over-organized large corporation. Robyn, you've been with Sportscraft for almost four years and you're years away from a top management job. This is a chance to do your own thing and end up with your own business—come aboard, eh?"

HOW THE SITUATION DEVELOPED

It was March 25, 1976, and Charles Boswell, an alumnus of the same California business school attended by Robyn Gilcrist, was trying to convince her to take a job as chief operating executive of Yellowtail Marine, a company Boswell had just bought. Boswell was president of CBG, Inc., a privately held venture capital firm which he had founded in 1964. Boswell's fortune was based on his ownership of the West Coast distributorship of a major earthmoving equipment company, and he had prospered—first on highway construction and the land boom in Southern California and more recently from his involvement with Alaskan oil development. He maintained, however, that the challenge in his life was new ventures and turnarounds.

Boswell first met Gilcrist in 1967 when, as president of the American Water Skiing Association, he presented her with the national championship. As they became acquainted, Boswell learned that Gilcrist had graduated in the top 5% of her MBA class. During the next three years, as she continued to win national events, he had kept in touch with her and over the past few years he had followed her career at Sportscraft. She had started in the marine division in promotions and marketing where she had increased total sales by 70% in just two years. Her next assignment was as marketing director of the Winter Sports Division. (Boswell wondered whether Sportscraft knew the difference between sea and ski.) More recently she had been assistant to the president of Sportscraft, and when Boswell had spoken with her in San Francisco, she had mentioned that she felt at a dead end and needed a more challenging position.

Boswell offered her a job that would leave her as president of Yellowtail by May 1977. Boswell had acquired Yellowtail from Olaf Gunerson, who

This case was prepared by Assistant Professor Kenneth J. Hatten. Harvard Business School case 376-235.

was something of a legend in San Diego. His inboard and outboard boats with their distinctive yellow sterns could always be seen there zipping about the harbor or bobbing up and down at their moorings looking as if they were raring to go.

As was his practice, Boswell had negotiated a deal which left the owner in place for 12 months while he took control of the board. As always, he intended to bring a new professional manager in to work with the retiring owner and he had thought of Gilcrist for this opportunity. She had extensive marketing experience in the water sports industry, and Boswell felt that Yellowtail would respond quickly if the company was more market-oriented.

Thinking back on it, Gilcrist realized that what had swung the deal was Boswell's willingness to allow her to buy into the business: $65,000 salary plus several generous fringe benefits and the rights to acquire up to 20% of the business over the next 7 years, followed by the chance to increase her ownership to a controlling interest in 10 years if things worked out. It seemed too good to be true.

Boswell had shown her Yellowtail's 1975 financial statements (see *Exhibits 1* and *2*) and told her that the company needed work. He said that sales had slipped from just over $10 million in 1973 to about $8.4 million in 1975. The oil crisis and the 1974 recession had cut deeply into the boat industry's sales. Although Gunerson was active, at age 73 he was not up to turning the company around himself and he wanted to retire. Boswell said he had already talked Gunerson into hiring a new advertising agency to beef up the company's sales in the summer of 1976. Happily, when Gilcrist accepted Boswell's offer, Gunerson and his wife had invited her to their home for a weekend and had held a dinner for her at the Green Dolphin Club, where Olaf introduced her to most of Yellowtail's managers as his new executive vice president and heir apparent.

Gilcrist had agreed to start work with Yellowtail on May 4, but on April 12, 1976, she received a call from Boswell telling her that Gunerson had died of a heart attack. He had been out in his favorite Yellowtail Corsair, a high-speed game fishing boat, when he had collapsed. Boswell wondered whether she could start earlier. After a call to Sportscraft's president, she agreed to start on April 14.

Boswell thanked her and said that he would appreciate it if she could get to the plant, deal with whatever needed doing, fly to San Francisco for a board meeting that same afternoon, and then return with him and his wife to Olaf's funeral on April 15. Boswell mentioned that after the funeral he would be flying to the Middle East for about 10 days. He said that if she could manage it he would like to see some kind of preliminary strategic plan for Yellowtail before he left. That way she could have about 14 days to work on it and develop a budget for the board's approval.

YELLOWTAIL MARINE

Yellowtail Marine was founded in 1926 by Olaf Gunerson when he acquired the White Bay Boatyard. Gunerson, who had been trained as a naval architect, initially offered a two-model line—a cabin cruiser and a game fishing boat. His choices were fortunate; first, because he met with almost instant success; second, because his boats appealed to the small segment of the West Coast population who had money to spend through the 1930s; and finally, because a special version of his game fishing boat was used by police departments, the IRS and customs agents, and the military.

When the United States entered the war in 1941, Yellowtail Marine was one of the firms selected to produce offshore patrol boats, naval launches, and a few other small craft. Because of its strategic task, Yellowtail Marine was able to maintain its place as a small boat builder and the company's products became widely known since many servicemen had used Yellowtails by the war's end.

During the 1950s Gunerson sought materials that would allow some measure of automation in the boat-building industry. He was one of the first to use fiberglass in pleasure craft and a pioneer in extensively using foam to improve flotation, a characteristic of Yellowtail's that became an important selling point.

EXHIBIT 1 Yellowtail Marine, Inc. Balance Sheet, July 31, 1975

Assets		
Current assets		
Cash	$ 8,000	
Accounts receivable	842,000	
Inventory	1,251,000	
Other	22,000	
Current assets		$2,123,000
Fixed assets		
Plant and equipment	2,511,000	
Less accumulated depreciation	989,000	
Net fixed assets		1,522,000
Other assets at cost	152,000	
Less amortization	22,000	
Other assets net		130,000
Total assets		$3,775,000
Liabilities and stockholders' equity		
Current liabilities		
Accounts payable	$ 665,000	
Short-term note	212,000	
Accrued liabilities (salaries, rents, property taxes, etc.)	78,000	
Current portion long-term debt	39,000	
Current liabilities		$ 994,000
Long-term obligations		
Bank of San Diego	52,000	
Mortgages	399,000	
CBG, Inc. (10 yr. subordinate loan)	1,200,000	
Long-term liabilities		1,651,000
Stockholders' equity		
Common stock (no par value)	782,000	
Retained earnings	$ 348,000	
Stockholders' equity		1,130,000
Total liabilities and stockholders' equity		$3,775,000

EXHIBIT 2 Yellowtail Marine, Inc. Income Statement, August 1, 1974 to July 31, 1975

Revenue		
Gross sales		$8,376,000
Less: discounts, returns and allowances		36,000
Net sales		8,340,000
Cost of goods sold		6,662,000
Gross profit		1,678,000
Operating expenses		
Selling and advertising	$710,000	
General and administrative	528,000	
Miscellaneous	21,000	
Total operating expenses		1,259,000
Operating income		419,000
Financial payments		
Bank interest	8,000	
Mortgage interest	32,000	
Lease payment	9,000	
Interest on CBG loan	$114,000	
Total financial payments		163,000
Income before tax		256,000
Taxes paid		88,000
Profit after tax		$ 168,000

In 1975 the company was predominantly serving the West Coast and the Rocky Mountain regions and offered a wide range of fiberglass and wooden craft from 14' to 40' long. The smaller boats (up to 26') were primarily outboard boats retailing at $100 to $275 per foot, which placed them in the medium-to high-priced segments of the market as *Exhibit 3* indicates. About 64% of the company's boats were outboards, another 35% were inboard/outboard boats selling for about $8,500, and the rest were customized or special order craft between 26' and 40' long selling for between $800 and $1,400 per foot. These boats were primarily game fishing boats, the Corsair, or an adaptation of the Corsair design for police or military use. Gunerson had deliberately fought to preserve a niche in these last two markets because he felt they had brought the company through the Great Depression and World War II. In 1975 he stated that the game and police boats were the only products that had increased sales since 1973. Yellowtail sold about 1,600 boats and employed 235 people in 1975.

Yellowtail was simply organized on a functional basis by Gunerson after World War II. The major functional areas in April 1976 were as follows: the boatyard, the production center, under the leadership of Robert McPhail, age 57, who had been with the company for 23 years; financial control and personnel, under Mark Lopez, a CPA, 59 years old, who had 15 years with Yellowtail; and marketing under Paul Lees, who had been

Exhibit 3 Sales of New Outboard Boats, Motors, and Inboard/Outboard Boats, 1972–1975

	1972	1973	1974	1975
Outboard boat				
Units sold	375,000	448,000	425,000	328,000
Average price per unit	$714,000	$726.00	$730.00	$801.00
Total dollars spent ($ millions)	$ 267.8	$ 325.2	$ 310.2	$ 262.7
Inboard/outdrive boat				
Units sold	63,000	78,000	70,000	70,000
Average price per unit	$ 4,885	$ 5,261	$ 5,524	$ 6,000
Total dollars spent ($ millions)	$ 307.8	$ 410.4	$ 386.7	$ 420.0
Outboard motor				
Units sold	535,000	585,000	545,000	435,000
Average price per unit	$ 808.00	$857.00	$850.00	$945.00
Total dollars spent ($ millions)	$ 432.3	$ 501.3	$ 463.3	$ 411.1

Source: Boating Industry, January 1976.

with the firm four years and was 36 years old. He had been the sales manager of one of Yellowtail's dealers before he joined the company.

THE PLEASURE-BOAT INDUSTRY

The pleasure-boat industry served almost one-quarter of the U.S. population in the mid-1970s.[1] This group included the yacht owners, insulated from the effects of the economic cycle, who cheerfully paid $150,000 to $300,000 and more for cabin cruisers and racing yachts; the $40,000-a-year middle-income families who aspired to the same fare but felt the pinch of hard times; and those with less who enjoyed boating but probably felt the pinch most of the time.

The industry was large with 1975 sales estimated at $4.8 billion, encompassing new and used equipment, services, insurance, mooring and launching fees, repairs, and boat club memberships. Across the country, *Boating Industry* claimed, almost 50 million people participated in recreational boating more than once or twice during 1975: 12 million people went water skiing, 34 million went fishing, 4 million went skin and scuba diving, and almost 10 million pleasure craft of all types and sizes plied U.S. waters. Retail sales increased from about $2.6 million in 1964 to almost $4.8 billion in 1975,[2] with 16,000 boating dealers and 6,000 marinas, boatyards, and yacht clubs serving the needs of boating families.

Although the industry's dollar sales increased, 1974 and 1975 were marred by an across-the board turndown in units sold. Inflation was a major factor in the industry's dollar growth as builders and manufacturers passed on their costs in an effort to maintain profit levels. Fortunately for the industry, used boat sales were brisk and used boat prices benefited from the increased cost of new equipment. A *Business Week* article stated:

[1]Frost and Sullivan, Inc., *The Pleasure Boat and Boat Equipment Market* (New York: June 1974) is a useful reference on this industry.

[2]*Boating Industry,* January 1976.

The continued high sales value of used boats, dealers agree, has loosened bankers' attitudes towards boat financing. "The collateral," one dealer notes, "is good." So apparently are the repayment habits of weekend sailors. Says a boat financing specialist for Seattle's Washington Mutual Savings Bank, which now advertises 10½% loans to boat buyers, "We have never had a repossessed boat and have hardly ever had a delinquency."[3]

The pleasure boat industry was historically a craft industry, regionally based because of the high cost of transporting boats overland, and cyclical in nature. At least until the mid-1970s it had been an easy business to enter because of its traditional labor-intensive nature.[4]

The industry was changing, however, partly because of the development of new materials—aluminum and fiberglass—which lent themselves to semiautomated and automated production processes and partly because of the investments of larger, well-capitalized corporations in the industry.[5] In the late 1960s and early 1970s a number of well-known boat firms were acquired by or merged with larger companies. *Table A* shows the extent to which the industry changed; only 5 of the 20 largest firms remained independent.

The merger and acquisition activity was prompted by the industry's steady growth through the 1960s and early 1970s, but the oil crisis in 1973 and the recession of 1974 and 1975 led to a shakeout. *Table B* shows how some raw materials prices changed over the period. Large and small firms were all affected, but it seemed likely that many small firms would not survive. It was estimated that outboard boat sales fell by almost 40% between 1973 and 1975. Boat trailer sales fell by about 25% in the same period and outboard motor sales fell by almost 20%.

It was expected that the industry would begin to grow again in 1976 (see *Exhibit 4*). It might grow in a different direction, however, since the energy crisis gave impetus to sailing over power

TABLE A Nonindependent Boat Manufacturers in the Top 40 Sellers

Manufacturer	Parent company
Chrysler Marine	Chrysler Corporation
Duo Boats	Bangor Punta
Jensen Marine	
The Luhrs Company	
O'Day Boat Company	
Starcraft Company	
Alcort	AMF
Crestliner	
Hatteras	
Slickcraft	
Boston Whaler, Inc.	CML
Ericson Yacht	
Columbia/Corando	Whittaker
Trojan Yachts	

TABLE B Prices of Chemicals, December 1972–1975 (per Pound)

Chemicals per pound	1972	1973	1974	1975
Styrene, monomer	.066–.0675	.09–.095	.19¼–22	.19
Polyester resin, unsaturated	—	.18½–20	.39 lb.	.36

Source: Chemical Marketing Reporter, December issues, 1972–1975.

[3]*Business Week,* July 28, 1975, p. 17.

[4]In 1973–1974 it was estimated that there were about 1,600 U.S. boat builders and manufacturers: 82% had less than 20 employees and more than 900 had between 1 and 4 employees. *Chemical Market Reporter,* July 20, 1974.

[5]Some large corporations, such as Chris Craft, set up regionally based plants around and across the country.

EXHIBIT 4 Expected Boating Industry Investment and Sales, 1965–1976 ($ Millions)

	Manufacturer			
	Plant expansion	New machinery and equipment	Marine dealer inventory (avg. daily)	Renovation and repair (older boats)
1976[a]	$19.40	$18.70	$241.00	$246.00
1975	16.90	16.90	204.55	210.00
1974	15.00	15.30	223.84	202.40
1973	14.10	14.40	193.23	190.60
1972	17.10	17.20	180.74	169.47
1971	8.20	9.45	156.90	158.00
1970	8.61	10.11	150.30	147.39
1969	10.30	12.98	160.30	141.06
1968	8.53	9.47	145.39	132.31
1967	8.14	9.24	142.53	127.68
1966	7.40	8.90	139.60	124.47
1965	8.13	8.74	135.70	120.38

Source: Peter B. B. Andrews, "What's Going to Happen in '76," *Boating Industry,* January 1976, p. 54.
[a]1976 data estimated.

boating. In 1975 only sailboats[6] and boats costing more than $45,000 gained in sales. This led some experts to predict that the sailing segment of the boating industry would grow at a rate between 15% and 20% through the remainder of the 1970s. They saw much of this growth coming in the low-priced end of the market, however, which was dominated by Snark with its foam sailers.

Other changes affecting the sailboat market included the following points:

If you're a sailor, you can listen open-mouthed to some of the cruise adventures young couples have these days; bubbling breathlessly and laughingly about getting underway while the "blue blazers" gape; stopping in the most improbable places. . . . To a traditional cruiser it all sounds a bit superficial and over-romanticized.

But if you're a sailing dealer and you expect to reach the new, young buying couples—the folks with money in their jeans and willingness to spend it on the outdoor life, the "freedom" sports—you better try to dig it.

Dealers seemed to be recognizing a nontraditional, nonnautical market of nonexpert but affluent sailors who were more interested in comfort, wall-to-wall stereo, and gourmet galleys than in sailing performance. These people were not interested in the organized life of the yacht club, but wanted hassle-free cruising. One type of sailboat that seemed to appeal to this market was the trailer sailer.

Trailer sailers were normally 20' to 26' long and allowed almost continental mobility, something few other livable boats offered. They cut maintenance costs considerably because the boat could be kept out of the water when not in use, and as *Table C* suggests, day-to-day maintenance costs could be substantial. Sales of trailerable boats slipped during the energy crisis, but were expected to pick up in the last half of the 1970s.

[6]The four most popular product classes had about equal dollar sales. Foam sailers sold for between $100 and $150; multiple hulls generally sold in the $1,000 to $3,000 range; sailboats ranged from $1,400 to $7,500 or more; and day sailers ran up to $5,000 or $6,000. Shipped value in 1975 was about $44 million.

TABLE C Rental Charges for Summer Berthing at Surveyed Establishments, 1973 ($ per Season)

Type of berthing	Flat charge		Charge per foot	
	Range	Average	Range	Average
Moorings	5–300	129	2–8	4.67
Breasted on docks	100–500	253	6–30	15.60
Slips	75–920	273	8–30	13.03
Tie-offs	90–400	297	5–10	7.50
Dry-stack	300–325	313	12–15	12.75

Source: David A. Storey. *The Massachusetts Marina Boatyard Industry 1972–1973*. October 1974/Bulletin #612. Massachusetts Agricultural Experimental Station. College of Food and Natural Resources, University of Massachusetts at Amherst.
Note: Typical season = 6 months.

The power boat segment of the industry was expected to resume growth at its historical rate or, perhaps, a little better. What the experts were more confident of was their prediction that among the surviving companies would be those more adequately capitalized firms that had the ability to widen their distribution systems and sustain volume production. This suggested that the power-boat segment of the industry would be split into two quite different businesses. Boats larger than 26′, would be at least partially handbuilt and virtually customized. Boats below 26′, would be semi-automatically or automatically produced.

In the under 26′, segment, manufacturers would have to continue to fight for uniqueness because new designs could be easily imitated. It might be that, like the auto industry, annual model changes would be more widely adopted—as a defensive as well as an aggressive strategy.

Males were thought to dominate most boat purchase decisions, certainly in the traditional markets. Surveys suggested that the typical male boat user was afloat at least twice the time of the typical female boat user. (The outboard market is described in *Exhibits 5* and *6*.) The sailing market seemed to be different if the profile of the typical reader of *Yachting* and similar magazines was coincident with the profile of the typical sailboat buyer: mostly college educated and in the growing 25–44 age bracket. There was a substantial readership, however, in the 55–65 age bracket. Most readers were interested in sailing as a recreational activity, and consistent with this theme, it was reported that most boat sales were made on weekends between 10 A.M. and 3 P.M

Aside from sales and manufacturing problems, the boating industry had other problems. Its executives often felt beset by governmental regulations. The Boat Safety Act of 1971 required boat manufacturers to keep records of their compliance efforts. EPA and OSHA had an effect. Motor boat noise levels were being reduced under government pressure. The Clean Water legislation affected boat sanitation systems. And, the chemicals used in boat manufacturing were found harmful to workers.

Among the problems facing the industry in 1976 was a shortage of marinas and service centers. To be successful, a marina had to be located in a heavily populated area. In these areas real estate values were high, especially when beach frontage was involved. One response was the dryland marina, but many owners had to have waterside service. Brand turnover was rising as dealers and OEMs (original equipment manufacturers) jockeyed for relative bargaining power and return on investment. As the industry entered its major selling season in 1976, dealers were conservative about the industry's sales prospects and OEM orders were slow. In boat sales, dealer conservatism could have been due to the problems of trade-ins. In 1975 about 46% of all new boat sales involved a trade-in.

Exhibit 5 Why Customers Buy Outboard Boats and Motors, 1970–1975

Buyers mentioning (in %)	1970	1971	1972	1973	1974	1975
Outboard motors						
Cruising	36.5%	32.6%	32.1%	31.1%	32.7%	40.0%
Fishing	55.4	47.0	36.1	36.4	33.0	42.3
Hunting	32.0	30.2	30.0	28.8	31.4	26.1
Skiing	54.1	50.4	49.2	49.3	47.7	40.2
All other	7.0	7.0	6.8	6.8	7.6	11.6
Outboard boats						
Cruising	41.4	37.2	36.9	40.5	37.9	38.8
Fishing	53.1	44.0	39.7	42.2	35.5	40.6
Hunting	37.7	35.8	29.9	36.9	32.9	25.9
Skiing	45.7	48.5	48.5	44.6	50.5	33.3
All other	6.1	6.5	5.9	5.9	6.7	9.9

Source: Boating Industry, January 1976.
Note: Percentages add to more than 100% because of multiple responses.

Exhibit 6 Top Markets for Outboard Boats and Motors, 1970–1975

	Outboard boats						*Outboard motors*					
Occupation of purchaser (in %)	1970	1971	1972	1973	1974	1975	1970	1971	1972	1973	1974	1975
Skilled workers	24.2%	21.6%	21.6%	21.8%	22.2%	22.4%	24.5%	22.6%	24.3%	22.4%	22.3%	22.6%
Clerical workers, salespeople	17.9	20.3	21.4	15.8	14.0	15.8	17.2	19.4	19.7	15.4	13.4	15.6
Managers, proprietors	15.9	13.7	11.3	15.4	19.3	19.8	14.3	12.9	11.8	14.5	19.3	19.1
Professional	17.0	18.1	15.9	24.7	20.5	16.7	17.6	18.8	18.2	25.7	22.3	18.5
Semiskilled workers	12.9	11.1	13.9	7.3	10.3	12.6	13.9	14.6	13.3	6.7	10.1	12.2
Farmers, farm laborers	2.4	2.4	2.2	2.2	2.6	3.1	2.6	2.6	2.5	2.4	2.8	2.9
Protective, service workers	7.9	7.8	7.4	9.2	9.0	8.7	7.9	7.1	7.3	9.1	8.5	8.1
Factory laborers	1.8	2.0	3.3	3.6	1.6	0.9	2.0	2.0	2.9	3.8	1.3	1.0
Total	100%	100%	100%	100%	100%	100%	100%	100%	100%	100%	100%	100%

Source: Boating Industry, January 1976.

(*Table D* details the types of service provided by a number of Massachusetts marinas.)

TABLE D Repair Activities at Surveyed Establishments

Type of repair activities	*Establishments*	
	Number	Percent
Wooden boats	81	69
Fiberglass boats	79	67
Inboard engines	81	69
Outboard engines	62	53

Source: David A. Storey. *The Massachusetts Marina Boatyard Industry 1972–1973.* October 1974/Bulletin #612. Massachusetts Agricultural Experimental Station. College of Food and Natural Resources, University of Massachusetts at Amherst.

WALKING IN AS PRESIDENT

When Gilcrist got to Yellowtail's boatyard, where the company's offices were located, she realized that it was already 8:15 A.M. and her plane to San Francisco left at 11:30 A.M. She had only two hours or perhaps a little more before she would have to leave. Gilcrist was eager to confirm Boswell's high opinion of her. She had to deal with what Gunerson had left, whatever had come up since, and the tasks Boswell had given her.

Because she was acting under a time constraint, Gilcrist decided to be specific and write the letters she needed to write, to make notes to herself and others as necessary. She liked to plan every action and clarify its purpose: What was to be done, by whom, and when? There might be other factors that seemed important; if so, she would be specific with respect to them. Gilcrist even decided to write out the substance of any phone calls she made and to plan her movements if she had to leave San Diego. She entered Gunerson's office, picked up his in-basket, and took it into the office Gunerson had set up for her. She felt it would be better to leave his office free until his personal effects had been returned to his wife. Then she went to work on the in-basket items.

ITEM 1

April 13, 1976

Ms. Gilcrist
President

Dear Ms. Gilcrist:

Normally we plan our show dates about 12 months ahead. This year we are running late. Which shows do you want us to participate in? I have attached a list of major shows from February through September.

Sincerely,

Paul Lees

Paul Lees
Marketing Manager

PL/wm

Attachment: Boat Show Calendar

ITEM 2

April 13, 1976

Ms. Gilcrist
President
Yellowtail, Inc.

Dear Ms. Gilcrist:

Mrs. Naumes, who was Mr. Gunerson's secretary, is very upset and will not be in for a few days. I'll try to help out where I can.

Cordially,

Sarah Clarke

Sarah Clarke

ITEM 3

April 13, 1976

Ms. Robyn Gilcrist
President

Robyn:

Welcome to Yellowtail. Sorry you have to start without Olaf.

Finish off the stuff Olaf left and fly to Miami to meet Stewart Marschal. He is a large dealer for Chris Craft in Florida. He is unhappy with the way they are dealing with him and may switch to us. Forget San Francisco but get back to San Diego for the funeral.

Let me have your ideas on Yellowtail's strategy before the funeral. We can go over it then and you'll have plenty of time to get set for the Board meeting on April 29.

Good Luck,

BOZ

Charles Boswell

CB:lhd

ITEM 4

April 14, 1976
8:27 a.m.

NOTE: Telephone call. Charlie Douglas, Yard Foreman.

. . . real glad I'm here. . . met at Gunerson's club and . . . plant. . . problem in the yard. Mr. McPhail (the yard manager) on vacation one more week. . . can't afford to wait. . . trouble. . . Outboard plant where space between the inner and outer skins filled. . . two foam injection units. . . one acting up. . . odd. . . new high pressure unit. . . first time trouble. Usually old one. . . problem hard to pin down. . . getting nine times normal number of air pockets in the hulls. . . only way to fix them. . . by hand. . . drill through the fiberglass skins and fill hole, then patch and smooth skin. Normally, one part-time man but now. . . have to stop production to fix boats already made. . . not sure whether it's injectors or men causing problem. . . McPhail fired Bob Lewis. . . with us 8 years. Last week <u>his</u> brother, Mike. . . works on foam injection was complaining. . . saying he would show us a thing or two one day. . . thinks men upset about Bob Lewis. . . knows he and McPhail. . . sharp words. . . number of occasions (lately). . . never had sabotage here Mike Lawson, Personnel Manager, said. . . that's what he thinks. Jack Patterson. . . shop steward, says men aren't doing it. . . doesn't want to push. . . always been straight but election soon. . . Lawson suspects trouble. Kendall, the organizer of the Boatyard Carpenters and Painters. . . here on Thursday, April 15. . . lives in San Diego. . . always stops here on the 3rd Thursday of the month on way back from Los Angeles. . . thought might have been the new foam, but both injectors using it. . . old one not having any trouble. . . not sure what to do next. . . needs help.

ITEM 5

ANDREWS, PETERS AND FINCH
Attorneys at Law

April 8, 1976

Re: EPA letter of April 5, 1976

Dear Mr. Gunerson:

As your legal advisor we believe that the law on your particular case is such that it would take years to force the company to comply with the "clean water" regulations. Even then, the annual costs for <u>continued</u> noncompliance would be about $12,000 if successful legal action was taken.

Cordially,

Patrick Finch

Patrick Finch

PF/tjb

ITEM 6

April 12, 1976

Mr. Gunerson
President
Yellowtail Marine, Inc.

Mr. Gunerson:

I could not find the exact information you asked for, but I have collected what I could.

The Boat Manufacturers Association prints estimated unit sales of outboard motors by city and state, and I have found estimates of the numbers of motors owned as of December 31, 1975. I think the Coast Guard Report Map may be more useful.

I'm sorry that the hull material report is only up to 1971, but the librarian said that government statistics are usually a year or two behind. It takes a year or two to work them out I guess.

Sincerely,

Robert J. Blake

Robert J. Blake
Marketing Manager

RJB/jt

Enclosures

ITEM 7

8:37 A.M Ms. Clarke knocks and brings a letter into the office saying as she comes in that Mr. Arch Towne of OSHA and two other men are in the foyer. Mr. Towne wants a representative of management and the shop steward to tour the plant with him and he asked for the president.

ITEM 8

OCCUPATIONAL SAFETY AND HEALTH ADMINISTRATION
Department of Labor
Government Center
San Diego Office
California

April 12, 1976

Mr. Olaf Gunerson
President
Yellowtail Marine, Inc.
San Diego, California

Dear Mr. Gunerson:

Your company has been selected for an in-depth investigation by our inspectors. As one of San Diego's leading marine businesses you are doubtlessly aware of the threats to worker safety commonly encountered in the boat building industry and we look forward to your cooperation during the inspections.

A team of inspectors under the supervision of Mr. Arch Towne will arrive on the morning of Wednesday, April 14 to give your boatyard a thorough going over. This letter will serve to introduce Mr. Towne the Senior Inspector.

Sincerely,

Marvin E. Sharppe

Marvin E. Sharppe
Regional Director

MS:dl

ITEM 9

MOUTON, LAMBE and WOLFE
Investment Bankers & Venture Capitalists
111 North LaSalle Street
Chicago, Illinois 60607

April 9, 1976

Mr. Olaf Gunerson
President
Yellowtail Marine, Inc.
San Diego, California

Dear Mr. Gunerson:

As I mentioned on the telephone on April 8, Saggitarius Inflatable Boats, Inc. is for sale at an attractive price. We would be delighted to meet your executive vice president whenever it is convenient for her.

Saggitarius is a new entry into the inflatable boat market, which is estimated to be growing at 20% per annum. The company had sales of $501,000 in 1975, its first full year of operations, and had a profit of $12,000 after meeting a number of start-up expenses. The company has a good distribution network in the Great Lakes area and a small leased plant, which is an old boatyard in Waukegan, near Chicago.

Our advisors think that the company needs an additional investment of $375,000 if it is to improve the quality of its products and ensure dealer reorders. However, our investigations show that the dealers are anxious to have the Saggitarius line.

Saggitarius makes eight outboard runabouts taking up to 100 horsepower, four dinghies, two life boats, and whitewater rafts, which are distributed mainly on the East Coast. The company's products sell for between $450 and $850.

We approached you initially to seek potential buyers with whom you were familiar, and when you said that Yellowtail might be interested itself, we were delighted. The asking price is $250,000. Management will continue if needed.

My partners and I are ready to assist you at your convenience.

Sincerely,

Roger Lambe

Roger Lambe

RL/ky

ITEM 10

ENVIRONMENTAL PROTECTION AGENCY
Southern California Office
San Diego

April 5, 1976

Mr. Olaf G. Gunerson
President
Yellowtail Marine, Inc.

Dear Mr. Gunerson:

On a recent inspection of the San Diego harbor our inspectors found high levels of cyanide and other chemicals in the bay off your boatyard. A closer inspection revealed that paint and other waste materials were being flushed out of your plant into the Bay.

Our inspector, Mr. Andrew Tozallowzki, will call you on April 19 at 9 A.M. if that is convenient, to discuss your plans for complying with the Clean Air and Water Act of 1971.

Sincerely,

George Davidson

George Davidson
District Supervisor

GD/jm

Study Questions

1. What are Gilcrist's responsibilities to the company? To the employees who might resent her sudden appearance? To Boswell?
2. How would you rank the issues she faces in terms of relative importance? Which are in conflict?
3. What long-term goals should she set for herself?
4. What should she do *now?*
5. How should she communicate her decisions?
6. What *risks* does Gilcrist face? What painful decisions should she make?
7. Should she immediately move to make the company more market-oriented? How?

CHAPTER 3

Audience Analysis

As the discussion in the previous chapter makes clear, you can't set achievable goals without persuading various audiences to help you achieve them. Audience analysis means understanding the interests, values, and goals of those people whom you want to influence to do something. It is perhaps the most critical and underpracticed skill in management. Success in business communications derives heavily from an ability to provide the framework for a motivated consensus—what organizational behaviorists call *participatory management.* Often, the course you choose matters less than the degree to which others are committed to achieving your goal. This means you must understand how they think; how they perceive their interests; what will move them to support you or, at least, stay out of the way. It also means you must give them something to believe in. This involves keeping your channels of communication open before, during, and after the decision-making process.

Audience analysis remains the most frequently and perilously ignored challenge in business communication. By the time you've decided what you want to accomplish, why you're the person to do it, and how to go about it, you'll probably see your recommendation as inevitable—and self-evident to others. Often, it won't be.

Start your audience analysis by posing a few key questions:

1. Who are my audiences?
2. What is my relationship to my audiences?
3. What are their likely attitudes toward my proposal?
4. How much do they already know?
5. Is my proposal in their interests?

WHO ARE MY AUDIENCES?

Defining your audiences may seem obvious. They are the people you want to act—the consumers who should buy your product, the boss whose sign-off you need, the employees who could achieve greater productivity. In almost any communication situation, however, the support—or at least the neutrality—of secondary audiences will be critical to achieving your goal. What opinion makers or other sources of information may shape consumers' behavior irrespective of your advertising campaign? Whom does the boss consult before making a decision? What individuals or groups may have more influence over your employees' attitudes than you do? In what order should you approach the various audiences who will pass judgment on your proposal?

Take the time to list every significant audience likely to have an influence on, or be affected by, your proposal. Divide these into *primary* and *secondary* groups. Then examine each of these audiences individually:

- *Primary audiences* include key decision-makers and others whose support you need to carry out your project.
- *Secondary audiences* include those who will be affected by your project and who, over the long term, may have some influence on the decision-makers.

Keep in mind that primary and secondary audiences may include further subgroups; "employees," for example, may have conflicts of interest between hourly and salaried. In addition, don't ignore *hidden audiences,* which include those who may not be in the group you're addressing or on the receiving end of your E-mail, but who will have influence over whether the course of action you're recommending is adopted. Consider the relatively simple communication situation described in Exhibit 1.1 (p. 6). An example of a hidden audience would be your boss's boss—someone you'll never see during the decision process but with whom you can nevertheless communicate. In your message to your boss, include the information she'll need to sell your proposal to her superior.

WHAT IS MY RELATIONSHIP TO MY AUDIENCES?

When advocating a strong point of view to audience members, you must adapt your presentation strategy to the realities of your relationship with them. Are you telling them or asking them to do something? Most business communication falls somewhere in between. You take one approach when delivering a proposal to a committee of superiors and another when assigning a task to an assistant. In her *Guide to Managerial Communication,*[1] Mary Munter offers a useful model of how to determine your approach to your audience:

As Munter observes, "The more you control, the less you involve; the less you involve, the more you control." Munter is really talking about two sorts of control here: information and executive power. (See *Exhibit 3.1,* Munter's Examples of Approaches to Various Audiences.) This is important: The more audience members feel they have contributed to a given decision, the more likely they will cooperate in carrying it out. However strongly you feel about your point of view, it will not prevail without support from the audiences whom you need to approve and implement it. This model also invites you to consider whether you are proposing *up* or *down.* Sometimes "tell" simply means a superior is issuing a legitimate and nondebatable executive order. Don't waste colleagues' time by arguing about what's already been decided unless there's a chance of changing it. Some rules of thumb for adopting your strategy:

[1] (Englewood Cliffs, N.J.: Prentice-Hall, 1992), p. 6.

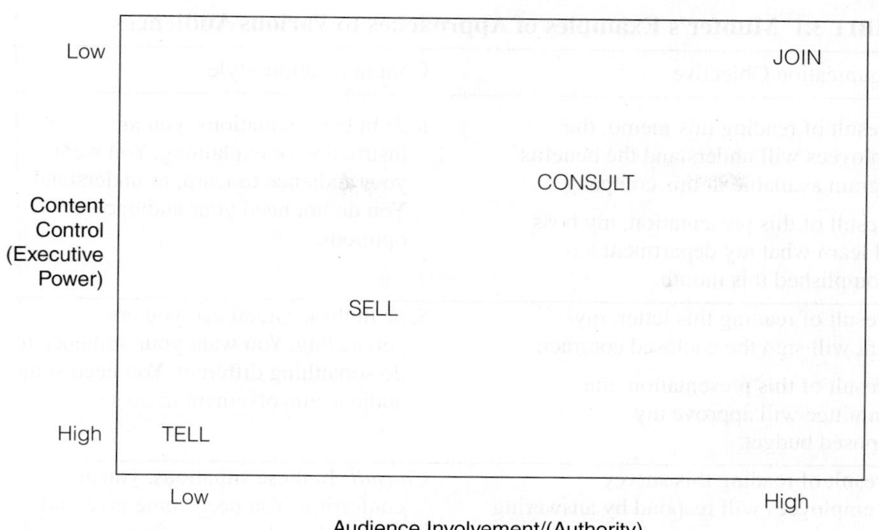

1. Use the *tell* approach when you are in complete command of the necessary authority and information. For example, you ask a subordinate to carry out a routine task.
2. Use the *sell* approach when you're in command of the information, but your audience retains the ultimate decision-making power. For example, you ask a customer to buy your product.
3. Use the *consult* approach when you're trying to build consensus for a given course of action. For example, you persuade colleagues to back your proposal to top management.
4. Use the *join* approach when your point of view is one among many. For example, you serve as a representative to an interdepartmental strategy session.

Generally, you're telling down and joining up. But not always. Often you'll find yourself soliciting the ideas of subordinates (consulting) or lobbying superiors for a favorable decision (selling). Successful advocacy of your point of view, as we will emphasize throughout this text, stands or falls on taking the proper approach to your audience.

WHAT ARE THEIR LIKELY ATTITUDES TOWARD MY PROPOSAL?

If you've defined your audiences correctly, the likely answer is, mixed. You've advanced when you've defined one audience as supportive, a second audience as neutral, a third as hostile. But closer examination will reveal that, even within these groups, attitudes vary. This is the time to do your preliminary research, whether that means sounding out a friend or commissioning a major survey.

EXHIBIT 3.1 Munter's Examples of Approaches to Various Audiences

Communication Objective	Communication Style
As a result of reading this memo, the employees will understand the benefits program available in this company. As a result of this presentation, my boss will learn what my department has accomplished this month.	*Tell:* In these situations, you are instructing or explaining. You want your audience to learn, to understand. You do not need your audience's opinions.
As a result of reading this letter, my client will sign the enclosed contract. As a result of this presentation, the committee will approve my proposed budget.	*Sell:* In these situations, you are persuading. You want your audience to do something different. You need some audience involvement to do so.
As a result of reading this survey, the employees will respond by answering the questions. As a result of this question-and-answer session, my staff will voice and obtain replies to their concerns about the new policy.	*Consult:* In these situations, you are conferring. You need some give-and-take with audience members. You want to learn from them yet control the interaction somewhat.
As a result of reading this agenda memo, members of the group will come to the meeting prepared to offer their thoughts on this issue. As a result of this brainstorming session, the group will come up with a solution to this problem.	*Join:* In these situations, you are collaborating. You and your audience are working together to come up with the content.

Positive

Audiences who already support you need to be motivated and given a plan of action. Let them know how important they are and what they can do to help you. Make their job as easy and rewarding as you can.

Neutral

These audiences are most susceptible to the tools of rational persuasion. Include them in the sequence of events and analyses that convinced you this was a good idea to pursue.

Hostile

These audiences probably won't ever actively support you. But by showing that you understand their point of view and explaining why you still believe in your project, you may move them to a position of neutrality.

When doing this analysis, you must pay close attention to individual and group motives. Some people will support you because they're your friends, irrespective of the merits of your idea. Don't let such support lull you into a false sense of security about the attitudes of your wider audiences. Others will support you for motives totally unrelated to your own. Be sure you understand what these motives are, so you can factor them into your planning.

Sometimes key members of your audience will oppose your proposal on its merits; they'll have legitimate reasons to believe it won't work or isn't the best approach. In either of these situations, you'll be best served to deliver your message frankly, while acknowledging your opponents' concerns and the merits of their arguments.

Sometimes colleagues will oppose you simply because your success will come at a cost to them. A boss may not want to be outshone; coworkers may fear that your level of performance could set a standard that will force them to work harder; subordinates may have ideological disagreements or may simply not like you. This is the hardest type of opposition to overcome, because such audiences are unlikely to admit the real grounds of their opposition. This may drive them to develop—and believe in—some very creative reasons to reject your plan. Consider two strategies in this situation. First, give your opponents a way out—perhaps by incorporating their suggestions, sharing credit, or supporting them in a corollary success. Second, gain the support of those with authority over people who have a practical or egotistical investment in your proposal's failure.

Most often, audiences will include positive, neutral, and hostile factions. Generally, frank acknowledgment of these differences provides the best opportunity for success. Give those who support you further reasons to do so, those who are indifferent persuasive arguments to get on board, and those who oppose you an explanation of how your proposals may be in their interests after all. Even acknowledging that opponents have a reasonable basis for their position can sometimes turn hostile audience members neutral.

HOW MUCH DO THEY ALREADY KNOW?

Nothing is more boring than reading a memo filled with familiar information. Nothing is more frustrating than listening to a presentation pitched over one's level of familiarity with the subject. Both experiences are likely to turn neutral audiences into hostile ones or supportive audiences into neutral ones. Before communicating, ask yourself some basic questions about each of your audiences:

1. What familiar information should I summarize to lay the foundation for my argument?
2. What additional information do they need to know to understand and judge my proposal?
3. How can I speak or write in language they will understand and respond to?

IS MY PROPOSAL IN THEIR INTERESTS?

This question cuts to the heart of audience analysis. Successful managers put themselves in others' shoes. If you were in your audience's position, what would motivate you to offer your support?

Analyzing your audience means identifying—first to yourself, then to them—how they will benefit by supporting you. Possible benefits are as various as human nature itself, but they include money, prestige, time saving, solidifying a friendship, gaining authority, avoiding conflict or embarrassment, improving status, making a job easier, and being on the winning side.

Sometimes managers have to send bad news, that is, news that can't be presented as being in the interests of the audience. We'll treat this situation more thoroughly in future chapters, but when you are facing a hostile audience, ask yourself a few key questions:

1. Why is this announcement or proposal going to hurt my audience? Having defined this clearly, you can at least show that you understand—and sympathize with—their point of view.
2. Can I demonstrate that my audience will suffer negative consequences regardless of whether my proposal is adopted? If so, you may be able to make the case that your strategy is the best of a bad lot, that the alternatives are even worse.
3. Having identified the grounds of the audience's opposition, can you find ways to soften the blow? Perhaps you can hold out hope that things may improve in the future. Doing so may allow you to position yourself as your audience's ally.

Given this audience analysis, revisit your goal. Are you still convinced it's valuable, achievable, and worth the costs? Perhaps your proposal needs revision before you have a realistic chance of selling it. Perhaps accomplishing it by different means would make it easier for your audiences to agree. In any event, make sure you send a consistent message to all your audiences. In the long term, your credibility as a source is more important than the adoption of any individual proposal. See Part Three, especially Chap. 17, Effective Speaking, for further discussion of how you can enhance your credibility with various audiences.

CONCLUSION: SELL BENEFITS, NOT FEATURES

Many managers believe that the sheer force of logic—the clarity of a particular cost/benefit analysis, for example—will convince others to support a given course of action. Most organizations (read: contexts) don't work that way. Effective advocacy means more than announcing the results of a trenchant analysis. It also means explaining the relevance of your proposal to the concerns, interests, and opinions of a wide variety of audiences: people from within different functional areas of the organization; parties in the public sector; specific colleagues, superiors, subordinates; and other individuals whose support will be needed before your proposal can be adopted.

The tools of rational persuasion will work only if their use convinces your audiences that the action you wish them to take will serve either their own interests or a greater good. This means selling benefits—what the audience will gain—rather than features, however fascinating, important, or elegant those features may seem to you. Customers may be supremely uninterested in the technology of a new management information system, which you know in detail. But they will be very interested in the savings of time and money that such a system can bring to their businesses. Hence, the first principle of message design: Ask not why you think your idea is great, but rather, What does my audience need to know or believe to support me?

In the following case, top management is sending some sobering news to audiences whose attitudes are bound to be mixed at best. How should Weymouth Steel factor audience analysis into its communication strategy?

CASE 3.1

Weymouth Steel Corporation

In early September of 2004, Weymouth Steel Corporation found itself with both good news and bad news to communicate to its salaried employees. The good news would affect all salaried employees, the bad news only some.When Chairman of the Board Carl Weymouth and his staff discussed the matter, they realized that they faced a familiar but difficult task in corporate communication—a task, moreover, that seemed to encourage reappraisal of some of Weymouth's traditional approaches to employee communication.

GOOD NEWS AND BAD NEWS

The good news was that nearly all salaried employees would be receiving salary increases and improved benefits. Provisions for retirement, vacations, medical and dental care, life insurance, and stock ownership were liberalized or improved in a variety of ways. While some of the changes derived from provisions of the most recent union contract, others resulted from Weymouth's ongoing adjustment of salaries and benefits. Ordinarily, such changes were communicated to employees through personnel bulletins and regular issues of the appropriate Weymouth publications—*Metal News* for salaried employees, *The Open Hearth* for hourly employees.

The bad news was that the company anticipated that it would have to terminate a sizable number of its employees—salaried as well as hourly. Long recognized as a highly cyclical business, the steel industry was enduring a long-term slump due largely to stiff competition from overseas companies. In the next eight months, Weymouth's business was likely to fall off 25%. At the same time, a variety of forces intensified the company's need for capital. To become more competitive with European and Japanese firms,Weymouth needed to purchase and install new processing machines and to construct state-of-the-art rolling and hot-strip mills.

In addition, their plants needed to satisfy federal anti-pollution standards. During the next five years, capital spending was expected to average $2 billion a year. Therefore, all areas of the company urgently needed to reduce costs.

This case is an update by Michael Hattersley of a case written by Linda McJannet. Harvard Business School case 393–014.

In recent years, Weymouth had initiated several major cost-cutting measures. They shut down several smaller and less efficient mills and processing plants. They deferred some plant modernizations, particularly those not necessary to meet environmental regulations. They restricted the use of overtime and temporary salaried employees. They encouraged efforts to reduce purchasing and supply costs. They limited travel and related expenses; whenever possible, meetings were to be held in company facilities. Ultimately, they would have to reduce the number of salaried employees.

No exact figure was set, and the company hoped to keep the number as low as possible; but as many as 2,000 salaried positions might be affected. Half of these might be painlessly eliminated through normal attrition, early retirement, and transfers. Whenever possible, open positions that could not be filled by transferring present employees would be left unfilled. The company planned to stay in touch with colleges through career days and faculty contacts, but actual recruiting on campuses was canceled for the balance of 2004. Nevertheless, when the painless methods were exhausted, 1,000 employees might have to be let go.

THE SALARIED EMPLOYEE

Salaried employees at Weymouth encompassed 20 different pay grades from file clerks to top management. Grades 1–10 included college trainees, maintenance workers, printing office employees, plant foremen, general foremen, plant superintendents, general engineers; grades 11 and up included the senior engineers and managers. It was assumed that the reductions would take place across the board; proportionally, no one grade would be significantly more affected than any other.

A salaried employee with one or more years of service would be eligible for a termination payment. He or she would also be paid for unused vacation for 2004 and any vacation accrued for 2005. Insurance coverage continued for one month after layoff and could be continued beyond one month by the former employee at reasonable rates. Unlike the hourly employees (10,000 of whom were laid off by October 31, as it turned out), salaried employees could not count on the Supplemental Employment Benefits (SUB) that were available to members of the United Steelworkers of America. Between SUB and state unemployment compensation, a union member who was laid off could receive a substantial portion of his or her former base pay for up to two years, depending on length of service. Salaried employees had a much smaller cushion against the hardships of termination. Weymouth managers were well aware of this fact and planned to do what they could to assist former employees in their search for a new job.

HOW TO COMMUNICATE THE NEWS?

Traditionally, the company made no general announcement of planned reductions of salaried employees, nor did it usually explain its reasons in any public forum. Employees were individually informed by their supervisors that their positions had been eliminated or that their services were no longer needed. James Harrison, VP for Public Affairs, had recommended that in such situations Weymouth should begin to take the initiative in openly communicating important information to its employees. Previous layoffs had been handled in the traditional way, Harrison pointed out, and the grapevine had exacerbated bad feeling. Instead of letting the press pick up a rumor about the layoffs, instead of letting the grapevine distort the reasons for the decision, he felt the company should go directly to its salaried employees with the full story. He urged that Weymouth explain the reasons for the decision and reassure all salaried employees that the company would do what it could to soften the blow.

When the matter was discussed by the staff in mid-September, Harrison's view was generally accepted; but the decision to take the initiative raised several questions. If some special communication(s) were to go out to the salaried employees, would the possibility of layoffs and the improvements in benefits be treated in the same document or in separate ones? How could the special communication(s) be coordinated with the regular channels—*Metal News* and *The Open Hearth,* personnel bulletins and the like? Who should sign—Byron Miller, Executive Vice President, Sandra Bernstein, VP for Personnel, or Weymouth himself? Should the company supplement any letter(s) with meetings, a teleconference, or explanatory videotapes? How best might the news be communicated to the outside world?

THE STAFF DEBATE

These questions sparked considerable debate. Bernstein argued for one letter; Harrison felt two letters were needed. No matter how carefully explained, he argued, the two messages would seem inconsistent; benefits would be immediately canceled out by anxiety and resentment over the possibility of layoffs. Weymouth agreed with Bernstein that one letter would serve. However, he stressed that employees and the media should both be considered key audiences; perhaps a letter and a press release were in order.

The staff did not entirely agree on the emphasis of any letter or memo to the employees. Harrison felt that employees needed to be informed about the impact of the industry downturn in general and about the various measures the company was taking to reduce costs. He also urged that any special communication include a strong and explicit expression of concern for the employees who might be laid off. Weymouth questioned whether information about other cost-cutting measures ought to be included; to someone who was about to lose his or her job, restrictions on travel and overtime might seem trivial or irrelevant. Bernstein was wary of attempting to express the company's concern; she felt such sentiments were awkward to convey and might seem condescending or hypocritical to some employees.

The staff also debated the source and the audience(s) of the special communication(s). Some argued strongly for a "corporate" communiqué, signed by Weymouth. Others felt that Bernstein of Personnel should sign. Everyone agreed that timing was important and that employees should know the company's plans before anything appeared in the press. They also recognized that both employees and the media were likely to have questions once these matters were openly discussed and that the company needed to have a response mechanism in place.

Weymouth was leaving for Japan the next day, but he felt the time had come to act on the staff's discussions. Harrison agreed to draw up an action plan and prepare the special communication(s) he deemed necessary.

Weymouth Steel Corporation: 2003 Fact Sheet

Sales	$6,702*
Net income	($307)*
Total assets	$6,973*
Employees	
Hourly	50,000
Salaried	10,000

*Figures in millions.

Study Questions

1. What key audiences need to be addressed in Weymouth's communication of good and bad news?
2. Where do their interests conflict? Overlap?
3. Most business communications involve good news for some audiences, bad news for others. What does this imply about how Weymouth should send its messages?
4. What is Weymouth doing—telling, selling, consulting, joining?
5. What media should Weymouth be using to send its messages?

CHAPTER 4

Point of View

Archimedes said, "Give me a lever and a place to stand, and I can move the world." To achieve anything, a manager must have a place to stand—a point of view. By *point of view,* we mean the perspective from which you assess a situation and present your findings and recommendations to your audiences. Whenever you set out to describe a problem or propose a solution, you must review the available information, the different and often conflicting values and interests that apply, and the opinions of other observers and participants. In doing so, you cannot and should not be neutral. To understand the situation, to make action possible, you necessarily focus on those facts, values, and opinions that you judge to be most important. By the same token, only if audiences grasp your point of view can they follow you through to your conclusions.

When you adopt a point of view, you are as likely to stimulate opposition as to reach agreement. In focusing on certain parts of the situation, you necessarily subordinate some elements. These may be precisely the facts, values, or goals that are paramount to other parties in the decision or implementation. But flushing out disagreement will be a service to your opponents and to the organization as a whole. You've helped set the stage for a consensus that accounts for the needs of the widest possible constituency.

Being explicit about your position is important when you're communicating with subordinates. You'll be a better manager for knowing precisely where they diverge from your point of view and why. Maybe they're right, and you need to modify your premises. Maybe they're wrong, and you can explain why. Maybe you have a basic disagreement that has to be resolved by a combination of dialogue and authority. In any case, making your point of view clear defines the territory and moves the situation closer to action.

Taking a clear stand is equally important when communicating with superiors. When making a recommendation, stating the solution you favor up front will help your audience focus on the merits—or weaknesses—of your argument. Even if your boss ends up disagreeing with the course of action you've proposed, you will have defined the terms of a productive discussion. Most weak reports, presentations, and communication assignments fail to get to the point. They tend to wander around among the data and possible solutions. In most management situations, a well-argued proposal, based on a clear point of view, is worth a thousand pieces of raw information.

A strong organization encourages its managers to express clear viewpoints for at least three reasons:

1. Providing a clear point of view aids the decision-making process. Many important organizational decisions involve complicated, amorphous situations; a firm stand gets the basic facts and arguments on the table and provokes reasonable alternative approaches.
2. Broad participation helps ensure long-term cooperation once a decision is reached.
3. Standing for something separates the managers from the functionaries. Even if your proposal isn't adopted, you've contributed some vision and impetus to the discussion. Perhaps some significant information you've unearthed, or a major argument you've made, will modify and improve the course of action adopted.

From the organization's point of view, putting various sensible proposals into competition and then choosing among them is crucial. Only in this way can the organization motivate its team and respond credibly to its full range of audiences: employees, unions, management, stockholders, consumers, government agencies, interest groups, and the public at large. A consistent message, familiar to everyone in the organization, provides the best opportunity to motivate your team and present a coherent, dynamic identity to the world.

Both individual and organizational characteristics make the clash of perspectives common in managerial communication. Your view may differ radically from that of another intelligent observer. The information you routinely seek or receive will be confined largely to that area necessary to perform your duties. While it's important to defend a point of view that serves the needs of your area or project, you won't be able to do so effectively unless you understand why others are likely to oppose you. Your point of view will carry maximum weight if it shows that you've factored in the reasonable arguments of your colleagues and opponents.

One caution: Generally, vigorous defense of a given point of view is an asset. But a manager has only so much credibility, energy, and goodwill to spend. Ask yourself if these assets will be increased or depleted by the time you've reached your goal. Why do you want to achieve it? Is it to benefit yourself, your colleagues, your organization, your society? The answer will usually be some mix of these. Deciding which, and in what proportion, will help you test your idea against your value system. In advocating your own point of view, don't pursue a goal that you, your associates, or the future won't be able to justify.

Communication brings your whole personality into play. You can easily convince yourself that you're pursuing a hard-headed business goal when, in fact, you're venting emotions. Once you've decided your goal is clearly defined, worthwhile, and achievable, ask: Am I the right person to achieve it? Envision the long-term consequence of imposing your point of view on others. Do you have the temperament, interest, and stamina to see the task through and harvest the results? Sometimes, even you would be better off if your undeniably terrific goal were achieved by somebody else.

BURKE'S PENTAD

Decades ago, Kenneth Burke developed an enduring model for analyzing how points of view can be translated into action (see Burke's *A Grammar of Motives* [Englewood Cliffs, N.J., Prentice Hall, 1945]). In Burke's terms, an *agent acts* in a particular *scene* through specific *agencies* to achieve a particular *goal.* Let's examine how these five terms relate to the communication model we've been offering in this text.

Agent (Our Source)

An agent is usually a person or a group, but it can also be a department, a division, an entire organization, or even a nation. In short, an agent is any entity that can choose whether or not to perform certain acts. Identifying an agent amounts to ascribing responsibility for past acts and delegating responsibility for future acts. Decisions about agents answer the question: "Who did, or should do, such and such."

When considering yourself, or your corporation, as an agent ask yourself:

1. Am I the right person to accomplish this task?
2. Have I specified the people and organizations that should act in this situation?
3. Have I explained why other agents should not be involved?

Focusing on agency is particularly appropriate when addressing issues like staffing, motivation, working relationships, training programs, and personnel development. A clear explanation from an agent-centered perspective can answer your audience's crucial question: *How does this affect me?*

Act (Strategy and Tactics)

This can include anything you do to achieve a specific goal. It may be a physical action, such as testing a specific product, but it always involves designing and delivering specific *communications.*

When considering yourself or your corporation as an *actor* ask yourself:

1. Have I been clear about what I want to see happen or have others do?
2. Have I given adequate motivation, guidance, and instruction?

Focusing on act will lead you to consider the important details of implementation: who should do what, in what way, in what order, at what time? This is the language of instruction kits, operating manuals, and implementation sections of an action plan. Used well, an act-centered approach can provide a road map for reaching your goal. Used poorly, however, an act-centered perspective may lead you to issue a series of clear instructions into a void, oblivious of your context or audience.

Scene (Context)

This refers to the setting for agents, acts, and other variables in a decision. Historically, agents in the business world have concentrated on resources and constraints (labor, supply costs, demand). But in the 21st century, the *scene* includes governmental regulations, media attention, social issues, and political developments in the global marketplace. Decisions that seem prudent in the parochial scene of a department or corporation may look short-sighted in the larger picture.

When considering the scene in which you are acting, ask yourself:

1. When, where, and under what circumstances should this act be carried out?
2. In what context will my recommendation be considered?
3. Have I chosen too large a scene, or issue, diffusing my efforts?
4. Have I chosen too narrow a scene, ignoring the full context?

Agency (Mostly Messages)

This means the tools to accomplish your act. It may include materials, processes, skills, and human resources, but it always involves motivating people to do things. Here is where choosing the right message to send, and the right medium by which to send it, becomes crucial to achieving your goal.

When considering agency, ask yourself:

1. Have I specified how the agents can perform these acts?
2. Are the resources and means available to achieve my goal?
3. Given the scene, will any of the acts necessary to achieving my goal end up subverting it?

Consider this example: wholesale firing of employees may make bottom-line economic sense in a downturn. Agency—absent context—might suggest simply sending the affected employees pink slips. However, consideration of the scene, for example, the value of maintaining long-term community trust, might lead the agent to fire fewer people or offer retraining programs.

Focusing on agency will lead you to consider the "how tos" and their consequences: how to assign particular acts to particular agents, how to allocate resources so that each subordinate agent can do her job, how to make sure the right resources or mechanisms are in place at the right time, what the best media for sending your messages are. Used well, an agency-centered approach can ensure that the systems are in place to achieve the desired result; used poorly, it can overemphasize technical, mechanical, or procedural matters.

Goal

Burke puts this point last, but obviously you will have defined it from the start, and perhaps revised it as you've moved through the pentad. Focusing on your goal helps you explain how achieving it will benefit the individuals and groups you need to persuade to cooperate. Ask yourself these questions:

1. Have I explained why my audience will benefit from supporting my proposal?
2. Have I identified the values that guide this course of action?
3. Is achieving my goal clearly worth the costs in time and effort?

Especially important here is the emphasis on communicating values, because whether you stand for something is critical to your credibility as an agent or source. Sharing with your audiences the values that motivate your action will motivate them as well.

Used well, an emphasis on your purpose convinces audiences that something needs to be done. Used poorly, it can stress that your goals are important to you but not to your audience.

Though use of the pentad can't guarantee that your point of view will prevail, it can help you present it clearly and persuasively. As a checklist, it encourages you to reexamine your assumptions about each aspect of the situation you face. It can help you identify where your point of view coincides or diverges from others'. In this way, it can identify which term of the pentad needs most attention or revision in a particular communication situation. It can help you adapt your messages to diverse audiences. Your decision to buy a new piece of equipment may be explained by long-term cost savings to the accountants, efficiency to top management, labor-saving to the employees, and reliable delivery to the marketing team. All of these arguments must be true and consistent; then they will meet the different needs of different audiences.

PUTTING YOUR POINT OF VIEW INTO ACTION

Almost all business communication is an attempt to see that, to the extent practical, your point of view prevails in a given situation. Suppose two managers consider a joint project. Manager A's point of view is that the company needs to reduce costs, while manager B worries about inhibiting capital development and delaying the adoption of new techniques. Manager A must convince manager B that cost reductions are more important than postponing the new technology. Manager B must convince manager A that keeping up with technical advances will be more cost-effective in the long run. Unless both managers clearly formulate and communicate their points of view, they'll be talking past each other and unlikely to arrive at a joint course of action. If you understand how you and others are seeing and weighing each term in an exchange, you have a better chance of framing a point of view that will be consistent, comprehensive, and persuasive.

In the following case, a manager's point of view collides with his corporation's culture.

CASE 4.1

Smith Financial Corporation

On February 10, 1997, Frank Miller walked into the offices of Smith Financial Corporation to assume his position as the director of data management in Smith's Information Services department. In this new position Miller was asked to fill a job vacancy that had been open for more than a year and also to help restructure and reorganize Smith's Information Services department. In the end, Smith Financial Corporation may have gotten more than they bargained for.

HISTORY OF SMITH FINANCIAL CORPORATION

Smith Financial Corporation was established in the late 1800s and had been servicing large Fortune 500 companies for more than 100 years. In 1997, Smith had over 15 offices both in the United States and internationally. Smith's main office was located in New England.

The Smith Information Services (IS) department included slightly over 100 employees and was broken down into two main subdepartments: Systems and Programming (S&P) and Network Services. The Smith Data Management Group was part of the S&P department and consisted of five individuals, each of whom had been with Smith between 3 and 15 years.

Prior to Miller's joining the company in 1997, the previous manager of the Data Management Group had resigned in late 1996. Between 1996 and 1997, the Data Management Group reported directly to Brian Jones, vice president of systems and programming, while the group searched for a new manager. *Exhibit 1* provides a partial illustration of the organizational structure of Smith's IS department immediately after Miller was hired.

The primary function of the Data Management Group had always been to manage the distribution, storage, capture, and flow of data throughout Smith Financial Corporation. While searching for a replacement to manage the Data Management Group, the company also identified the need for a person who could come in to "shake things up" and help break some of the organization's cultural habits. It was time for a change. In February of 1997, Miller was hired to assume the position of assistant vice president and director of data management.

This case was prepared by Christopher Bortlik, © 2003.

EXHIBIT 4.1 Smith Financial Corporation Information Services Department Partial Organizational Chart February 10, 1997

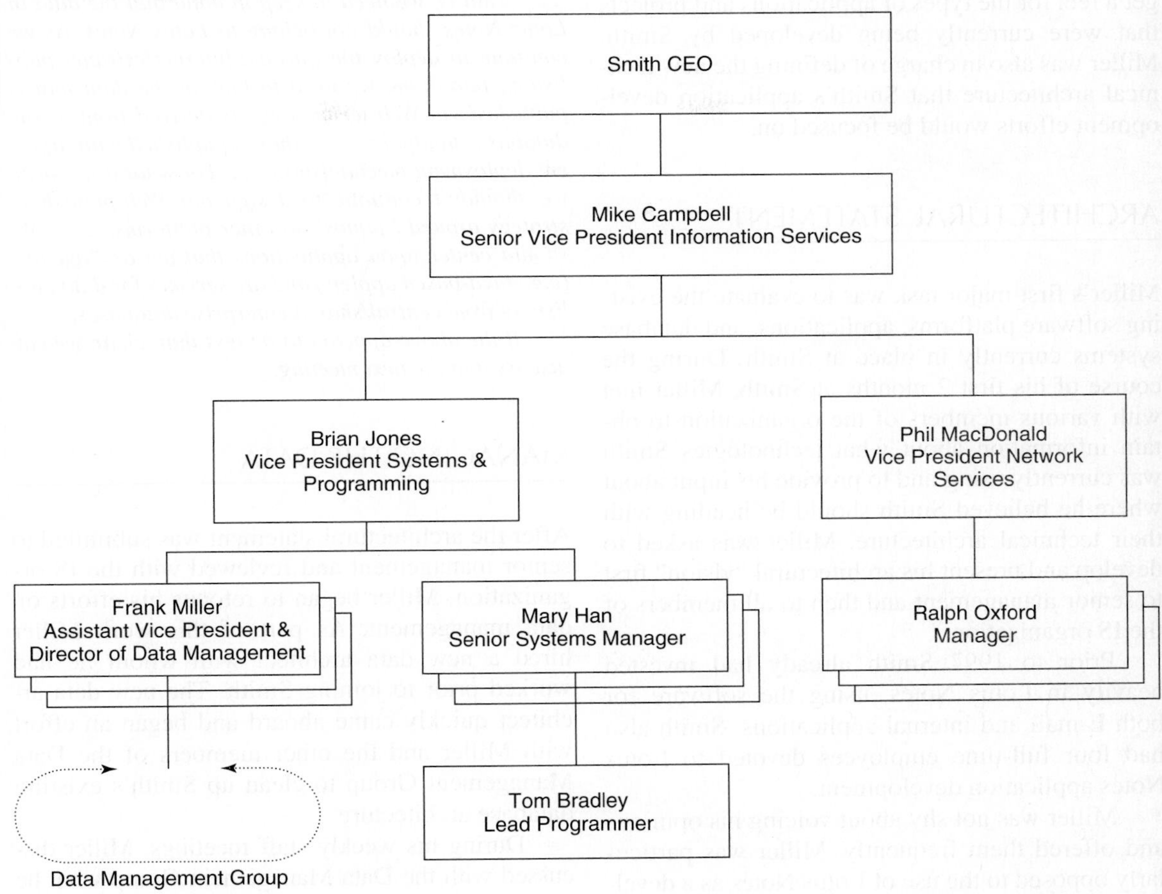

FRANK MILLER'S BACKGROUND

Prior to joining Smith in 1997, Frank Miller had been working as a consultant for more than 10 years. Throughout his 20-year career, Miller's primary focus was data management. Miller also had been published on a few occasions in industry trade magazines, writing about issues related to data management. Miller was knowledgeable about Microsoft products and frequently attended Microsoft conferences to help keep his technical skills sharp.

WELCOME TO SMITH FINANCIAL CORPORATION

Frank Miller entered the Smith New England office on Monday morning February 10 dressed in casual attire; his pepper-gray hair tied up with an elastic band. There was a buzz in the office as members of his staff introduced the new data manager to the S&P department, and people discussed Miller's technical background and skills with him. A new office was soon constructed for Miller and furnished with amenities such as leather chairs.

Miller moved into his new position and began to attend the various weekly project meetings to get a feel for the types of applications and projects that were currently being developed by Smith. Miller was also in charge of defining the new technical architecture that Smith's application development efforts would be focused on.

ARCHITECTURAL STATEMENT

Miller's first major task was to evaluate the existing software platforms, applications, and database systems currently in place at Smith. During the course of his first 2 months at Smith, Miller met with various members of the organization to obtain information about what technologies Smith was currently using and to provide his input about where he believed Smith should be heading with their technical architecture. Miller was asked to develop and present his architectural "vision" first to senior management and then to all members of the IS organization.

Prior to 1997 Smith already had invested heavily in Lotus Notes, using the software for both E-mail and internal applications. Smith also had four full-time employees devoted to Lotus Notes application development.

Miller was not shy about voicing his opinions and offered them frequently. Miller was particularly opposed to the use of Lotus Notes as a development and communications tool. During his architectural statement Miller spoke of the "sun setting" on Lotus Notes at Smith and recommended that Smith migrate to Microsoft Exchange. A few weeks after this presentation, the lead Lotus Notes developer left Smith to pursue opportunities elsewhere, stating that he did not see a future for himself at Smith.

Miller also directed his comments to members of IS management and offered the following comments during an E-mail exchange discussing the use of Lotus Notes for applications:

Folks . . . some "food for thought". . . .

I know that I am forever the "thorn in your side" about terminology and data/technical design, but that is my "calling" . . . . So, with that in mind, here goes . . . .

We should not look to Lotus Notes applications as we go forward as sources of data; they are not databases. . . . That is, we need to keep in mind that the data in Lotus Notes should not belong to Lotus Notes. As we continue to deploy the intranet/Internet/extranet publishing paradigm, we need to look at the data that is published via Web technology, as derived from a true database standpoint . . . shared/published with different deployment mechanisms. . . . For what it is worth, we shouldn't continue to design our Web-publishing strategy around "jumps" to other platforms. . . . We should center upon applications that act as "agents" (e.g., java-based applets) and are services for data publishing from central/shared/enterprise databases.

If the above appears to be less than clear, we can discuss it at the next meeting.

MANAGING THE DATA

After the architectural statement was submitted to senior management and reviewed with the IS organization, Miller began to refocus his efforts on data management. As part of this work Miller hired a new data architect with whom he had worked prior to joining Smith. The new data architect quickly came aboard and began an effort with Miller and the other members of the Data Management Group to clean up Smith's existing database architecture.

During his weekly staff meetings, Miller discussed with the Data Management Group what he saw as wrong with the existing systems. When members of his staff stepped in to explain why things were done in a particular way, Miller pushed these comments aside as "excuses" and spoke of how he was brought in to "fix the problems."

On many occasions Miller also shared his thoughts with other S&P managers. One such exchange occurred between Mary Han and Miller. Han needed an urgent change to resolve a critical business problem. After much discussion, Miller agreed to Han's proposal and offered the following explanation to the entire S&P department about why he was allowing this change although he was opposed to it:

Mary and I have reviewed the proposed solution, and, in light of the need, an exception to sound data management practice will be allowed in this case . . . the new environment and processes that will be forthcoming will prevent this type of "work around" solution in the future.

Frank Miller

TO PUSH OR NOT TO PUSH

In July 1997 Smith began to implement electronic commerce activities via the Internet with its customers. The Smith IS department was faced with two different options: to develop an Internet application internally (with assistance from outside consultants) or to purchase a third-party tool that would enable Smith to "push" information to its customers via the Internet.

Miller was asked to lend his consulting skills and knowledge to Tom Bradley who was heading up the Internet development activities at Smith. Miller and Bradley had different technical opinions on this matter: Miller was in favor of purchasing the third-party tool while Bradley recommended developing the applications in-house.

After reviewing the pros and cons of both proposals, senior management sided with Miller and granted authorization for Miller to purchase this third-party "push technology" from Interpush for $45,000. During negotiations with Interpush, Miller learned that the company was in the process of being acquired by another company and that the president of Interpush was leaving to start his own company. Miller decided that this information did not need to be shared with his manager (Jones) or the senior vice president of the IS department (Mike Campbell), since he did not believe that this information pertained to what Smith was looking to do with the product.

After a few weeks of working with Interpush to develop a customized version of the product for Smith, and after paying the full $45,000 contract, users of the product at Smith found the product to be too difficult to use, and Campbell was forced to abandon the use of this product. In August 1997, Internet development efforts were refocused, and Bradley's group set off to develop the Internet application internally with assistance from a consulting resource that was brought in to work with the team.

Shortly after Campbell decided not to implement the Interpush product, Campbell received an E-mail about the sale of Interpush. Campbell forwarded this announcement to the team and added the following comments:

> Sounds like we made the correct decision not to implement Interpush.

After reading the announcement sent to him by Campbell, Miller responded to Campbell and the group:

Mike . . .

Agreed, that is, of course, the point of team decisions . . . however . . . just for the record. . . .

Their sale is nothing we were not informed about . . . and, doesn't affect their viability as a push technology company. . . . In fact, as I read the article it points out the strengths they are pitching to . . . i.e., Corporate Customers. . . . We were hoping to use their development/technology versus developing it in-house via Microsoft's integrated push solution.

The fact that Netscape and Microsoft are integrating the technology underscores its viability. Of course when/if we integrate push (whether purchased or developed with the Microsoft toolkit) . . . it will likely cost the same amount of investment to develop and implement.

Great article, though.

Thanks for the copy . . .

Frank

THE END OF THE LINE

By mid-August 1997 it appeared that Miller had effectively alienated most people within the Smith IS organization. Miller received a written warning in June that his current "treatment of others" would not be tolerated any longer. Miller had 3 months to "shape up or ship out." Even after these warnings, members outside of the IS organization commented to Campbell and Jones how "unprofessional" Miller was acting during meetings with them, particularly when the discussion was not going his way. A number of people within the Smith IS organization left the organization and many others stated that they were prepared to leave if Miller stayed on.

By September things were getting further out of control. Meetings involving Miller and others in the organization were getting more contentious. On one occasion Ralph Oxford and Miller nearly engaged in a physical altercation. Campbell and Jones were left with no other choice. Miller was terminated in September of 1997.

Miller's termination after only 6 months with Smith left the entire organization in a state of shock and disbelief. How did someone who started with so much potential and hope to change things for the better end up being terminated only a few short months later? What could Miller have done differently to avert this fiasco?

Study Questions

1. How well does Miller's style and tone serve him in his E-mail explanations of why Lotus Notes isn't serving the company well? How would you do it differently?
2. How well does Miller communicate his goals for the future of data management at Smith Financial Corporation?
3. How sensitive is Miller to the knowledge levels and concerns of his various audiences?
4. Could you suggest a communication strategy that would have served Miller better?
5. What does the case suggest about the problems that can arise in clashes between various corporate cultures?
6. What role does personality play in communication? How can you, as Socrates recommended, learn to "Know yourself" better?

CHAPTER 5

Message: Content and Argument

This chapter concentrates on how you can design a message that will most likely achieve the results you wish with the full range of interested audiences. Successful message design depends on *content* (what you have to say) and *argument* (how you build your persuasive case).

CONTENT

Although *content* includes everything you know or have to say, at the beginning of your communication effort, you should be able to boil it down to a single sentence. Refer back to *Exhibit 1.1, Sample Communication Analysis* (p. 6).

Message: I want to take my vacation during a busy period.

Your basic message, in other words, consists of a clear statement of your goal. Each of your audiences must understand that goal to engage in communication with you. (Remember Drucker's admonition that communication isn't what's *said*, it's what's *understood*.) But because achievement of your goal will have different consequences for different audiences, this message requires modulation, for example:

To your boss I've arranged for my work to be covered by colleagues.
I can keep on top of the job by putting in more hours before and after the vacation.

To colleagues Schedules and deadlines can be rearranged to make this possible.
I'll repay the favor.

To everyone Personal considerations make it crucial that I go at this time.
Others have been given similar consideration.

All of these submessages are explanations of your main message, that is, *arguments* that support it. They justify *how* your goal can be achieved and *why* each audience should support you.

Often, business communications are more complex than the above example suggests. Often, you're in possession of a mass of data, all of which should inform your argument, but not all of which is essential for each audience to know. In these typical situations, you want to digest the data into salient points, then decide which points are most important to which audiences. At the same time, you need to be prepared to back up any generalization with evidence and to demonstrate why any given body of data has led you to a particular conclusion.

ARGUMENT

Finding the phrase that encapsulates your central message should be the first step in planning business communication. Then turn to audience analysis to determine how to develop it. Few managers can press a button and command automatic agreement with their positions. Usually, to achieve enough consensus to proceed, you must gain the support of your primary audiences, assuage the concerns of your secondary audiences, acknowledge and neutralize opposing points of view, and explain why your approach is more feasible than reasonable alternatives. This means advancing a logical proposition that can be defended by an appeal to evidence or to your audiences' interests and values.

Given good audience analysis, persuasive message design depends on the effective use of logic and evidence. There are two types of logical argument: deductive, which moves from the general to the specific, and inductive, which moves from the specific to the general.

Deductive logic pairs a major premise ("We need a safer workplace") with a minor premise ("My proposal will make our workplace safer") to draw a conclusion: "Therefore, we should adopt my proposal." Before using deductive logic, you need to conduct both an internal and an external reality check.

- *Internal:* Logical consistency doesn't necessarily equal truth. Perhaps your major premise is faulty, and others don't agree that the workplace is unsafe. Perhaps your minor premise is faulty, and your proposal won't really make the workplace safer. Both (or all) your premises must be acknowledged by your audiences before a deductive argument can be used to persuade them.
- *External:* Have your premises excluded elements that make them only partially true or irrelevant? Perhaps making your workplace safer will cost your company a crucial margin of profitability. Perhaps a different proposal would make the workplace even safer.

Most deductive arguments, of course, will involve more than two premises, but every one should pass these tests.

Inductive logic is the method of the researcher who assembles all the evidence, then seeks out the simplest explanation or conclusion. This has been the predominant approach of western science. In business, inductive argument often outlines a series of problems, then proposes a general solution: "Our salespeople promise products manufacturing can't supply. Manufacturing designs products no one wants to buy. Accounting tells us profitability is down. Therefore, we must establish a high-level strategic planning committee."

The inductive argument, like the deductive one, works only if each piece of evidence passes key tests. Are all the problems real—have we received one letter from a disgruntled customer, or a chorus of complaints? Are all the relevant facts included—has tension between sales and manufacturing propelled us toward an important technological breakthrough? Do all the facts bear directly on our argument? Perhaps the industry is suffering a general downturn, and our profitability holds up well by comparison. If all these factors have been considered, is the solution apt? We may need a new CEO rather than another level of bureaucracy. We may need to redefine the business we're in.

Both inductive and deductive arguments share the same basic structure. The essence of this method could be described as having three parts: *given* (major premise), *since* (minor premise), *therefore* (conclusion).[1]

Given:	That we all agree on this basic problem (deductive) *or* That we have assembled this body of data (inductive),
Since:	Addressing this problem will benefit us (deductive) *or* These data demonstrate the following trend or principle (inductive),
Therefore:	We should take the following course of action.

This three-part structure resembles a syllogism, the central strategy of Socrates, whose development of rational argument has dominated western thinking since the fifth century B.C. It has served as the central engine of mathematics for 2500 years. Use this tool to display your *major* arguments. Don't get bogged down mapping every assertion that plays a role, no matter how small, in your considerations. Consider the following functional definitions:

1. The *given* lays the foundation you believe your listeners or readers will grant for the argument, whether this is a general principle or a body of data. It answers the question, *What problem* and/or *evidence* do we agree that we have?
2. The *since* introduces the second step in your argument: a principle or a statement that links the *given* to the *therefore.*[2]
3. The *therefore* states the conclusion or course of action you want your audience to accept.

In the following pages, we will examine how informal syllogisms provide the basis for most business argument. As you review them, keep in mind the following general principles:

1. You should approach your audience as a *partner* who helps choose the criteria for generating argumentation. Bringing out too elementary or too many arguments will bore and alienate your partners; having too complex or too few arguments will frustrate them.

[1]For more details, see Stephen E. Toulmin, *The Uses of Argument* (Cambridge, England: Cambridge University Press, 1964), especially Part 3.
[2]Toulmin (op. cit.) calls it a "bridge."

2. When you review your overall argument, be sure to emphasize those parts that will be most important to your audience.
3. Once you've outlined an argument to yourself, consider how the audience can best receive it. Often you're better off starting with the *therefore,* so that your audience knows from the start where you're going.
4. Often, you'll find that the *since* is the most difficult to discern in your own and others' arguments. This is because, to the best-informed person, the *therefore* will seem to follow inevitably from the given. Keep in mind that your audience doesn't usually have all the information you do and hasn't thought it through as thoroughly. Use this model to help yourself clarify the *since.* This will remove unnecessary barriers from your partners' paths.

It's often hard to break down our thinking into the basic *given, since,* and *therefore* units, because they've become instinctive to us. This is especially true when we are arguing from *definition,* which relies on conventions and symbols whose meaning is agreed upon by a group. For example:

Given:	The stoplight is red, and
Since:	Red lights mean that I should stop,
Therefore:	I will stop at the red light.

Still, once we've considered the basic structure of an argument, these sorts of decisions are pretty easy to analyze. Most managerial arguments are more complex.

Demonstrating the logic that has brought you to a conclusion can be crucial in helping your audience to arrive at the same point. Very often, managers argue from *cause* and *effect:*

Given:	That we are losing customers to Sprint, and
Since:	Sprint has increased its market share through aggressive pricing,
Therefore:	We should reduce our prices.

This typical managerial argument combines content and clarity, though it must guard against excluding evidence, for example: "But lowering prices will eliminate our profitability."

Almost as often, managers argue from *experience,* meaning that similar situations will produce similar results:

Given:	In the past, higher interest rates have discouraged home buyers, and
Since:	Interest rates are going up,
Therefore:	We face a decline in home sales.

In the early 19th century, John Malthus argued that improvements in nutrition and health care would result in a burgeoning population that would end up starving. While the human population of the earth has increased 10 times since his prediction, actual famine is less common today than in the first half of the last century. Malthus neglected to consider that improvements in agriculture might outpace population growth. This points out the danger of presuming that old rules apply to the future, or that current trends will go on forever. The above example neglects the fact that interest rates may be driven up by higher demand. In the current market, demand for homes may be great even though interest rates are rising. Here again we need to apply the tests described in the above discussion of deductive and inductive logic.

Often, managers make arguments from *identity:*

Given:	Our quality is the same as that of our competitors, and
Since:	Their market share went up when they began advertising quality
Therefore:	We should advertise quality.

Perhaps your competitive advantage depends on lower price. When the argument depends on identity, the *since* asserts that the two situations being compared share enough similarities to ensure that they will produce the same outcome. But such arguments don't work as consistently as arguments from definition or cause and effect, because other factors may be at work.

At other times, managers argue by *analogy:*

Given:	Our employees are very upset, and
Since:	A boiling pot is likely to explode,
Therefore:	We should address their concerns immediately.

Arguments by analogy aim to place a vivid image in the audience's minds and can often be used effectively to stress either the positive or negative consequences of a given course of action (but they risk appealing more to emotion than to logic).

The standard syllogism depends on *classification:*

Given:	Socrates is a man, and
Since:	All men are mortal,
Therefore:	Socrates is mortal.

This type of argument harks back to syllogisms based on *definition,* but in the business world, it's easily subject to abuse. For example:

Given:	One of the candidates we're considering is an MBA, and
Since:	All MBAs have marketing training,
Therefore:	We should hire the MBA candidate as Marketing Director.

Such an argument needs to protect itself against all sorts of external evidence, for example, the argument that another candidate has superior skills, education, and/or job performance.

This suggests that we need to add another factor to our given-since-therefore formulation—*unless:*

Given:	Lower cost will give us a competitive advantage, and
Since:	Greater experience lowers the cost per unit,
Therefore:	We can lower costs by adding experienced workers,
Unless:	This will destroy our margin of profitability.

Experienced workers may cost so much more than the ones we have that they will eat up any gains we make on productivity. Arguments, to be persuasive, need to proceed through clear, convincing syllogisms. But no argument will persuade that doesn't take account of the "unlesses" that are in the minds of the audience.

Evidence

As the above discussion makes clear, both deductive and inductive arguments depend on evidence. In business, evidence includes the following:

Facts and Figures

These data are the core of most business arguments: Our sales are going down, our employee surveys demonstrate the following attitudes, our costs bear the following relation to our profits. Arguments from this common type of evidence stand or fall on accuracy, but accuracy is not enough. Some managers presume that facts and figures are always useful in and of themselves. Databases, decision trees, regression analyses, or econometric models may provide useful data that should enter into a manager's argument for a certain course of action. But the correctness of the calculations is one thing; demonstrating their relevance to the situation at hand is quite another.

Remember that *the facts don't speak for themselves.* Every colleague has seen statistics manipulated to the advantage of the manipulator. Most significant managerial decisions require the interaction of people with different sets of data, areas of expertise, and interests. Cite only those facts and figures that will be as persuasive to your audience as they are to you, and take care to explain their relevance to your argument. Also be sure to present this type of evidence in enough detail for your audience to be convinced, but no more, and in a form they can digest.

Appeal to Common Knowledge

"Everybody knows that marketing promises product on a schedule we can't meet." This may be news to the sales force. Business people, like social or political groups, tend to associate with others of similar responsibilities, backgrounds, and views, from whom they derive their biases. Don't cite evidence based on universally acknowledged "truths" until you've tested them against those members of your audience least likely to agree with you.

Anecdotal Evidence

Examples can provide powerful support for your argument: Here's an instance where a customer refused to buy our product; here's a situation where this policy hurt someone we were trying to help. When you use anecdotal evidence, however, make sure it meets two tests: that it's *representative* of a larger pattern and that it's *relevant* to the concerns of your audience.

Appeal to Authority

This can take several forms, from citing the tried-and-true practices of the past to pointing out that a superior wants things done this way regardless of the consequences. Appeal to authority can constitute evidence that overwhelms any number of facts and figures, common knowledge, or anecdotes because a tradition or directive is an objective factor in the decision-making process. If you're arguing for change, you bear a heavy burden in convincing your audience to sail into uncharted waters. If you are carrying out the commands of a superior against the wishes or common sense of your audience, you should be prepared to explain how this course of action fits into the larger picture, or why the pressure is irresistible.

Use of *logic* and *evidence* will help you shape your argument; they will be even more useful in testing what you've already prepared. When you are sending E-mail, editing your document, or reviewing the notes for your presentation, ask yourself:

1. Will my readers or listeners accept my given?
2. If not, what can I provide so that they will? Do I need to insert a prior argument to establish my *given?*
3. Is my *since* a convincing link between the *given* and *therefore?* If not, create a new *since.*
4. What rebuttal (the *unless*) could be strong enough to shake your *since?* Can you guard against this prospect by adding more evidence?
5. Should I qualify my *therefore* out of deference to contrary views in my audience or because it's not a certainty?
6. Are there parts of my argument so obvious that belaboring them will seem patronizing?

In personal as well as business conversation, people tend to be strong on the *given* (we have a problem, we agree on the following set of facts) and the *therefore* (we should take the following steps). Generally, they fall down on the *since* or the *unless:* Why should we take the course of action I recommend?

We've stressed the role of logic in message design so heavily here because clear thinking is the crucial precursor to clear communication. But the most irrefutable logic in the world won't necessarily carry the day in many business situations if you don't consider the emotional, contextual, and human-interest factors that will also affect the outcome. So once you've designed your logical argument, test it against the following criteria:

Assumptions

Assumptions can cut both ways in a logical argument. Ask yourself during the process of message-design: does my audience share my assumptions on this subject? People at different levels of an organization tend to hang out with people who agree with them and, therefore, share similar assumptions. Managers may presume hourly employees are loyal and grateful for their jobs, while the hourly workers may assume their managers are a bunch of out-of-touch jerks. Analyze which assumptions you share with your audiences and which you don't. Refer to shared areas of agreement without beating them to death. Acknowledge differences frankly and address them in your message.

Proof

As we've emphasized before, the content of your argument (facts, figures, anecdotes, appeals to shared assumptions) is almost invariably subject to interpretation. You may be able to prove beyond contradiction that market share has risen, but you may not be able to prove to the satisfaction of all your audiences *why* this is the case. Each will have a vested interest in believing it's due to their contribution. When designing your argument, be clear to yourself and to your audiences about what you can *prove* and what you're *inferring.*

Inference

Most arguments, however much proof they amass, end in inference: "Therefore, mine is the best solution." Almost all business situations involve too many factors to lend themselves to a purely logical solution. Some of the data you have to rely on—the best available—will still be soft. The fact that your market is growing, for example, doesn't mean it will continue to do so. The fact that your product is the best value doesn't guarantee a competitor isn't about to underprice you. Inference means drawing the most *plausible* conclusion from the proofs you've assembled. Be prepared to acknowledge in your message when you're moving from proof to inference.

In the following case, ask yourself: How should Wilson design his messages to meet the needs of his various audiences?

CASE 5.1

Cuttyhunk Bank (A)

Walking to his office in downtown Boston on a gorgeous May day in 2002, Richard Wilson felt better than he had in weeks. Two months ago, he had become chairman and chief executive officer of Cuttyhunk Bank; the transition had been hectic and stressful. A large part of his time had been taken up with efforts to convert Cuttyhunk, which was under federal charter, to a state bank. Only yesterday he had ended a long series of negotiations to merge with the small Harbor State Bank in suburban Roslindale. Over the last decade, many small banks in New England had been acquired by megabanks such as Fleet. These mergers usually had resulted in major layoffs. Often this involved senior staff at the acquired banks who had developed long-term relationships with their customers. Wilson believed the state charter, facilitated by the merger with Harbor State, would make it financially viable for Cuttyhunk to survive and preserve its record of community service.

Wilson found himself thinking, "If I'm lucky, I might be able to get away early this afternoon to try out my new sailboat on the Charles." There were no urgent matters pending except a call from a reporter that he hadn't had time to return. Wilson assumed it concerned the opening of a new branch next week, and he thought he could answer the reporter's questions and be out of the office by noon.

This hope was dashed when Wilson entered his building. The office was in an uproar. Every phone seemed to be ringing. His office staff, however, was gathered in the far corner of the room, staring at a newspaper. Nancy Brock, the assistant treasurer, ran up to him with a copy of the *Boston Herald* thrust out in front of her. With a look of horror on her face, she said, "Read this."

There, on the front page of one of Boston's major newspapers, was an excerpt from a confidential interoffice E-mail Brock had sent the previous week to the bank's branch managers. The passage dealt with how managers should handle inquiries from bank members (depositors and borrowers) concerning their attendance at a bank meeting where a vote would be taken on the proposed merger with Harbor State Bank. The excerpt read:

> Also, although they are "entitled" to come to the meeting, we naturally do not want to encourage this. If they don't remember whether or not they have given us a proxy, tell them that they probably have (either by signing the sig. card or returning the special form back in January '01) but that, in any event, there is no need for them to complete a proxy now, nor are they under any obligation or requirement

This is an update of a case written by Sally Seymour, Associate in Communication. Harvard Business School case 387–031.

> to attend the meeting. *Just don't tell them in so many words that they shouldn't attend, because legally, they may.* Tactful discouragement is the line to take if the subject comes up. For your information only (don't get into this with customers), as soon as we convert to the state charter, depositors and borrowers will no longer be considered members and will no longer be entitled to attend meetings and vote.

Wilson's first thought was "How did this get into the newspapers?" He quickly realized, however, that he didn't have time to pursue that question. Those increasingly ringing phones, his staff told him, were calls from angry customers demanding to know what the bank was trying to hide and why members were being denied their voting rights.Wilson had to act and act fast. He had to come up with an answer to the phone calls and a letter to all members as soon as possible, explaining the bank's position.

BACKGROUND ON CUTTYHUNK BANK

After 150 years as a Massachusetts-chartered mutual savings bank, Cuttyhunk Bank converted to a federal charter in 1983. At that time, management thought the change might facilitate interstate mergers, since the merged bank would be subjecting its operations to national supervision rather than supervision from another state. Management also thought that the change would guarantee continuation of the broad powers essential for the bank's long-term strategies.

Unfortunately, the expectations failed to materialize. The Federal Home Loan Bank Board required far more complex and expensive appraisals for real estate than did the Commonwealth of Massachusetts. While the tighter regulations may have resulted from flagrant abuses elsewhere in the country, Cuttyhunk saw no reason why it should bear the competitive burden of expensive and time-consuming appraisals.

Also, Federal Home Loan Bank Board regulations severely limited commercial loans to Trustees. While Cuttyhunk management also opposed "sweetheart" insider deals, it didn't want to be prohibited from having the benefit of the business judgment and wisdom of many outstanding people simply because the bank had made loans to them. Cuttyhunk management felt that it was natural for its clients to want to do business that would benefit the bank they were associated with and that these relationships were a fact of life throughout the banking industry.

Even more important, shortly after Cuttyhunk went federal, the law was changed to allow Massachusetts banks to expand to other New England states. The banking industry had undergone deregulation in a number of areas in the 1980s. The New England Experiment—the first of several regional experiments—allowed banks in Maine, Vermont, New Hampshire, Connecticut, Massachusetts, and Rhode Island to engage in interstate banking transactions as long as there was reciprocity between states. This meant that a bank in Massachusetts could merge with a bank in Connecticut only if the Connecticut bank was allowed to do business in Massachusetts. Some states (Vermont was one) chose not to take advantage of the relaxed regulations. During his 20-year tenure at Cuttyhunk,Wilson had seen many small banks turned into branches of corporate monoliths as a result of the deregulation.

Finally, most state savings banks in Massachusetts had begun to reap considerable profits in the 1990s, thanks to lower interest rates and the booming housing market. Therefore, Cuttyhunk decided to go back to a state charter by merging with the small Harbor State Bank, which had $9 million in assets, three employees, and one office in Roslindale. The merger would allow Cuttyhunk to convert to a state charter without paying a million dollars to be insured by the state.

The merger, however, had to be approved by the bank's members. Under federal charter, depositors are members entitled to one vote for every $100 on deposit. While the conversion to a state charter would have no impact on the bank's current depositors or borrowers, once the bank charter changed, depositors and borrowers would no longer be considered members with the right to attend meetings and vote on proposals.

Two weeks before, on April 25, Wilson had sent a letter to all members, notifying them of the upcoming meeting on May 27 when members could vote on the proposal to merge with Harbor State Bank (see *Exhibit 1*). Wilson emphasized in his letter that members were under no obligation to attend and that those unable to attend would have their proxies voted in favor of the charter change and the acquisition "unless you indicate otherwise."

Wilson didn't expect a large turnout since at the first annual meeting only two members showed up and at the second, only one member did. In neither case were any questions asked or

EXHIBIT 1 Wilson's Letter to Bank Members

April 25, 2003

Dear Member:

You recently received a legal notice of a Special Meeting of the Members (depositors and borrowers) of Cuttyhunk Bank, to be held on May 27, 2003, at 3:00 p.m. at 68 Jefferson Street, Boston, Massachusetts.

This meeting has been called for several reasons. One is to seek approval of the conversion of Cuttyhunk Bank from a federal savings bank to a state-chartered savings bank regulated by the Massachusetts Commissioner of Banks. It is important to note that this does *not* mean conversion to a stock form of organization. Cuttyhunk Bank will remain a mutual savings bank, just as it has always been. The conversion to a state charter will enhance Cuttyhunk Bank's ability to serve its customers and remain a viable, competitive financial institution.

Also, your deposits in Cuttyhunk Bank will continue to be insured by the Federal Deposit Insurance Corporation. In addition, once the conversion has taken place, deposits in excess of the FDIC limit of $100,000 will be insured by the Deposit Insurance Fund of Massachusetts as well, thereby improving our already strong deposit insurance protection.

The second item on the meeting agenda concerns our merger with Harbor State Bank, a small savings bank located at 1234 Main Street in Roslindale. Harbor State Bank is being merged into Cuttyhunk Bank, and this action will have no effect on you as a Cuttyhunk Bank customer.

Although federal law requires that we notify all members of the bank when such a meeting is scheduled and while you, as a member of Cuttyhunk Bank, are entitled to attend this meeting, you are under absolutely no obligation to do so. Almost all of our members have already provided us with their proxy votes, either by signing an account signature card or by returning special proxy forms early in 2003, and these proxies are still in force. At the Special Meeting, these proxies will be voted in favor of the conversion to a state charter and the merger with Harbor State Bank. If you do attend the Special Meeting, you may vote in person if you wish, even if you have previously signed a proxy.

Once again, please be reassured that both the conversion from federal to state charter, and the merger with Harbor State Bank, will strengthen Cuttyhunk Bank and allow for a stronger, more competitive institution to serve all its customers.

Sincerely,

Richard G. Wilson

Chairman of the Board and
Chief Executive Officer

any comments made. Yet, shortly after the notice of the May 27 meeting went out, branch managers had received dozens of phone calls from members confused about what the change in charter would mean and whether they should attend the meeting. The branch managers had asked Nancy Brock for some guidance on what to tell the members. Wilson had told Brock that he thought it wasn't worth depositors' time to attend the meeting, since all the issues were clearly stated in the letter they received. However, members were entitled to vote and they couldn't be told not to attend.

Feeling that the situation called for a quick response, Brock went off to write an E-mail to the branch managers. Someone leaked it to the press, and Wilson now faced a crisis that was growing bigger by the minute.

Study Questions

1. How do you evaluate the message Wilson gave Brock? Brock's E-mail? The April 25 letter?
2. Did flaws in the use of content, logic, evidence, or argument lead to this problem?
3. What messages does Cuttyhunk Bank need to send out now? How?

CHAPTER 6

Structure

Both deductive and inductive logic appear, to varying degrees, in all business communication. They should provide the building blocks—that is, the paragraphs—of your argument. But describing how you've reached your conclusions may not be the best way to shape the argument so that your audience can hear it. As a general rule of thumb, several other considerations should also govern the design of your message:

1. Make your goal and point of view clear from the start so that, whether they agree with you or not, your audiences can follow your argument.
2. Demonstrate that you understand the decision-making context by outlining the conflicting viewpoints of your audiences and citing reasonable opposing proposals.
3. Show why your solution is best.
4. Acknowledge and neutralize reasonable alternatives.
5. Conclude by outlining next steps, and emphasize the long-term benefits to your audience of adopting your proposal.

COMBINING CONTENT, ARGUMENT, AND STRUCTURE

In Chap. 2, Setting Goals, we discussed how to rank your priorities. When determining the structure of your document or presentation, you need to decide how to organize your points under a few main headings that will be memorable to your audience. Consider the following example:

Great Lakes Stores has recently lost market share to Galaxy Stores for the following reasons:

1. Galaxy has a colorful advertising approach.
2. Galaxy remodeled its stores to attract new customers.

3. Galaxy increased its media exposure by 20 percent.
4. Great Lakes is hampered by poor control over inventories, purchasing, and promotion.
5. Great Lakes reduced its advertising budget.
6. Great Lakes has a spotty record of maintaining store cleanliness and organization.

These points, properly supported, provide the meat of your argument, or the middle. While you prepare your communication, start by listing this key evidence. But in and of themselves, these points don't sufficiently organize the information or point toward a course of action. After identifying your evidence, organize it into an *argument*, and frame a clear structure:

Topic/Purpose

I. If we don't change our practices, Great Lakes Stores will continue to lose market share to Galaxy Stores. (*Introduction*)

Given

II. Great Lakes stores has been losing share to Galaxy for the following reasons:

   A. *Great Lakes' internal problems*. Poor control over purchasing, inventories, sales promotion, cleanliness, and organization has meant that customers are alienated and often can't find what they want. (*Body*)

   B. *Galaxy's superior marketing*. While Great Lakes has reduced its advertising budget, Galaxy has spent more on media, produced better ads, and remodeled its store to attract customers. (*Body*)

Since

III. While improving Great Lakes' performance will cost more initially, this cost will be more than offset in greater long-run profits. (*Body*)

   A. Costs
   B. Benefits

Therefore

IV. We should take the following courses of action. (*Conclusion*)

This model shows how *argument* (given, since, therefore) and *structure* (introduction, body, conclusion) combine to organize your information and form a persuasive argument.

DEVELOPING AN ACTION-ORIENTED STRUCTURE

Consider the following situation: The dean of students has asked you to evaluate the role of graduate students who serve as resident assistants (RAs) in campus housing. You've surveyed administrators, resident students, and the RAs themselves. In reporting your findings, you could rely on the following outline:

I. Introduction outlining the purpose of your report
II. Administrators' views of RAs
III. Students' views of RAs

IV. RAs' self-perceptions
V. Conclusions and recommendations

This outline makes sense; it allows you to include all relevant information. But what if all three groups you've surveyed have similar views? What if everyone thinks that the RAs are caught in the middle? In this case, the structure outlined above would yield a very repetitive discussion and would not highlight your findings. A structure based on the different functions of the RAs, rather than the views of the different groups, might look like this:

I. Introduction: RAs are currently forced into conflicting roles.
II. The RA as liaison between administration and students.
III. The RA as organizer of dorm activities.
IV. The RA as monitor of campus regulations.
V. Conclusions and recommendations.

In following such an outline, you would blend evidence from all your sources to support your analysis of the RAs' effectiveness in their three main tasks.

Neither of the above structures would help much, however, if you knew the dean wanted specific recommendations on how to improve the effectiveness of RAs. She would know where to look for your recommendations, but your main headings would give no hint of what problems needed to be addressed, or the solutions to them. To highlight your recommendations, you might choose the following structure:

- *Recommendation*. This provides the *what*, emphasizing the reason your audience should pay attention to you and the goal you wish to achieve.
- *Rationale*. This provides the *why,* the history and facts that support your recommendation.
- *Implementation*. This provides the *who, when,* and *how,* in other words, a schedule of how to proceed, assignment of responsibilities, and a time line to measure success.

Such a structure can be applied to a long report, a memo, a speech, or a short E-mail message. It has the advantage of grabbing the audience's attention, demonstrating that you understand the situation, and showing that you have a plan to achieve your goal. All the elements covered earlier can be included in this format. Point I will fall under recommendation; points II, III, and IV under rationale; and point V under implementation. For example:

I. *Recommendation:* We need to clarify the roles of RAs so that they can do their jobs better while suffering less stress. We can do so by:
   A. Offering more training to RAs in managing conflict.
   B. Encouraging RAs to report only serious infractions.
   C. Appointing additional RAs in Taylor Hall.

II. *Rationale*
   A. RAs constantly find themselves negotiating conflict, both between the students and the administration and among students.
   B. RAs' main role is to provide support and informal counseling to students, but current regulations require them to betray student trust by reporting minor infractions.

C. Dissatisfaction with RAs is highest in Taylor Hall because the RAs there are overburdened.

D. While some have argued that the current system is working well, the RAs themselves disagree, and we need their long-term allegiance to continue recruiting qualified candidates.

III. *Implementation*: Outline specific steps to redefine the role of RAs and provide them with more support.

While this structure does not apply to all business situations, it will work in most because it turns a report into a *plan of action*. During even a cursory examination of it, both your analysis and your recommendations will jump out. Your findings and logic will be immediately evident to your audience.

SELECTING A PERSUASIVE STRUCTURE

At the beginning of this section, we offered a generic structure for a business communication containing a clear statement of your goal, the development of a partnership with your audience in problem solving, arguments in favor of your proposal, discussion of why other reasonable solutions are inferior, and a course of action that will accomplish your purpose. All these elements need to be included in any document or presentation that goes beyond a mere recitation of the facts. But how you *organize* these elements depends heavily on your audience's attitude, as we began to consider in Chap. 2. Sometimes, when communicating, you need only to *inform* your audience of certain facts; more often, you need to *persuade* them. Following are some tools that can help you create a structure that matches your arguments to the needs of your audience.

One-Sided versus Two-Sided Presentations

A supportive or neutral audience will often respond well to a simple statement of your case, especially if the subject is noncontroversial—a minor policy change, for example, or a routine procedure. But if, as is often the case, your ideas are in competition with others', you need to take a two-sided approach to include your audience in the discussion. Consider the following arguments for buying restaurant A rather than restaurant B:

One-Sided

1. Good location within walking distance of shopping mall and cinemas
2. Parking not ample but adequate
3. Right size
4. Higher costs justified by ease of financing

This presentation simply lists the evidence in support of your position. If your credibility is high and your audience's knowledge of the situation is low, it may suffice. But if you are competing with another proposal, you need to build this evidence into a comparative argument:

Two-Sided

1. Superior location. Restaurant A is between the mall and the cinemas, while restaurant B is a mile away.
2. Restaurant A's parking lot is adequate, and overflow can park in the mall next door. Restaurant B has more parking, but the lot is rarely full.
3. Both restaurants have seating for 300; restaurant A has a lounge, while restaurant B doesn't.
4. Although restaurant A will cost more, the expense will be justified by greater patronage. Restaurant B's lower cost is also offset by a nontransferable mortgage.

This structure not only offers more evidence for your recommendation, but also anticipates counterarguments and the likely concerns of your audience. These are the essential elements of persuasion.

Pro-Con versus Con-Pro Order

Given that you're in a situation where persuasion is necessary, you need to determine whether you should first present the arguments for your proposal or respond to those against it. As we discussed in our coverage of audience analysis, members of a supportive or neutral audience will want to hear the pro arguments first (though they'll also want to be sure you've considered the downsides), while skeptical or hostile audience members won't pay attention to your positive arguments until their concerns have been addressed. Either way, you'll increase your credibility with your audience by recognizing the merits of opponents' arguments while simultaneously noting weaknesses and offering rebuttals.

Deductive versus Inductive Order

In a deductive argument, the given is a general premise, such as "We need a safer workplace." In an inductive argument, the given is a set of facts and figures: "Here is the evidence that we suffer more workplace actions than our competitors do." Deductive arguments follow the pattern of assertion then support. Inductive arguments follow the pattern of support then assertion.

Inductive structures are probably less common in business than are deductive ones, but they can be refreshing after sustained doses of assertion. Citing evidence first can show respect for your audience and lead them along the path you took to reach your conclusion. But even while you use an inductive approach, don't leave your audience members totally in the dark about where you are going, or they'll be unlikely to follow. Often, a combination of the two approaches will work best; for example, "We need to make our workplace safer because recently we've suffered the following series of accidents."

Ascending versus Descending Order

All the above structures require a decision on how to order your arguments. An ascending order puts your most powerful point last; a descending order puts it first. As always, in deciding what order to choose, consider what matters most to your *audience*.

An informed audience, interested in the topic, will probably want to know your strongest supporting data or argument immediately. If you decide to put your strongest points first, however, you must handle the remaining arguments so that they don't seem trivial. Make their subordinate status clear, treat them briefly, and reaffirm your strongest arguments in your conclusion.

Less engaged or less informed audience members may respond more readily to the end of the communication, after their interest has been aroused. Here, you need to accumulate evidence that a situation requires action before you can sell them on your solution. Still, your introduction has to grab their attention—perhaps by citing a startling fact or figure—and you need to drive your main point home forcefully in your conclusion.

To summarize this discussion of *persuasive structures:*

Audience	*Argument*
	One-sided
Interested	Pro-con
Supportive	Deductive
Informed	Descending
versus	versus
	Two-sided
Unengaged	Con-pro
Hostile	Inductive
Uninformed	Ascending

As we suggested in Chap. 4, interested, supportive, informed audiences invite a *tell-or-sell* approach, while unengaged, hostile, and uninformed audiences require a *consult-or-join* approach. However, most business situations are more complicated than any graph can describe and will fall somewhere between these two extremes. Managers often find themselves telling hostile audiences things they don't want to hear or consulting with supporters to determine the best course of action.

Addressing a hostile audience is obviously the most difficult communication task. Psychologically, it's likely to put you on the defensive, which will, in turn, drive you to explain how right you are. Resist this approach and stay as objective as you can. Try to understand the conscious and unconscious sources of your audience's opposition. Use the two-sided, con-pro, inductive, ascending structure.

USING THE POWER OF NARRATIVE

In Chap. 5, we discussed how to define your content and make the most effective use of argument. The previous portions of this chapter suggest how you can build an audience-sensitive structure. We invite you to review that material now, then measure it against the following discussion of how to impart your argument with narrative drama, which is the oldest means of holding an audience's attention. Narrative drama may seem to belong to literature, but business situations, too, can—and usually do—have dramatic elements and consequences. Vividly portraying the bind the

RAs find themselves in, for example, may be the first step toward solving a serious problem. Once you've defined the basic structure of your argument, you should consider how to make the situation as real and compelling to those you are trying to persuade as it is to you. Often, too, you'll find yourself speaking at inspirational or ceremonial events where narrative will be much more compelling than argument.

Consider the millions of words and images that have washed over you in a lifetime. Of all the conversations, books, movies, newspaper articles, stories, rumors, pictures, emotional encounters, dreams—which do you remember most vividly? Why can we recall childhood ghost tales more clearly than the cause of disagreement that happened yesterday? Why, of all the anecdotes you hear weekly from friends, colleagues, and the media, is there one you make sure to retell? What combination of message (argument) and shape (structure) ensures that meaning migrates from one person to the next? Given the transformations from Neanderthal signs and mumblings to E-mail, what has remained the same about the structure of human communication?

If we consider children sitting around a campfire to hear a ghost story, we're at the root of what makes certain human communication structures memorable. The audience thrills to the danger, courage, generosity, horror, and triumph. The villain suffers horrible mutilation and wanders the woods as a lost soul, howling after curfew. The camp counselor has made her point that it's risky to sneak out of the campsite after dark (this is her argument, though it may never appear overtly in the tale). The campers will remember, embroider, and pass along the tale, to share pleasure, to convey information, to earn an audience and the prestige of being the teller.

The original human communications share the same situation and structure as the campfire ghost story. The earliest information available to us packaged in language—carrying essentially the same meaning as when it was created—has come down in the form of parables that define values and modes of action for a culture. The earliest books of the Bible tell adventure stories of the clash between good and evil which established standards—with a rationale—for human conduct. The *Iliad* inculcates a style of behavior, a definition of justice, and a view of the moral universe that laid the foundations for the staggering intellectual and cultural achievements of ancient Greece. During the same period, Confucius and Buddha were promulgating similarly enduring world visions by means of parables.

All these interpretations of reality were packaged as memorable stories, passed from mouth to mouth. Tales were told from generation to generation for thousands of years. At first, essential communications were stored in old people, later in tribal officers, later in bards and teachers, and finally in a new medium—writing. Since then, they have metamorphosed into poems, plays, philosophical tracts, textbooks, scientific studies, historical records, movies, comic books, television shows, and video games. Throughout, they have held their audiences by:

- Defining a value at stake for the culture or community
- Starting in the middle
- Using vivid, concrete images
- Putting familiar information in a new light
- Establishing clear direction and forward motion
- Overcoming obstacles
- Developing suspense

- Showing character in action
- Creating a firm sense of closure
- Respecting the audience's expectations of timing
- Ending with a moral
- Addressing the next steps

These characteristics of good narrative are of more than historical interest; they catalog the structural principles of effective business communication today. We can best discuss them in terms of *opening strategies, building strategies,* and *concluding strategies.* One important point to consider when you structure your argument: Research has consistently demonstrated that audience attention is high at the beginning, goes down in the middle, and rises again at the end. Make sure that you emphasize your main points in your opening and in your conclusion. Effective use of narrative allows you to appeal to your audiences' *humanity*—their hearts as well as their heads.

Opening Strategies: Getting Attention

Demonstrate That There's a Defining Value at Stake

Any business communication has a purpose. That purpose, and its relevance to your audience, should be clearly defined in your first few sentences. The more clearly you emphasize the importance of achieving your goal—without exaggerating—the more closely the audience will follow your argument. Be especially careful to show why this value is one your audience does, or should, share.

Start in the Middle

In most business situations, a thousand preliminaries, starting with the founding of the company or your own birth, have eventuated in the current decision that has to be made. But listing all of these chronologically will put your audience to sleep by the time you arrive at your main point. Some of these factors may be crucial in deciding how to reach your goal. But work them into your argument *after* you have your audience's attention, not before.

Start with a Vivid, Concrete Image

If you can find a way to boil your argument down to a memorable picture—in words or graphics—this can rivet your audience's attention and, moreover, help you keep focused on your central argument. Sometimes this means saying, "Put yourself in the following situation." Sometimes it means portraying the severity of a current problem by offering an example. Sometimes it means showing how an abstract situation affects real human beings. The key to success in such an opening is to create a visual and emotional picture, then put your audience inside it.

Put Familiar Information in a New Light

By evoking something your audiences know but then giving them a new way of looking at the situation, you can gain both their attention and their respect at once. This may mean demonstrating that a problem is an opportunity, that a hallowed tradition no longer applies, or that you're in a different business than you thought. By creating a new perception of the situation, you have signaled that you are setting out on an adventure that your audiences will want to join.

Building Strategies: Holding Attention

All the opening strategies above share one characteristic: Each creates interest in what is to follow. Once you have achieved that dramatic momentum, don't give it up. Only a few techniques are crucial to holding your audience's attention.

Signal Where You're Going Next and Why

Once you've defined your central argument in your opening, identify the issues you need to address to reach a conclusion. In other words, provide a brief outline of the upcoming document or presentation. This will reassure audience members early that you are going to cover all the bases, and it will allow them to follow you more closely. As each new topic arises, specify clearly how it fits into, and advances, your argument.

Overcome Obstacles

Great stories portray protagonists who defeated enemies of their community, achieved the object of their quests, or restored peace and order to their world. This is a pretty good catalog of the challenges facing managers from day to day. Confronting, and overcoming, obstacles to achieving your goal can inject the excitement of an adventure story into a routine memo.

Maintain Suspense

We keep turning the pages of a good book because we want to know what will happen next. This can be as true of a debt refinancing proposal as of a terrific detective story. By defining an important challenge vividly, you can generate suspense about how it can be resolved.

Character in Action

Audiences identify more with people than they do with abstract information. Sometimes, it's most effective to describe a proposal or situation in terms of its effect on a particular individual. Sometimes that individual is you. You might, for example, describe how you once held views identical to your audience's and the sequence of events that's caused you to change them. Sometimes, the protagonist of your narrative should be someone else—a representative audience member, for example, or a customer who will be affected by the adoption of your proposal.

Rarely should all these attention-holding strategies be used at the same time in a business communication, and none is sufficient, in and of itself, to build a compelling argument. Generally, speeches, that are heard only once, require greater use of dramatic technique than do documents, that can be reviewed several times and passed on. An image or situation that sounds vivid when heard may seem overwrought or tiresome when read over several times. Once you've identified the main structural elements of your communication, check to be sure they can accommodate the necessary information. But if you make appropriate use of dramatic structure, your audience, like those children around the campfire, won't want you to stop.

All these building strategies are designed to *direct* attention, keeping your audience interested, and then to *focus* attention on the key messages you want to deliver. Invariably, your audience will want to know: Where are we ultimately headed and why?

Concluding Strategies: Letting Go

A successful conclusion feels inevitable, complete, and expected. It distills the preceding information and imagery into a clear solution and a credible course of action. Follow a few basic rules to develop conclusions that will have maximum impact.

Create a Firm Sense of Closure

When audience members realize you're about to finish, their attention level goes up. Take advantage of this by signaling your conclusion clearly. This is easier to do in writing, where the approaching white space is obvious, than in speaking, where you must be more explicit.

Respect the Audience's Expectations of Timing

Samuel Johnson said of Milton's *Paradise Lost,* "No one ever wished it longer." People have read, heard, and watched thousands of narratives and presentations by the time they become members of your audience. It's very easy to become entranced with your own prose or voice and to begin to ramble. Make sure you've condensed your argument into the minimum number of words. A corollary: Make sure your conclusion itself ties up your argument without wandering. Statements such as "That's it" will leave your audience feeling let down. On the other hand, statements such as "In conclusion" followed by more subsidiary or supporting information will cause the audience's attention to peak too soon.

Draw the Lesson or Moral

Take advantage of heightened audience attention to drive your main point home. Don't merely summarize what you've said so far; emphasize the important consequences for the audience members who have paid attention.

Address the Next Steps

Most business communications constitute a call to take some action. Once you've convinced an audience of the merits of your proposal, show them what specific actions will be necessary to achieve your goal. This will assure them that what you want is not only desirable, but also achievable. It will also raise audience members' confidence that they have a significant role in your plans, and that you are qualified and prepared to lead them forward.

The following case tests a manager's ability to select persuasive arguments and a persuasive structure for a change he wishes to make.

CASE 6.1

McGregor's Ltd. Department Store

James McGregor, President of McGregor's Ltd., a department store in downtown Boston, was considering how best to inform his staff of a new policy on employees' discounts. McGregor had decided to change the discount policy to conform with current practices in other stores. Every staff member would be affected by the proposed changes, some adversely, some beneficially. The information sent out by the Personnel Department would therefore have to be tailored to the different groups. Most of his 721 employees would receive an improved discount, but McGregor was concerned about the reaction of the managerial staff. This group stood to lose its generous discount, yet without its full cooperation, the new plan could become a bone of contention rather than a liberalization of an old policy.

McGregor was debating whether to write a memo to all managerial staff or to call small groups into his office and personally explain the reason for the change. He did not relish the prospect of justifying the new scheme to 114 people—thirty-four executives and eighty buyers. The task would be time-consuming, and the news would reach some departments before others. McGregor felt the decision should be made known to all managerial staff at the same time and should be relayed to the sales force as rapidly as possible. He wanted to see the new policy put into operation without delay.

This case is an update by Linda McJannet of a case prepared by Alison Eadie under the supervision of Professor Thomas J. C. Raymond.

HISTORY OF MCGREGOR'S LTD.

McGregor's department store had a reputation for being rather old-fashioned and traditional. Founded in 1871 by McGregor's great-grandfather, a first-generation Scottish immigrant, the store had remained under tight family control. In 1961, under the tenure of James McGregor's father, the store went public, but much of the stock remained in family hands.

The influence of the founder, who put great emphasis on personal service, was still felt in many areas of the business. Chairs were available in most departments for footsore customers. Goods were delivered free of charge to account customers within thirty miles of Boston, regardless of the amount of purchase. One customer of long standing had fruitcake from the food hall delivered every week, although the cost of delivery far outweighed the value of the cake. Generous credit terms were extended to account customers.

James McGregor, who took over the business from his father three years ago, did not want to destroy the old-world charm that distinguished McGregor's from other department stores in Boston.

He knew customers highly valued the personal services and enjoyed the atmosphere of gracious living that characterized the store. But he also felt the image projected by McGregor's was detrimental in some respects.

Many young people thought the store catered to older people, although its merchandise was up-to-date and the store had a boutique that sold teenage fashions. The juniors department had recently been taken over by a top-notch young buyer. Although the store had tried some promotions to attract younger customers, McGregor felt they had not been entirely successful. He worried about overreliance on a middle-aged and elderly clientele, which had serious implications for the store's future.

McGregor was also concerned about what he viewed as the firm's long-term financial performance. Although business had improved since he had taken over (*Exhibit 1*), and this year's increase in sales was above the average for retail stores (4.9%), he would have liked to see greater efficiency, a more rapid turnover of goods, and greater profitability.

McGregor's did not attempt to compete with Filene's bargain basement, Wal-Mart, or other stores offering slashed prices. Instead, it sold unusual and often more expensive goods. Imports were a major feature of McGregor's merchandise. It boasted the largest selection of foreign china and glassware in Boston, including a wide range of Wedgwood, Crown Derby, Royal Worcester, and Coalport china from England, Noritake china from Japan, and Waterford crystal from Ireland. Although this type of merchandise always sold, it sometimes took a while for the shelves to clear. McGregor believed a greater reliance on special sales would be necessary to speed up turnover.

Partly behind McGregor's thinking was the memory of the turbulent wave of mergers in the late 1980s that shook U.S. retailing to its core. The company that continued to do business as usual had often become a takeover target. Allied Stores and Federated Department Stores had been the two large department store chains in the U.S. After Robert Campeau, a Canadian tycoon, acquired Allied Stores in 1986, Federated Department Stores became the battleground. Over the years, Federated had managed to retain its image as a "Grande Dame" among its peers, and it was still the largest U.S. department store chain at the end of 1987. However, Federated had long been

EXHIBIT 1 Statement of Earnings and Retained Earnings, Year Ending June 30

	Current Year	Previous Year
Revenue		
Net sales	$46,103,603	$42,887,073
Costs and expenses		
Cost of merchandise sold	27,064,915	25,176,665
Selling and administrative expenses	10,910,348	10,149,161
Interest expense	301,871	319,440
Subtotal	38,277,134	35,645,266
Earnings before provisions for income taxes	7,826,469	7,241,807
Provision for income taxes		
Federal	3,710,284	3,451,427
State	389,246	362,089
	4,099,530	3,813,516
Net earnings	$ 3,726,939	$ 3,428,291

considered vulnerable because it "rested on its laurels" and appeared to ignore changing demographics and emerging forms of retailing. Further, its management failed to control a high expense structure and bring the autonomously-operated divisions together. A bidding war for Federated Department Stores arose between Robert Campeau and D. H. Macy. It ended in May, 1988, when Robert Campeau completed the acquisition of Federated at a cost of $8.8 billion. (Subsequently, many analysts thought that chain prices had been inflated in the overheated market of the mid-eighties.) Although the wave of mergers had died down, for McGregor the lesson of the acquisition of Federated remained: even when the company was doing well, it was better to prevent trouble than to wait until it came up.

One area in need of updating, according to McGregor, was personnel policies. Many employees concurred with customers in labelling the store old-fashioned. Despite the competitive wages paid by the store, McGregor's sometimes had trouble recruiting younger salespeople. McGregor decided that to create a less stuffy image and to attract younger staff, he should modify some of the more hierarchical personnel practices. He felt a young and dynamic sales and managerial staff would attract younger customers. One of his top priorities was to overhaul the employees' discount program.

THE CURRENT EMPLOYEES' DISCOUNT PROGRAM

When McGregor took over, the program was complex and inegalitarian. The size of the discount depended on the position of an employee within the firm, i.e., the higher the rank, the greater the discount (*Exhibit 2*). Six possible discounts existed. Salespeople had to verify the percentage of any purchase to be discounted by checking the employee's ID before deducting the appropriate discount from the full price.

In addition to taking employees' time, the system made no business sense. Discounts at the upper end of the scale were eating into profit margins, and beyond, on some type of goods. Major electrical appliances, calculators, cameras, and typewriters, for example, often had profit margins of 10 percent or less. Executives receiving a third off the price of a color television set were severely damaging the profitability of the Appliances Department. At Christmas time, particularly, managerial staffs spent heartily in some of the low-profit-margin departments.

At the other end of the scale, McGregor felt salespeople, maintenance workers, and clerks were not getting a fair shake. He was particularly anxious to include cleaners in the discount program. They had previously been left out because

EXHIBIT 2 McGregor's Existing Employee Discount Scheme

Grade	Position	Discount %	No. of Staff
1	Executives—vice presidents, managers, etc.	33⅓	34
2	Buyers	25	80
3	Supervisors, executive secretaries	20	97
4	Sales staff with more than 10 yrs. consecutive service	17	29
5	Sales staff with more than 5 yrs. consecutive service	15	62
6	Other sales staff, maintenance workers, van drivers, clerks, cafeteria workers	10	349
7	Cleaners	0	70
	Total work force		721

their working hours did not coincide with store hours. The premises were cleaned in two shifts, after the store closed at night and before it opened in the morning. Incidents of "lost" merchandise in several departments had led sales personnel to suspect the cleaning staff of shoplifting. Although no allegations had been substantiated, McGregor hoped extension of the discount to cleaning staff would reduce the amount of "lost" merchandise.

He also hoped the new policy (as it was more generous for most employees) would encourage spending on high-profit-margin goods such as clothes and accessories. The new policy would increase the involvement of employees in the store and in the type of merchandise being sold and, if the incentives were sufficient, it should lead to a significantly greater volume of sales.

THE NEW EMPLOYEES' DISCOUNT PROGRAM

The new policy proposed by McGregor brought McGregor's more in line with other department stores (*Exhibit 3*). It abolished the hierarchical structure. Every employee would receive exactly the same treatment: the discount would vary according to the goods purchased, not the status of the purchaser.

Instead of six tiers, the new program had only three. A 10 percent discount would be given on lowmargin goods, such as large electrical appliances, calculators, typewriters, cameras, film, and food. A 15 percent discount would be given on books, records, stationery, household goods, clocks, toys, china, linens, sporting goods, small electrical appliances, and furnishings. Finally, 20 percent would be given for clothing, fabrics, cosmetics, costume jewelry, purses, belts, and scarves. Items on which the store made virtually no profit (e.g., candy and tobacco) would be sold at retail price.

McGregor believed the new system made sense because it was simpler. Salespeople would no longer have to figure out one of six discount possibilities. They would deal with only one or two at most, since all the goods in one department would tend to be sold at the same discount. The new system also made financial sense. Low-profit-margin goods would be sold at realistic prices, and high-profit-margin ones would sell faster. In overall financial terms, McGregor was not sure how the change would affect the company. He kept records of employee spending, but these were not divided according to departments (*Exhibit 4*). Most of the spending was done by executives and buyers. This reflected in part their greater purchasing power, but it was also encouraged by the over-generous discounts for upper-level employees. McGregor believed the financial difference to the company would be significant when the 33⅓ percent and 25 percent discounts were abolished. Though the actual cut in any one manager's spending power would be small, he estimated the store would save about $19,024, mostly in the Appliances Department. He arrived at this figure by discounting all executive and buyer purchases at an average of 15 percent.

McGregor believed in the new plan. He now had to convince executives and buyers of its merits and gain their support to implement the changes. Some of the younger staff, he knew, welcomed change and modernization in the store. A few of them had even suggested more radical moves, such as trimming McGregor's somewhat top-heavy

EXHIBIT 3 Employee Discount Schemes at Other Boston Stores

Filene's	20% standard rate for all goods for all full-time employees
Jordan Marsh	15%, some variation according to merchandise
Lord and Taylor	20% standard rate on all goods for all employees
Sears, Roebuck & Co.	10% and 15% depending on type of goods
The Harvard Coop	5–30% depending on type of goods
Bradlee's	No discount

EXHIBIT 4 Employee Spending Habits for Most Recent Fiscal Year

Grade	Total Bill	Per Person Average		Total Discount	
1	$53,856	$1,584	(34)	$17,950	(33⅓%)
2	91,520	1,144	(80)	22,880	(25%)
3	88,774	915	(97)	17,755	(20%)
4	17,864	616	(29)	3,037	(17%)
5	29,462	475	(62)	4,419	(15%)
6	122,848	352	(349)	12,285	(10%)

management structure. But most of the executives and buyers had been with McGregor's for many years and were devoted to its traditions. McGregor knew he could expect resistance, but he was not sure how much. He certainly did not want news of the proposed changes to reach the sales force in general before he had the full agreement of executives and buyers.

Before taking action, McGregor explained his plan to Allen Lee, a younger buyer who had been with the company for three years. He laid out some of his reasoning and asked for Lee's thoughts. Lee agreed that many salespeople viewed the discount program as old-fashioned, even unfair, and that they needed to attract a younger salesforce in order to attract younger customers. He also agreed that the new program would save some money for the company, but he wondered if the resistance it would meet was worth the savings. On the issue of fairness, for example, many senior executives thought the current system was fair: those employees with the greatest responsibilities enjoyed the greatest discounts. Further, if McGregor stressed the $19,024 savings, the executives might wonder why it should come out of their pockets, especially since the store was doing well. Finally, he suggested that if saving money was McGregor's main motivation, he might look to more significant ways to cut overhead and administrative expenses. McGregor promised to consider Lee's comments, but he said he was still convinced the outdated employee discount program was the place to start.

Study Questions

1. Once McGregor has chosen his arguments, what structure will work best in this situation? One-sided or two-sided? Tell or sell? Given, since, therefore? Recommendation, rationale, implementation? Storytelling?
2. In arriving at his decision to modify the discount program, McGregor considered many arguments in its favor. Identify his arguments with a suitable key word. Which seem most cogent and persuasive to you?
3. What attitudes are the executives and buyers likely to have toward the new discount program? Which of McGregor's arguments are likely to seem most persuasive to them? Can you devise new arguments that might be more acceptable to them?
4. In designing his communication to his senior managers, should McGregor concentrate on one or two issues, or should he discuss all the issues that had a bearing on his decision?
5. Do you find merit in Allen Lee's suggestion that there might be more meaningful ways to cut costs and overhead than McGregor's new discount program? What might they be? What arguments support your view?
6. Suppose you disagree with McGregor about instituting the new program as it is described in the case. What changes would you make? Or would you leave the current plan in place? What arguments and what structure would you choose to persuade McGregor to modify or abandon his new program?

CHAPTER 7

Choosing Media

Since most business communications involve a variety of audiences, you may need to use a number of different channels to accomplish your goal. You may want to talk to a colleague, hold a meeting with representatives of other departments, send a written proposal to a superior, solicit advice from a friend via E-mail, make a videotape for employees, train supervisors as presenters, establish a website, or prepare an external public relations campaign. Some important business communications require that all these media, and more, work in tandem.

Often, choosing media requires decisions on how best to send a message upward (to superiors) or across (to colleagues). But communication channels upward are usually narrow (conversations, E-mail, meetings, memos), and conversations across are usually routine. By contrast, communications down or out, especially in a large organization, often involve multiple media. We'll deal with conversations out (to shareholders, the press, and the public) in later chapters. Here, we're primarily concerned with downward communication in large organizations. We'll also concentrate on the toughest communication challenge: sending a message the audience doesn't want to hear.

Peter Drucker provides a good starting point; he argues that downward communication is impossible.

> [Downward communication] cannot work, first, because it focuses on what we want to say. But we know that all [the communicator] does is utter. Communication is the act of the recipient. . . . [All] one can communicate downward are commands, that is, prearranged signals. One cannot communicate downward anything connected with understanding, let alone with motivation. This requires communication upward, from those who perceive to those who want to reach their perception.
>
> This does not mean that managers should stop working on clarity in what they say or write. Far from it. But it does mean that how we say something comes only after we have learned what to say. And this cannot be found out by "talking to," no matter

how well it is being done. "Letters to the Employees . . ." will be a waste unless the writer knows what employees can perceive, expect to perceive, and want to do. They are a waste unless they are based on the recipients' rather than the emitter's perceptions.[1]

Here, Drucker returns to a central point in his argument about communication: Subordinates hear only what they want to hear. People don't want to get bad news. They don't want to learn that they must lose their jobs or change their traditional practices. Still, often, management has to send precisely these messages. How can it send them, and what media work best when one is conveying painful messages? Sending good news is easy, and managers will do it in person, to share in the credit and good feeling. Sending bad news is harder.

Let's examine several typical situations in which the manager has to send bad news, and the media through which this can be communicated.

The most extreme situation: *you're fired.* While it's true that a large corporation can send out a bunch of pink slips, by and large, dismissal is a one-on-one situation, or should be. Managers tend, for obvious reasons, to avoid this situation, but handling it well can contribute significantly to their credibility. Before deciding how to communicate this message, the manager must consider whether the firing results from *performance* or *context.*

- *Performance.* This is the toughest situation personally, but the easiest bureaucratically, if certain criteria have been established ahead of time. Have you, as a manager, established clear standards for success—sales record, production, or other measurable standards of performance? If so, regardless of whether the firee is willing to believe it, you're in the enviable position of saying that your action can be based upon a verifiable and agreed-upon contract.
- *Context.* This is tough bureaucratically, but easier personally: "Our market is shrinking, we need to reduce the workforce, and you're one of the ones to go." While performance arguments often apply in these cases, there are other factors that can ease the pain: lack of seniority, the availability of an early retirement plan, or help in finding the next job.

Less extreme cases of bad news include "We have to become more productive," "We're not performing up to standard," "We have to change our tried-and-true practices," and "You must learn new skills to keep your job." In each of these situations, consider whether you should argue from performance, context, or both. Be as specific as you can about the consequences of failure *and* the rewards of success.

CHOOSING THE MEDIA TO SEND TOUGH MESSAGES

As a rule of thumb, it's fair to say that the more personal your communication medium, the more likely your message will reach your audience. In a one-on-one conversation, you can gauge your audience's reaction moment by moment, modulate your approach, and respond to individual questions and concerns. Obviously, however, this is impossible in the situation where, for example, a CEO is sending a message to thousands of employees.

[1]Peter F. Drucker, "Managerial Communication," *Management: Tasks, Responsibilities, and Practices* (New York: Harper and Row, 1974), p. 490.

Generally, you're well advised to choose the most personal medium, or combination of media, capable of carrying your message. Here are some examples:

Personal Conversation

While you won't always be able to talk personally with each member of your audience, you can usually do so with some of them, for example, key decision-makers or those you've designated to carry your message to the wider audience.

Electronic Communication

Often, a telephone call, a text message, or an E-mail will take much less time than a face-to-face meeting and will achieve a better result. On the other hand, electronic communication can often serve as an easy way to avoid tougher but more effective modes of communication such as public speaking, negotiating sticky issues, or personal confrontation. See Chap. 15 for suggestions on the appropriate use of electronic communication.

Small Group Meetings

Often, you or your delegates can meet with your audience in small enough groups that each individual still can have his or her say. Sometimes, this situation can be better than one-on-one meetings, because extreme views may be counterbalanced by more moderate views expressed by members of the group.

Large Group Meetings

While more unwieldy than small group meetings, these can still demonstrate that the leader is willing to face the troops and, at least symbolically, share the tough times with them.

Live Broadcast

This is usually done by in-house network, satellite hookup, or public media. While relatively impersonal, this can convey immediacy, a consistent message, and a sense of urgency.

Videotape

The leader can at least be sure that all audience members see his face, hear his voice, and interpret gestures and body language.

Letter

While pretty impersonal, this medium allows the leader to share the information and analysis that led to a particular decision. An additional advantage is that it can be sent to the employee's home and allows time for reflection.

Word of Mouth or the Grapevine

This medium is the least personal and the most prone to inaccuracy. But the manager will ignore at her peril the fact that this medium will have a crucial impact on the outcome of almost every business communication situation. While you're talking to one colleague in your office, others will be speculating on what you're discussing, and some of those speculations may be passed on as facts. Rumors about layoffs rippling through an organization may become wildly exaggerated. Everyone likes to talk about personalities and drama. The successful manager accepts the existence of the grapevine, and uses it in two important ways:

Know What's on It

Your immediate subordinates are unlikely to tell you that employees further down the line are saying you're a jerk. But you or your assistant may have friends in another department who'll give you the lowdown if they don't fear the consequences.

Make It Work for You

This is a delicate proposition, and it can often go awry. But there are times when you may *want* rumors to be circulating through an organization. You might leak information that layoffs are coming, so that when the actual news is announced, it doesn't seem as bad as expected. A subordinate who's heard that salaries are capped this year may be happy with a modest raise. These sorts of tactics, however, should be used sparingly and wisely; even a slight abuse of them can damage your credibility.

Negotiation

This medium deserves special discussion, because it's both very difficult to do well and the centerpiece of many, if not most, business communications. Whether you're talking to a large union or discussing your workload one on one with your boss, you're negotiating. A classic study of negotiations, *Getting to Yes,*[2] is worth reading for any student of management. It offers specific techniques for defining your goals, understanding the needs of your negotiating partner, and finding areas of agreement. While the technical details of conflict resolution are beyond the scope of this book, the golden rule is *start by finding common ground.*

Modulating Your Media Choices to Your Message

Sending tough messages downward requires particularly careful attention to choosing the appropriate media. Especially when giving bad news to loyal employees, design your choices to convey the message as personally as possible. Large layoffs, for example, may best be handled by a more human approach than sending people pink slips. In smaller companies, you might choose to hold an all-employee meeting and have the CEO or president explain the painful changes personally. In a larger company, you might convene a manager's meeting and provide department heads and their immediate subordinates with an explanation for the downsizing and instruct them to convey to the employees the company's gratitude for their services

[2]Roger Fisher and William Ury, *Getting to Yes: Negotiating Agreement without Giving In* (New York: Penguin Books, 1983).

and explain the help the company will give employees to retrain them or help them find employment elsewhere. In either case, you might decide to supplement this effort with a letter to every employee thanking them for their services and explaining why these painful decisions are necessary.

Crisis communications, which we'll discuss in more detail later in the book, are a special case. Sometimes managers need to get news out very fast. Consider the situation of organizations that had their headquarters in the World Trade Center on 9/11. Some companies had much of their management staff wiped out. The remaining employees didn't know if they had a job, if the company was going to survive, where or when they should report to work. In this, or even a less disastrous situation, multiple media are crucial to communicating your messages effectively. In such a situation, sometimes the best means to reach your employees is through the public media. It's critical in a crisis situation that credible company spokespersons are available to the print and television press, and that they arrive at a preliminary plan of action very quickly. Managers should also be sure that they have the means available (E-mail for example) to reach all of their reports at home as soon as possible, and that those reports have the means to contact their subordinates immediately.

Factors to consider when deciding what media to use to convey your messages include:

Urgency

How soon does the employee or audience need to get this message to function effectively?

Formality

What level of information and direction does the receiver of the message need? What means of communication is most likely to acknowledge their importance and dignity?

Permanency

While you can't always tell everyone immediately how they should respond to a situation, you should let them know when you can tell them and how long the situation or crisis is likely to last.

Feedback

Especially in a crisis, it's important that employees know how to find out important follow-up information. Staffing a telephone response line or creating a regularly updated website may help here.

Complexity

Different audiences need different levels of information. Choose the media appropriate to the complexity of the message and the needs of the recipients.

Cost

Mass E-mails are cheaper than mass mailings, and press conferences that take up a great amount of executive time are more expensive than using free press via a clear press release or an interview. Perhaps a company-wide teleconference will cost less than flying in all the executives from overseas. Consider cost by measuring it against the urgency and complexity of your message.

Habit

How is your audience used to hearing from you? Familiar modes of communication are usually best unless the urgency of the situation dictates otherwise. In fact, the choice of an extraordinary medium can by itself convey urgency and importance.

Efficiency

Especially in crisis communication situations, ask yourself: Is this the fastest way to get out the basic information that will do the job? Other media will give you the opportunity to deliver more detail or message refinements later, though you want to be sure your message is consistent throughout the communication campaign.

Follow-up

Before you've sent out the urgent message, make sure you have the systems in place to deal with the consequences.

Usually, several media will be operating at once. The grapevine will be buzzing in a mass communication situation. Sometimes media can be combined creatively to achieve the maximum personal communication possible given the size and situation of the audience. A CEO who can't pull all the workers off the floor simultaneously for a satellite broadcast, for example, might choose to videotape a meeting with a representative range of employees, then show the results to the rest as time permits.

These are some considerations to address when you are choosing media in a tough downward communication situation:

1. *Consistency.* If possible, make sure all members of the audience get the same message.
2. *Timeliness.* Get the message out ahead of the grapevine. The longer rumors have to develop, the harder they'll be to counter.
3. *Modulation.* Large audiences contain subgroups that will be affected differently by your announcement. Make sure each receives a message tailored to its needs and interests while avoiding inconsistencies or appearances of double-dealing.
4. *Feedback.* Anyone receiving a message, especially a negative one, will want to respond. Make sure a mechanism is in place to air and address questions and concerns.
5. *Follow-up.* Once an action has been announced, make sure the systems exist to carry it out as expeditiously as possible.

Although this chapter and the following cases focus on the common situation of having to send bad news downward, most of the principles described here apply to delivering good news as well. Obviously, this is an easier task, but it still requires specific skills, including the following.

1. Take every opportunity to personally congratulate those responsible for the success.
2. In your messages, be sure to emphasize how all members of the organization will benefit personally from the positive development.
3. Consider how the changes likely to result from the good news will affect the existing organizational structure. Good news for the company may not be good news for everyone involved. Communicate information such as promotions or changes in job descriptions using the same media but with messages modulated to meet the different concerns and likely responses of disparate audiences.

The following case addresses a situation where bad news is forcing organizational change.

The Timken Company

Burt Jones, director of employee relations, believed he had a challenge that played to his strengths. Eight months from now, in August 1986, The Timken Company, America's largest bearing producer and a major alloy steelmaker, faced one of the toughest labor negotiations in its history. Global competition had flooded The Timken Company's markets; the company had been running up losses for the first time since its founding. Top management had decided on a radical restructuring of the company. Substantial numbers of the salaried and hourly workforce had been laid off since the American steel industry had gone into a tailspin in 1981 and 1982; more employment cuts lay ahead. George Arris, group manager for labor relations, had instructed Burt to prepare an action plan for next year's employee communications program to submit to The Timken Company's president.

Burt knew he had a case to make for employee restraint in the 1986 negotiations. Employment in American steel had dropped by over one half since 1979. Foreign producers were selling better-quality steel than that produced by the Americans, and trade information indicated that the Japanese were targeting bearings for a major push. Although government subsidies and modern plants contributed to the competitiveness of foreign steelmakers, a more decisive factor was their dramatically lower wage rates. Burt was convinced he had a persuasive argument for spurring productivity and avoiding a strike that could only cause more lost jobs.

Several factors, however, stood in his way. Company management embraced a range of views on the scope—even the utility—of an employee communications program. Like many older American manufacturers, The Timken Company had a conservative employee relations tradition predicated on preserving "management's right to manage." Moreover, Timken workers had granted substantial concessions in the last contract. Burt wondered whether the company could "go to the same well" again.

Early signals from the United States Steelworkers, which represented 31% of the U.S. Timken workforce, were not positive. The union was avoiding early confrontations with industry leaders such as U.S. Steel, which could count on substantial earnings from its subsidiary, Marathon Oil. Instead, the union was concentrating on weaker companies to achieve a favorable settlement pattern. In December 1985, the Steelworkers issued "Confronting the Crisis: the Challenge for Labor," a report that offered a frank assessment of the prevailing crunch in the steel industry. It implied a sharp distinction between steel companies on the verge of bankruptcy, which would

This case was prepared by Michael Hattersley, Lecturer in Communication. Harvard Business School case 387–035.

be offered concessionary packages, and producers such as The Timken Company, which would be expected to make up for previous concessions in the August 1986 negotiations (see *Exhibit 1*).

At various points in Burt's career with The Timken Company, he had worked in personnel administration and logistics, labor relations, and employee communications. He had familiarized himself with corporate communications practices at analogous companies and in other industries. He knew that many American manufacturers, especially in newer growth industries, were looking to Japan for employee relations models. The Timken Company itself was experimenting with innovative management practices at its new Faircrest operation —the first totally integrated steel plant constructed in the United States in 30 years. Many bright and effective managers at older steel and bearing plants were pressing for a more liberal management-employee communications policy. On the other hand, Burt sensed that as an older manufacturing firm with a successful tradition of conservative management and cool union relations, the Timken Company could not shift its employee communications policy without risking a major—and potentially destabilizing—impact on management techniques, employee relations, labor relations, and the legal obligations inherent in a union contract.

As Burt and his colleagues met to discuss the scope, audience, structure, media, message, and goals of the 1986 program, several late developments affected their deliberations. Management had asked for a program to sell the company's new structure to the workforce. Preliminary figures indicated that the company's 1985 results would show stagnant sales and another small loss. Finally, Burt was informed that the company planned to announce an 8% across-the-board pay cut for salaried workers early in 1986.

HISTORY OF THE TIMKEN COMPANY

Henry Timken (born in 1831) founded The Timken Roller Bearing Axle Company of St. Louis, Missouri, in 1899 with himself as president and his sons William and Henry as principal officers. The key to the company's success was Henry Sr.'s invention of a tapered roller bearing that could relieve friction regardless of the angle from which the load was applied. Although tapered roller bearings had at that time just recently become available in Europe, Henry Timken's patented design was demonstrably superior to any other bearing in the marketplace.

The Timken Company originated as a supplier to wagon and carriage builders, but the automobile had already made its appearance. When rising demand required building the company's first factory, the family decided to locate it in Canton, Ohio—roughly halfway between steel suppliers in Pennsylvania and auto shop customers in southern Michigan. The Canton plant produced its first bearings in 1902, employing between 30 and 40 persons in the early years. These were lean times for the company, but Henry Ford's invention of the automobile assembly line in 1908 generated a rapidly expanding market for Timken products.

The following three decades witnessed important product line expansion.TheTimken Company's first steel mill was constructed to overcome supply shortages caused by World War I. By the early 1920s, the companywas producing high-grade alloy steel as an independent product line as well as for its own use. To accommodate this growth, the company added new plants throughout Ohio and opened divisions in Great Britain and France. In the 1930s, The Timken Company developed a high-quality, removable rock bit, which made it a major supplier to the mining, quarrying, and construction industries.

The Timken Company's stock was first issued to the public in 1922, but the family maintained its lead role in managing the corporation. Generally, a Timken served as chairman of the board to provide continuity and a long-term view. The family helped carry the company and most of the employees through the Great Depression.

The Second World War inaugurated a period of unprecedented prosperity and innovation. New plants were opened in Ohio, the Carolinas, and South America. In the 1960s, before the era of environmental protection legislation, the company took the lead in installing scrubbers to reduce smokestack pollution and voluntarily curbed the discharge of industrial wastes into waterways. By 1981 The Timken

EXHIBIT 1 United Steelworkers Issues a Report on the Steel Industry Crisis (1985)

Findings quoted from "Confronting the Crisis: the Challenge for Labor," prepared for the United Steelworkers by Locker/Abrecht Associates, Inc.

1. The Reagan Administration's policies have greatly magnified the industry's problems. The government has promoted the rise in the value of the dollar, which has promoted imports, shifted government expenditures away from steel intensive industries and supported high interest rates.
2. Recent research done for the USWA has revealed that the Reagan Administration has subverted implementation of the Voluntary Restraint Agreements (VRAs) program by granting excessive quotas, thereby raising the penetration level to 24.5 percent from the promised 20.3 percent. This means that in 1985 imports will rob the domestic producers of shipments equal to almost four million tons, further weakening job and income security.
3. We see no reasonable economic scenario which would allow steelworker employment to return to the levels of the late 1970s. While the rate of job loss can be expected to slow down, more layoffs are likely.
4. Steelworkers have already made enormous sacrifices towards improving the viability of the industry. Seventy-two percent of all operating cost reductions since 1982 have come from lowering employment costs.
5. Contrary to what most people believe, we have found that *steel usage*—the total amount of steel used in the U.S. economy—has not *significantly declined.* Traditional approaches to measuring steel demand fail to take into account *indirect imports* (imported manufactured products which contain steel). When these goods are included in the demand figures, steel usage in the U.S. has remained relatively constant with only a two percent drop over the past eight years. Based on this insight, we have concluded that the amount of steel consumed in the U.S. remains more than enough to sustain the domestic steel industry at its present size.
6. The integrated producers have experienced major operating losses each year since 1982. During this period, a massive surge in direct and indirect imports drove down prices, shipments and revenues. Costs also dropped in this period, but not enough to offset the decline in revenues. For the first time, U.S. producers could not pass along higher costs by raising prices.
7. The integrated producers continue to operate some plants that are losing money because the one-time shutdown costs, especially those related to USWA severance benefits, are very high.
8. Imports have been the main source of downward pressure on prices. The most reliable data available estimates that since 1982, actual domestic prices were cut from $518 to the present $467 per ton, a 10 percent drop.
9. Some of the integrated producers are threatened with an immediate cash shortage which could lead to bankruptcy. This threat is intensified by huge debt payments which in 1985 alone cost the industry at least $500 million.
10. Despite major cost reductions achieved in the last three years, the cost gap between domestic and foreign integrated producers has not narrowed, primarily because of the artificially high dollar favored by the Reagan Administration.
11. Over the past ten years, the domestic integrated industry has been more profitable than producers in West Germany, Britain, and France, all of whom lost money on an operating basis. These foreign producers survived because of subsidies, protection or other forms of government support. The governments in these industrialized countries have recognized the need to sustain their own distressed industries and steelworkers. The U.S. government refuses to recognize the importance to this country of its integrated producers and their employees, thereby withholding subsidies or protection.
12. Among the integrated producers, there have been tremendous gains in labor productivity in recent years. According to a leading analyst, man hours per ton have fallen from 8.3 in 1980 to 6.1 in 1984, a 27% drop.
13. Our research identified three simple government programs that in 1985 could have provided domestic producers with an additional *10 million tons* in shipments—enough to make the industry profitable. If instituted these programs would have raised operating rates to 79 percent of capacity, prices by at least five

EXHIBIT 1 (continued)

percent, the profit per ton by $23 or more and increased employment by about 15,000 workers. These programs are: proper implementation of the VRAs, 20 percent restriction on indirect imports and public investment programs.

14. Growing competition has forced the integrated producers to rely increasingly on flat rolled products for revenues and profits. To remain viable, these producers must be competitive in this market. Imports and possible future mini-mill competition must be met head-on and defeated, or the integrated producers will not survive.
15. Overtime hours have steadily increased to the point where they presently constitute the equivalent of 13,900 full-time steelworkers.
16. Poor management performance has plagued the industry for years, especially in the areas of capital investment, marketing, quality control, maintenance, product development and labor relations. A very entrenched corporate culture has not been able to adapt to the long-term crisis now confronting the industry.

Company employed over 21,000 people in 19 plants worldwide and earned after-tax profit of $101 million on sales of $1,427 million (see *Exhibit 2*).

TROUBLED TIMES: THE EARLY 1980S

In 1981, The Timken Company, under Chairman William R. Timken, Jr., and President Joe Toot, Jr., took its greatest gamble. It committed $500 million—equivalent to two-thirds of net worth—to construct the most advanced steelmaking plant in the world. Nearly 900,000 square feet in size, the new Faircrest Steel Plant near Canton would increase the company's smelting capacity by 50%, to 1.5 million tons per year. The plant was expected to be fully operational by 1986.

Just as construction of Faircrest was putting substantial strains on The Timken Company's capital structure, sudden realignments in the global market for bearings and steel in the early 1980s dried up demand for the company's products. Neither The Timken Company nor any other American steel producer was prepared for the dramatic shift: American manufacturing and heavy industry had become uncompetitive both overseas and at home. The factors that hurt other areas of the American economy—a strong dollar, sluggish domestic demand, increasingly sophisticated foreign competition, outdated facilities —hit American steel and related industries particularly hard. "We couldn't believe," said one senior Timken manager, "that this could happen so fast. Suddenly, the sky fell in on us." What was difficult for management to grasp was unbelievable to the workforce, which had grown accustomed to continually greater employment opportunities, better working conditions, and fatter paychecks.

EXHIBIT 2 Impact of Economy on the Timken Company, 1981–1985
($ in thousands except per share data)

	1981	1982	1983	1984	1985
Net sales	$1,427,158	$1,041,361	$937,320	$1,149,908	$1,090,674
Income (loss) before taxes	183,846	(21,037)	759	51,612	(34,545)
Total income taxes (credit)	82,731	(18,036)	229	5,555	(27,579)
Net income (loss)	101,115	(3,001)	530	46,057	(6,996)
Net income (loss) per share	9.01	(.27)	.05	3.91	(.32)
Dividends per share	$3.40	$3.00	$1.80	$2.00	$1.80

Between 1981 and 1983, sales plummeted from $1,427 million to $937 million. Net income dropped from a profit of $101 million to a $3 million loss in 1982 and returned to the black in 1983 by an amount of only $530,000 (*Exhibit 2*). The results included substantial layoffs of hourly employees, reductions in salaried ranks, and a considerably tougher approach to negotiations with the union.

THE RECESSION'S IMPACT ON LABOR RELATIONS

The first test of unionized employees' response to the company's new economic situation came with the 1982 contract negotiations for Faircrest, which would be opening in stages over the next several years. This highly automated, state-of-the-art facility would employ far fewer workers to achieve the same production levels as older plants. Furthermore, plans for the plant called for assignment flexibility, which would require concessions from the union in the form of relaxed work rules. These were substantial concessions to ask of one of the nation's largest and most powerful unions.

The Timken Company's history of labor relations was like that of other conservative American manufacturers. The older Ohio plants had been unionized in a series of tough labor struggles during the 1930s and 1940s, led by I. W. Abel, a Timken electrician who later became president of the United Steelworkers. After the Second World War, negotiations had tended to produce fat settlements. Although generous, these were contracts the company could afford, and Timken employees remained among the best-paid manufacturing workers in the country. No major strike had hit the company since the late 1960s; partially as a result, the 1970s had been a decade of almost unparalleled prosperity for The Timken Company and its workforce. As one company official observed, "Employees' biggest problem in those years was whether they could get a Saturday off to spend with their families."

The Timken Company's negotiating pattern had always been to keep the union at arm's length. Generally, the company's offer was not put on the table until week six of an eight-week negotiation. By five o'clock on the last day, the union either accepted the company's final package or walked out.

The Timken Company had mounted vigorous and successful anti-union drives at its newer plants. By 1982 most unionized workers were concentrated in the older Ohio facilities. Newer plants in Ohio, Colorado, and the Carolinas had remained nonunion. Compensation packages for nonunion workers, however, closely followed union settlements.

During the 1982 Faircrest negotiations, the United Steelworkers were feeling the pinch of current economic conditions as acutely as were the steel companies. Early signs indicated that membership was heading into a steep decline; job flexibility and automation were no longer as threatening as they had appeared only a few years before. Indeed, flexibility and automation were emerging as American industry's only response to the tide of foreign competition. After an initial vote that went against the company largely due to lack of employee interest—it was held during the annual Cleveland-Pittsburgh football game—the Faircrest contract was approved by a substantial majority of unionized employees in a second vote in October 1982.

This concessionary pattern persisted in the companywide 1983 negotiations. Impressed by the severity of the company's competitive situation, the United Steelworkers approved a reduced-wage agreement with a restitution feature triggered periodically over the three years of the contract. Both the union and the company saw the agreement as a temporary expedient to carry The Timken Company and its workers alike over an extraordinary economic slump.

ORIGINS OF TIMKEN'S EMPLOYEE COMMUNICATIONS PROGRAM

A crucial factor in the success of the 1983 negotiations, many managers agreed, was The Timken Company's new employee communications program.

"Our War on Competition" (OWOC) was conceived in 1982 as an effort to educate employees about the competitive situation; its second purpose—although never explicitly acknowledged—was to prepare the way for a concessionary 1983 contract. The program featured: (1) videotaped messages from senior management, with follow-up discussions led by supervisors for groups of about 30 workers; (2) the ACTION program—periodic meetings between supervisors and employees to solicit suggestions for improved productivity; (3) a motivational campaign of bulletin board messages and posters, generally displayed near the time clocks or in other well-traveled areas; (4) a program to reward successful employee suggestions with modest bonuses; (5) articles in regular company publications; and (6) a few spots on Canton-area radio, with a public-service emphasis. The videotaped messages generally featured Joe Toot, Jr., or Personnel and Logistics Vice President Bob Lang. They emphasized the company's recent loss of market share and the need for each individual worker to help the company grow more competitive.

All Timken employees, salaried and hourly, union and nonunion, were pulled off the plant floors for one hour to watch each videotape and to participate in a follow-up question-and-answer session. The employee relations department compiled the evaluations prepared by discussion leaders and summarized the results for management. In general, response from the workforce was positive. Although employees clearly perceived the attempt to soften them up before negotiations, they were impressed that the company was, for the first time, attempting to reach them directly. The Timken Company's leadership judged the program a success, and following signing of the 1983 contract, OWOC persisted—although at a considerably slower and more sporadic pace. (*Exhibit 3* offers a brief outline of the 1985 OWOC program.)

REORGANIZATION

By 1985 Timken's management had spent three years exhorting workers to improve productivity. The various feedback channels established by OWOC indicated that workers felt it was management's turn to make sacrifices. The company's leadership agreed that The Timken Company's management structure should be reorganized. Senior officials, like other salaried employees, had taken a 6% pay cut in 1984, but the company's chairman and president decided that, in the existing climate, more radical surgery was in order. In July 1985 they hired McKinsey and Company, which had extensive experience in major corporate restructurings, to assist in a reorganization of the company.

From its earliest days, The Timken Company had evolved as a highly centralized company. Its steel operations had originated as suppliers to the bearing factories and remained integrated into, and subordinate to, the original management structure. Steel and bearing operations were organized regionally rather than functionally or by product line. In one respect, this had caused "the tail to wag the dog." Historically, bearing employees had been paid less than steel employees, but, under the umbrella of the United Steelworkers, they had achieved parity at The Timken Company.

In consultation with McKinsey, the company's leadership developed a reorganization plan. Separate operations would be developed for bearings and steel. Each would operate as an autonomous unit headed by one executive vice president. Corporate headquarters would be divided into four operational centers: (1) finance, (2) technology, (3) strategic management, and (4) personnel administration and logistics. Each would be headed by a vice president. All six vice presidents would report to the president of The Timken Company, who retained responsibility for coordinating all operations. Several intermediate managerial levels would be stripped away, which would bring leaders more directly in contact with operations and streamline the company's structure.

In the fall of 1985 The Timken Company began to implement the reorganization. The company instituted an early retirement and layoff program designed to reduce salaried employment by 500. Layer by layer, managers were promoted, demoted, retired, or reassigned. The process was a painful one, and disruptions in many operational

EXHIBIT 3 1985 "Our War on Competition" Program: A Brief Outline

	Months—1985												1986
Elements	Jan.	Feb.	Mar.	Apr.	May	June	July	Aug.	Sept.	Oct.	Nov.	Dec.	Jan.
ACTION II 1984		E											
"State of the Company" management meeting		M											
Letter from Joe Toot, Jr.			E										
O.W.O.C. videotape—Joe Toot, Jr.			E										
Department visits						E[a]							
"State of the Company" management meeting								M					
O.W.O.C. videotape—VP for Marketing								E[b]					
Divisional meeting to all levels (supervisors separate)										E			
ACTION III Program											E		

Note: *On-going programs:* "TIMKEN" magazine, "Update," bulletin boards, Timken clock posters, community radio, in-plant displays.
Audiences: M = management;E = employees.
[a] To be accomplished during the year 1985.
[b] August–September, following "State of the Company" management meeting.

areas were inevitable as individuals, departments, plants, and even whole divisions waited to see for whom they would be working.

THE 1986 EMPLOYEE COMMUNICATIONS PROGRAM

It was in this atmosphere that Burt Jones and his colleagues were charged with developing an employee communications action plan. The company was instituting a traumatic management reorganization, facing major negotiations in July, laying off substantial numbers of experienced employees, and reducing the incomes of the rest.

Burt's collaborators in this task included his boss under the pre-reorganization regime, Group Manager for Labor Relations George Arris; his boss under the new dispensation, Director of Communications Jim Oaks; Director of Labor Relations Don Simonson, who together with Arris would be conducting the upcoming negotiations for the company; and Burt's assistant, Bill Drozda. Once the 1986 program had been designed, each of its elements would be scrutinized by Personnel Administration and Logistics Vice President Bob Lang and President Joe Toot, Jr.

The shift of employee communications from labor relations to communications might signal that the program now had a broader mandate than simply preventing a strike, but that mandate had yet to be precisely defined. Meeting regularly, the employee communications team identified the elements of a comprehensive communications action plan. One problem facing the communications group was to define the long-term purpose and scope of the program. OWOC had originated as a vehicle to inform workers of an extraordinary situation requiring extraordinary sacrifices. Important segments of senior management still regarded it as an occasional expedient, useful during periods preceding negotiations. As the "extraordinary" situation had become permanent, however, so had OWOC. It was supported by some members of management as a motivational device, by others as a sign of greater openness on the part of the company, and by still others as a wedge to insert more participatory, personalized management.

Defining an employee communications policy, the group realized, required them to choose among competing constituencies. Any decision on communications policy had important implications for employee relations, labor relations, management style, and strategic direction. All of these policy areas were currently undergoing vigorous evolution—often being pulled in different directions. Openness about the company's financial situation, for example, might be important to the credibility of the communications program, but it would fly in the face of The Timken Company's traditional—and successful—relationship with the union; the company had never opened its books.

Communications policy also had important implications for the company's management style. Some managers at the plant level, and especially at Faircrest, were convinced that the employee involvement program had proved itself at Faircrest and should be reinforced by a vigorous communications program. Others believed that since Faircrest employees had been carefully selected, a management strategy that succeeded with this sophisticated workforce could not easily be transferred to other plants in the company. Also, many managers thought that OWOC, with rewards and messages directly from the top, worked outside the traditional chain of command and tended to undermine the authority of supervisors on the factory floors. Both the content and the structure of a future communications program were therefore the subject of intense debate.

Shaping an effective program also demanded consideration of the audience management wished to reach. In light of the upcoming negotiations, the primary audience was unionized workers. For the purposes of a long-term program, however, the audience had to be defined as all hourly and salaried employees of The Timken Company. Could a message be tailored that was appropriate to all these constituencies? This concern was coupled with another. Workers who felt their jobs threatened, and who were being geared up by their union for negotiations, were not in the mood to hear exhortations to greater effort from a management that was preparing the ground for concessions.

Burt and his colleagues felt they had a good grasp of worker attitudes toward the company's current situation. OWOC aside, few Timken workers could be oblivious to the crisis in their industry. They had watched neighboring plants in allied industries close their doors, and they were aware that many American steel companies were on the verge of bankruptcy. At the same time, however, they were deeply suspicious that top management was setting them up. In previous economic downturns, The Timken Company had been relatively impervious, and many workers couldn't believe that conditions had changed so suddenly. Rumors circulated that The Timken Company was about to be broken up and sold to the Japanese, that new contracts were being shunted to nonunion plants down South, or that the company's recent losses were really the result of accounting gymnastics. One comment reported from a worker was characteristic: "You tell me that we're suffering from global competition; then I see the machine next to mine pulled out and sent to Timken France. You're exporting our jobs."

Early signals from the union—the employees' major alternative source of information—were increasingly bellicose. United Steelworkers' President Williams had been quoted as saying that, in the current industry shakeout, certain companies would go out of business and jobs would be lost, but that the survivors would continue to pay good wages. Union cards were circulating at nonunion plants in South Carolina and Ohio. At other plants, managers were reporting increasingly bitter grievance disputes over work rules and seniority; isolated cases of vandalism had occurred. The local Canton union newspaper, the *Golden Lodge News,* which characteristically attacked management in general, was beginning to launch assaults against individual company leaders.

Definition of the audience for a long-term communications program was complicated by the widely varying situations at individual plants. Workers at the older, less-efficient steel plants felt their jobs threatened by Faircrest. Workers at unionized bearing plants worried that work was being diverted to their nonunion counterparts. Some employees felt management was cynically pitting plants against each other to see which would be the survivors. The communications team pondered whether a single communications program could successfully appeal to such a diverse audience.

Still, many managers hazarded the opinion that, on the whole, workers were less belligerent than they had been before the 1983 negotiations, which had concluded successfully for the company. Words like *depressed, stunned, afraid,* and *emotionally paralyzed* were more common than *angry* or *defiant* in assessments of workers' attitudes. "Our task," said one senior figure, "is to manage anxiety. We must tolerate a realistic concern in the present, while holding out legitimate hope for job security in the foreseeable future."

Considerations of scope and audience led the team to define clear goals for the 1986 program. Majority opinion here was represented by George Arris, who argued that a continued OWOC or its successor should support the company's business objectives: to hold the line on or reduce employment costs, to protect management's right to manage, to be fair to employees, and to avoid a strike. Others, representing different constituencies, proposed other objectives: to foster a participatory management structure, to educate employees about the international economic pressures faced by the company, to motivate greater efficiency and productivity, and to give the workers a sense of partnership with the company.

Once goals had been defined, a message had to be devised that would achieve them. To date, OWOC's central message had been that Timken employees needed to work smarter if they were to win their battle against competition. Some managers felt this message had grown thin with repetition. Others felt events had superseded it. All agreed it could be more sharply focused. The message had to convince workers that the competitive crunch was not the company's fault.

One possibility was to direct employees' attention exclusively to the threat posed by foreign competition. Such a message had the advantage of emphasizing the United States' patriotic struggle to preserve its manufacturing base. The facts in general would support this approach. As one manager summarized it, "In steel, we're competitive domestically but not internationally. In bearings, we're killing our domestic competition, but foreign competition is killing us." Faircrest was beginning to produce specialty alloy steel as good as or better than any other being made in the world, but The Timken Company was still having trouble beating Japanese prices. Korea was also emerging as a major competitor to American industry in both steel and bearings. While it was conceivable to match Japanese technology and efficiency, it was hard to imagine matching Japanese employment costs, which at $12 an hour were roughly half those prevailing in American industries. It was inconceivable to compete with Korean companies that were paying $4 an hour or less. In these circumstances, business would continue to go offshore. The challenge was to get as much of the business as possible that was going to remain in the United States.

Another possible approach for the 1986 program was to tie competitiveness more directly to job security. The company could send employees the message that if they worked harder their jobs would be safe. As serious as the competitive challenge had become, The Timken Company had held its own better than most comparable American manufacturers, and management was convinced that shrewd policies and a spirited team effort could position the company as one of the survivors. As President Toot pointed out, the Timken family had stuck by the company through hard times before and would do so now. No one could confidently predict at what employment level The Timken Company might stabilize, or when. However, job security was probably the most powerful motivation the company had to offer.

Finally, OWOC could be reconceived as an educational program designed to inform employees of the international competitive situation, the current position of American heavy manufacturing, and the strategy of The Timken Company. This approach envisioned challenging the union as the employees' primary source of economic information and achieving a real partnership between management and labor. It at least implied inviting workers to see the company's operations as a whole and to participate in management decisions. Historically, the company had been resistant to devices such as quality circles. Most of The Timken Company's leadership regarded such strategies as faddish and at best inappropriate to the plant environment.

Although most leaders felt that OWOC had accomplished its initial purposes well enough, managers at the plant level had complaints about the structure of the program. Most felt it was inordinately time-consuming—especially the ACTION component, which required each supervisor to speak individually with every worker reporting to her or him and also to submit a detailed report. Many plant-level managers felt they needed more training in how to present the videotapes effectively and handle the follow-up discussions. They complained that when they forwarded questions raised at the sessions to their superiors, the responses they received to pass on to the workers were often either unconvincing or confusing. Others asserted that their credibility had been undermined through repeated appearances by top company officials, and that it might be wise to turn to convincing outsiders for information on the competitive situation.

Many plant managers also questioned the top-down structure of OWOC. The work situation varied considerably from plant to plant, and different messages were appropriate to different audiences. Why not decentralize OWOC, they suggested, so that each plant could put its own particular spin on the message, and then gradually evolve an individualized communications program?

OWOC had employed videotape messages, question-and-answer sessions, one-on-one meetings, and a bulletin-board campaign to convey its messages on beating the competition. Granted that further training could be given to videotape presenters —and a smoother mechanism developed to respond to workers' questions—should the 1986 program use the same media mix? Other possibilities included letters to workers, focus-group meetings, plant-floor tours by senior management, video conferencing, and company-sponsored employee events.

The company could also reach the workforce through the local and national press by means of news releases, paid spots, and media events. Most employees, especially unionized employees, were concentrated in a few media markets. An external public relations campaign would provide the company with a powerful opportunity to reinforce its main points. A downbeat message carried on the public media, however, might undercut the company's general marketing and public relations strategies.

If videotapes, posters, and meetings continued to serve as the program's vehicles, how could their design support the central messages? Videotapes to date had usually featured senior executives as talking heads. Once, President Toot had appeared walking through a factory. For the most part, however, the tapes had resembled speeches from the Oval Office. Some managers felt other formats should be explored, such as interviews with customers, suppliers, or competitors. Perhaps a program based on the imagery of battle and competition should aim for snappier, more aggressive graphic effects. Similar considerations applied to launching any external public relations campaign.

BURT'S CHALLENGE: SATISFYING TWO AUDIENCES

Burt and his colleagues searched for a formula that would establish clear priorities for the 1986 program, create effective delivery channels, and attract the broadest possible consensus within the company. As they worked, they were increasingly aware that perhaps their most important audience of all was The Timken Company's top leadership, which would soon have to approve their proposals.

Study Questions

1. What key messages does The Timken Company need to send to its workforce?
2. Does The Timken Company need to change its management or communication practices in order to achieve its goal?
3. Once you've developed a plan of action and a strategy to communicate it, what will sell it to top management?
4. What media mix should you use to convey your messages?

CHAPTER 8

Style and Tone

Once you've designed your message and decided how to send it, the most delicate task still lies ahead: choosing language that's audience-sensitive, clear, forceful, persuasive, and memorable. You have selected the points you want to make, the order in which they should appear, and the appropriate media, but what language will simultaneously achieve accuracy, brevity, clarity, and vigor? The answer to these questions will lie in your mastery of style and tone.

Since specific choices about language can be made only as you draft and revise a communication, this chapter follows those on audience analysis, setting priorities, point of view, message design, and choosing media. Remember, however, that important decisions about style and tone should be made early in the genesis of your communication. Your interpretation of the context, your role as the source of communication, your goal setting, your understanding of your audience—all these should determine your style and tone from the beginning. You will be revising and rehearsing constantly to make sure the communication has the style and tone you planned. Style and tone aren't frills to be added at the last moment; they embody fundamental assumptions about you, your subject, and your audience.

GENERAL CONSIDERATIONS

Style can be defined as the art of packing the maximum amount of meaning into the minimum possible number of words. A clear, vigorous style makes your content accessible and convincing; a murky, lifeless style obscures and weakens it. Style also raises the question: Am I fitting my language and my choice of media appropriately to the situation? Is it formal or informal, a jargon-laden conversation among technicians who share my vocabulary or a presentation to a general audience? *Tone*—telling, selling, consulting, or joining—will determine your audience's responsiveness and commitment (see Chap. 3). Effective use of tone largely consists in conveying your respect for your audience's position or situation. It can mean something as apparently insignificant as tone of voice. Many people sound harsh or authoritarian even when the content of their communication is conciliatory. Others sound tentative when issuing an order. The only way to modulate these habits is to solicit and incorporate feedback from your peers in class and on the job. An inappropriate or unattractive tone creates resistance to you and your message; an appropriate tone invites understanding and assent. We are often persuaded not by arguments, but by an approach that wins our trust and respect for the communicator.

As a reader, you may have noted the studied simplicity of Hemingway or the complexity of Henry James, the restraint of a *New York Times* editorial, or the flamboyance of the tabloid press. As a manager, you may assume that only a professional writer needs to be conscious of style and tone. But style, whether conscious or not, is an integral part of all human discourse.

Naturally, the style and tone of managerial communications differ from those appropriate to literary, scientific, technical, or casual communications. But as you consider the spectrum from issuing clear instructions to writing good advertising copy, you may conclude that the business communicator needs to master as broad a range of styles as the novelist or news writer.

Most textbooks stress that the ultimate criterion of style and tone is *appropriateness;* the style should suit the source, audience, and occasion. We agree. Familiar shoptalk to one audience may strike another as incomprehensible jargon. Some occasions invite humor and informality; others require high seriousness. Sometimes you want to pass along the bare facts; other times, you want to grab the audience's attention at all costs. Success in these situations depends on your use of appropriate style and tone.

Under the pressure of time and other responsibilities, managers sometimes forget to adapt their style and tone to the audience; but just as often, a conscious effort to find the appropriate language goes awry. In carefully explaining technical matters to a nontechnical audience, you may come across as condescending. In acknowledging the burdens imposed by a new policy, you may sound apologetic. In deferring to a superior, you may convey a devastating lack of confidence, or you may please the superior while making your peers wince.

Achieving appropriateness does not mean laboriously contriving a new style and tone for every situation. Rather, you can cultivate a style and tone that are lucid, direct, vigorous—and thus appropriate for most situations. This is largely a matter of eliminating unnecessary words; constructing clear, declarative sentences; and avoiding undesirable or exaggerated overtones.

STYLE

A forceful style starts with correct, concise use of the language: accurate grammar, precise words, well-built sentences and paragraphs, active verbs, and a clear thesis or thread that runs from the beginning to the end of your communication. This means drawing on all the resources of effective communication we've discussed in previous chapters, but we especially encourage you to review the sections on clarity, brevity, and vigor covered in Chap. 1. Also, see Chap. 16, Effective Writing, for suggestions on how to draft, organize, and edit good prose. Here we'll concentrate on general principles that will help you capture and hold your audience's attention.

Forget correct English for a moment, though, and consider what we mean when we say someone has *style.* Typically, we're suggesting the person possesses some combination of flair, elegance, economy, and completeness either externally (in appearance) or internally (force of personality or intellect) or both. The same applies to prose. We tend to think of style as a quality of creative writing, but it's equally important in business communications. Although the conventions that govern business writing are more constrained than those governing novelists, most fine business writers appreciate literature and learn from it.

How can correct, routine business prose be transformed into prose with *style,* that is, with flair, elegance, economy, and completeness? Here are a few considerations:

Compelling Concept

Your writing will never be better than the idea you're trying to express. Stylish writing flows from an arresting concept that runs from beginning to end in a communication and governs all the constituent parts.

Memorability

People will remember striking facts, vivid images, and apposite comparisons or metaphors.

Facts

A simply stated fact, if important or surprising, can grab audience members' attention and motivate them to follow your argument. You've immediately established dramatic momentum, an element of mystery, because the audience will be asking: How will he prove this? Where is he going? or What can we do about this?

Images

If a good picture is worth a thousand words, a good image can be worth a thousand data points. The smaller and more technical your audience, the more important your data and your interpretation of them. The larger your audience, the less you can expect them to follow detailed argument, and the more you should aim to plant a few decisive images in their minds. A public relations or advertising campaign, for example, aims to plant positive images of the product or company and to counter existing negative ones. But even your technical audience will remember your main point better if you can encapsulate it in a picture that stays in the mind.

Comparisons

These can be used to demonstrate either similarity or difference. Comparisons based on similarity are most useful when carrying a technical message to a general audience. If you can show that something unfamiliar works the same way as something familiar, the audience will be more likely to understand, follow, and remember you. Comparisons based on difference can throw your ideas into bold relief.

Metaphors

When Ronald Reagan said it was "Morning in America" he was using a form of comparison most common in literature: metaphor. The image of dawn carried with it feelings of renewal, optimism, and rebirth. It also conveyed in three words a political and economic program. Metaphors are among the most powerful tools in language for condensing meaning and planting it permanently in the minds of your audiences.

Whenever you use one of these stylistic devices, make sure it's emphasizing, not distracting from, your main point.

Language

Like all sound, the English language is part music. How it jumps off the page or sounds in the ear, its words and rhythms, will heavily determine its impact. Even when reading to ourselves, we're hearing in our minds. Reading your document aloud can be the single best test of its style. Your ear will catch awkward sounds, repeated words, grammatical inaccuracies, obscurities, and holes in your argument that the eye might never see. Nothing tunes your ear better to the music of good language than reading or hearing good prose or poetry, whether you find it in *The Wall Street Journal* or at your local coffeehouse.

More than most languages, English is multilayered. Its foundation, Anglo-Saxon, derived from early German and consisted primarily of short, vigorous nouns and verbs: *man, trust, life, hope, stand, grasp, build, drive, speak.* Later, English adapted a vast number of words from Latin (often via French) to meet the needs of an increasingly sophisticated society: *human, fidelity, vivaciousness, aspiration, maintain, apprehend, construct, transport, orate.* By and large, Anglo-Saxon words are shorter and more concrete, Latinate words are longer and more abstract. No important concept in business or other areas of modern life could be expressed completely without the use of Latinate words, but vigorous English depends on choosing the Anglo-Saxon word when it will do the job. This will give your language a natural boldness and rhythm.

Variety

Your style can be vigorous and correct, yet still strike the reader as boring. This will usually be due to repeating the same sentence structure over and over, as in "We face a crisis in our overseas markets. Different countries like different types of packaging. Sales representatives are meeting resistance. Small distributors won't give us shelf space. Our product doesn't fit their traditional displays. They say we must change our coloring."Two factors make this tightly packaged information uninviting to the reader:

First, each sentence follows an identical grammatical structure: subject, verb, object. While this is the basic structure of a clear declarative sentence in English, and should be a model for the majority of your sentences, using the same pattern over and over will lull the reader into a sense of monotony.

Second, each sentence is short and of essentially the same length. *Style* contains the idea of flexibility, surprise, and connection. While most teachers of business writing emphasize the virtues of short sentences, often only longer constructions can pull ideas into clear relation. Consider: "We face a crisis in our overseas markets. Our representatives are meeting resistance because different countries like different packaging and coloring. As a result, small distributors won't give us shelf space." Here, the shorter sentences emphasize key points, while the longer sentence adds variety and makes connections. Causality is clearer, the reader feels greater interest, and the stage is set for action.

Once again, when deciding on an appropriate style, consider the situation. Is it formal or informal, business, social, or a mix of both? Are you communicating with colleagues who understand your style or with relative strangers? The professional style you use to address stockholders should be considerably different than the one you employ for an informal address at a company picnic. Untranslatable American slang might mystify a group of international executives. Jargon that serves as shorthand to communicate with fellow computer buffs might be incomprehensible to your own boss. Choose a style appropriate to your audience. While designing your message, consider how they talk to you, and to each other.

Finally, always check your prose, written or spoken, against the basic tenets of style-masters Strunk and White (*The Elements of Style,* Allyn and Bacon, 1995; referenced in *Harvard Communications Update,* February 1999):

1. Choose a suitable design (message and medium) and hold to it.
2. Make the paragraph the unit of construction.
3. Use the active voice.
4. Put statements in a positive form.
5. Use definite, specific, concrete language.
6. Omit needless words.
7. Avoid a succession of loose sentences tied together with conjunctions.
8. Express coordinated ideas in similar form.
9. Keep related words together.
10. In summaries, keep to one tense.
11. Place the emphatic words at the end.

TONE

While a clear, vivid, forceful style will generally serve you well, some matters of tone and tact deserve special attention. Controlling tone is easier in speaking than in writing or electronic communication. When you're speaking face to face, you can supplement words with expressions, vocal emphasis, and body language; you can also adjust your approach depending on the reactions of your audience. A written document must stand on its own, and it can be studied, reread, and passed on. Here are some suggestions for making sure your tone is working for, rather than against, you:

Develop an Ear for Tone, and Suit It to the Subject and Occasion

Listen to the tone of documents you receive or presentations you hear. Suppose, as a plant manager, you received the following memo from your CEO about a recent decision to centralize purchasing:

> As you have been personally informed, a new purchasing policy will go into effect on Oct. 3, following this year's peak buying season. At that time, you will notify Mr. Lyman, the new Vice President in charge of purchasing, of all contracts in excess of $10,000 one week in advance of the day on which they are to be signed.
>
> The company's increasing difficulty in securing essential new materials has necessitated these changes. It is to your and the company's advantage to comply with the new procedure. We expect your complete cooperation.

This language sounds authoritarian. The future imperatives ("you will notify"), the flat assertion of points that may be in dispute ("it is to your . . . advantage"), the "big me-little you" in the final sentence ("We expect your complete cooperation")—all express expectation of unquestioned obedience. Such a tone is increasingly uncommon and inappropriate in business. Moreover, the writer expresses a certain contempt for the reader by offering no evidence for the claims ("Increasing difficulties . . . necessitated").

There are times when a manager needs to command, but the habit can come too easily and can become counterproductive, especially in tone:

> In order to operate these tennis courts properly with a minimum of administrative interference, the following rules and procedures have been developed and are promulgated for information and compliance. . . .
>
> Since caretaking will schedule this area for cleaning last on the evening shift, it is imperative that all play be terminated by 10:50 P.M. and that locker rooms be vacated no later than 11:15 P.M.

The writer seems to have attempted a nonauthoritarian communication, explaining the reasons for the deadlines. But the tone of the words here subverts good intentions. "Compliance," "imperative," "terminate," and "vacate" all convey command. Other factors make the announcement sound pompous: the polysyllabic phrases ("administrative interference"), the frequent compounds ("rules and procedures"), and the legalistic vocabulary ("promulgated") are out of proportion to the topic and make the communicator sound self-important.

The expression of authority makes more sense in the following announcement of organizational changes due to the merger of two engineering firms:

> I wish to admonish each of you that the organizations, as promulgated for each group, do not represent a downgrading or a diminution of certain senior personnel who will be operating within a new structural hierarchy.
>
> As with any change, a certain amount of uncertainty always tends to creep to the fore, and usually a certain amount of random confusion ensues. Your indulgence and cooperation in allowing the dust to settle are sincerely appreciated.

This writer's heart is clearly in the right place; she wants to explain, reassure, offer guidance, and thank those who cooperate. But "admonish" and "promulgate" still sound authoritarian, while the rest of the passage is filled with redundancies ("structural hierarchy," "random confusion," "downgrading/diminution") that convey a defensive unwillingness to speak clearly. As a result, the writing, in Shakespeare's phrase, "protests too much." Say something once and people will usually believe you; say it three times, and they'll wonder if you believe it yourself. Readers of the above memo who never worried about losing status may begin to do so now.

Avoid Condescension and Accusation

Few things alienate an audience faster than a condescending or an accusatory tone. Many common phrases convey condescension to one degree or another:

"Please feel free to call if . . . "; "Please do not hesitate to contact me if. . . . " These imply that you're so august, your audience will think twice before disturbing you. *Better:* "Please call me if. . . . "

"I am sure you will understand"; "I know you will agree that. . . . " These usually precede a disputed assertion. Omit such phrases and provide specific support for your view.

"As vice-president in charge of operations, and on behalf of the entire management team, I would like to thank you . . . "; "During the recent employees' annual meeting we were indeed impressed with your comments and questions. . . . "

Such language focuses all the attention on the imperial communicator, none on the audience he's trying to praise. These examples suggest why we quoted Peter Drucker in the last chapter to the effect that it's very difficult to communicate downward.

Avoid also language that attacks the competence, intelligence, or honesty of your audience. People react defensively to an accusation, however unintentional; further communication may become impossible. Don't impute blame unless the case is clear and compelling. Watch out for:

"You're wrong, mistaken, inaccurate."

"You allege, claim, deny."

"You failed to notice."

"You forgot."

"At this point, the only sensible thing to do is. . . . "

Instead of trying to make your opponent look like a fool, which will only harden opposition, ask him to respond to countervailing evidence that seems important to you: "My understanding was. . . . " You may prevail, or you may unearth new information that changes your view.

Avoid Exclusive Language

A manager who refers constantly to "my plans" communicates a different message from one who refers constantly to "our plans." Inclusive language can do much to bring the audience over to your side.

Similarly, sexist language excludes a part of one's audience. When we say, "If a manager wishes to accomplish his goal, he should . . . " we really mean "*he or she* should." While overuse of *he or she* can get cumbersome, there are a number of ways around it. *Men* and *mankind* have perfectly acceptable substitutes in *people* or *humankind*. "Each manager submits his sales report at the end of the month" can read, "Each manager submits a sales report at the end of the month." Replace the masculine pronoun with *one* or *you.* In a long text, you can do as we have done here, alternating *he* and *she.*

Be careful, as well, to avoid insulting minorities in your audience. Even if you're a white male addressing a group of white males, most of them will think you're a bigot if you make racial or ethnic slurs. Also, statements such as "I'm sure all of you would rather be home tonight with your wives or girlfriends" will exclude those members of your audience who are female or gay as well as those heterosexual males who are currently unattached.

Avoid Flattery

Superiors deserve and appreciate praise as much as colleagues and subordinates do, but keep it honest and specific. Otherwise, your boss may start to smell insincerity, and your coworkers may learn to hate you.

Use Humor When Appropriate

We've all seen humor used well in informal situations such as conversations with friends or social gatherings like weddings or club meetings. Along with drama, it's the main reason people keep watching television. Nothing pulls people together, or endears them to the speaker, like a good laugh. Organizations like Toastmasters can give business people good practice in using humor to win over an audience. There's a role for humor as well in more serious situations, such as making a sales pitch or advancing an important proposal. Here the most common humorous strategy is to make fun of yourself; especially if you're a superior, subordinates will like the fact that you can recognize your own weaknesses. But don't use a joke or a selfdeprecating reference unless you're sure it will work. Another point: Jokes work better in speaking than in writing—although they're a very successful social element in E-mail.

Different managers can employ different styles and tones successfully in the same position. Naturally assertive people and naturally empathetic people may get similar results. Managers cannot re-create their personalities completely to fit a new job—and if they do, the falsity of their tone will be evident.

Part of managerial success is due to choosing the jobs that fit your personality. Remember Socrates' crucial advice: know thyself. If you're a hard-driving personality you may be the right person to run a manufacturing facility or work as a stock trader. You may not be the right person to direct employee relations or to represent the company at a contentious press conference. In your job choices, as well as your communication strategies, play to your strengths, modulate your approach to the situation, and know when to delegate or pass off the task to a colleague whose personality is better suited to the job.

For more detailed discussion of how to apply considerations of style and tone to specific communication situations, consult Chap. 16, Effective Writing, and Chap. 17, Effective Speaking.

In the following case, a manager at headquarters needs to advise a local manager about style and tone—and perhaps operational issues—related to alleged environmental problems at the plant.

CASE 8.1

Vanrex, Inc.

Alison Hitchcock, Director of Corporate Communications for the Vanrex Company in Chicago, had just received a report and a packet of news clippings from John Rubin, General Manager of Operations at Vanrex's chemical manufacturing plant in Hayestown, Oklahoma. A small but vocal group of Hayestown residents had been complaining about air pollution from the plant site, and their complaints had received extensive coverage in the local press. In response to these complaints, officials from the state Department of Health and Environment (ODH&E) and the Environmental Protection Agency (USEPA) had inspected the site. They found the plant in compliance with regulatory requirements, but the complaints continued. Frustrated, Rubin sent Hitchcock his report and asked for her advice. As she read the report and the accompanying news articles, she noted the extent of Rubin's operational problems and his proposed solutions and considered how he might improve relations with the community. She also kept in mind Vanrex's Corporate Environmental Statement, which committed the company to being a "good neighbor" (see section I of *Exhibit 1*).

This case was prepared by S. Lindsay Craig, Associate in Communication. Harvard Business School case 380–158.

BACKGROUND ON THE HAYESTOWN PLANT

Vanrex manufactured and marketed paint for homes, businesses, and institutions; it also supplied coatings for manufactured products and automotive parts. As a result of diversification, Vanrex also manufactured paint cans, aerosol cans, brushes, rollers, and other paint applicators. The Hayestown plant was located on the west side of the city and employed 253 of the city's 43,256 residents. When it was built in 1906, the site was well out in the country. Now, because Hayestown had expanded, residential housing partially surrounded the plant.

Two different sources affected air quality near the Hayestown plant: fugitive dust and stack emissions. The plant site occupied approximately eighty acres, little of which was covered by vegetation. The raw materials were all dry; prior to recent improvements, up to 15% of the raw materials were often lost into the atmosphere. The wet waste materials from various plant processes dried quickly when deposited on the sludge piles. These conditions, plus the dry Oklahoma climate, created the problem of "fugitive dust," air-borne particulate matter from any source other than a flue or stack. The other sources of emissions at the plant were the approximately twenty process stacks,

EXHIBIT 1 Hayestown Plant Report by John Rubin (Excerpts)

I. Corporate Environmental Statement

It has been the policy of Vanrex to meet or exceed the state and federal regulations. In addition to these requirements, it has been the intent of the company to be a good neighbor. It does not matter that the plant originally was situated on the outskirts of an urban area that has grown out and around the plant. Residential neighbors are located fairly closely on all sides and public concern in environmental matters is at a higher level nationally than ever before. The company believes that an effort has been extended to solve the continuing problems, has consistently been found in compliance by ODH&E and USEPA, and has extensive projects planned over the next year that will improve the overall problem. In this way, the company plans to be a good neighbor.

II. Existing Conditions

A. Process Stack Emissions

All process sources were evaluated by ODH&E two years ago. The several sources that were found out of compliance at that time have been brought within compliance by installation of control devices, better maintenance of existing devices, or deactivation. Some of these have occasionally experienced problems which have caused them to emit greater quantities than allowable. These sources will be discussed in detail.

1. **Calciner scrubber.** This source, Stack 3, was fitted with a venturi scrubber with a cyclonic separator two years ago. The system was designed to use water from the process and to return it to the process. The system cleaned the stack gases well when operating; however, it experienced plugging problems and chloride stress-cracking of the fan impeller. As a result, the scrubber was inactive part of the time. In January of last year, it was replaced with an ejector-type scrubber, which was certified for compliance in March.
2. **Dryer/calciner scrubber.** This source, Stack 7, was equipped with parallel dual-cyclone separators and a venturi scrubber with cyclonic separator for a water surge volume. Plugging has been a frequent problem in the operation of this system, resulting in too little water being supplied to the venturi, resulting in poor scrubbing.
3. **Hydrogen sulfide incinerator.** For some years the hydrogen sulfide formed in one of the processes had been burned in an incinerator that was vented into a common stack with the kilns. A project was begun in January to replace the old incinerator with a new incinerator and a separate stack. The incinerator design was changed during the project to meet the 20 percent maximum opacity on incinerators (Oklahoma Regulation 28-19-41). That is, the emissions from the incinerator may not block more than 20% of the sun's rays. The unit has been in operation for only about two weeks, so the optimum operating conditions have not been completely determined, and the 20 percent maximum opacity has not been attained. The incinerator manufacturer is conducting tests to determine these conditions. The results of these tests will be added to the appendix of this report when they become available.
4. **Kiln scrubbers.** There are two small kilns. A portion of the stack gases is routed through scrubbers to clean the gas stream for use in another process. The remainder of the gas stream was passed through cyclone separators to a common stack with the hydrogen sulfide incinerator.
5. **Electrostatic precipitators.** A roasting kiln in this plant is served by a three-section electrostatic precipitator and 150-foot stack. In the past, occasional electrical problems associated with the electrostatic precipitator have caused a slight plume from the stack. Several minor changes have been made, with little improvement.

B. Fugitive Dust

1. **Raw materials and residue.** The most apparent sources of fugitive dust are the coal and ore piles and the large residue pile in the northwest part of the plant site. Other residue piles are located near the center of the plant and the north side of the water treatment plant surge pond, where dredgings from the pond are dumped until they are sufficiently dry to haul.

EXHIBIT 1 (continued)

2. **Process plants.** Many leaks in process plants contribute to the total emissions. Feed stock handling at the plant has been a particular contributor. The coal and ore are crushed and further ground and stored prior to feeding the kilns via a belt conveyor. Considerable loss from the belts was noticed, as well as from the outlet end seal of the kilns. Some feed and product loss can be attributed to other process plants, but the plant handling of coal and ore has been proven to be the major contributor.

III. Proposed Solutions

A. Process Stacks

In the past, several of the stack emission control devices have exhibited occasional problems, from poor operation to actual shutdown. These problems have been under study for some time and solutions have been completed or will be in the near future. These include the following:

1. Improvements will be made in the scrubber by increasing the scrubber liquid supply by a factor of four to five, which will reduce solid buildup. This should be completed by September.
2. Improved operational control for most designated emission sources has been achieved. More work is needed in this area to reduce the number of outages on scrubbers, etc.
3. Electrostatic precipitators must be improved. Over $10,000 has been spent and $172,000 is pending for future work.
4. Plant wastewater must be routed to the large kiln scrubber, where scrubber operation and wastewater treatment are enhanced.

B. Fugitive Dust

1. Progress is well under way to move most ore storage indoors to reduce fugitive dust from this source.
2. Use of binder material on plant roadways has begun on a test basis and will continue in an expanded form once evaluations are complete.
3. A water spray program is being established to control fugitive dust on some of the bare ground areas.
4. Air drying has been eliminated.
5. A tree planting project is in the test stage and will become active next spring when evaluations are complete.
6. Grass seeding for the undeveloped area on the north plant site is planned for next spring.
7. The ball mill vent has been recycled back to the kiln and additional studies are being done to see if further improvement is necessary to abate the problem.
8. Cyclone dust from the scrubber system has been rerouted back to the beginning of the ore feed cycle.
9. The outside overhead conveyor has been covered to eliminate wind-blown dust from this source.
10. Large amounts of spillage in the outside kiln area have been cleaned up to help eliminate fugitive dust.
11. New sealer materials have been tested on the fan housing joints for the scrubber fan. The situation has improved, but additional work needs to be done in this area.
12. The kiln has been rebricked to improve the seal at the discharge end.
13. The ball mill operation has been improved by rearranging inflow to get better wetting of the kiln discharge with less dusting.
14. Binding of some feed stock for the kiln should reduce fugitive dust. Additional work is scheduled in this area.

The above list of projects are all believed to have merit. Some will have a major impact on reducing fugitive dust and a favorable impact on efficiency, since raw materials will not be lost.

EXHIBIT 1 (continued)

C. Management Reorganization

For many years, environmental control at Vanrex was accomplished by a foreman and five operators, all concerned with the operation of wastewater treatment facilities. When any new facilities were added or modification of existing facilities was necessary, a project engineer was assigned to the project from inception through installation and start-up. Once facilities were operational, plant operating personnel took over unless operation wastewater was involved. Since August of last year, an environmental manager has had an environmental supervisor and a chemist with one or more technicians under his direction. Further changes to enhance the environmental program at Vanrex are as follows:

1. The environmental group of the Vanrex Chemical Division has been strengthened to provide more assistance at Hayestown and other plants.
2. The environmental group will establish control over all new projects that are part of the pollution control effort.
3. There have been several personnel changes to improve control of the environmental aspect—that is, to better integrate the operation of the production and pollution control facilities. Pollution control facilities have not always received equal attention, as they will henceforth.
4. Plant supervision will continually review the operation of the plant from the viewpoint that production and pollution control must be viewed with equal interest and must be an integrated operation.

IV. Summary

The above projects represent the program Vanrex has undertaken in an effort to alleviate the problems it has experienced. As may be seen, the programs undertaken are quite varied and are an attempt to improve the whole gamut of possible problems. The work on process stack scrubbers may show a gain sooner because they are so visible; however, improvement in opacity or operational capability is about all one can expect. The attack on fugitive dust will require more time because of the nature of the projects. Growth of vegetation can take a long time, while some of the projects will make an immediate impact.

Ambient air testing will be continued to determine the effect of fugitive dust programs. Stack testing will be carried out as required and in consultation with ODH&E. In an effort to determine the corrosive qualities of windblown particulates and gases, a program has been initiated to test painted coupons in areas in and around the plant.

In conclusion, Vanrex has made and will continue to make a major effort to improve the dust and stack gas problem. In addition to the actual work involved, an active program will be waged in public relations so the public knows what is involved and what Vanrex is doing about it.

including the kilns and incinerators, many of which had been equipped with scrubbers, precipitators, or other devices installed over the years to capture, recycle, and otherwise reduce particulate emissions. These devices did not always operate at maximum efficiency, but, when inspected by state and federal agencies, the plant had usually been found in compliance with relevant air quality standards.

Hitchcock was aware, however, that as a result of increased consciousness of the dangers of acid rain, a strong Clean Air Act was being debated in Congress. The Act, which seemed likely to pass, would commit the country to much stricter standards for particulate emissions, especially for sulfur dioxide. Over the next fifteen years, the new standards would require industry to reduce existing sulfur emissions by ten million tons, or 77%.

RESIDENTS' COMPLAINTS

Several types of complaints had been lodged with the plant and the environmental authorities by area residents. First, residents often charged that emissions from the plant increased at night. According to Rubin's report, day and night levels of dust and stack emissions had been tested, and no differences were found. The plant processes were continuous and ran most economically and efficiently at maximum rates. As the plant had only recently become profitable, it would be impractical to operate at reduced rates for any period of time. In addition, six hours to several days were required for raw materials to be processed into finished products, and once operating conditions were established, any attempt to alter the process on an overnight cycle would cause poor quality and low production.

Rubin's report conceded, however, that training for the night operators and foremen might not be equal to that on the day shift. In addition, he acknowledged that nighttime breakdowns or other problems might not be corrected as quickly as during the day. A training foreman at the plant site had been appointed to prevent the first possibility, and work schedules had been restructured to prevent the second. Rubin noted, however, that most complaints about night emissions came from the west side of the plant. He speculated that an optical illusion might be involved: "In the morning with the sun rising in the east, the plume from stack 17 does block early sunlight and appears relatively dark when people first go out. During the day and evening with the sun setting in the west, the light reflects from the plume on the west side of the plant and it looks lighter."

A second complaint of the residents was the "rotten egg" smell and the health hazards associated with sulfur dioxide (SO_2). Sulfur dioxide is generated when hydrogen sulfide (H_2S) is incinerated, the only legal method for disposing of this toxic gas. Sulfur dioxide is not toxic, but it is classified as an irritant to the eyes and respiratory tract and has a strong suffocating odor. Given proper weather conditions, Rubin reported, concentrations of SO_2 were sometimes strong enough to annoy people and occasionally cause discomfort to anyone with respiratory problems. But, he reported, the County Health Department had found no evidence of any further health hazard. Sulfur dioxide is also a major contributor to acid rain: water (H_2O) + sulfur dioxide (SO_2) = sulfuric acid(H_2SO_4).

Finally, residents were concerned about property damage. Many believed the emissions from the plant were damaging the paint on their cars and houses. Their perceptions about the effect of plant emissions on their property intensified their concerns about possible effects on their health. As one resident put it, "This stuff literally eats metal. You can't tell me that it doesn't damage lungs."

Hitchcock read and reread Rubin's report on the neighbors' complaints, existing conditions at the plant, and his plans for improving control of the dust and stack emissions (*Exhibit 1*). She also perused the newspaper clippings (*Exhibits 2–5*) he had enclosed. Now she had to decide what she should advise Rubin to do about the persistent complaints and the unfavorable press coverage.

EXHIBIT 2 "Vanrex Subject of Complaints," by Evan Lynn, Staff Writer, *Hayestown Clarion*, May 4

It billows from smokestacks at the Hayestown Vanrex chemical plant, drifting over homes with the wind, permeating storm windows, discoloring the paint on homes, and corroding the finish on cars, nearby residents will tell you.

It is a mixture of sulfur dioxide, sulfur trioxide, and hydrogen sulfide, say Middlesex County health officials.

Vanrex officials say smokestack emissions do not exceed state guidelines and are not harmful to the health of nearby residents. Some westside residents don't believe it.

A group of about 50 westside Hayestown residents who live in the vicinity of the Vanrex plant met with state health officials in Hayestown Monday claiming emissions from the plant are getting worse and demanding to know what can be done.

Peter Jurger, an engineer with the state Department of Health and Environment, told the group he would tour the Vanrex plant today. "In the last three weeks we've gotten more complaints about Vanrex than [we've gotten] in the last two years," Jurger said.

Bob Jackson, 111 Canton St., a westside resident for five years, said he gets "pretty much a daily residue" from the plant. The residue ranges from "a fine mist" to "floating pieces of carbon like a snowstorm." "The outside corrosion is obvious. Nobody could argue with that," Jackson said.

Henry Young, another homeowner near the plant, told Morris the residue from the plant deposited overnight "reacts like an acid on my car." "This stuff literally eats metal," he said. "You can't tell me that doesn't damage lungs."

Mitch Wood, 310 N. Canton St., said his son, a third-grader at Parkside School, contracted two separate cases of bronchial pneumonia this year. Wood said he believes emissions have aggravated the child's respiratory problems. The family moved to a home near the plant a year earlier, he said. Parkside Elementary School is across the street from the plant.

Wood believes emissions from the plant are getting heavier. "Just these last couple of weeks, I drive past the plant and it just takes your breath away," said Wood, a welder.

Another westside resident, Pam Cohen, said she and her husband are prepared to move out of the neighborhood, probably at a financial loss, if something isn't done to curb these emissions. Their 9-year-old son, David, has missed 30 days of school this year suffering from respiratory disorders, Mrs. Cohen said. When the family lived near Lincoln School—up until two years ago—David suffered considerably less from respiratory problems, she said.

John Rubin, General Manager of Operations of the Hayestown Vanrex plant, said emission levels at the smelter have been improving over recent years. He said at one time there were no state regulations limiting emissions by plants such as Vanrex. Current regulations do not require zero emissions, Rubin said.

"I would like to say that we have it in our power to eliminate what they're complaining about. It's a difficult situation. I think the public outcry is more forcible now than it has been in the past—and maybe rightfully so," Rubin said.

The plant routinely tests conditions in the plant to ensure that employees working closest to noxious substances are not exposed to dangerous levels of those substances, Rubin said. He said it is a "pretty safe assumption" that if conditions inside the plant are safe, then conditions in the neighborhood surrounding the plant are also safe.

Rubin said Vanrex had been informed of today's health department inspection of the plant last week. He said he expects the plant to be found in compliance with all pollution regulations.

EXHIBIT 3 "Rubin: Smoke Emission to Drop but Sulfur Rotten Egg Odor Will Stay," by Evan Lynn, Staff Writer, *Hayestown Clarion,* May 25

John Rubin, installed last August as plant manager at the Hayestown Vanrex Chemical Division, says residents maddened by the plant's smokey sulfur emissions can expect a future decrease in those emissions. "But it's going to be a gradual improvement," the 43-year-old Rubin predicted.

Local Vanrex executives will be in Oklahoma City Tuesday to discuss the findings of a May 8 state inspection of the plant with officials of the Air Quality Division of the state Department of Health and Environment.

The meeting and earlier inspection, state officials said, was prompted by a significant rise in the number of complaints about Vanrex smokestack emissions. Inspectors found no pollution laws being violated at Vanrex, the state announced after the May 8 inspection.

At the meeting Tuesday, state and company officials will discuss the volume of complaints about Vanrex smokestack emissions and consider ways the company can lessen its pollution problem, Rubin said.

When Vanrex, at the corner of Fifth and King Streets, opened its chemical plant in 1906, the site was well outside city boundaries. The area around the plant had not been developed. Since then, Hayestown's westward residential expansion has pushed beyond the plant site. Many of the city's higher-priced homes were subsequently built within a few blocks of Vanrex's billowing smokestacks. Hayestown Elementary School was built by the Hayestown School District virtually in the shadow of the plant.

As the population density increased in the vicinity of the plant, the number of complaints about plant smoke and its accompanying "rotten egg" smell also increased, Health Department records show.

Rubin said the new incinerator will not alleviate the "rotten egg" odor from the plant. The odor is caused by sulfur dioxide, he said.

Vanrex has additional projects in the works aimed at reducing the amount of pollution produced by the Hayestown plant, Rubin said. One project involves planting trees on barren areas of the Vanrex complex.

Dust from the plant grounds combines with emissions from the plant to aggravate the air pollution problem, Rubin said. He said he believes when people living near the plant find dusty particulate matter on their cars and houses, the majority of the matter consists of dust from the plant grounds and not from the emissions.

Plant officials hope trees on the ground will hold down blowing dust, he said. However, the trees planted so far will not grow large enough to have an impact on the pollution situation for four or five years, he added.

Rubin said the plant has discontinued the use of a warning siren at night. Activation of the siren—which emits a shrieking, whining sound known to many who live near the plant—is a federal requirement when certain moving equipment is operated in reverse, he said.

The decision to discontinue use of the siren at night came last week. Plant officials decided that activating the siren at night does more harm than good, Rubin said.

The plant has begun watering down coal stored outdoors, and storing more chemicals indoors, to keep coal and chemical dust from blowing around the neighborhood, he added.

Rubin said he believes the appearance that emissions from the plant are heavier at night is at least partially an optical illusion, caused by heavy night air that keeps trapped smoke lower to the ground and makes it more visible.

The new hydrogen sulfide incinerator will be required by state law to reduce opacity—a gauge of the amount of particles in smokestack emissions—to below 20 percent, Rubin said. Twenty percent opacity is an indication that 80 percent of light rays will travel through the smoke, he said. One hundred percent opacity would mean that no light shows through.

The old incinerator, because it was built before 1975, was required only to reduce opacity to below 40 percent, he said. Vanrex was found in compliance with the 40 percent requirement May 8, he added.

Rubin said he believes some complaints about plant emissions can be attributed to a toughening of state pollution laws that have spawned increased public awareness of industrial pollution.

The evening before the May 8 inspection, in a backyard session with state Department of Health and Environment inspectors, about 50 westside residents complained about the plant.

Among the complaints:

That smoke emissions had been getting worse in recent months.

EXHIBIT 3 (continued)

That emissions levels increase at night, when most people—except those living within range of the winds that carry the smoke—are sleeping and unaware of the problem. That those living in the path of the smoke emissions find a corrosive, dusty film on their cars and houses.

"This stuff literally eats metal," said Henry Young, owner of a home near the plant. "You can't tell me that it doesn't damage lungs."

"I've heard those comments. I just don't think it is true that the emissions are greater [today]," said Rubin, who served stints at the Hayestown facility from 1958 to 1961 and from 1966 to 1973 before returning to take charge of the plant last year.

Rubin said improvement in emissions levels should come with installation of a new hydrogen sulfide incinerator in July. The plant's present hydrogen sulfide incinerator, which dates back to the 1940s, produces the hanging smoke and pungent sulfur odor usually mentioned in complaints about the plant, he said.

Despite increased complaints, Vanrex emissions levels have actually decreased due to installation 2 years ago of a scrubber on a high-temperature reactor that produces barium sulfide, Rubin said.

"I did a study in 1959 or '60 and there were three to five tons of particulate waste coming out of that unit every day," he said. "That's all collected in the scrubber now."

"Emissions levels still are high," he said, "because the hydrogen sulfide incinerator does not quite work properly. It's not as efficient as it should be. Also, the smokestack is corroding pretty badly."

The new hydrogen sulfide incinerator, along with a new smokestack, should reduce the level of visible smoke, comprised of sulfur particles discharged by the plant, Rubin said.

With installation of the new incinerator, which is governed by stricter pollution guidelines, the result should mean less smoke, but not necessarily right away. It takes a while for a plant to adjust to new equipment and make it work properly, he said.

There is no way Vanrex will become totally free of the smoke that currently billows from its plant. There are no requirements, state or federal, that require a plant to run emission free, he said. But as far as the plant officials now know, there is nothing emitted by the Vanrex smokestacks believed to be dangerous in the quantities currently pouring out, Rubin said.

"We know what it [the product being emitted] is and the general amount. It's not known to be hazardous. I've got bronchial asthma and I'm a lot better off here than I was in Chicago," he said.

EXHIBIT 4 "Emission Reduction Promised," by Evan Lynn, Staff Writer, *Hayestown Clarion*, June 2

Local Vanrex Chemical Plant executives met with state Air Quality Bureau officials Tuesday and promised to submit a plan to the state by August 18 to reduce plant smoke emissions. The promise came despite renewed admissions by the state that inspections of the Vanrex plant have uncovered no violations of state pollution laws.

Vanrex will voluntarily submit a "comprehensive plan for resolving [pollution] problems at the plant," said Patricia Lopez, Chief of Air Engineering and Enforcement with the Air Quality Bureau, a subdivision of the state Department of Health and Environment. "Then we will review it and see if it is acceptable to us," she said.

The meeting in Oklahoma City Tuesday was set to discuss increased pollution complaints citing Vanrex smokestacks in recent months, state officials said. The increased complaints prompted a state "visual" inspection of the plant earlier this month that turned up no pollution law violations, the officials said.

The August 16 date was set to allow Vanrex to install a new hydrogen sulfide incinerator to replace the plant's current hydrogen sulfide unit, Lopez said. The current unit, which dates back to the 1940s, "does not quite work properly," said John Rubin, Vanrex plant manager.

The new incinerator is scheduled to be installed in July, company officials said. The new unit should reduce smoke emissions, but not the sulfurous "rotten egg" smell at the plant, Rubin said.

Sulfur emissions from the hydrogen sulfide incinerator are cited in most public complaints about plant emissions, Lopez said.

EXHIBIT 5 "Officials Disappointed with New Smokestack," by Evan Lynn, Staff Writer, *Hayestown Clarion,* August 15

Local Vanrex officials say they are unhappy, so far, with the pollution-cutting performance of a new hydrogen sulfide incinerator and smokestack at the company's westside chemical plant. Some westside Hayestown residents are also unhappy with the performance of the new equipment, which was installed last month at a cost estimated at more than $160,000.

Company officials installed the new equipment expecting it to substantially reduce the amount of black, sulfurous smoke spewed into the air by the chemical plant at Pine Street and Angle Road.

Victor Fitzwilliam, 1715 Pine St., said Saturday the incinerator and smokestack have "not helped much" in reducing the amount of pollution billowing from the chemical plant. Fitzwilliam lives about two blocks from the Vanrex plant.

"I can't see much improvement, but I'm going to reserve judgment until I see how it's working when school opens," said Pam Cohen. Mrs. Cohen's house at 311 Lincroft Ave. is also two blocks from the plant.

Vanrex spokesperson Marshall Painter said a representative of the company that designed the incinerator will be in Hayestown midweek to try to find out any operating problems with the unit.

"We're still trying to get the equipment to operate as guaranteed by the firm that designed it. We're aware it's not helping the situation in the neighborhood yet," Painter said. He said the company officials still believe the equipment can be made to reduce pollution levels from the plant to an acceptable level.

Patricia Lopez, a spokesperson for the Oklahoma Department of Health and Environment, said Saturday she is aware the new equipment is not working the way it is supposed to. Lopez said her department has not yet conducted a pollution compliance test on the new incinerator because the state is aware the company is trying to correct problems with the unit.

To meet state pollution guidelines, the new unit must reduce the opacity of smoke released through the burning of hydrogen sulfide to 20 percent. So far the new unit has reduced opacity of smoke from the hydrogen sulfide process to 30 percent, Painter estimates.

Opacity is a measure of pollution's density determined by measuring the amount of light that can pass through the pollutant. A higher amount of opacity translates into a higher level of pollution.

Vanrex's old hydrogen sulfide incinerator was governed by more lax pollution standards because that unit was built before stricter standards were put into effect, company officials said.

Vicky Moreno, 422 Buell Terrace, who hosted a May 7 meeting with state pollution officials to complain about Vanrex pollution, said Saturday she has surveyed several westside residents and found no one who is happy with emission level reductions since installation of the incinerator and smokestack.

Some residents believe pollution from the plant has increased since installation of the new equipment, Mrs. Moreno said.

Results of the survey have been passed on to officials of the Department of Health and Environment, she said.

Study Questions

1. What is the problem at the Vanrex plant? Is it just a problem of perception or of the residents' desire for zero emissions? Are there real problems with the control of stack emissions and fugitive dust?
2. What steps have been taken to reduce emissions at the plant?
3. What common features of technical language are exhibited by Rubin's report? Cite some specific examples. See pgs. 245–248, "Effective Writing."
4. What differences do you note between Rubin's style and tone and those of Evan Lynn, the reporter for the *Hayestown Clarion?* Which style is likely to have greater impact on the general public?
5. Has Rubin been presenting the company's position and actions to the public effectively? Why or why not? How might a change in style or tone help him improve his communication?
6. What steps might Vanrex take to improve its image and community relations in Hayestown? What groups would be appropriate audiences for the company to address? What message should it communicate? What media should it use?

PART TWO

Applications

CHAPTER 9

Giving and Receiving Feedback

Giving and receiving feedback are essential managerial skills. A manager's tasks include directing, coaching, and evaluating the work of subordinates. Informally, managers review and respond to the performance of those who work both over and under them every day, clarifying expectations, praising success, and correcting misunderstandings. Most companies require formal appraisals once or twice a year to evaluate performance and encourage growth. Since a manager's own results depend heavily on those whom she or he supervises or reports to, effective feedback benefits the giver as much as the receiver.

In addition, as the previous discussion has suggested, listening to your audiences before, during, and after a business communication will often determine whether your message achieves your goal. This means receiving constant feedback: the data you need to build your case, the preconceptions of key audiences, how your proposals are coming across, what reasonable alternatives are possible, why important constituencies are likely to oppose you, whether superiors are merely nodding their agreement or actually implementing your proposals. Thus, seeking and wisely interpreting feedback are essential to your personal success as a manager and communicator.

Two major factors inhibit both downward and upward feedback in many business communication situations.

First, nobody likes to get bad news. Any manager wants to hear that she or he has done a good job. It's very easy to send verbal or nonverbal signals that you don't want to be criticized. As a result, subordinates, colleagues, or superiors may be reluctant to share crucial information that may help you redefine your goal, revise your communication strategy, or use your energy in a more productive direction.

Second, hierarchical organizations have a tendency to become less and less receptive to both downward and upward feedback. Several factors inhibit feedback in organizations.

Human beings prefer to command rather than confer. Immediate subordinates easily adapt to this style. Consequently, habits or systems develop that prevent managers from getting the information they need or understanding the concerns of those who are working for them. Often, this can result in drastic losses in morale and productivity.

Managers like to hoard information because it gives them a sense of power. Sometimes extra information will give them a leg up over a colleague or additional authority over a subordinate. Most of the time, however, successful managers share information widely because they benefit if others know what they need to know to do their jobs. Numerous studies have demonstrated that information hoarding by middle managers is one of the greatest drags on productivity in large organizations.

Everyone is prone to tell the boss what she wants to hear.

Listening takes time. Busy managers with the best intentions in the world often flub opportunities to get invaluable feedback from subordinates. Managers may send unintentional messages that they're too busy to be bothered, not respond to subtle hints, or simply fail to schedule regular feedback opportunities. Surveys of most organizations regularly demonstrate that, by and large, managers feel their superiors really don't care much about their opinions. Top managers are often surprised to hear this.

Successful organizations maintain and improve internal channels designed to drive accurate information both downward and upward.

GENERAL CONSIDERATIONS

Both *giving* and *receiving* feedback are among the high arts of management, and demand very special skills. Several key factors determine the effectiveness of most managerial feedback, whether it's informal day-to-day coaching, formal performance evaluation, or talking to your boss. As you provide feedback to superiors, peers, and subordinates, keep the following four factors in mind:

Timing

Delayed feedback rarely works. Over time, the specifics may have faded from memory, or, more likely, have been transformed in the mind to shore up individual egos. The recipient may wonder why you've waited so long; has the incident rankled all these months? Occasions also exist where feedback can come too soon. If a presentation has clearly not gone well, the communicator may need time to salve his wounds before he can hear suggestions for improvement. The most timely feedback is a regular flow while a project is underway. This can prevent feedback from becoming an extraordinary—and often painful—experience for both parties.

Objectivity

Total objectivity is impossible, and even often undesirable, as we discussed in Chap. 4, Point of View. Still, effective feedback provides concrete support for judgments that inevitably have a subjective element. Were projects completed on time? Were agreed-upon goals met? Did a communication have the desired effect? When and where did the receipient display the particular strength or weakness under discussion? Without such specifics, your feedback won't be credible or interpretable. Saying "Here are the objective results of your actions" or "Here's how your actions have affected me" will sound less accusatory than "You're failing." Saying "You're doing a great job" will be less effective than "Here are the types of accomplishments I want you to keep delivering."

Empowerment

Feedback must focus on things the recipient has the power to change, whether the recipient is a boss who can approve a project or an employee who's been slacking off. Most people can't change basic personality traits such as timidity or hotheadedness, but they can learn to modify their behavior to accomplish goals or perform more effectively. They're most likely to do so if you've given them the tools to do the job. Have you provided the boss with the information to make your case? Have you given a subordinate the resources to meet specified goals?

Trust

While people occasionally learn valuable lessons from someone with whom they don't get along, feedback is always more readily accepted if it comes from a trusted source. A foundation for trust cannot be established in a single exchange; it develops by experience, over the life of a working relationship. But skillful managers use each feedback opportunity to contribute to the fund of trust and mutual respect. The best single tool for building trust is legitimate *praise.* Managers and employees alike too rarely receive congratulations for a job well done. If you've recognized their accomplishments, people are more likely to heed you when you point out their deficiencies. An equally powerful tool, over the long term, is *honesty.*

GIVING FEEDBACK TO PEERS AND SUBORDINATES

The following guidelines can improve your informal, day-to-day experiences as a giver of feedback as well as your formal evaluation of subordinates.

Evaluate Strengths and Weaknesses in Light of Agreed-upon Goals and Objectives

This basic principle undergirds the "management by objectives" school of performance evaluation, but it applies in a commonsense way to all effective feedback. Workers' performances cannot be usefully evaluated unless the specific tasks and overall objectives they were charged with are reasonably clear. Arriving at mutually agreed-upon, or at least mutually understood, goals and criteria for performance is itself an important part of providing effective feedback.

Commend Where Possible

A totally negative critique not only disheartens the recipient but also is easy to ignore. He will likely shrug it off on the grounds that successful communication with such a harsh superior is impossible. Remember that praise and affirmation are more powerful motivators for most people than is criticism. Don't neglect these important management communication tools.

Be Specific

General comments such as "Great job" or "Poor presentation" won't be of much use. Instead, refer to specific instances, and describe the particular virtues you noticed or the specific problems you encountered: "The change you proposed will save us a great deal of paperwork" or "Your recent presentation needed more preparation and better graphics."

Strive for a Matter-of-Fact Tone

When you are providing feedback across or down, it's easy to sound obsequious, coy, apologetic, or condescending. Use superlatives sparingly, and avoid, except in extreme instances, questioning the recipient's competence or motives. As much as possible, keep yourself out of the picture. Statements such as "As one who appreciates good writing," or "I hate to be a nitpicker, but . . . " will make you sound like a prima donna.

Avoid Overkill

Most subordinates appreciate a frank and thoughtful response to their work, but there's a limit to how much anyone can absorb at one time. Focus on the most significant issues. A clear point of view on your part will ensure that you put minor points in their proper place.

Practice What You Preach

It's hard to complain about another's interpersonal skills if your own are somewhat lacking. It's unwise to point out missed deadlines if you are known to procrastinate. A badly written critique or an incoherent oral response to a subordinate's written or oral report won't command much authority.

SOLICITING FEEDBACK

When do you need feedback, and how can you get it?You need feedback in the *planning stages* to determine the attitudes of your audiences and the feasibility of achieving your goal. This means gathering factual information to support your case and sounding out those you need to persuade. Determine their bias (positive, neutral, or hostile); their familiarity with your topic; and their likely questions, concerns, and objections. How you solicit this feedback will depend on the size and variety of your audiences. If you're trying to persuade one person, you may feel out her views ahead of time in informal conversations and by asking others what types of arguments and approaches she has found convincing in the past. If you're addressing a small group, you may test your ideas against representative members whom you trust. With large audiences, such as all the employees of a corporation or the general public, you may need to conduct focus groups or to commission a professional survey.

Often, eliciting feedback during the planning stages gives you a double advantage; not only does it provide you with information you need to develop your communication plan, but also it can begin to build advocacy ahead of time with influential members of your future audience. Irrespective of audience size, you need feedback on each communication before you deliver it. This may mean asking a colleague to edit a memo or practicing a speech in front of your partner.

You need feedback during the *execution stages* so you can adjust your message according to the reaction you're getting. Build in as many response opportunities as possible. You'll keep your finger on the pulse of the audiences; by engaging in a dialog with you, they will become invested in the process and may develop a commitment to help you achieve your goal. Opportunities for feedback during the execution stages include inviting written responses, seeking out informal one-on-one reactions to formal communications, inviting questions from the audience, conferring in small groups, and polling large audiences.

You need feedback during the *follow-up stages* to ensure that your plan is being executed. Many a manager has promulgated a great plan, to universal applause, and then seen nothing happen. Before you send a message, determine how you will measure its success. Then put mechanisms in place to provide you with a regular series of updates on whether you're making progress toward your goal. These can include data (Are sales going up?), fixed deadlines (Have all the branch offices reported back by the specified date?), specific results (Did the union sign the contract?), or attitude surveys (Have my audience's views changed in the direction I wish since my communication?).

RECEIVING FEEDBACK

Hearing is even harder than telling, because few pieces of feedback you receive will be entirely positive, especially during performance evaluations. Here are some guidelines:

Listen First

As a recipient of feedback, you must cultivate the habit of listening to your sources. Anyone who has devoted time and thought to reviewing your work has earned the right to be heard. You can't benefit from responses that you haven't understood.

Strive to Understand Your Respondent's Goals

Whether you're listening to bosses or subordinates, you won't fully understand them unless you temporarily set aside your own goals and focus on what they want to accomplish. While ideal feedback is explicit, keep in mind that secondary or subtle purposes may be in play. Ascertain what your source wants out of this interaction. A boss who is mildly suggesting a change in your project or approach may actually be issuing an order. A subordinate's memo reviewing a recent meeting may be intended to set certain decisions in stone.

Don't Get Defensive

Most of us must make a conscious effort to receive criticism constructively. Our impulse is not to listen, but to devise a self-protective reply. We interrupt our respondent to explain the constraints on us; we try to direct attention back to our goal or interest. Such responses will provoke the reaction "She just doesn't want to hear me," and they will rarely serve you well. At the same time, listening should *not* be passive; ask questions that clarify your respondent's remarks. You'll communicate courtesy and appreciation by following your source's train of thought rather than directing it. Save your main reactions until you've elicited your respondent's point of view.

EVALUATING FEEDBACK

Evaluating feedback means evaluating your sources. Are they reliable? Do they have your best interests at heart, or are they pursuing their own agenda? Are they likely to be flattering you? Does their response demonstrate an adequate knowledge of your subject?

People giving you feedback on a specific performance-period, communication, or proposal may respond in three ways:

1. They can report their experiences as workmates, readers, or listeners.
2. They can identify strengths and weaknesses.
3. They can suggest improvements in your analysis or plan of action.

In receiving such feedback, first, look for *misunderstanding:* Have your words, proposals, or actions been misinterpreted? If so, you probably need to modify your communication strategy. Second, look for *valid arguments against your position:* Has your respondent discovered real flaws? If so, perhaps you need to go back to the drawing board. Third, look for unanticipated *grounds of opposition;* these can help you reshape your message or performance. Perhaps your behavior or proposal will hurt your respondent in a way you hadn't considered. Fourth, value those *suggestions on how you can perform or communicate better.*

Two quotes aptly summarize the challenges of giving and receiving useful feedback. Rosabeth Moss Kanter and Derick Brinkerhoff write, "No amount of human relations techniques can change the fact that evaluations represent the exercise of power and authority by superiors over subordinates."[1] Admiral Hyman Rickover, the developer of the nuclear submarine, once said, "Always use the chain of command to issue orders, but if you use the chain of command for information, you're dead."[2] Kanter and Brinkerhoff are saying that no one enjoys the boss's criticism. Rickover is warning: "Don't believe yes-men." Managers must exert constant sensitivity to the human situations of those to whom they are giving feedback and of those who are giving feedback to them.

Consideration of feedback also leads to a more general observation implicit in the previous eight chapters. Effective business communication is not something you "add on" at the end of a decision-making process. No business strategy will succeed unless communication considerations are factored in from the beginning of your planning. At each step along the way—examining yourself as a source, analyzing your audiences, defining your goal, considering the context, shaping your message, choosing your media, achieving appropriate style and tone—you need to reexamine your project in light of the feedback you've received. At any point, you may find that, to succeed, you have to revise your original approach.

The following case and Dotsworth Press (case 15 in Part Three) explore the uses and abuses of feedback, including performance evaluation in business situations.

[1] See "Appraising the Performance Appraisal," *Sloan Management Review,* Vol. 21, 1980, pp. 10–11.
[2] *Newsweek,* Oct. 10, 1994.

CASE 9.1

Bailey & Wick

In early spring, 2005, the Executive Committee of Bailey & Wick, a first-tier New York accounting firm of 150 accountants and 200 staff, approved the hiring of HK Communications to explore the issue of giving and receiving feedback at B&W. In particular, HK Communications was asked to report to B&W management on whether associates were receiving enough useful feedback on their work from partners. A year before, at B&W's fall retreat, an Associate Retention Committee had noted "the lack of formal and informal mentoring, training, or feedback—either positive or negative." B&W had also ranked low in a nationwide poll on associates' job satisfaction and career advancement prospects.

Two questions most concerned the Executive Committee: (1) Was the firm losing prominent candidates for promotion because insufficient attention was being paid to associates' development? (2) Was productivity being hampered because partners were not helping associates improve performance? The Professional Development Committee—two partners, four associates, and a director—felt the feedback issue merited serious review. HK's job: to assess the situation and propose options to the decision makers.

This case was prepared by Michael Hattersley, © 2006.

HK'S METHODOLOGY

The consultants planned to interview a representative cross-section of B&W's executives on the issue of partner-associate feedback. But before speaking to anyone, they needed to define clear goals for the project. After two meetings with the Professional Development Committee, HK decided to focus on five key questions:

1. *Was there a problem?* Apprentices are always grumbling about their jobs, and there is bound to be a good deal of grousing in a service organization where the competitive edge is sharpened by the implied message: UP OR OUT. Generally, associates who survived the three-year review could stay on until year seven, when they either left or attained partnership. Suppose there were weak links in professional nurturing; were they really damaging the performance of associates, particularly those willing and able to succeed at B&W?
2. *If the problem was real, how, specifically, was it hurting the firm?* Was B&W actually losing associates it wanted to retain? If partners were not providing effective feedback and if associates were therefore not performing at capacity, were partners doing work that associates should be performing and thereby wasting billable hours

on routine tasks—and thus risking burnout? Did a lapse in professional development suggest a lapse in total quality management?

3. *Was this a perception problem, a question of no feedback, or of not enough feedback?* Juniors always want more attention and affirmation from seniors. Given the times and apparent uncertainties, was the perceived need for more and better feedback satisfiable? How did partners see their side of the feedback equation?
4. *What reasonable range of actions could improve partner-associate feedback?* Would a renewed effort at consciousness-raising be enough? In the relatively informal world of B&W, could feedback mechanisms be institutionalized?
5. *Were the benefits of any given solution worth the costs?* Perhaps many associates would welcome improved coaching and critiquing; yet would the results justify the investment of partners' time and B&W's resources? How good were the B&W partners and associates at giving and receiving feedback? How much training would be required to realize any sustainable change? To what extent, in a horizontal organization like B&W, was resistance to confrontation a cultural norm?

Beyond these questions, HK also planned to approach the interviews with a flexible definition of "feedback" itself. The word had a wide spectrum of meanings at B&W—from the offhandedly responsive to the directly judgmental—and the consultants didn't want to inhibit free exchange in the interviews by narrowing the use of jargon. "Feedback" also included the single most important appraisal associates received: their performance evaluation, conducted twice a year for the first two years and annually thereafter. In years one and two, the review assessed basic competence within the associates' departments. The third-year review was especially important, because it was conducted by all the partners, many of whom by that time had worked with a given associate. Historically, such reviews had involved both a discussion and a written evaluation. More recently, the written feedback had been discontinued; instead, two partners visited the associate and summarized the review. The consultants' brief charged them with examining the effectiveness of feedback outside the review process, but they wondered if such a distinction could actually be made. Perhaps if the reviews were functioning better, there would be less demand for day-to-day feedback.

Feedback really included any reactions partners gave associates. Most often, this meant editing of associates' draft audit reports or other documents. But it also included every partner-associate interaction: praise or criticism of a task, comments on a client interaction, warmth or coolness at a social occasion, responsiveness to associates' questions, greetings in the elevators or hallways, even name-recognition. Which of these mattered, and which, if any, could be influenced by the firm?

INTERVIEW RESULTS

Simple ground rules applied to the interviews: any questions could be asked; confidentiality would be maintained in reporting results. Fourteen interviews were conducted, seven with associates (three female, four male) and seven with partners (two female, five male).

After collating the interview results, HK Communications decided that two composite views essentially represented the Alpha and Omega of the feedback issue:

Alpha (mid-level associate):

> I never know what's wanted of me or how I'm doing. Frankly, I need more affirmation, if only for self-respect. I spend too much time here worrying about people's expectations of me—worrying if they think I'm just slacking off, worrying whether no news is good news. There's too much stress. I work for everybody and nobody. What one partner likes, another hates. When I manage to get a response from a partner on my work, I can't tell if it's a casual suggestion or a coded but devastating critique of my performance in general. Of course I know that my reports are going to be refined by my seniors; but how do I know if it's a good draft or hopelessly inept? My evaluations are particularly hard to read. They're incredibly

general, like: "We think you're doing fine. Just do better. We think you could improve your client presentations." How? I have peers who come out of their reviews serenely confident that they're going to make partner. Some of these have been eased out. But most associates report hearing the same things I did. I think I'm pulling my weight but I want to know, specifically, how I can do better. Most of us know we're not going to make partner, and for many of us, that's not even the goal. We want to learn, contribute, and be respected while we're here. If we didn't have to spend so much time second-guessing and reading partners' minds, we'd be more productive. If partners spent a little time giving us feedback, we'd be better at what we do, and save the firm money. I'm not looking for a formal report card—I'd dread that. I'd like some direct, honest assessment of my work on a major project.

Omega (senior partner):

Let's face it: accountants aren't good at direct teaching of subordinates. We're not educating associates, we're looking them over. Training is a secondary consideration, especially the first two years, when we need to get a lot of grunt work out of them. They're in boot camp, and they know it. It's the exceptional associate who's productive before year three. But you can tell quickly whether someone has it or not. The one who reaches out, finds training and mentoring, is the one who gets the plum assignments. The partners are looking for that as they decide who has to go, who's partner material, and who can be productive for a few years before she or he moves on. It's often said that the way to become a partner at B&W is to start somewhere else. We're probably not good at nurturing, but the truth is, it's easy to find someone out there to fill a gap. Juniors always want to change the rules, to box seniors in and guarantee their own security. But a busy partner has little time for wet-nursing and schoolmarming. It's easier to rewrite a bad report than use it as a training vehicle. If there's to be more direct feedback, it should go to associates who are going to be around here for a while.

Most of HK's interviews fell between these two extremes, and helped to round out the picture. Some samples:

Associate:

If I'm concerned with a problem about my work, I ask. I've always gotten a straight answer. But many associates are very unsure of themselves, and a good many of them are suckered by the p.r.—that B&W is committed to training—and they become disillusioned very quickly. They want assurance that they're doing well when often they're not. I started going for feedback because I got badly burned in my first evaluation. I'd had no indication that I was doing poorly; then I got slammed in my review. Maybe that was a good sign—they thought I could improve. Half of us came here for the experience, the other half to make partner. Maybe one or two of my class of twenty actually will. This isn't kindergarten, and partners shouldn't have to do remedial education. But let's take a competent associate who may not be partner material in the current climate. An hour of focused feedback a month would make that person so much more productive—maybe, even, happy in his work—and save the partner a lot of time currently spent running around with a pooper scooper.

Senior partner:

When I came here years ago, I worked with two of the younger partners. One took pride in teaching, in marking up the product and getting me to see the relevance of detail and the importance of craftsmanship. The other took no interest at all; she essentially ignored me. With her, I had to get better on my own. This is a big organization. You have to develop a thick skin; it's a meritocracy. While we value collegiality, we don't necessarily foster it; winnowing out is part of the process. Actually, among peers, we have a lot of feedback, but there's a structural problem. When an associate clearly isn't going to make it, it's harder for a partner to take interest. We need a senior associate group to do training of juniors. And the junior partners could do more. I accept the associates' claim that "if you give me useful feedback I'll do a better job and save the firm money." But I accept it abstractly. I welcome juniors who visit my office to ask for advice, but I know it's intimidating. That's part of the job.

Mid-level associate:

We suffer a lot from attrition. Lots of the best associates seem to be leaving. One senior associate I knew was particularly willing to provide feedback to younger associates. She saved the firm a lot of time and money. But this commitment to training didn't show up in her performance review. She received mediocre evaluations and ended up leaving the firm. Our main competitor has an associate committee that's in-the-know about partners' personal styles and walks you through the feedback. Maybe partners here should sit down with associates after each major transaction and tell them what worked and what didn't—not a long meeting, just a brief review while the memory is still fresh.

Partner:

Today's clients want senior people and fewer people. It's difficult to foist new associates on impatient clients. Why waste trained talent? Recently, we've created a Professional Development Staff— but their real title should be: "How to Help Decent Associates Who Won't Make Partner." The ones who will make partner are too good and too busy. We've hired a lot of people we shouldn't have, people we know aren't going to make it here. We're also losing people we need to keep because the pipeline has gotten too narrow. We haven't admitted to ourselves that we've gotten "partnered up" and sometimes mislead the associates about their chances. The truth is, associates have become disposable, and the smart ones know that. So we don't project excitement and communicate our enthusiasm downward. We're not building loyalty because we can't satisfy the expectation that would generate.

Senior associate:

Most corporations today recognize that they get a big payback from training employees. People who feel some sense of ownership clearly do a better job. But there's clearly a caste system here: associates don't feel they're on the same team as the partners. There are code words: everyone not partner is "staff"; we don't "work with someone," we "give them an assignment." It's not "our client," it's "my client." It's not in the firm's interest to signal someone they're not going to make it until the last possible moment: carrot and stick, like anywhere else. Otherwise, what performance would you get out of them?

Junior partner:

Consciousness-raising isn't enough; it seems to me we have to institutionalize feedback. One idea currently floating around is to have associates give anonymous feedback to the partners. But do we really need more forms to fill out? Any institutionalized feedback would have to be tailored from department to department, and who has the time for that? Maybe there should be a new class of billable time—training hours. It's never going to work until you build it into the system. Still, why should partners do training unless they get some credit for it? A lot of the top people here are brilliant eccentrics who can't be told what to do. When I needed feedback, I didn't wait. I asked for it, and I got it. But for many people, this place is too courtly and too chilly.

IMPLEMENTATION

HK decided there were two ways B&W could go. One was to continue current practice. Although it generated anxiety among the associates and probably caused some good prospects to leave while they were ahead, it worked. On the other hand, B&W could reorganize its feedback processes to develop permanent talent, using more carrot, less stick. Steps the firm might implement to improve feedback included:

1. Encouraging partners to be more responsive to associates' requests for feedback;
2. Teaching associates how to solicit feedback, perhaps in initial orientation sessions;
3. Adding a third category of "training hours" to billable and pro-bono hours;
4. Rewarding senior associates who provided feedback by crediting them in their evaluations;

5. Institutionalizing feedback by requiring seniors to provide it to juniors after each major project;
6. Requiring each department to propose, then implement, a feedback program appropriate to its size and needs; and
7. Encouraging partners to see themselves less as independent craftsmen, more as team leaders. Any significant change in feedback practices would require the sustained and active support of top management.

Study Questions

1. What are the most important ways people communicate with one another in a complex, high-pressured organization?
2. What are the trade-offs among responsibility, legitimate self-interest, and training at Bailey & Wick?
3. What are the differences between how juniors can talk to seniors and how seniors can talk to juniors?
4. What institutional changes in communication practice could benefit this organization? How might they be communicated?

CHAPTER 10

Managing Meetings

Running and participating in meetings are two of the toughest managerial tasks to do well. Meetings can consist of anything from two colleagues who've unexpectedly dropped by your office to large, formal gatherings of decision-makers or constituencies. Many managers' reputations have been made or damaged by how they conducted themselves at a single meeting.

Meetings ensure that every aspect of communication will be brought into play: conflicting goals and perceptions, force of personality, contextual constraints, questions of power and authority, even the primitive human need to feel included, heard, and valued. A meeting is often the place where an individual finds out if he is included in the community or where she stands in the pecking order.

MEETING PREPARATION

Whether you're running a meeting or attending it for the first time as the most junior member, several key questions can help focus your preparation and participation:

Do I want to call or participate in this meeting at all? Sometimes calling a meeting—even a regularly scheduled one—can invite more problems than it solves. Sometimes *not* attending a meeting where you're expected can send an important message.

What do I want out of this meeting? Reflecting on this question may lead you to decide that obtaining authorization for your particular requisition matters less than being perceived as a team player or getting a superior to see your point of view.

How can I influence the agenda? An advance agenda and supporting documents will always influence, and often dictate, the outcome of a given meeting. Can you order the items under discussion or influence the agenda setter so that your concerns occupy a favorable position? Perhaps you want your proposal to be discussed early, when people's attention is high. Perhaps you want it discussed late, when it's less likely to be subject to scrutiny.

What can I learn at this meeting? Most often, you'll go to a meeting primarily concerned about being heard or achieving a specific result. This may prevent you from practicing the most useful habit at any meeting: *listening*. Whether or not you ultimately support them, people will remember and value you for hearing and understanding their concerns. Equally important, by listening without prejudice, you will often identify reasonable grounds of opposition to your point of view, gain information that may support your cause, or discover unexpected allies.

Am I fully prepared? Do you understand the likely views of other participants in advance? Do you possess the necessary information to answer tough questions? Have you thought about how your concerns fit into the bigger picture? Are you flexible enough to consider a powerful argument that cuts against your interests?

MEETING PARTICIPATION

Several techniques can make your meeting participation more successful. For example:

1. Don't sit as a block with other people who agree with you. This can create an us-against-them situation that may only harden opposition.
2. Don't always lay out your whole case immediately. Providing the general outlines, inviting comments, and then fleshing out your proposal can provoke useful feedback and give your colleagues the sense that they've contributed to the final product.
3. Circulate supporting materials ahead of time. This can give colleagues a chance to get back to you with questions or disagreements that you can address, or that may lead you to revise your proposal.
4. Show respect and understanding for viewpoints you disagree with.
5. Build alliances. Often a colleague will go along with you on a close call if you've done the same for her in the past.
6. It cannot be said too many times: Know as much as you can about how other participants feel *before* you walk into the meeting.
7. Build executive support. To the extent possible, make sure that superiors (in or out of the meeting) back your proposal or are at least willing to consider it.
8. Ensure and monitor follow-up. See that clear responsibilities and deadlines are assigned.

Much of your work as a business person will be done in groups. One useful reference: J. Richard Hackman, ed., *Groups That Work (and Those That Don't)*. A briefer synopsis: Michael E. Hattersley, "Checklist for Conducting a Perfect Meeting," *Management Update* (July, 1996), p. 10.

ROLE-PLAYING IN MEETINGS

Going into the meeting, consider what role you'll play. We're all typecast by others who know us through our business dealings, but you can *choose* the character you want to play on specific occasions. A little conscious planning can make the difference between success and failure. Even in the world of non-hierarchical organizations and virtual offices, meetings are still the main stage on which managers display their strengths, reveal their weaknesses, and shape their images in the eyes of their coworkers. Otherwise brilliant performers who can't handle meetings well hurt their chances to move up and cut themselves off from crucial resources.

Planning your role ahead of the performance can help avoid these pitfalls. Good managers have a general meeting strategy as well as a specific plan for each individual occasion.

Your Role-Playing Strategy

How do you come across at a meeting? Do you typically talk too much or not enough? Do you play a fixed, predictable role at every meeting, or do you adjust your strategy to particular needs and circumstances?

Start by defining what sort of meeting participant you typically are. Possible categories include:

- **The Joker** who tries to break the ice or insert disguised barbs
- **The Gatekeeper** (not always the leader) who tries to keep to the agenda
- **The Devil's Advocate** who regularly challenges an emerging consensus
- **The Critic** who sees the problems with others' ideas but has none better to offer
- **The Agenda Setter** who regularly puts new ideas and issues on the table
- **The Consensus Builder** who draws others' ideas together into a course of action
- **The Cheerleader** who encourages any sign of progress
- **The Mimic** who always echoes others' comments
- **The Monomaniac** who rides the same hobbyhorse at every meeting
- **The Outsider** whose comments and body language convey detachment or contempt
- **The Leader** (not always the person running the meeting) who all tacitly agree has the final word.

Think for a minute about which of these categories your colleagues would put you in. Is it the one you'd choose for yourself?

Anyone who consistently plays only one of these roles, even the most constructive ones, is probably not handling meeting participation optimally. Good managers are able to play the constructive roles listed here—Gatekeeper, Agenda Setter, Consensus Builder, Cheerleader, Leader, even Joker and Devil's Advocate—depending on the context of each individual meeting.

Do another exercise. Think of the people you meet with regularly. What roles do *they* play? If you pay close attention to participants' typical *roles* as opposed to what they happen to be saying at the moment, you can often cut right to the heart of the issue under discussion very quickly: "Ken (the Devil's Advocate) points out some problems we're going to have to face but most of us clearly agree this is the best plan" (spoken by a Consensus Builder). Understanding what roles you and others play will make you a much more effective meeting participant. Consider these variations and strategies:

The Joker

Employed well, this can be an especially useful role in meetings that tend toward tension or conflict. A witty observation can remind all the participants what they have in common—a shared desire for success or a collective obstacle. But this role should be employed only when you're sure it will have the right effect. Humor easily verges into sarcasm, and you don't want to be identified as the group cynic or the class clown. If you find yourself in a meeting with an inveterate Joker, be prepared to point out, gently, when the jokes are getting in the way of necessary progress.

The Gatekeeper

Try to play this role if you're leading a meeting. Identify an emerging consensus and get it on the record. Make sure specific tasks are assigned to accomplish it. If an issue appears unresolvable, point out that it's time to move on and look for solutions outside the session. If you're attending a meeting run by a Gatekeeper, don't let him shut down discussion before views crucial to your position are thoroughly aired.

The Devil's Advocate

Sometimes, a self-satisfied meeting consensus needs to be challenged by a dose of reality. When necessary, this should be done crisply and succinctly. Often, pointing out how others will view your group's actions will help you shape a better policy or a more acceptable way to present it. Sometimes it may be wise to suggest that doing nothing is preferable to doing something half-baked. But don't let yourself get typecast as someone who enjoys argument for argument's sake. When dealing with a dedicated Devil's Advocate, it can sometimes help to say something like, "While Meg is always good at identifying pitfalls, I think we've taken her concerns into account here."

The Critic

The Critic is related to the Devil's Advocate but often has a more destructive agenda. Sometimes, people argue just because they don't want to see another succeed. Don't attack someone else's idea unless you're pretty sure you have a better one; otherwise you'll develop a reputation as a carper or, worse, a back-stabber. When dealing with a Critic, accommodate the strong points in his argument but be prepared to challenge either a specific criticism or a general pattern of obstruction.

The Agenda Setter

No good meeting or series of meetings survives for long without one. Generally, this should be the Leader's role. Providing an agenda and supporting materials ahead of time can move things along more quickly. But if you're the Leader, make sure you've included the legitimate concerns of all participants. If someone else is setting the agenda, whether it's the Leader or a creative colleague, get your ideas in ahead of the meeting so you're sure to get consideration and build support.

The Consensus Builder

Everyone should be prepared to play this role at almost every meeting. It's key to achieving leadership. The person who spots an emerging consensus and shows how it can be put into action will gain the gratitude of his colleagues, build alliances, and store up capital for the future. If you think an established Consensus Builder is on the wrong track, acknowledge her talent in this area and then play Devil's Advocate.

The Cheerleader

This is another role everyone should play from time to time; just don't overdo it. We all underestimate how much others crave praise and inclusion, and they should get them when they're deserved. An effective Cheerleader will point out the common ground between two apparently opposed positions and can evolve into a Consensus Builder. When possible, tie your comments to others' previous remarks and give credit where credit is due. Even if someone presents your idea as his own, consider that imitation is a form of flattery and that most participants will remember who raised the proposal first. Also, it never hurts to make the boss look good unless you risk becoming known as a flattering sycophant (or unless the boss is dead wrong).

The Mimic

Usually, this type is a failed Cheerleader. It's important to be willing to support others' good ideas, but avoid becoming a parrot. If you agree with someone, you can usually say so while at the same time adding value by fleshing out her ideas or describing how they can be implemented. If you encounter a persistent Mimic in meetings, you can often gently deflect the habit by saying, "Yes, Jane already made that point well, but we need to consider. . . ."

The Monomaniac

Some people have one idea (or gripe) that they will push relentlessly at meeting after meeting. Soon their colleagues will be able to repeat every word of the set speech and will grow increasingly irritated at the wasted time. If you find yourself falling into this role, do one of two things: drop the predictable patter, or, if you're convinced your idea is a good one, sound out other participants individually to discover why it isn't catching fire. Perhaps there are insurmountable obstacles to achieving it, or perhaps you're pursuing it in the wrong forum. When confronted with a Monomaniac, be prepared to challenge him, but if his idea has some merit, suggest how it can be implemented more effectively.

The Outsider

Often in meetings, you'll encounter a participant who consciously or unconsciously signals her detachment from the proceedings. This is often demonstrated by silence or body language, and can be as simple as edging a chair back from the table. If you find yourself in this role, ask why. Is it because you regularly disagree with what's happening (in which case, perhaps you should get another job), or simply because you're shy and unwilling to participate? If it's the second, consider what more constructive roles you could play. When dealing with an Outsider, it's often productive to directly invite him into the discussion. It may turn out he has good ideas he's been reluctant to express.

The Leader

Leadership is usually earned, and is most often the result of playing the right roles at the right times over a long period. Almost every one of the above roles has its place; even the Monomaniac or the Outsider may eventually be proved right. Usually the Leader is the person who's running the meeting by virtue of experience and authority. But a wise administrator recognizes when another Leader is emerging in the meeting, and studies carefully why that's happening.

Remember, whatever role you're playing, *few ever wished a meeting went on longer.* Make your point and get out; your colleagues will be grateful. Also, *avoid being predictable.* Becoming more conscious of the roles you and your colleagues play can help you operate outside of the box. A willingness to support an opponent's good idea, for example, can solidify your long-term reputation for wisdom and objectivity. In short, don't play any role all the time.

MEETING CHECKLIST

Most executives spend a tremendous amount of their time—often too much—managing meetings. Broadly defined, "meetings" range from discussion with a colleague who has dropped by your office to a major press conference to the CEO's appearance before stockholders at the annual company convocation. But certain rules for running a successful meeting apply in any situation. These can be broken down into what you should do before, during, and after, since all meetings require preparation, execution, and follow-up. To review the material covered in this chapter, ask yourself the following questions:

Before

1. **What are my goals for this meeting?**
   Are you looking to inform, elicit ideas, or make decisions? Each requires a different preparatory strategy. Think through—even write down in a sentence or two—what your ideal outcome would be.
2. **Should I call this meeting at all?**
   Many meetings cause more problems than they solve and waste everyone's time. Participants who feel nothing has been achieved may be resentful or uncooperative. Often issues or decisions addressed in meetings could be better solved by personal contact or executive fiat. Even standard, regularly scheduled meetings can be canceled if the manager decides the participants' time would be better spent elsewhere.
3. **Have I provided everyone with a clear agenda in advance?**
   A shared agenda not only encourages preparation, but also allows you to determine what order of discussion is most likely to help you achieve your goals. Sometimes it's wise to put the most difficult issues first, especially if they need a thorough airing. Other times, your best course may be to put the tough questions at the end, after people have spoken their piece and are ready to end the meeting.
4. **Have I sounded out the key participants ahead of time?**
   Generally, key players don't like surprises. If they feel bulldozed or cornered, they're likely to be uncooperative. One-on-one conversations ahead of time may cause you to rethink your agenda or help you build support for your proposals.
5. **Have I provided the participants with enough advance information to make informed decisions?**
   Much meeting time can be wasted bringing people up-to-speed. When everyone operates from the same body of information, you're more likely to achieve consensus and to make actionable decisions.

6. **Have I anticipated likely objections?**
Don't get ambushed in a meeting on an important point you hadn't thought of. Often, polling participants ahead of time can help avoid this problem. If you know some meeting members will likely oppose your goals or proposals no matter what, be prepared to show you understand their objections and have thought through why, on balance, your course of action is superior to reasonable alternatives.
7. **Have I built support on high?**
In advance of any meeting, make sure your superiors endorse the general line of action you intend to take.

During

1. **Summarize the purposes of the meeting off the top.** A crisp summary will minimize digressions and the introduction of unexpected or irrelevant material. It will also authorize you to keep the meeting on track.
2. **Let everyone have their say.** Even in meetings where participants are of significantly different status within the organization, show you value the opinions of each. Invite people who haven't spoken to contribute in their areas of expertise. You're more likely to get everyone invested in the meeting's result.
3. **Don't allow anyone to dominate the meeting by giving long or irrelevant speeches.** Recognize when someone is riding a hobbyhorse or pushing a personal agenda. Be willing to redirect the discussion to the main point tactfully, but with as much firmness as necessary. The other participants will be grateful.
4. **Be prepared to learn.** No matter how carefully you've prepared a meeting, new information may pop up that should change your course of action. You'll gain respect and authority by demonstrating you're not tied to a script.
5. **Gain closure on each issue as soon as you sense an emerging consensus.** No one wants to spend more time in a meeting than absolutely necessary, and most participants will be grateful to a leader who makes a decision and moves on.
6. **End each meeting with a summary of what the group has gained from it.** Summarizing may mean saying: "We've decided A, B, and C, but we need to give further consideration to X,Y, and Z." This way, participants will have some sense of achievement and know what's expected of them. You also will have set a productive agenda for the next meeting. When possible, end the meeting earlier, rather than later, than expected. Few meetings achieve much after the first two hours, at the maximum.

After

1. **Follow up quickly with minutes.** Their arrival will remind participants what they've agreed to do.
2. **Meet with members who didn't get heard or who felt unsatisfied with the results.** Not only will such conversations provide you with feedback, but they

also will help you prevent smoke from becoming fire or soothe the egos of those whose support you may need in the long run.

3. **Send participants a memo on next steps.** A marching document will reinforce everyone's sense that something has been accomplished and will provide a road map for future action. It may also reassure any dissatisfied members that their issues have been heard and will be addressed in the future.
4. **Provide any resources you've promised.** Participants will be frustrated if they've been assigned a task but aren't given the means to accomplish it. If it proves impossible to deliver the resources, explain why.
5. **Act as quickly as possible on any decisions that have been made at the meeting.** This provides key evidence on the effectiveness of any executive. In the end, people are judged much more by what they do than by what they say.

As a participant, contribute to meetings only when your comments are pertinent to moving the discussion forward. As a meeting leader, guide others to do the same. You'll enhance your reputation as an efficient executive.

FURTHER READING

Effective Meeting Skills by Marion E. Haynes (1997, Crisp Publications, 90 pp., $10.95, Tel. 800-442-7477)

How to Hold Successful Meetings: 30 Action Tips for Managing Effective Meetings by Paul R. Timm (1997, Career Press, Inc., 96 pp., $7.99, Tel. 800-227-3371)

How to Make Meetings Work by David Straus and Michael Doyle (1993, Berkeley Publishing Group, 300 pp., $6.50, Tel. 800-631-8571)

We've Got to Start Meeting Like This! by Roger K. Mosvick and Robert B. Nelson (1996, JIST Works, 294 pp., $14.95, Tel. 317-264-3720)

CASE 10.1

Lincoln Park Redevelopment Project

Ann Clarke believed this afternoon's meeting could be the turning point in a major eastern city's effort to rejuvenate its ailing center. Incidentally, it might also mark an important step forward in her own career. In one form or another, the Lincoln Park Redevelopment Project had been on the drawing boards for ten years. Its goal: to replace blocks of pornographic theaters, drug dealers, and strip joints with hotels, boutiques, a convention center, legitimate theaters, and services for the homeless who would be displaced. With yesterday's agreement by a Dallas developer to take a major equity position in the convention center, it appeared the final piece was in place.

BACKGROUND

Clarke, a new MBA in hand, had joined the State Department of Economic Development (DED) six years before. Largely because of her engineering background, she had been made Project Director of a series of construction and renovation efforts sponsored jointly by the state and private investors. In her first four years with DED, she had overseen the construction of a large parking garage, the conversion of a food-processing plant into a candy factory, the building and dedication of numerous bridges, and the renovation of depressed shopping districts in towns all over the state.

Two years ago, with the support of her boss and mentor, Harry Silverman, DED's Vice President of Economic Development, she had been appointed Coordinator of the Lincoln Park Development Project (LPDP). A year later her title had been upgraded to Vice President in recognition of her effective performance and the importance of the project. She now reported, not to Silverman, but to the Secretary of DED.

Her two years in charge of LPDP had been both exhilarating and frustrating. For the first time in her career, she had found herself working daily with major figures in business, construction, architecture, city planning, and politics. She regularly appeared with the Mayor and Governor at press conferences, negotiated the language of environmental impact statements with representatives of major law firms and community groups, and reached binding understandings over the phone with nationally known developers.

On the other hand, it seemed that every time LPDP was ready to go, some important piece fell out of the puzzle. Just as she had taken over the project, a major investor had backed out due to a drop in the stock market. No sooner had he been replaced than a prestigious national chain had cancelled its plans to build the project's flagship hotel. Demonstrators in a residential neighborhood abutting the project had forced a new round of public hearings. But now that the convention center was set, the momentum in favor of the project seemed inexorable.

Clarke had also done everything she could think of to build public support for the project. She had arranged press conferences featuring the Governor and the Mayor to emphasize LPDP's economic and social benefits. She had met repeatedly with representatives of the area's neighborhood associations, public agencies that provided social services, the police, clergy from adjacent religious institutions, leaders of the Coalition for the Homeless, even the owners of the porno theaters and strip joints.

She had also established a website featured prominently in all project publicity, and had been surprised to discover she had to assign a full-time assistant to monitor and respond to the volume of inquiries and complaints it drew. Most of the hits came from locals concerned about how the renovation would affect them personally, but a significant number came from regular visitors from out-of-town, worried that the character or—as several put it—the 'funkiness' of Lincoln Park would be destroyed.

PLANNING THE MEETING

As she considered the attendees at the upcoming meeting, Clarke found her confidence increasing that all would go well. They fell into two groups: city and state officials, who could make the key recommendation to move forward; and representatives of the developers who would do the building.

The project had been made possible by taking the interests of both these groups into account. The city and state had negotiated a complex package of tax breaks that virtually guaranteed the developers a fair return on their investment. The developers had agreed to help fund the renovated theaters and services for the homeless which made the project popular with the affected communities. "Going ahead" meant closing the deals already worked out with current property owners who had agreed to sell, and taking the remaining areas of the project through the state's right of eminent domain.

Clarke felt she could count on the enthusiasm of all the officials who were attending the meeting. Cora Martinez, the city's Director of Urban Development, had served through two administrations and had been working on the project since its inception. John Lundt, DED's counsel, had negotiated the complex web of contracts with the developers and current property owners, and had probably invested more hours in the project than anyone else. Ivan Zidonis, DED's Director of Public Affairs, had been briefing representatives of the press for years, trying to convince them that the project was moving forward. Ben Burdett, a consultant under contract to DED, had led a changing team through the seemingly endless series of design changes, resource inventories, wind tunnel experiments, sewage treatment plans, and public hearings that had resulted in the Final Environmental Impact Statement. John Philipson, Chief Architect, had negotiated a compromise between the requirements of the developers and the demands of the city's leading arts organizations. He emerged with designs that satisfied both his constituencies and his own aesthetic sense. Floyd Chen, whom Clarke had promoted from Office Manager to be her assistant, had served as her representative at innumerable meetings, and had a refreshing faith in the project's inevitability, characteristic of someone who had only been working on it for a year. Clarke had also invited her old boss, Harry Silverman, who had seen the project through its often discouraging early stages. This might be Silverman's valedictory appearance at DED, since he had all but agreed to run as the Democratic Party's candidate for City Council President in the upcoming elections.

Clarke was a little less familiar with the attitudes of the developers who would be attending, but they too had every reason to move ahead. Sam Shiavone, who would be developing the majority of the hotel and office space, had stuck with the project even through a serious downturn in the real estate market. Clyde Shultz, representing the Dallas convention center developer, had barely been able to contain his desire to get moving during Clarke's phone conversation with him two days ago. Olga Mason, President of the Clendennon Theater Organization, had been working for twenty years to convert the porno movie houses back into legitimate theaters, as they had been before the Second World War. On balance, Clarke believed the developers would be as positive as the officials.

THE MEETING

After calling all the participants yesterday, Clarke's secretary had set the meeting for 4:00 P.M. to accommodate everyone's schedules. By a few minutes later, all the attendees had assembled near the long table in DED's glass and black marble conference room except for Harry Silverman. Clarke took her place at the head of the table, with Floyd Chen at her side, and waved everyone who was gathered around the coffee and pastry counter to take their seats.

"By now you're all aware of the good news," Clarke began. "Ten years of hard work is about to pay off." Her assistant, Chen, began to pass thick packets of paper down either side of the table. "Floyd is handing out the memorandum of understanding I initialed yesterday with Dallas Development. My proposal, as I E-mailed you yesterday, is that we announce in the next couple of days that we're breaking ground, say, next month. The quicker we move, the less likely we'll get any stay orders from current owners making a last-ditch effort to save the sleaze trade." "We tend to get your E-mails the day before something has to be decided," Martinez remarked drily.

"We're ready to move," said Shultz. "Although Dallas has only been in formal negotiations for a couple of months, you probably know we've had our eye on the convention center piece for a long time. We're ready to buy the design, with some minor modifications that we believe will save the city and state some dollars in the long run."

Clarke noticed several participants glancing up from the paper before them. "Sorry, folks. This is Clyde Shultz, Construction VP for Dallas." Nods were exchanged all around.

Ivan Zidonis spoke. "Welcome onto the team, Clyde. My job is to see we get the best possible press out of this. Ann, how did you figure the announcement?"

Clarke paused only a second. "I guess you'd set up a press conference, the sooner the better. I'd take the lead, and John could follow with the architectural big picture. Maybe Clyde should be there, since he represents the final big player."

Zidonis nodded, though Clarke thought he looked a little more reserved than usual. The door to the conference room swung open and Harry Silverman entered. "Sorry I'm late, Ann. Urgent meeting with the Secretary." He took an empty seat halfway down the right side of the table. While Clarke filled him in, most of the others continued to leaf through the memorandum of understanding with Dallas.

But Olga Mason's eyes were on Clarke. "Ann, the convention center's commitment is to renovate the Lido Theater. What agreement do we have on that?"

Floyd Chen jumped in. "Same deal we have with the hotels and the office complex: ready to open, to our standards, at the same time as the center."

Mason continued calmly. "We've left it to the center contract, but I thought we'd agreed that the Lido, since it's on a side street, would need a longer-term subsidy to get it up and running. We were figuring on slightly more experimental fare there."

Shultz looked up in surprise. "That'll be the theater closest to the center, in fact a part of the building. Our idea was a little more Las Vegas."

Chen persisted. "There's room for maneuver here. It'll be three years minimum before we finalize companies or theater management. We don't need Wayne Newton's signature on the dotted line to go ahead with this project."

"Well, maybe Green Day," Shultz chuckled. "We're into the nineties."

"Excuse me a moment," said Zidonis. "I have to make a quick call."

Sam Shiavone spoke for the first time. "No one has been more eager to move on this than we have. Frankly—and I'm surprised it's taken this long— some of our investors have begun to get antsy. The sooner the better, as far as we're concerned."

For the first time since the meeting began, John Philipson looked up from the memorandum of understanding. "Ann, I wish we'd had a chance to talk about this ahead of the meeting, but there's some language here I'd like the legal beagles to take a look at. One of the biggest concerns of the neighborhood community groups is that we don't create deserted alcoves for muggers to work out of. I'm not sure we're covered here."

"They appear to be in full compliance with the environmental impact statement," Ben Burdett interjected.

Shultz made a point of looking Philipson straight in the eye. "Mr. Philipson, we've worked together before. No one has greater respect for the integrity of your designs than Dallas. One of the reasons we've brought you in is that we're convinced you couldn't design a building that didn't improve the urban environment. We're willing to accommodate any reasonable concern you express."

Cora Martinez gave Shultz's emphasis a moment to sink in, then assumed an expression that expressed some irony about her own words. "We're all committed to the long-term welfare of this city. There's hardly an organized group here that hasn't endorsed this project or been brought on board. The neighboring communities want the homeless, the prostitutes, and the drug dealers off the streets. The construction unions want the work, and we have about the best minority hiring program in the country. We're one of the few cities in the United States that really needs more hotels and office space right now. But the welfare of this city includes its political health as well. There's an election coming up."

"What does that mean?" Chen asked. Martinez smiled reflectively.

Clarke decided to take charge again, as Zidonis slipped back into the room. "We're going to be facing issues like the alcoves or the types of performances right up until every brick is in place. But I think we have the resources and the goodwill here and now to bring this off. I'm asking for a consensus to move."

In the following moment of silence, all eleven participants leaned forward a little. "Let's go," said Shultz.

"Yes," said Shiavone.

"We're ready," said Burdett.

"Not quite," said Mason.

"Let's talk a little more," said John Lundt, DED's counsel.

"No," said Philipson.

"No go-ahead today," said Zidonis.

"Sorry, Ann," said Martinez.

Clarke looked to Silverman for support. He smiled but shook his head. "Ann, I think we need a little more time to chew on this."

Study Questions

1. How well did Clarke prepare for this meeting? What, if anything, should she have done differently?
2. How well has she used electronic communication?
3. What agendas did the various participants bring to the meeting?
4. Are there any lessons you can draw from the case about how to manage crossfunctional teams?
5. What should Clarke do next?
6. What general lessons have you learned from meetings you've participated in or led?

CHAPTER 11

Communicating Change

All the situations covered so far in this book involve upward, lateral, downward, and outward communication challenges. All, in one way or another, concern managers who are asking others to change, or who are being asked to change themselves. Change messages say things like: buy a new product, trust my organization, work harder, share authority, face financial changes, live by new rules. Most individuals' natural reaction to such communications will be to think of ways to subvert them. As Woodrow Wilson once said, "If you want to make enemies, tell people they have to change." But identifying the barriers to receiving this sort of communication can help shape a successful strategy. These barriers include the following:

HABIT. People naturally prefer to do things and think about things as they've always done. Habit—a routine approach to a repeated task—is usually a tremendous time and energy saver. No one wants to think through every step of brushing his teeth or purchasing a trusted product every day. Habits also foster a sense of security, which almost invariably will be threatened by change.

TIME CONSTRAINTS. Successful managers and employees are very busy. Those who aren't have found other ways to fill their work hours with private tasks or regular conversations with colleagues. People have to give something up to change their behavior, whether it's altering their work routine or searching out a better service provider.

CONFLICTING MESSAGES. When a change message comes from top management, employees simultaneously receive and generate countermessages, such as "This won't work," "There's a better way," "They don't really mean it," "This is a low priority," or "This violates our rights." Messages aimed at clients, customers, or the general public via media will generate challenges, whether from competitors in the form of advertising or from critics who are expert in the field.

LACK OF CONSEQUENCE. People generally won't change unless the consequences of not doing so will be serious. Internally, this sometimes means enforcing discipline or changing job descriptions. Externally, this means convincing audiences that it's worth their time and effort to change. Plans of action that don't consider, impose, and communicate consequences are generally useless.

LACK OF RESOURCES OR SUPPORT. Too often in organizations, people are told to change without being given the means to do so. Too often, organizations ask external audiences to change behavior without giving them a sufficient reason to do so.

ENTRENCHED LEADERSHIP. Leaders often issue change messages without understanding the views or problems of those whom they expect to follow orders. Obviously, the best way to encourage desired behavior in subordinates is to practice it yourself.

LACK OF FOLLOW-UP. Internally, people in the process of changing their behavior need reinforcement and clear standards by which to judge whether they're succeeding. Externally, organizations need objective measurements of whether their change messages are being received.

LACK OF RISK ASSESSMENT. Change involves risk, and a manager who seeks to initiate or impose change without considering potential negative consequences may be wading into deep water. Change messages are much more likely to be heard if the sender has considered both why they may be unwelcome to some members of the audience and how that resistance can be understood and overcome. Conversely, receivers of change messages should not be yes-people; it's a major part of their job to alert their superiors to consequences of which they may be unaware. Both givers and receivers of change messages need to measure what will be gained against what will be lost, including trust.

Each of these barriers needs to be considered when an organization announces change. A successful change message tells employees why they have to change, how change will save them time, why opposing arguments are wrong or inferior, what will happen if they don't change, that they'll be provided with the tools to do the job, that management understands their position, and how their new performance will be evaluated. Attending to these fundamentals can make the change message a summons to adventure and opportunity rather than an additional drudgery. Most significant organizational changes also have to be sold to external audiences: clients, constituents, suppliers, competitors, the media, and the public at large. Communicating change successfully—internally or externally—depends on convincing your audiences that they, and the organization as a whole, will benefit from the result.

CHANGING FROM THE MIDDLE

Every manager wants to change something about her or his job. It's relatively easy to identify your goal: You want to receive more support and resources from superiors, gain more cooperation and understanding from subordinates, initiate a new project, change the way your company does business, or get promoted. *Managing change* became a popular business buzz phrase of the 1990s, but two recent serious studies of the issue take dramatically different approaches.

Recent work by Professors M. Lynne Markus, now of Bentley College, and Barbara Bashien at the Claremont Graduate School and Professor Patricia Riley at the University of Southern California (USC) has suggested five ways to make sure your change projects have a greater chance of success:

Make Sure You're the Right Person to Make the Change

Do you have the authority and credibility to bring about change? If not, but if you have a good idea, then you need to find senior allies who have better contacts and access to resources. Be prepared to share credit, but create a paper trail so that your contribution isn't lost in the chorus of praise when you succeed.

Don't Delegate Management Responsibilities to Consultants

Often, consultants are called in to tell companies something they already know or to deliver the bad news: You have to change, become more productive, lose your job. Use them as advisers, not messengers or managers. Consultants tend to be buffers between the change leader and those who have to implement the change. When misused, consultants can create a decision-making black hole. Executives who delegate change to consultants often do so because they're unwilling to make necessary transformations in their own priorities or management styles.

Tie the Change Project to Strategic Corporate Initiatives

Too often, changes are tied to narrow goals such as cost cutting, gains in efficiencies, or narrow technological advances. The researchers found that the most successful change projects were tied to a broader corporate strategy. Savings, efficiencies, and technological progress, while important selling points, are less important than convincing top management that the change will help achieve major organizational goals.

Involve Human Resources and Technology Specialists Early

Many brilliant project ideas have gone nowhere because the right people weren't involved or because communication failed. Changing anything from technology to staffing will probably require support from outside your area of expertise. Get the information you need from consultants and the buy-in from those who can find the right personnel to do the job.

Maintain an Optimistic Environment

"Some say that a crisis atmosphere promotes success," the study's authors write.[1] "But crisis often creates fear. Fear drives out optimism." Whenever possible, emphasize what those whose cooperation you need will gain from the change, or at

[1]Barbara J. Bashien, M. Lynne Markus, and Patricia Riley, "Preconditions for BPR Success, and How to Prevent Failure," *Information Systems Management* 11, #2 (1994), pp. 7–13.

worst, why this change is better than alternatives. Giving others a stake in your success will keep them encouraged and focused on results.

CHANGING FROM THE TOP

The California study provides a reasonable list of how-tos, but in a recent *Harvard Business Review* article, "Leading Change: Why Transformation Efforts Fail," Harvard Business School Professor John P. Kotter looks carefully at the dark side. Pulling together his experiences with over 100 corporations, large and small, U.S. and international, he concludes that change efforts often fail due to a lack of focus, patience, and follow-through: "The most general lesson to be learned from the most successful cases is that the change process goes through a series of phases that, in total, usually require a considerable length of time."[2]

Kotter's study concentrates on corporatewide changes: total quality management, reengineering, right-sizing, restructuring, cultural change, and turnaround. He identifies eight steps to transforming an organization:

1. *Establishing a sense of urgency;* that is, examining marketing and competitive realities and identifying and discussing both crises and opportunities;
2. *Forming a powerful guiding coalition* so that a tight team has the power to lead the change effort;
3. *Creating a vision* to direct the change effort and developing strategies to achieve it;
4. *Communicating the vision,* both by sharing direction and strategy as widely as possible, and by ensuring that coalition members set a good example;
5. *Empowering others to act on the vision* by removing obstacles and encouraging risk taking;
6. *Planning for and creating short-term wins* by identifying, rewarding, and recognizing even small steps toward the goal;
7. *Consolidating improvements and producing still more change* by changing systems, structures, policies, and employee development and by constantly reinvigorating the process with new projects, themes, and change agents; and
8. *Institutionalizing new approaches* by communicating the connections between new behaviors and corporate success and promoting successful change agents to positions of power and leadership.

Kotter suggests that skipping even one of these steps can lead to failure or, at best, more of the same. He quotes the CEO of a large European company: "[Make] the status quo seem more dangerous than launching into the unknown."[3] Sometimes this means actually seeking out bad news: "One CEO deliberately engineered the largest accounting loss in the company's history, creating huge pressures from Wall Street in the process. One division president commissioned first-ever customer satisfaction surveys, knowing full well that the results would be terrible."[4] Such steps, while risky, at least create a broad-based awareness of the case for change.

[2] J. Kotter, "Leading Change: Why Transformation Efforts Fail," *Harvard Business Review,* March–April, 1995, p. 59.
[3] Ibid., p. 60.
[4] Ibid., p. 60.

Kotter concludes: "There are still more mistakes that people make, but these eight are the big ones. . . . In reality, even successful change efforts are messy and full of surprises. But just as a relatively simple vision is needed to guide people through a major change, so a vision of the change process can reduce the error rate. And fewer errors can spell the difference between success and failure."[5]

Clearly, the Claremont-USC study focuses on middle managers trying to bring about change, while Kotter analyzes top management trying to change whole organizations. Robert Kent, also of Harvard Business School, wisely warns about the dangers of "CEO-ism" in business students; that is, a tendency toward grandiose strategies that the middle manager wouldn't have the power or resources to realize. But the middle manager who understands the big picture and gets on the right side of change is less likely to get left behind by it and more likely to graduate to top management.

Whether they're aware of it or not, managers are always being challenged to change by their superiors and their subordinates. Top executives constantly search for ideas and for allies in their vision. Subordinates constantly suffer frustration with bosses who don't communicate their vision and include them. Great projects regularly fail from a lack of what the great New York master builder Robert Moses called *lack of executive support*. Both of these studies offer significant opportunity for introspection on how to initiate change and how to be a successful partner in a change process.

Both the California study and Kotter's work suggest there are two major types of organizational change efforts: top-down and bottom-up. *Top-down* approaches presume that change will generate conflict between the needs of the organization and the interest or habits of employees. They also often presume that change must be initiated quickly—either to sidestep resistance or to address pressing problems. For example, managers charged with turning around a failing enterprise may decide on the necessary changes, then rely on power and authority to force them through. Although this heavy approach has taken its knocks in recent years, it still tends to be the U.S. model for achieving change.

Japanese companies, by contrast, tend to adopt a *bottom-up* approach to change. When a problem is identified, a fairly low-level manager or task force tackles the job of preparing a response. These managers develop their proposal and present it to successively higher levels of the organization for suggestions and approval—an approach known in Japan as *ringi*. When the plan has been approved at all levels in a given department, it is sent to other concerned departments for review. Only then, after a broad consensus has developed, is the plan recommended to top management. More and more U.S. companies are adopting the ringi approach.

Some situations are so important or urgent that they demand a top-down approach. But the ringi system ensures that by the time the changes are made or the product is launched, everyone is on board. Kotter's eight criteria provide a useful guide for how to determine the right mix between a bottom-up and a top-down approach to change.

FOLLOW UP

This topic requires additional emphasis because doing a good job of communicating a change you've decided upon is only the first step in making it happen. Any

[5] Ibid., p. 67.

change, whether from the bottom, the middle, or the top, will cause both foreseeable and unforeseeable consequences; be prepared for both.

Foreseeable Consequences

Significant change means that people at all levels of the organization will have to rethink their job responsibilities and/or improve their performance. Make sure you've:

Provided the information that enables people to understand what you need from them, and

Provided the support so people have the means to accomplish their new tasks and responsibilities.

Unforeseeable Consequences

This may be the toughest part about communicating change. The key factors are:

Monitoring results. If one person in the chain of command isn't up to speed, it can hold up change in the whole organization. Make sure you can identify the problem areas quickly and fix them.

Responding quickly. Have a response mechanism in place to answer questions and provide unanticipated resources. Depending on the size of the organization, this may mean hotlines, regular review meetings, a website, or management retraining.

In the following case, managers at headquarters need to introduce centralized planning to division managers accustomed to decentralized decision making.

CASE 11.1

Hammermill Paper Company

Content through its first sixty years to gather strength and assume leadership in a single business (the manufacture and sale of fine and printing papers), Hammermill Paper has for the last twentyfive years radically expanded its operation with the acquisition of a complex array of businesses. A decentralized operating philosophy was adopted: acquired companies continued to make all decisions on operating matters, while Hammermill Corporate controlled and allocated capital. Diversification allowed the company to grow from its original pulp and paper mill in Erie, Pennsylvania, to a national network comprised of five distinct businesses and twenty-four operating companies. Such a pattern of decentralized growth can create numerous problems in decision making, communications, and motivation of employees; stability and familiarity in policy and planning inevitably give way to change and uncertainty. Disparate companies managed by self-reliant individuals with long service have to forge new relationships to maintain the integrity of the corporate structure.

As Hammermill's organizational structure became increasingly complex (see *Exhibits 1-A* and *1-B*), the need for enhanced communication, among divisions and between division managers and corporate headquarters, grew. With more layers of people to manage and a greater variety of decisions to make, company leaders like Albert F. Duval, President and CEO, and Donald S. Leslie, Jr., Executive Vice President, realized that a new, more formal planning process was essential to ensure that performance would be measured against specific goals for each division and location. While such corporate planning seemed vital to Hammermill's continued expansion and prosperity, implementation would not be easy. How could decentralized, autonomous divisions (each run with an entrepreneurial touch) be yoked to one another through a centralized plan that controlled the allocation of capital and assigned specific goals and objectives? Could the principles of decentralization and formal planning coexist harmoniously in the corporation's philosophy of management? The first step toward answering these questions was to introduce the new planning process to the division managers so as to explain its necessity and to address their concerns.

RECENT CORPORATE HISTORY

Twenty-five years ago, Hammermill Paper Company appeared much as it did when founded just before the turn of the century. Although the number of

This case was prepared by Frank V. Cespedes and S. Lindsay Craig, Associates in Communication, and research assistant Terrance Cheeseman. Harvard Business School case 380-014.

EXHIBIT 1-A Hammermill Organizational Structure

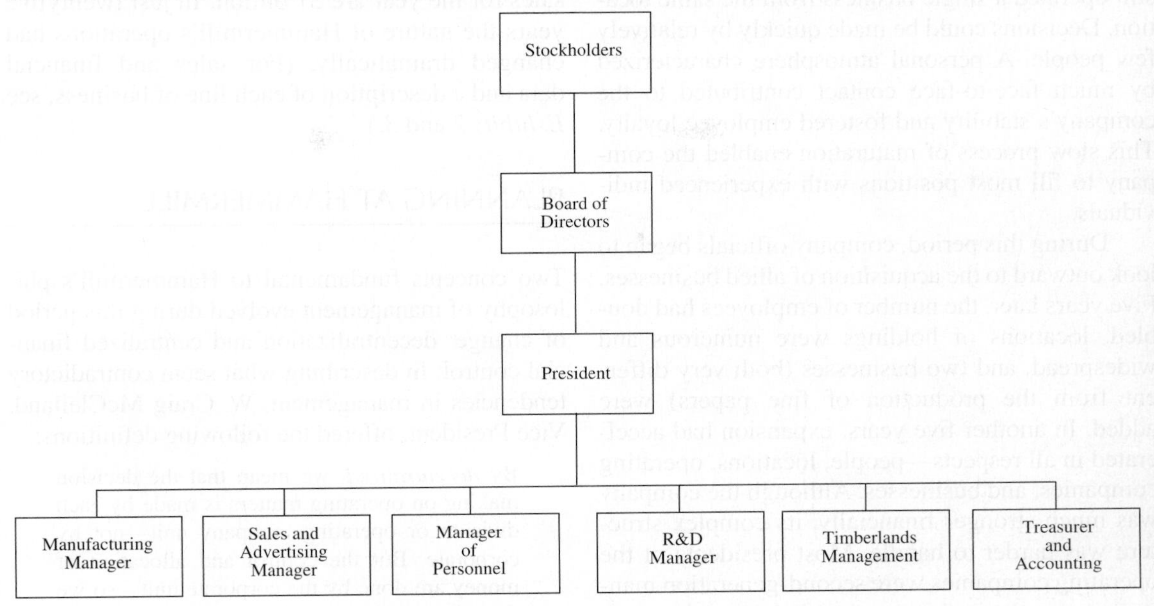

EXHIBIT 1-B Revised Hammermill Organizational Structure

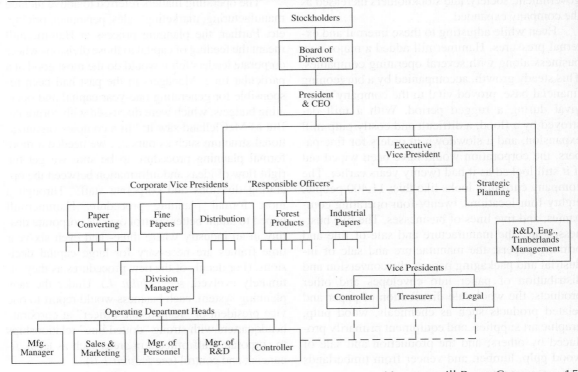

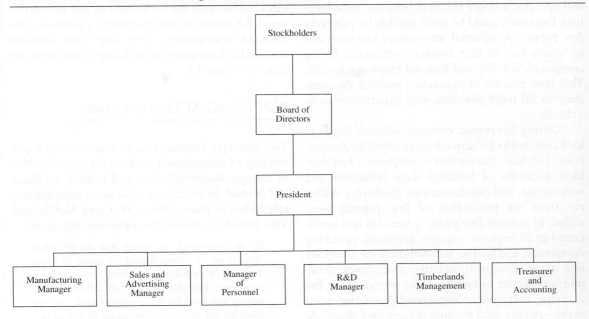

Stockholders

Board of Directors

President & CEO

Executive Vice President

Strategic Planning

R&D, Eng., Timberlands Management

Vice Presidents

Controller

Treasurer

Legal

Corporate Vice Presidents

"Responsible Officers"

Paper Converting

Fine Papers

Distribution

Forest Products

Industrial Papers

Division Manager

Operating Department Heads

Mfg. Manager

Sales & Marketing

Mgr. of Personnel

Mgr. of R&D

Controller

employees had grown steadily to 2,100, the company still operated a single business from the same location. Decisions could be made quickly by relatively few people. A personal atmosphere characterized by much face-to-face contact contributed to the company's stability and fostered employee loyalty. This slow process of maturation enabled the company to fill most positions with experienced individuals.

During this period, company officials began to look outward to the acquisition of allied businesses. Five years later, the number of employees had doubled, locations of holdings were numerous and widespread, and two businesses (both very different from the production of fine papers) were added. In another five years, expansion had accelerated in all respects—people, locations, operating companies, and businesses. Although the company was much stronger financially, its complex structure was harder to handle. Most presidents of the operating companies were second-generation managers—people used to running their own shops. At first, plans and policies from headquarters were not always well received. Further, pressures from government, society, and stockholders increased as the company expanded.

Even while adjusting to these internal and external pressures, Hammermill added a major new business along with several operating companies. This steady growth, accompanied by a burgeoning financial base, proved vital to the company's survival during a rugged period. With a mill destroyed by a flood, a difficult and costly pulp mill expansion, and a slowdown in orders for fine papers, the corporation would have been wiped out if it still looked as it had twenty years earlier. The company currently looks like this: 11,400 people, eighty-four locations, twenty-four operating companies, and five lines of businesses. The five businesses are: the manufacture and sale of fine and printing papers; the manufacture and sale of industrial and packaging papers; the conversion and distribution of paper into envelopes and other products; the wholesale distribution of paper and related products such as chemicals, wood pulp, graphic art supplies, and equipment primarily produced by others; and the production and sale of wood pulp, lumber, and veneer from timberlands owned or managed by the company. Projected sales for the year are $1 billion. In just twentyfive years the nature of Hammermill's operations had changed dramatically. (For sales and financial data and a description of each line of business, see *Exhibits 2* and *3*.)

PLANNING AT HAMMERMILL

Two concepts fundamental to Hammermill's philosophy of management evolved during this period of change: decentralization and centralized financial control. In describing what seem contradictory tendencies in management, W. Craig McClelland, Vice President, offered the following definitions:

> By *decentralized*, we mean that the decision making on operating matters is made by each division or operating company unit—not by corporate. But the control and allocation of money are done by the corporate unit—so we describe our business philosophy as that of decentralized operations and centralized financial control and planning.

The operating matters referred to above include manufacturing, marketing, sales, personnel, pricing, etc. Further, the planning process at Hammermill meant the feeding of capital to those divisions where corporate leaders felt it would do the most good at a particular time. Managers in the past had been responsible for generating one-year capital and operating budgets, which were discussed with corporate. But as McClelland saw it: "In a complex organizational structure such as ours . . . we needed a more formal planning procedure to be sure we get the right flow of ideas and information between the operating divisions and corporate staff." Through a more formal planning procedure, Hammermill hoped to attain better control over its corporate destiny in an industry where three- and even six-year time frames are necessary for large capital decisions. (For details of the new procedures as they ultimately evolved, see *Exhibit 4*.). Under the new planning system, each business would report to one vice president or "responsible officer" at corporate headquarters with strong "dotted line" relationships to corporate staff officers in areas such as legal, financial, and control (see *Exhibit 1-B*).

EXHIBIT 2 Hammermill Paper Company Sales

Financial Highlights	Current Year	Last Year
Sales	$912,294,000	$787,032,000
Net income	26,059,000	19,525,000
Per common share		
Primary	$3.35	$2.51
Fully diluted	3.14	2.37
Common dividends paid	9,976,000	9,752,000
Per share	$1.32½	$1.30
Shareholders' ownership	264,181,000	247,883,000
Total assets	583,092,000	542,535,000

Breakdown by Business (in millions)	Sales	Operating Profit	Assets at Year-End
Fine and printing papers	$278.3	$23.5	$246.7
Industrial and packaging papers	166.1	18.5	130.3
Converted paper products	92.6	4.9	33.9
Wholesale divisions	382.1	12.1	87.7
Forest products	60.4	9.5	44.2

However, corporate managers foresaw some resistance to the new planning procedures from the division managers. Most of the managers were in their forties and fifties; they had long service in their respective companies, but were relatively new to Hammermill. (Most of the companies had been acquired by Hammermill less than ten years ago.) Their business experience has been shaped in the smaller companies that they either had founded or had entered as the second generation of managers. Donald Leslie noted that "one of the most difficult things for the managers to accept was that their goal under the new planning philosophy was not necessarily growth, which is the natural assumption of the entrepreneur." There were no MBAs among the division managers, but many had graduate educations and extensive experience in the manufacturing and marketing functions of their businesses. Their track records were good. Moreover, for five years the managers had planned annual budgets for their divisions, but not in a formal planning mode where they had to deal with issues and goals.

Craig McClelland described the atmosphere among the managers:

> Some of the managers welcomed planning, because they realized they had real problems trying to run a company on a one-year budget when their businesses often involved three-year time frames. The introduction of a new paper machine, for instance, is a three-year decision. However, most of the managers felt that corporate involvement in any matters except legal and financial reports was a nuisance or a threat. The planning process shifted emphasis from budgeting and number punching to issue definition and goal setting; more staff work was required, and most divisional managers do not have large staffs. They felt, "How do you expect me to run a business and do planning at the same time?"

EXHIBIT 3 Hammermill's Five Lines of Business

Fine and Printing Papers Many grades of paper for writing, printing, commercial, and converting applications are manufactured, with Hammermill Bond perhaps the most widely known. Other independent divisions within the fine papers group include the Beckett Paper Company, which produces book cover and text papers, as well as embossed and other fancy-finish papers, and the Strathmore Paper Company Division, which produces cotton fiber bond and writing papers, and artists' papers, pads, markers, and brushes.

Industrial and Packaging Papers The Thilmany Division manufactures a wide range of light-weight craft specialty papers. Thilmany's sales of $152 million account for over 90 percent of this business group's revenue. Its principal products include carbonizing base paper used for business forms; polyethylene-coated paper sold for the manufacture of composite cans; asphalt-coated backing paper used with fiberglass insulation materials; and other specialty papers used for packaging and wrapping. The Manning Division is a small specialty mill that manufactures pulp and specialized papers principally from hemp fiber imported from the Philippines and Ecuador. Finally, the major business of the Akrosil Division consists of the coating of film, paper, and other materials with silicones in the production of release liners used with contact adhesive.

Converted Paper Products Of the six converting divisions, four specialize in the manufacture and distribution of envelopes, making Hammermill one of the largest producers of envelopes in the United States. The other two converting divisions make a variety of rolled- and folded-paper products for the electronics, communications, and business equipment industries.

Wholesale Distribution Hammermill owns three wholesome businesses primarily in fine and printing paper and, to a lesser extent, in ink, film, chemicals, binding, and related graphic art equipment. These companies have offices and warehouse facilities in fifty-one cities located throughout the United States and generally sell the products manufactured by companies other than Hammermill. Historically, this group has accounted for the largest percentage of annual sales and paced last year's upsurge.

Forest Products The final area of business in the corporate structure (and one with a promising growth record) is forest products. The major portion of this group's operations resulted from acquisitions, although one highly profitable facility was the result of internal expansion. Hammermill owns or controls approximately 422,000 acres of timberlands in Pennsylvania, New York, and Alabama. These lands also provide sawtimber for its six hardwood and pine lumber sawmills, and Hammermill is a major supplier of raw materials to the premium furniture industry. Nearly 34 percent of these sales are for export. Each division of Hammermill's forest products group was highly competitive and became a substantial factor in the various product markets.

> You finally can't generalize about types of response to planning, but when we introduced the topic we didn't expect them to leave the room cheering, that's for sure.

Donald Leslie provided this additional contextual information about the introduction of planning at Hammermill:

> Before we formally introduced planning, the managers knew something was going to be done about a planning process, but they had not received any outline of the steps involved or the goals or specific purposes. It was simply in the air and part of the grapevine. When we did communicate the process to the managers,we had to deliver this message: we were not asking, "Do you think we should have planning?" or, "How should we have planning?" Rather, we were saying, "We've studied planning, we need it, here's why, this is our preliminary procedure—it will undoubtedly evolve, but for the time being this is the framework in which we want to operate." So you see we had to communicate a decision and the basic framework, but we also had to make clear how and why planning was flexible. And a problem was how to communicate the concept in this manner to a wide variety of people with different backgrounds.

EXHIBIT 4 Excerpts from the Planning Procedures Manual

Note: Each year since the introduction of planning, the Planning Procedures Manual has been revised, with new material added and old material changed or deleted as the corporate planning staff adjusts and fine-tunes the planning process. This exhibit, consisting of excerpts from past manuals, should therefore be considered a representative sample of Hammermill's Planning Procedures Manual, rather than a verbatim duplication of the document.

Section I. Planning Process

A. Introduction

Planning within Hammermill is designed to be an ongoing, two-way process. Corporate and operating company planning should be closely intertwined. The intention is to avoid the limitations of a planning procedure based strictly on the consolidation of independently compiled operating company plans. Planning is not a task done once every three or four years as part of a major capital project. It is a continuing process of revising and updating goals, strategies, and prospective results.

There are four fundamental questions that are common to almost any planning procedure:

1. *Present Situation*—"Where are we now and how did we get here?"
2. *Long-Range Goals*—"Where do we want to go?"
3. *Strategies*—"How are we going to get there?"
4. *Planned Accomplishments*—"What will be achieved in the short and intermediate term?"

The purpose of the Hammermill planning/budgeting procedure is to provide an efficient and effective means for the corporation and the individual operating companies to deal with these questions.

B. Overall Approach

1. *Corporate and Operating Company Planning*—Hammermill is a highly decentralized company. A formal planning process can be painful in terms of time and frustration. The process must be a practical one. Heavy analytical work and goal-setting activity cannot be allowed to impinge on operational, motivational, and measurement factors inherent in the decentralized corporate structure. Because of the decentralization and diversification, the planning process is designed to achieve heavy interaction between the chief executive's office, the responsible officer, the operating company manager, and the planning staff. But the operating companies are responsible for their own plans and analyses. Corporate concern is for the "fit" of the operating company plans with the corporate direction.
2. *Long-Range Planning Technique*—There is a sequence of steps that can be followed to move through the strategic planning process. As indicated in *Chart 1-A* at the end of this section, there are three major steps: Analysis, Goal Formulation, and Development of Strategic Plans.
3. *Goal Formulation*—As illustrated in *Chart 1-A,* the main linkage between the corporate and operating company planning process is at the goals step. Based on the fundamental issues facing the corporation, the formulation of a set of corporate goals provides the framework within which supportive operating company goals can be developed.
4. *Responsible Officer*—The responsible officer at headquarters (i.e., the appropriate corporate vice president) plays a very important role in the planning/budgeting process. It is important to recognize that planning/budgeting is a two-way process. The responsible officer, therefore, has the responsibility to work with the operating company manager and find agreement on a set of goals and strategies for the existing operating companies. These must conform with the needs and capabilities of the particular business group and the corporation. The responsible officer has primary responsibility in the goal and strategy development stage for each operating company within his or her business group and for the particular business group as a whole. It follows that he or she is accountable for the accomplishment of the agreed-upon operating company and business group goals.

(continued)

5. *Fall Planning Sessions*—The culmination of the annual planning/budgeting sequence for the operating company takes place during the month of November, when the fall planning sessions are held. At this meeting the operating company manager and/or the responsible officer discuss with corporate management the goals and the strategies on which the three-year fiscal plan is based. Preliminary agreement is reached regarding the operating company's budget for the next year and its direction for subsequent years.

C. Three-Year Fiscal Plan

The three-year fiscal plan, along with the annual operating budget and the annual capital budget, documents the planning process. It is in the three-year plan that the blending of broader, longer-term goals and strategies with more immediate, operating steps takes place. Three fundamental purposes are fulfilled:

1. A budget that projects as accurately as possible performance for the next fiscal year is provided to meet control and measurement needs.
2. Projections for the second and third years require the quantification of longer-term goals and strategies for the company. The impact of a strategy and the movement toward a goal are reflected in pro forma financial statements.
3. The three-year plan provides the basic data for analysis and discussion of operating company plans at several stages within the planning process. In addition, the consolidation of the operating company plans provides the information with which the ability of the corporation as a whole to achieve its goals can be evaluated.

D. Planning/Budgeting Sequence and Timetable

To accomplish the annual planning/budgeting task within Hammermill, a ten-step process has been defined. *Chart 1-B* at the end of the section summarizes the ten steps, along with the timing and the people responsible.

Section II. Corporate Guidelines

There are two types of corporate guidelines that will be made available to the operating companies at the start of their three-year plan activities each year. A set of *Goal Guidelines* will be delivered by the responsible officer to

CHART 1-A Steps in the Strategic Planning Process

Corporate	Operating Company
I. Analysis	I. Analysis
1. Financial track record	1. Financial track record
2. Comparisons	2. Comparisons
3. Strengths/weaknesses	3. Strengths/weaknesses
4. Issues (problems and opportunities)	4. Issues (problems and opportunities)
II. Goal formulation	II. Goal formulation
1. Track record	1. ROA
2. Return to investor	2. Growth
3. Access to capital markets	3. Cash flow
III. Development of strategic plans	III. Development of strategic plans
1. Internal plan	1. Internal plan
2. External (acquisition) plan	2. External (acquisition) plan

Source: Hammermill Paper Company.

(continued)

EXHIBIT 4 (CONTINUED)

the operating company. The goal guideline is a critical ingredient of the two-way planning process. The second type of guideline is the *Planning Assumption.* Along with the planning/budgeting worksheets, a set of planning assumptions will be delivered to the operating companies each June. These are intended to bring greater uniformity to the general economic, price, cost, and availability assumptions used in the operating company plans.

A. Goal Guidelines

The goal formulation process is the primary linkage between the corporate and the operating company planning efforts. A great deal of exchange of information and discussion is required to make sure that individual company goals are congruent with corporate goals. Goal guidelines initiate the process that begins with the May management meeting and culminates with the fall planning sessions.

The guidelines are typically expressed in financial terms:

A return on assets (ROA) target,

A growth target,

A cash flow target.

They will be ranked according to priority or desired emphasis. The targets or the priorities may change as the time frame moves from the short to the long term. The priority goal guideline for one company may be a step-by-step improvement in ROA performance. Growth could be quite a secondary consideration—at least for a period of time. Another company may be asked to maintain historical levels of ROA performance but really strive for growth. Net cash usage for a period of time would likely be appropriate.

CHART 1-B
Hammermill Planning/Budgeting Sequence

	STEPS	CONTENT	COMPLETE BY CLOSE OF...	MAR	APR	MAY	JUN	JUL	AUG	SEPT	OCT	NOV	DEC	JAN	FEB
1	Corporate Review and Planning	Blue Book Update Goal and Issue Revisions	3rd Week. May				Corporate Management and LRP Staff								
2	Management Meeting	Communicate Corporate Guidelines (Goals, Goal Guidelines, and Planning Assumptions)	4th Week. May					Corporate Management							
3	Res. Off. Initiates Planning Process with Op. Co. Mgrs.	Distribution of Planning Assumptions; Budget & Planning Worksheet Distribution; Strategy Formulation	4th Week. June						Responsible Officer						
4	Operating Company Plan Development	Complete Capital Budget, Annual Budget, and Three-Year Fiscal Plan	1st Week. Oct.								Operating Company Manager				
5	Responsible Officer Review & Approval	Prepare Planning Summary Charts & Goal Achievement Summary	2nd Week. Oct.				Responsible Officer								
6	Corporate Staff Analysis	MAC: Review Capital Budget; Controller's Staff: Prel. Consolidation; Planning Staff: Plan Summary & Commentary	1st Week. Nov.				Corporate Staff								
7	Fall Planning Sessions	Final Agreement on Operating Co. Goals, Discuss Strategies; Prel. Approval of Operating Budget	4th Week. Nov.					Responsible Officer							
8	Revisions, as Needed	Operating Company Plan and/or Capital Budget	1st Week. Dec.		Responsible Officer and Operating Company Manager										
9	Consolidation and Corp. Review of Annual Budget	Evaluate "Fit" with Corporate Goals	2nd Week. Dec.				Corporate Management and Staff								
10	Consolidation and Corp. Review of Three-Year Plans	Evaluate "Fit" with Corporate Goals	4th Week. Feb.					Corporate Management and Staff							

(continued)

EXHIBIT 4 (CONTINUED)

The goal guidelines are intended to initiate the goal formulation process at the operating company. Typically, the target and even the priorities would be changed before they became agreed-upon "goals" at the fall planning sessions. Furthermore, the targets, the priorities, i.e., the roles or missions, developed for the operating companies can be expected to change from time to time. Specific circumstances, capital availability, problems, and opportunities are ever changing. This requires that goal formulation be correspondingly flexible.

B. Planning Assumptions

On June 1 each year, the corporate staff will distribute three-year fiscal plan forms to each operating company. At the same time, the corporate staff will also submit a set of *Planning Assumptions* for the operating companies to use in developing their three-year fiscal plans. Planning assumptions will be established for the following factors:

1. General economic climate

a. Real growth

b. Inflation

c. Special features

2. Construction prices

a. Equipment

b. Material

c. Labor

3. Prices and availability of raw materials

a. Pulp

b. Chemicals

c. Other raw materials

4. Energy costs and availability

5. Wages, salaries, and fringe benefits

6. Transportation

The purpose to be fulfilled by these assumptions is threefold. To provide for comparability and understanding of large numbers of plans, certain inputs should be uniform from one operating plan to another. The market price of pulp is an obvious example. The second point is that the plans provide a database for purposes of simple consolidation into a corporate total and for analysis of the impact of specific strategies or real movement toward goals. Uniformity of assumptions about the general economic environment, energy availability, etc., is important in this regard.

Section III. Plan Review

A. Responsible Officer

No later than the close of the first week in October, the responsible officer should receive the operating company's three-year fiscal plan, the annual operating budget, and the capital budget. Prior to this, he or she will have also received a set of summary charts from the director of corporate long-range planning. The first chart in the set is designed to illustrate the historical trend and future plan for eight critical financial measurements:

Sales	Return on sales
Pre-tax profit	Asset turnover
Capital expenditures	Return on assets
Working capital	New cash flow

(continued)

EXHIBIT 4 (CONTINUED)

By the end of the second week in October, the responsible officers should complete their reviews and summary analyses. The complete set of plan documents including the annual budget, the capital budget, the three-year plan schedules, and the responsible officer's analysis and summary charts should be forwarded to the corporate controller's staff, who will handle the further distribution to the planning staff.

B. Corporate Staff Analysis

Three elements to the corporate staff work must be accomplished to prepare for the fall planning sessions:

1. Review of the capital budget.

2. Preliminary consolidation of the operating company three-year plans by the corporate controller.

3. Issue analysis by the planning staff.

One week prior to each planning session, the director of corporate long-range planning will submit to each participant in the session a packet containing the following:

An agenda,

A list of points for discussion (based on analysis by the planning staff),

Responsible Officer Analysis,

Summary Analysis,

Goal Achievement Summary,

History of Budgeted Sales and Profit vs. Actual,

Preliminary Corporate Consolidation (received from corporate controller).

C. Fall Planning Session

The culmination of the operating company planning process is the fall planning session. It is the principal opportunity for corporate management and the operating company manager to discuss in depth the future direction of each specific company—the problems and opportunities, the appropriate goals, the major strategies, and the capital requirements.

A typical agenda will include the following four items:

1. Operating company performance compared with goals,

2. Operating company long-term issues and goals,

3. The three-year fiscal plan (including annual operating and capital budgets),

4. People development.

Prior to the close of each session there will be either preliminary approval of the annual operating budget or a request for a revision. In addition, there should be agreement on a set of goals for the operating company and an understanding of the nature and timing of broad strategies designed to achieve the goals.

Study Questions

In thinking about this case, put yourself in the position of managers in corporate headquarters sometime shortly before the initial attempts at communicating the need for and benefits of planning to other people in the organization.

1. How should corporate headquarters communicate the new planning procedure to the organization? Who should constitute the primary audience for communications about the planned change?Are there important secondary audiences? What role should written communications play in introducing the change? What role should oral communications play?

2. Who should be the primary source for communications about planning with each audience? What role should the CEO play? What role should the "responsible officer" play? In general, who should be the primary spokesperson(s) for the change?
3. What are the most important changes introduced by the new planning procedure? From the perspective of corporate headquarters, what are the advantages of and potential problems with planning? From the perspective of the division managers, what are the benefits and potential concerns? If you were a corporate manager, what arguments could you offer in response to their concerns?
4. What features of the new planning procedure should be included in an initial announcement? How detailed should this information be? Should the target audience receive the entire Planning Procedures Manual or just excerpts (*Exhibit 4*)? Can you provide that exhibit's information more concisely? How?
5. Study the company's organization chart (*Exhibit 1-B*) and the different flows of information introduced by planning. What individuals or groups might be important channels of communication concerning planning? How might feedback be arranged?
6. Given the concerns and informational needs you see as important for your target audience, what style, tone, and argumentation are appropriate in a communication explaining the planned change?

CHAPTER 12

Communicating with External Audiences

Since we will be dealing extensively with external communication in the following chapters, we focus here on two specific situations: a small company trying to persuade a small community, and a larger company trying to persuade the government and the general public.

A generation ago, corporations mostly needed to develop a good product, price it well, find a way to market it, and keep stockholders happy. But as far back as Teddy Roosevelt's trust busting, business has had to become responsible to an increasingly large number of external constituencies: consumers, the government, the media, and the general public. Increasingly, even during conservative political climates, regulators, activists, and the press are unlikely to go away. All these constituencies will be addressed in the following pages. This chapter concentrates on a typical example of external communication: the corporation that needs to persuade an audience with veto power.

Even the most responsible corporations often face a NIMBY attitude, that is, "Not in *my* backyard." Citizens who recognize that a certain service needs to be performed would prefer it done elsewhere. Communities are constantly balancing the benefits of hosting a particular business—jobs and ancillary income—against the costs, such as increased pollution or aesthetic consequences. How should a company approach a community or regulatory agencies with decision-making power to argue that the benefits outweigh the risks? How can the company best convey that it understands its audiences' concerns? Many of the challenges an executive faces in convincing an internal audience—understanding their interests, overcoming resistance to change—also apply to dealing with external audiences.

Many managers believe that they will never have to deal with the press. Often, they regard it with hostility. Most think press relations are entirely the domain of their company's or agency's public relations department. But in fact, senior executives say they spend more time on communications than on other tasks, and a significant component of that time is devoted to press and public relations. Junior managers need to be highly sensitive to press relations for the following reasons:

- *Often, free press can be the best way to acquaint the public with your product or service.* To cite only one example, the amount Microsoft spent on advertising Windows 95 was dwarfed by the value of the free publicity it received from international news coverage.
- *Your particular area of expertise may unexpectedly become something your organization needs to promote or explain.* Line workers at auto companies have been drafted to extol quality improvements in advertisements; accountants may be called to the CEO's office for briefings on a potentially embarrassing news report or an upcoming press conference.
- *Public relations considerations need to be addressed at the beginning, not the end, of a planning process.* Business history is replete with examples of companies that invested vast sums to develop products, ideas, or services that couldn't be sold because of public resistance to the concept, the configuration, or the public image of the company. General Motors' Tacos, for example, could be the best in the world and still not jump off the shelves.
- *Junior managers become senior managers who will eventually have to deal with the press directly.* As both marketers and corporate citizens, organizations have to explain themselves to the public constantly through advertising, press releases, and press conferences. Junior managers who understand this aspect of their work are likely to become senior managers faster.

These premises lead to several conclusions:

1. *A successful manager understands how the press works.* Successful managers tend to follow the press in general, and how their organization is playing in particular. Members of the press tend to trust companies and individuals with a track record of accuracy and accessibility. To cite only two examples, both Johnson & Johnson and Perrier survived charges of contaminated products because they had a record of reliability and accessibility and addressed the problems immediately. In both cases, and many others, stonewalling would have been disastrous to the company's image of wholesomeness and purity. Most press stories last only a few days, but they can leave an indelible impression in the public's mind. Many managers tend to believe they can "snow" the press with their greater expertise, but this strategy rarely works. Most reporters are hard-working professionals who will carefully check out an expert assertion or who know someone who can.
2. *A successful manager understands what the press needs.* What the press needs is a story, and bad news generally sells better than good news. Companies and individuals are most likely to have to deal with the press when something has

gone wrong. This suggests a couple of lessons. When you have good stories, give them to the press to establish a record of credibility; many media outlets will print or broadcast a press release from a reliable source more or less verbatim. Consider how private decisions may look if they should become public. If something has gone wrong, take the initiative in announcing it, explaining it, and telling the world how it's going to be corrected.

3. *A successful manager understands press jargon*. Reputable reporters will stick to their verbal agreements on how information you provide them is to be used. How you will be quoted depends on the ground rules you establish at the beginning of an interview. *Deep background* means the reporter can reflect the information in her story without possible attribution. *Background* means that you can be referenced as "a reliable source." Any other comment, however apparently casual or social, can be quoted directly and attributed.
4. *A successful manager should be able to generate an attention-grabbing, accurate, and well-constructed press release*. While many managers may not be regularly mailing out press releases themselves, most will be contributing to them and need to understand how they work. A good press release is extremely formulaic and follows the structure of a good news story:
   a. The first paragraph states the main point clearly and emphasizes its newsworthiness. For example: "Acme Corporation announced today that it is releasing the best tire ever available on the world market."
   b. The second paragraph provides a quote from a reputable source: "Acme President Rudy Roadrunner said, 'Not only does this tire surpass all our competitors' in endurance, quality, and safety; it's also available at a lower price.' "
   c. The third paragraph provides evidence that the claims made so far are true: "In repeated tests against our competitors . . . "
   d. The remaining paragraphs provide background information on the product, the company, and Rudy Roadrunner, and they demonstrate a track record of credibility. They may also include testimonials available from respected independent sources.

Obviously, the formula of an effective press release will vary depending on the nature of the news to be announced. But the pyramid structure suggested by this example always applies: Move from the most important and specific to the least important and most general information. Busy editors often run a press release more or less verbatim and just cut it off when they run out of space. The easier you make their jobs, the more likely they are to cover your story.

Once you've written or contributed to a press release, decide who's most likely to run it. This can cover the gamut from extremely specialized trade magazines to the national or international media. Consider the use of venues other than print and broadcast media as well; perhaps there's a room on the Internet where interested parties are likely to gather.

5. *A successful manager understands the role of the press in crisis management*. This includes knowing how to provide effective interviews and understanding when and how to hold a press conference. Certain rules apply to both:

a. Identify your central message, make sure you can back it up, and stick to it.
b. Prepare materials in advance—press releases, statements, supportive studies—that the reporters can take away with them and study or quote later.
c. Never say more than you know to be true. If you don't know, say, "I don't have that information at the moment, but I'll get it to you as soon as I do"—then follow up.
d. Make sure your team is behind you. This means making sure not only that top management of a corporation agrees on a message, but also that other potential press sources (for example, subordinate employees) have the same information you're dispensing to the public, believe it, and are unlikely to leak contradictory and embarrassing information.
e. Provide the press with the most credible and informed access possible. Reporters will always want to get to the top. They'll be more likely to cover the comments of a CEO or a Cabinet secretary than those of a press agent or an underling. But they will understand that a high official may need to refer technical questions to an informed specialist.
f. Anticipate, and be prepared to respond to, the most difficult questions.
g. Don't become hostile or defensive; experienced reporters are experts at smelling *anxiety*.
h. Make your answers brief, quotable, and to the point. Rambling and repetition are likely to get you into trouble or open new lines of inquiry.
i. If you're facing a problem you've caused, however inadvertently, be prepared to acknowledge your error and describe clearly what you're prepared to do to correct it.

All these rules apply as well to internal organizational communications about situations likely to become public. Superiors will almost always appreciate savvy advice from subordinates about how to handle public relations situations, whether these are opportunities or problems. One work worth consulting on crisis communication is Laurence Barton's *Crisis in Organizations* (Cincinnati, OH: Southwestern Publishing Division, 1993).

The following cases address a company that needs to persuade a community and a company that needs to persuade the government and the country.

Oxford Energy

In early May of 1987, Philip Rettger, Vice President of The Oxford Energy Company, was trying to organize a presentation. On May 11 he would be appearing in Derry, New Hampshire, at a public forum to talk about Oxford's proposal to build and operate a plant that would generate electricity by burning discarded tires. As he began to outline his thoughts, Rettger wondered what strategies could persuade the Derry residents to vote for this proposal.

THE OXFORD ENERGY COMPANY

Founded in 1984, Oxford had established a niche in the American energy market by adapting a technology developed in Germany in the 1970s. The company's Modesto Energy Project in California, scheduled to begin operations in the summer of 1987, exemplified the company's business and would be the United States' first large-scale waste-tire-to-energy plant. Located next to the world's biggest pile of scrap tires (33–40 million tires), the Modesto plant was projected to consume approximately 4.5 million tires per year and generate 14 megawatts of electricity—enough to meet the power requirements of about 15,000 homes. Tests to date confirmed that the plant would easily meet California's stringent air-quality standards.

In addition to the Derry site, Oxford was considering developing tire-to-energy plants in Sterling, Connecticut, and Lackawanna, Pennsylvania. Plans were also on the drawing board for a California facility that would generate energy from rice hulls. Like the tire-burning plants, this facility would solve an environmental problem by converting rice industry waste into electricity and usable by-products. Oxford had also developed several conventional hydroelectric power plants.

In August 1986, Oxford Energy made its first offering of common stock (see *Exhibit 1*). But in the annual report for that year, President and Chairman of the Board Robert Colman cautioned stockholders not to expect immediate profits: "Our projects are capital-intensive, with long-term development cycles. Thus, short-term earnings are not the Company's primary objective, nor should they be the principal standard by which Oxford's overall performance is measured." Nevertheless, the consolidated balance sheet for 1986 showed solid growth and increasing profitability (see *Exhibit 2*).

THE TIRE WASTE DILEMMA

Each year, Americans discard approximately 200 million tires. As a result, by 1987, two billion

This case was prepared by Lecturers in Communication J. Janelle Shubert and Michael E. Hattersley. Harvard Business School case 390-085.

EXHIBIT 1

This announcement is neither an offer to sell nor a solicitation of an offer to buy any of these securities. The offering is made only by the Prospectus.

New Issue

1,000,000 Shares

OXFORD ENERGY

The Oxford Energy Company

Common Stock

Price $6.50 Per Share

Copies of the Prospectus may be obtained in any State in which this announcement is circulated from only such of the Underwriters, including the undersigned, as may lawfully offer these securities in such State.

Bear, Stearns & Co. Inc.

Alex. Brown & Sons
Incorporated

The First Boston Corporation

Donaldson, Lufkin & Jenrette
Securities Corporation

Hambrecht & Quist
Incorporated

Kidder, Peabody & Co.
Incorporated

Lazard Frères & Co.

Morgan Stanley & Co.
Incorporated

PaineWebber
Incorporated

L. F. Rothschild, Unterberg, Towbin, Inc.

Salomon Brothers Inc.

Shearson Lehman Brothers Inc.

August 20, 1986

EXHIBIT 2 The Oxford Energy Company and Subsidiaries Consolidated Balance Sheets

Assets		
Current Assets:	December 31 1986	December 31 1985
Cash and marketable securities (including $2,500,000 of securities at December 31, 1986, purchased under agreement to resell)	$5,962,480	$1,870,724
Receivables:		
Deferred project costs	—	1,287,122
From affiliates	684,678	650,000
Miscellaneous	16,751	105,489
Other	70,148	20,135
Total Current Assets	6,734,057	3,933,470
Noncurrent Assets:		
Property, equipment, and leasehold improvements, net	157,199	66,422
Investments in projects	547,756	66,514
Advances and deferred costs related to projects	2,040,831	1,001,640
Advance receivable	—	75,000
Other	298,046	68,103
Total Assets	$9,777,898	$5,211,149

The accompanying notes are an integral part of these financial statements.

Liabilities and Stockholders' Equity		
Current Liabilities:	December 31 1986	December 31 1985
Accounts payable and accrued liabilities	$ 387,685	$ 586,232
Accrued income taxes	552,247	—
Current portion of promissory note	—	1,300,000
Total Current Liabilities	939,932	1,886,232
Promissory Note	1,200,000	500,000
Subordinated Note Payable to Affiliate	—	1,500,000
Redeemable Preferred Stock, 1400 shares issued and outstanding at December 31, 1985, redemption value of $1,000 per share	—	1,400,000
Commitments and Contingencies		
Stockholders' Equity		
Common stock, $.01 par value; 100,000 shares authorized and issued in 1985; 25,000,000 shares authorized and 6,399,947 shares issued at December 31, 1986	63,999	1,000
Additional paid-in capital	6,625,330	99,000
Retained earnings (deficit)	948,637	(175,033)

EXHIBIT 2 (CONTINUED)

Less 5,000 shares held in treasury, at cost, in December 31, 1985	—	(50)
Total Stockholders' Equity	7,637,966	(75,083)
Total Liabilities and Stockholders' Equity	$9,777,898	$5,211,149

The accompanying notes are an integral part of these financial statements.

waste tires had accumulated in dumps, creating eyesores, fire hazards, and breeding grounds for mosquitoes and other vermin. Most landfills refused tires because of their tendency to float to the surface; consequently, many tires were dumped illegally along country roads, on farmland, or in vacant lots. A bolt of lightning or a youngster with a match could easily convert a tire dump into an inferno which was difficult to extinguish, and often poured polluting smoke into the atmosphere for days or weeks.

President Colman was fond of saying, "We prefer to look at scrap tires not as a national problem, but as a national opportunity." By 1987, Oxford's approach to tire disposal was beginning to receive wide attention. In February, *Business Week* observed, "One way to clean up the blight is to burn the tires. Pound for pound, they hold more energy than high-quality coal." In April, the U.S. Department of Energy endorsed Oxford, saying, "The particular advantages of the [technology used by Oxford] are its long history of 12 years of successful operation and its environmentally clean operation."

THE DERRY PROJECT

On Halloween night, 1984, a tire pile 15 miles from Derry was torched by pranksters. The blaze took hours to control, and the rubble smoldered for days. The town officials were concerned and discussed how they could possibly safeguard the pile in the future. But it wasn't until the late summer of 1986, when they were approached by Oxford Energy, that a solution was available.

Derry, with 28,000 residents, was the fastest-growing town in New Hampshire; its population had doubled over the previous 15 years. Most of this growth was due to an influx of white-collar workers from Massachusetts who were attracted to the town's relaxed pace, low taxes, and easy access to New Hampshire's spectacular woods and mountains. Because Derry was just over the Massachusetts state line, the commute to Boston took less than an hour. Seventy-five percent of Derry's employed population worked in Massachusetts.

"We were interested in Derry as a possible site," said Gordon Marker, Executive Vice President of Oxford, "because the town showed a great deal of leadership. The town had a high-quality staff that was interested in technology. This was evidenced by the approval they had already given to Power Recovery Systems for building a plant that would convert trash to energy."

Oxford was proposing to build a $50 million plant which would bring in $7 million in revenues annually by selling electricity to UNITIL Services Corporation, an independent utility in New Hampshire. Oxford would pay the town of Derry $350,000 annually to lease the land on which the plant was built and pay the town $2 per ton for the tires processed at the plant—an additional $90,000. It was estimated that the plant would create about 25 jobs. Craig Bulkley, Derry Town Administrator, along with other officials and citizens, was enthusiastic. "Derry needs to encourage industry as well as residential growth," said Bulkley.

Although the discussions with the town were still preliminary, in October of 1986 Oxford funded a trip to West Germany for Derry Public Works Administrator Rodney Bartlett to tour the plant that had been operating there for almost a dozen years. Said Marker, "Technologically speaking, the operation is actually very simple; that's the beauty of it. It's clean, it's quiet, and it works. But seeing is believing." When Bartlett returned he reported that the plant in West Germany was indeed "very clean and very quiet. There's no shredding and a very small amount of by-product, most of which can be recycled."

At a Town Council public hearing on December 16, Malcolm Patterson of the State Department of Waste Management, who had also visited the West German plant, said that he was impressed with the facility and that there were no doubts that what Oxford was saying about the technology's ability to burn tires cleanly and safely was true. Around this time, the State of New Hampshire issued a 267-page report endorsing Oxford's technology as a solution for the state's tire waste problem.

January 7, the Derry Town Council approved, by a vote of 6 to 1, Oxford's plan to "... build and operate an incineration plant that will burn 4.5 million tires annually to produce 12,000 kilowatts of electricity."

"This was a real step forward," said Rettger, "but there were a lot of steps left to complete." Oxford still had to obtain the approval of the town attorney and an independent engineer, and get the required permits from the state environmental agencies. In addition, Rettger knew that any opposition would probably result in still another approval step: a referendum vote.

May Casten, former selectman of Derry, had told reporters after the Town Council vote that she would launch a petition drive for a referendum on the plant. Said Casten, "I don't know of anything that burns that doesn't smell. I'm not happy to have Derry be a tire dump for New Hampshire." Neither Rettger nor Marker was particularly surprised by this "not in my backyard" position. Said Marker, "There's always opposition to any energy plant anywhere in the country. There are always some people who say we shouldn't burn anything, and no amount of evidence will convince them otherwise." But Rettger and Marker had to be concerned about how to use what they felt was very strong evidence to persuade the majority of the citizens that the plant would be safe and beneficial to their community.

Part of the difficulty in responding to plant opponents was how to talk about the technical incineration process in a way that was accurate but also understandable to the average citizen. Said Rettger, "Derry has an image as a small, sleepy village in southern New Hampshire. But, actually, it is a small city with a well-educated, relatively affluent population. These are well-read, well-informed people who know, at least in a general kind of way, about emissions controls, scrubbers, by-products, and so on. You can't talk down to them. But you can't fund trips to Germany for all of them either."

Another problem, said Rettger, was that even though this plan had been " . . . kicking around Derry, very publicly, for over eight months, there were still people who felt like they didn't know enough to really support the idea. While we were disappointed that there would be a referendum, it wasn't totally unexpected. This is a very politically active community; people want to feel like they understand what's going on—like they have a say in what happens. I can't say I'm thrilled about the prospect of more meetings but, on the other hand, the more information they get from us, the more straight answers instead of speculation or rumor, the better our chances of getting approval."

While the petition drive continued, the Town Council met on February 4, 1987, and under their charter authorized Mayor Paul Collette to sign a long-term contract with Oxford Energy. "We've definitely got a problem with discarded tires and we're not going to take care of it by sitting here doing nothing," said Collette. In the meantime, Town Attorney Barbara Loughman and the independent engineer, Roy F. Weston, also endorsed the project. The deal was still contingent on approvals from the state environmental agencies, which Rettger estimated would take 6–12 months.

In late March the petition drive closed with enough signatures to call for a referendum vote, which was scheduled for May 19.

PLANNING FOR THE MAY 11 MEETING

Derry planned a week-long series of public meetings beginning on May 11 with a gathering in a high school gym. Other meetings would be held in private homes. The purpose of the meetings, according to Mayor Collette, was to have Oxford explain the plant and answer questions from residents.

Because Oxford had been participating in meetings in Derry for several months, booklets describing the proposed plant were already in the hands of hundreds of citizens (see *Exhibit 3*). What Rettger wondered was how well the booklet answered the kinds of questions that had prompted the referendum vote. In addition to safety, pollution, and aesthetic questions, which Rettger felt were covered in the booklet, some citizens had started asking, "What's in this for us?" Scott Gerrish, Derry At-Large Councilor, urged citizens not to belittle $350,000 in additional revenues. "That's more than three times the revenue we get from Hood Plaza and three times what we get from Hadco," he said, referring to a local shopping mall and a Derry manufacturer.

What also concerned Rettger was assessing the intensity of the opposition—how emotional this issue had become and for which people. Said Rettger, "When the Council voted back in January, the lone dissenter was Richard Buckley, Councilor for the district where the plant would be built. What he said then was, 'There are just too many unanswered questions.' So we figured, fair enough; we'll try to answer them. But by the time the May 11 meeting was announced, May Casten had started saying we had misled the town because the plant would be larger than the one operating in Germany. We had used the West German plant as an example of the technology that would be used and had funded Craig Bulkley's trip so someone could see how that technology worked. Our brochures say clearly that the German plant is smaller."

An indication that the issue had become an important one for some people was the rumor that surfaced a week before the first meeting: the West German plant had been shut down. With reporters and officials crowded into the Mayor's office, a Derry resident who spoke German phoned the plant. The call, which lasted about twenty-five minutes and cost the town about $30, verified that the plant was still operating.

Rettger believed he could limit misinformation on the grapevine by establishing himself as an absolutely credible source. "I like doing presentations," he said. "I believe in our technology and I think it's a good way for towns like Derry to solve waste problems. Presentations help people to put faces with facts; if they can see you and talk with you, sometimes you can reach them; then there's a chance they'll listen and make informed decisions. Presentations are the life-blood of our work."

"But," he continued, "sometimes it's difficult to know where to start. At 7:30 on May 11, I have to be in that gym, ready to tell the Oxford story and ready to answer heaven only knows what kinds of questions."

EXHIBIT 3

INTRODUCTION

Oxford Energy, a company specializing in the development of alternative energy projects, is in the process of building a series of small-scale electrical generation facilities around the country which will be fueled by whole scrap tires.

The project proposed for southern New Hampshire will provide a stream of benefits to the host community, including:

- Approximately $350,000 per year of payments in lieu of property taxes for a 12 MW facility;
- 80+ construction jobs and 25 permanent jobs, representing an annual payroll of nearly $1 million; and
- Residual heat which can serve other business clients in the area.

The project will be constructed and its operational safety and environmental compliance guaranteed by a major turnkey contractor such as General Electric, the contractor on Oxford's California facility. They will utilize a technology with a long-term history of success, reliability, and safety. The process will produce neither smoke nor odor and must meet stringent air quality and other environmental impact limitations.

All aspects of the project, including environmental control, design, operations and financing, must be approved in a series of state review procedures. These reviews, which will include public hearings for local input, must find that the project will not have a significant environmental impact. The state approval will only permit construction to commence. Additional testing to ensure air quality compliance is required before full-scale operations are allowed.

EXHIBIT 3 (CONTINUED)

PROJECT DESCRIPTION

ELECTRICAL GENERATION PLANT

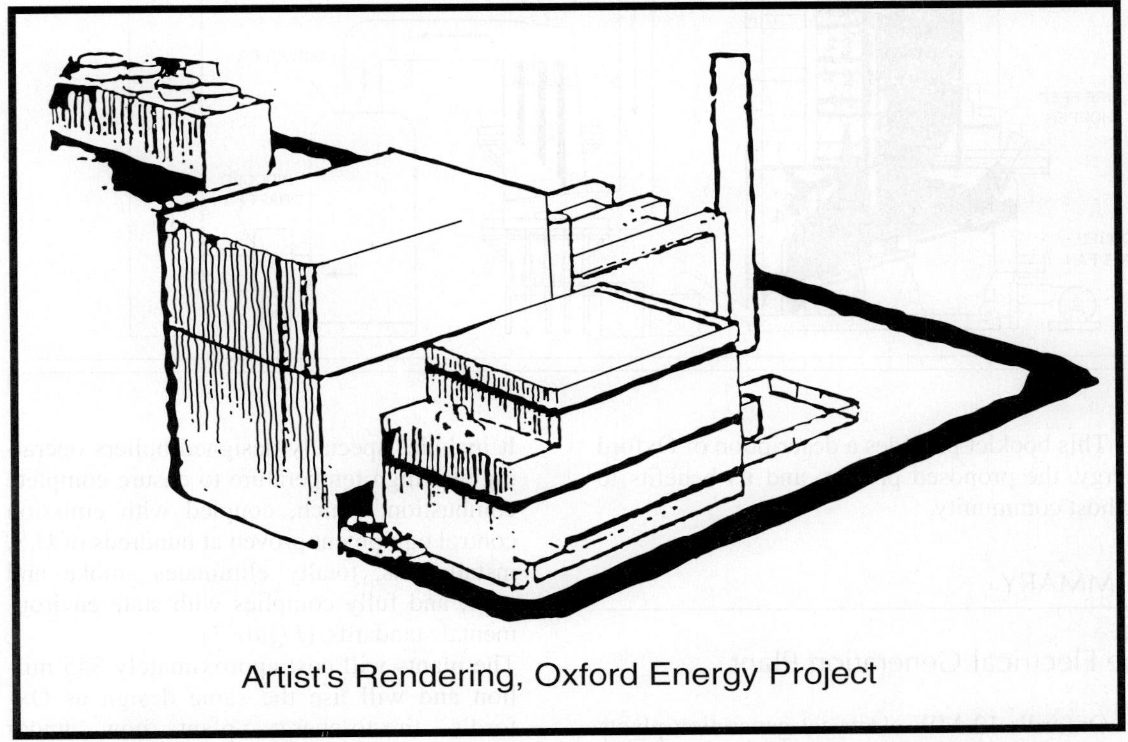

Artist's Rendering, Oxford Energy Project

OXFORD ENERGY COMPANY

MAY 1987

FIGURE 1

SCHEMATIC: TIRE INCINERATION PROJECT

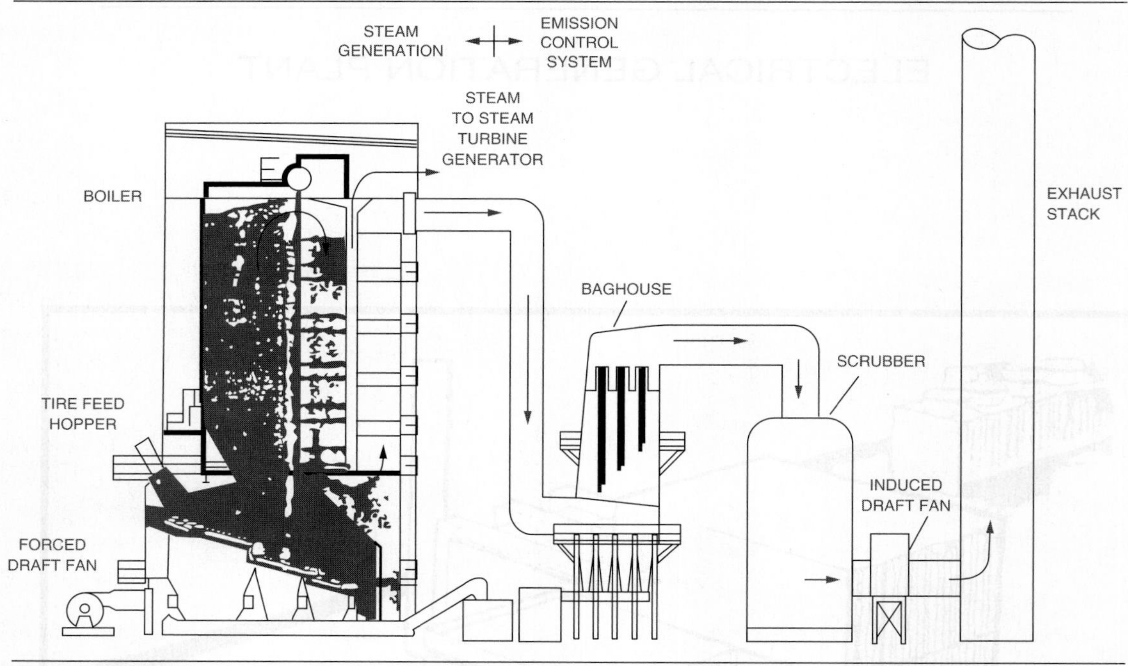

This booklet provides a description of Oxford Energy, the proposed project, and its benefits to the host community.

SUMMARY

The Electrical Generation Plant

- Oxford's 12 MW electrical generation plants are small-scale, located on 6–12 acre sites, using whole discarded tires as fuel to produce steam and electricity (*Exhibit 4*). Typical oil or coal power plants, which use hydrocarbon fuels much like tires, fall in the 300–800 megawatt range.
- The design for these plants has been demonstrated over 15 years of successful operation. It includes specially designed boilers operating at a high temperature to ensure complete combustion, which, coupled with emission control equipment proven at hundreds of U.S. installations, totally eliminates smoke and odor, and fully complies with state environmental standards. (*Figure 1*)
- The plants will cost approximately $45 million and will use the same design as Oxford's tire-to-energy plant now under construction near Modesto, California. The General Electrical Company, selected as general contractor, equipment supplier, and operator, fully warranties the technology and its performance. The Modesto plant design has met California's stringent air quality standards necessary for issuance of its construction permit.

EXHIBIT 3

Benefits to Host Community

- The electrical generation plant will provide an estimated $250,000–$350,000 per year in local community receipts.
- Approximately 25 permanent jobs will be created, with priority to residents.
- The annual payroll is estimated to be nearly $1 million.
- During the 16–18 month construction phase, an additional 80+ jobs will be created.
- The benefits—local revenues, permanent jobs, payroll—are long term. The plant's operation will be secured by a long-term electricity sales contract.

Compliance with Community and State Regulations

- Before it can be constructed or operated, the energy plant will be required to meet all federal and state air, noise, and waste regulations to assure maintenance of community environmental quality. Environmental performance must be tested and verified for compliance before start of operations. Waste management and air quality permits have been granted to Oxford for a site in Danville, New Hampshire.
- The enclosure of most machinery within a building structure and the erection of sound attenuating walls, if required, will assure absence of noise impact and compliance with stringent state and local noise regulations.
- Landscaping of the plant will be developed and maintained in accordance with Planning Board guidelines to assure minimal impact on the community.
- All waste products will be containerized and transported away from the site for recycling or landfilling.
- The plant will involve relatively low volume truck traffic, an estimated 20 loads per day.
- Fuel storage will be strictly maintained to state and community standards; a fire protection system is built into plant design.

Air Quality Concerns

- As shown in *Figure 1*, the plant will emit pollutants at the same rate as about 1000 home heating systems.
- *All* emissions from the plant will be several to hundreds of times lower than the levels considered harmful to humans, plants, or animals as specifically defined by health agencies, as shown in *Figure 2*.
- Because of the highly efficient emission control equipment used, the facility will emit pollutants at a rate similar to many other "clean" industries. This is demonstrated for one pollutant, sulfur dioxide, in *Figure 3*.

About The Oxford Energy Company

- Oxford Energy is headquartered in New York City, with offices in Boston and on the West Coast.
- Oxford is a public company traded in over-the-counter markets.
- Oxford Energy has a record of success in the development, financing, and operation of small-scale, renewable energy projects.
- The company is staffed with energy experts and professionals with specialized expertise in alternative energy project development and financing.
- Oxford presently has 20 renewable energy projects across the United States in various stages of development, construction, or operation, aggregating over $200 million in additions to local tax bases. Collectively, these projects will generate over 500 million kilowatt hours of electrical power annually.

FIGURE 2

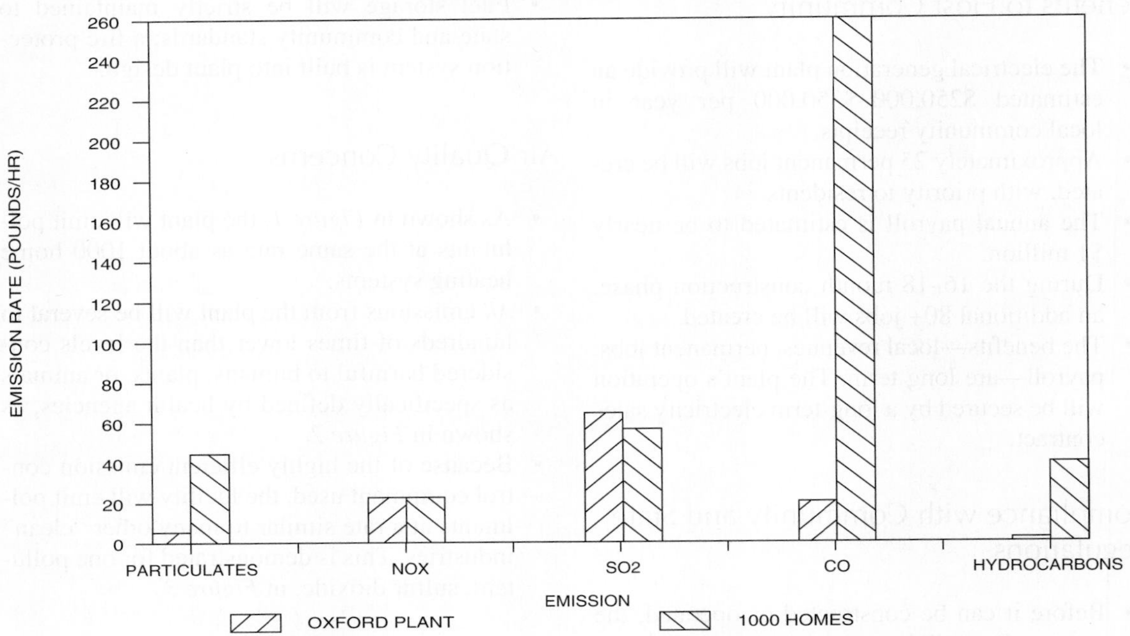

The Oxford Project Team

In addition to its own staff, Oxford brings together world-renowned expertise for its tire-to-energy facilities:

- General Electric—provides high-quality equipment, turnkey construction, and plant performance and environmental guarantees.
- Radian Corporation—one of the largest and best-known environmental consulting firms in America.
- Fichtner Consulting Engineers—internationally recognized engineering and design firm.
- Morgan Stanley and Bear Stearns, two major Wall Street investment banks, will provide debt placement services.

Plant Description

Oxford tire-to-energy projects range in size from 12–28 megawatts. The following describes a 12 megawatt configuration.

A 12 MW electrical generation plant consists of two identical boilers using whole discarded tires as fuel. The steam from the boilers will be fed into a single turbine generator to produce electricity. The electricity will be supplied to the existing electrical grid, where it will be purchased on a long-term contract by the local utility, UNITIL.

The facility will produce about 90 million kilowatt hours of electricity annually. The boiler building will be approximately 70' wide, 100' long, and 90' high. The turbine and generator will be housed in a smaller adjacent building, approximately 40' wide and 100' long. Equipment to clean flue gases will be located in the rear of the main building, with discharge into the 115-foot-high exhaust stack.

The scrap tire fuel will be delivered to the facility and by-products removed by 15 to 20 trucks per day. A plant of this size will consume 4.5 million discarded tires per year. Taking into account seasonal variations in tire consumption and disposal, a varying stockpile of the tire fuel will be

FIGURE 3

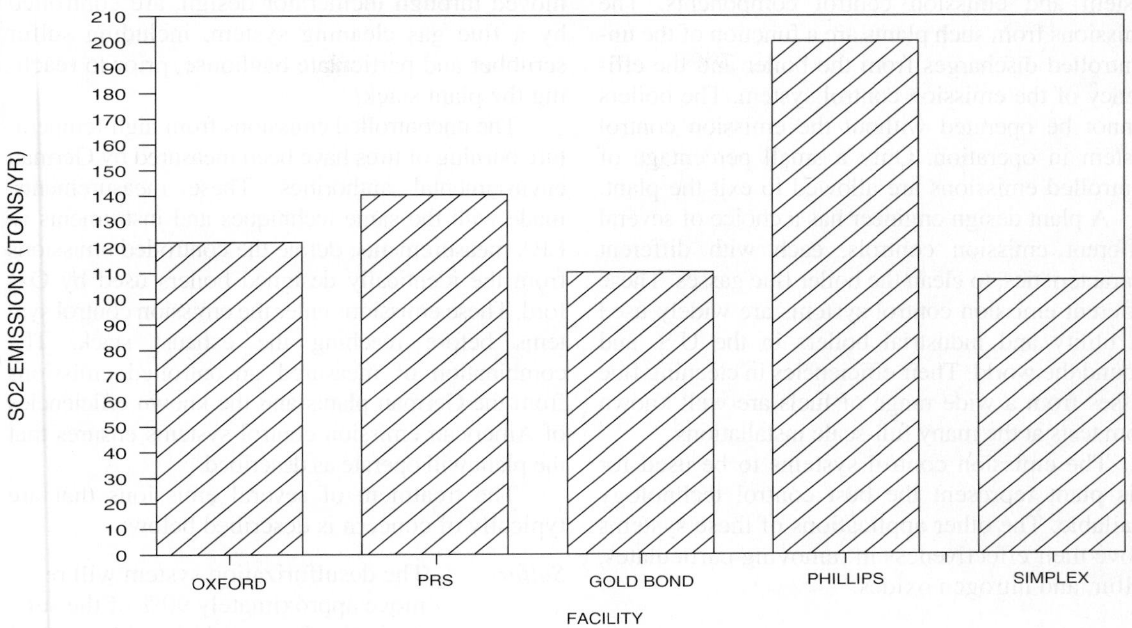

maintained on-site. These tires will be stored in separated, confined piles protected by the plant's built-in fire protection systems. The site will be landscaped to minimize visual impact.

The plant will operate approximately 7500 hours per year, or about 85 percent of the time. The facility will be shut down for preventative maintenance periodically to ensure reliable, safe operations. Operation will be on a 24-hour-a-day basis.

Tires will be fed to the boilers by conveyor. Once in the boiler, the tires will instantly ignite and begin the total combustion process. As the tires move down an inclined grate in the incinerator section of the boiler, all combustible components will be burned until only steel belts and metallic slag remain. This waste, amounting to about 1000 cubic yards per year, will be stored in closed containers and removed for off-site disposal.

Hot gases from the boilers will be used to produce steam for the turbine generator. Exhaust gas from the boilers is directed to a pollution control system, including a flue gas desulfurization system and a fabric filter baghouse, designed to ensure full compliance with state and federal air quality standards. The baghouse will remove over 99% of the particulates emitted by the boilers. The small amount of emissions resulting from the plant will be maintained in strict conformance with state and federal regulations and will be invisible, without odor, and unnoticeable to local residents.

The plant will utilize existing water supplies or its own wells for process water needs of about 250 gallons per minute. The small amount of waste water generated will be discharged to a water treatment system or evaporated in the plant's systems.

Proven Technology

All the components of the plant have been tested in years of full-scale operation. The proven capabilities of the systems give the air quality review agencies, the turnkey builder, Oxford, and the community assurance that the plant will perform as predicted.

All thermal power plants include a combustion system and emission control components. The emissions from such plants are a function of the uncontrolled discharges from the boiler and the efficiency of the emission control system. The boilers cannot be operated without the emission control system in operation. Only a small percentage of controlled emissions are allowed to exit the plant.

A plant design engineer has a choice of several different emission controls, each with different characteristics, to clean the boiler flue gasses. These different emission control systems are widely used on utility and industrial boilers in the U.S. and around the world. Their efficiencies in cleaning flue gasses from a wide range of fuels are well known from tests at the many full-scale installations.

The emission control systems to be used for this plant represent the best control technology available. The other applications of these systems prove their effectiveness in removing particulates, sulfur, and nitrogen oxides.

ENVIRONMENTAL CONSIDERATIONS

Air Quality (Figure 4)

The Oxford electrical generation plant is designed to satisfy all state and federal air quality regulations and guidelines. The controlled emissions from the plant will have no noticeable impact on air quality (See *Figure 4*). The Oxford facility under construction near Modesto, California, has been granted air quality certification with more stringent requirements than are normal for other states. A similar permit has been awarded the proposed Danville, New Hampshire site.

Minimization of environmental impact starts with the design of the facility itself. The boilers are specially designed to burn tires completely. Thus, the black smoke and odor usually associated with burning tires, which is the result of the release of unburned hydrocarbons, are not produced by this plant. The system itself, through its efficient incineration chamber, also minimizes production of nitrogen oxides and other emissions. Particulates and sulfur oxides, which cannot be removed through incinerator design, are controlled by a flue gas cleaning system, including sulfur scrubber and particulate baghouse, prior to reaching the plant stack.

The uncontrolled emissions from high-temperature burning of tires have been measured by German environmental authorities. These measurements, made with the same techniques and instruments as EPA measurements, define the controlled emissions from the identically designed boilers used by Oxford. These emissions enter the emission control systems before reaching the exhaust stack. The combination of measured uncontrolled emissions from the German plants and the known efficiencies of American emission control systems ensures that the plant will operate as described.

The treatment of several emissions that are typically of concern is described below:

Sulfur — The desulfurization system will remove approximately 90% of the sulfur in the flue gas. If the older power plants in the United States had such desulfurization systems, there would be no acid rain problem. Many smaller industrial facilities, which burn oil without sulfur scrubbers, emit many times more sulfur dioxides than the proposed plant.

Dioxins — Dioxins are destroyed when exposed to temperatures in excess of 1800 degrees Fahrenheit for one second. The plant maintains such temperatures for over three and one-half seconds. Dioxins are destroyed before exiting the boiler.

All of the plant's emissions are similarly treated or controlled to ensure that the plant will not have an impact on the health and welfare of the area.

An environmental impact assessment of the facility was completed and reviewed by the New Hampshire Air Resources Agency as part of their issuance of a permit for the Danville site. This

FIGURE 4

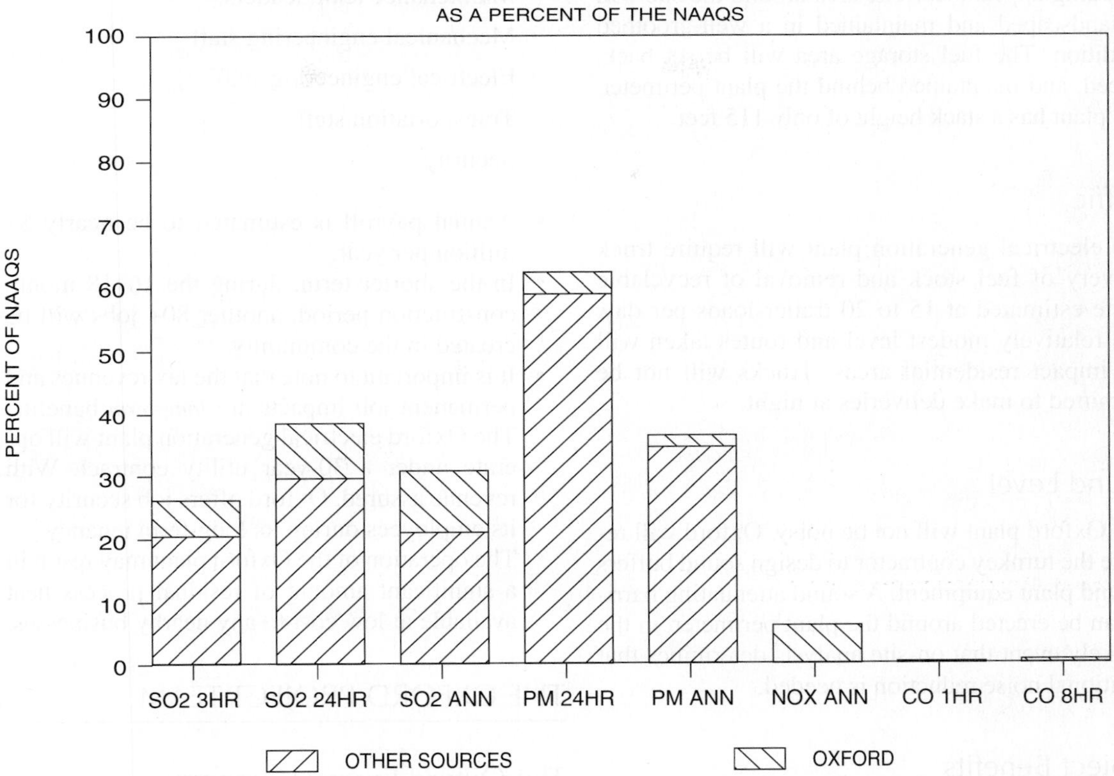

impact assessment has been revised for the Derry site under consideration, with the results shown below. The analysis was conducted utilizing New Hampshire's air quality impact analysis modeling guidelines following a meeting with the staff. The results assume the proposed PRS facility is in full operation in assessing the additional impact of the Oxford Energy facility.

Waste and By-Products

The residues from the combustion of tires are highly recyclable. The steel belts that remain as slag can be used by metal reprocessors. Gypsum, the by-product of the desulfurization system, is a component of wallboard and concrete. The fly ash removed from the flue gasses can be used as fertilizer or as a component of paints. Only when the recycle markets are depressed would we look to landfilling—off-site—of the by-products. No residue from the facility will be landfilled in New Hampshire.

With respect to sewage, the plant can be, and in the case of the Modesto plant was, designed to have no waste water discharge. The maximum discharge would be 20 to 30 gallons per minute of clean, but salty, water. Since the discharge contains no metals, toxics, or sludges, it can be easily handled by the existing water treatment equipment. The final design determination of zero-discharge versus 20–30 gpm of salty water will be made in concert with the sewer authorities.

Appearance

Oxford will comply fully with community standards regarding appearance. The area around the site will be landscaped and maintained in a well-groomed condition. The fuel storage area will be set back, fenced, and maintained behind the plant perimeter. The plant has a stack height of only 115 feet.

Traffic

The electrical generation plant will require truck delivery of fuel stock and removal of recyclable waste estimated at 15 to 20 trailer loads per day. The relatively modest level and routes taken will not impact residential areas. Trucks will not be permitted to make deliveries at night.

Sound Level

The Oxford plant will not be noisy. Oxford will require the turnkey contractor to design sound buffers around plant equipment. A sound attenuating barrier can be erected around the plant perimeter, in the unlikely event that on-site analysis determines that additional noise reduction is needed.

Project Benefits

The location of an Oxford electrical generation plant will provide a substantial flow of short- and long-term benefits to a host community.

Benefits to Community

- The community will receive an estimated $350,000 per year in property taxes and/or other payments from the plant.
- Approximately 25 permanent jobs will be created by the project. Local residents will be given priority in the hiring of plant staff. Permanent positions include:

  Plant manager

  Administrative and clerical staff

  Shift supervisors

  Ash operators

  Materials handlers

  Maintenance team leaders

  Mechanical engineering staff

  Electrical engineering staff

  Transportation staff

  Security

- Annual payroll is estimated to be nearly $1 million per year.
- In the shorter term, during the 16–18 month construction period, another 80+ jobs will be created in the community.
- It is important to note that the tax revenues and permanent job impacts are *long-term* benefits. The Oxford electrical generation plant will operate under a 30-year utility contract. With revenue assured, Oxford offers job security for its employees during its long-term tenancy.
- The operation of the Oxford plant may result in a significant amount of residual process heat available at low cost to any nearby businesses.

THE OXFORD PROJECT TEAM

The Oxford Energy Company

The Oxford Energy Company is headquartered in New York City and has offices in Boston, Massachusetts, and on the West Coast. Oxford is a public company whose stock is traded over-the-counter.

Oxford Energy, its principals, and affiliates have substantial experience in the design, construction, operation, and financing of small-scale energy projects. Oxford employs a staff of energy specialists experienced in all aspects of project development—identification, site specific analysis, engineering, community and agency liaison, environmental mitigation, finance, construction, and operations management.

The principals of Oxford Energy have a record of success in energy development projects. Oxford concentrates solely on alternative and renewable energy project development, and presently has 20 projects in various stages of development, construction, or operation. A partial list of projects in which Oxford, or its principals, has played a significant role follows:

- A 14.0 MW electrical generation facility using whole discarded tires as fuel, located near Modesto, California. This $37 million plant was financed with private capital and a public sale of Industrial Revenue Bonds. The bonds were underwritten by Morgan Stanley and backed by a major international bank. The construction phase, with General Electric as general contractor, commenced in December 1985, with completion scheduled for September 1987. When in operation, the plant will generate 96 million kwh of electricity annually.
- A $120 million, 850 ton per day waste-to-energy facility in Stanislaus, California. Oxford was selected by the county to develop the project and subsequently entered into a purchase and sale agreement with Ogden Martin Systems to construct, own, and operate the facility. Tax-exempt bonds totaling $100 million were sold in December 1985. Construction will commence in mid-1986.
- A 15.0 MW hydroelectric facility located on the Merrimack River in Lawrence, Massachusetts, constructed at a cost of $30 million. The facility, one of the first private power plants in the country, began commercial operation in 1981. It produces 75 million kwh annually.
- 5.3 MW of hydroelectric facilities consisting of eight separate power stations located on New York City's reservoir system. These facilities will be constructed by General Electric and owned and operated by Oxford.
- 11.8 MW of hydroelectric facilities on the Contoocook River in Concord, New Hampshire. Generation commenced at this series of three plants in 1983. When construction of the $29 million system is completed in 1987, the plants will have the ability to produce 46 million kwh annually.
- A 1.0 MW hydroelectric plant on the Nashua River in Nashua, New Hampshire. Generation commenced on this $3 million facility in December 1984. The plant produces 4.5 million kwh annually.

Oxford utilizes world-renowned firms in the development of its projects. These include:

- General Electric Company, which serves as general contractor for the Modesto tire-to-energy plant. General Electric provides detailed design, turnkey construction services and guarantees all aspects of the plant's performance, including compliance with all environmental regulations;
- Radian Corporation, which provides guidance, analysis, and consultation to assure that all environmental standards are satisfied; and
- Fichtner Consulting Engineers, an internationally recognized engineering firm which provides conceptual design and construction management services.

General Electric

Oxford's association with the General Electric Company assures high-quality equipment and construction techniques for the project. Under its agreement with Oxford, General Electric will guarantee all aspects of plant performance, including electrical generation and adherence to environmental and air quality standards. General Electric brings to the project:

- A 100+ year history of excellence in the engineering, construction, and performance of power stations.
- Proven technology in General Electric manufactured electrical generation and emissions environmental control equipment
- Extensive depth and breadth of engineering expertise to assure efficient, reliable, and safe design
- General contracting and construction management capabilities with utilization of local subcontractors
- Years of operation and maintenance experience in all aspects of electrical generating stations

- Guarantees on construction completion, equipment performance, and compliance with environmental regulations

Radian Corporation

With a staff in excess of 1000, Radian is one of the largest environmental consulting firms in the United States. Major areas of expertise include:

- Regulatory analysis and environmental permitting
- Environmental impact assessment
- Solid and hazardous waste management
- Ambient air monitoring
- Evaluation and optimization of pollution control systems
- Source sampling and complete analytical services

Fichtner Consulting Engineers

Since 1922, Fichtner Consulting Engineers, based in Stuttgart,West Germany, has been active in providing public utilities, industrial firms, and government agencies with professional engineering services in the field of energy engineering and the economic usage of energy and heat.

Fichtner is one of the leading independent international consulting firms operating in the following fields:

- Steam power stations for the public and industrial sectors, covering the whole range of fuels and outputs
- Diesel and gas turbine power stations
- Heat supply stations and district heating stations
- Industrial cogeneration stations
- Transmission and distribution of electric power
- Treatment, handling, and disposal of waste materials
- Refuse incineration and energy from waste plants
- Environmental protection technology

Fichtner Consulting Engineers employs a permanent staff of over 400, including more than 300 qualified and experienced engineers, scientists, economists, and ecologists.

Fichtner USA, the domestic subsidiary, is based in Atlanta, Georgia. In addition to its core staff, it draws on head office personnel resources as dictated by project requirements. The subsidiary specializes in energy-related projects that involve the generation, storage, or management of conventional, nonconventional, and renewable energy resources.

Study Questions

1. How should Rettger prepare for his upcoming Derry presentation?
2. How would you analyze his probable audience?
3. What main topics would you suggest for Rettger's speech? How would you organize them?
4. How effective is Oxford Energy's brochure? Does it include unnecessary repetition or overly technical language?
5. What questions should Rettger be prepared to answer?

CASE 12.2

NutraSweet

"By the summer of 1983 we were basking in glory," said Robert Shapiro, President of the NutraSweet Group of G. D. Searle and Company. "We had a wonderful product that provided a solution to a real public need. People were dissatisfied with the choice between sugar and saccharin. Aspartame was the most tested product ever; nothing could be said against it."

In the 1960s, G. D. Searle developed aspartame, an amino-acid compound 200 times sweeter than sugar. After a turbulent, decade-long regulatory review, the Food and Drug Administration (FDA) approved aspartame for use in dry foods in 1981, and the company marketed it under the brand name "NutraSweet." The small NutraSweet Group that launched the product had solved novel marketing and pricing problems, and NutraSweet leapt in sales from $74 million in 1982 to $336 million in 1983. Although G. D. Searle expanded manufacturing facilities rapidly, production could not keep pace with demand.

In December 1983, the NutraSweet Group, which was headquartered near Chicago, got a request from a local CBS affiliate to do a story. The inquiry seemed to be routine; Shapiro and other executives had been carrying out an aggressive schedule of promotional appearances and welcomed the opportunity to do another. Preliminary contacts with the CBS station, however, made it clear that the reporters were raising informed and skeptical questions about NutraSweet. Further contact between G. D. Searle and the staff of the CBS Evening News in January 1984 revealed that Dan Rather, anchor of CBS Evening News,was planning a three-part series on NutraSweet that could raise product safety questions. Since the history of artificial sweeteners had been plagued by health concerns and abrupt product withdrawals, senior management took the threat of negative coverage very seriously.

This case was prepared by Michael E. Hattersley, Lecturer in Communication. Harvard Business School case 389-142.

THE SEARCH FOR A LOW-CALORIE SWEETENER

Aspartame had been subjected to extraordinary regulatory scrutiny between its discovery in 1965 and its first appearance on the market in 1981. In part, this was due to the controversy that had surrounded artificial sweeteners since the nineteenth century. In 1879 two Johns Hopkins University scientists discovered saccharin, a non-caloric coal tar derivative 300 times sweeter than sugar. Although saccharin had a bitter after-taste, it appealed strongly to an increasingly calorie-conscious America. By 1907, when President Theodore Roosevelt proclaimed, "Anyone who says saccharin is injurious to health is an idiot," the sugar substitute was available in a wide variety of canned goods. The Wilson administration, elected in 1912, inaugurated a tougher regulatory atmosphere and saccharin was banned because of health concerns, only to be proclaimed safe again during World War I sugar shortages. Saccharin's checkered approval history foreshadowed the fate of other non-sugar sweeteners.

Although its producers managed to keep saccharin on the market, the search continued for more satisfactory sugar substitutes. In the early 1950s Abbot Laboratories introduced cyclamate, and in 1953, with the introduction of cyclamate-sweetened No-Cal, the diet soda industry was born. In 1958 the Cumberland Packaging Corporation began marketing the cyclamate-based tabletop sweetener Sweet 'n Low. During the 60s, cyclamate, which lacked saccharin's bitter aftertaste, became the nation's best-selling sugar substitute, flavoring canned and baked goods, sodas, candies, cereals, toothpaste, and even cosmetic products. But in 1969, after tests indicated that large doses of cyclamate were associated with cancer, genetic damage, and testicular atrophy, the FDA banned the sweetener. Cumberland Packaging switched Sweet 'n Low to saccharin, which itself remained suspect to many scientists. This history of regulatory reversals created a troubled climate for the introduction of a new sweetener.

In 1965, while working on an anti-ulcer drug, a researcher at G. D. Searle and Company, a prominent pharmaceutical firm, licked his fingers. The sweet taste he noticed was produced by aspartame. It appeared that the search for the perfect non-sugar sweetener was at an end.

Aspartame is a synthetic compound of two amino acids, which are constituents of normal dietary protein. When consumed, aspartame breaks down into phenylalanine and aspartic acid, and methanol. Phenylalanine (fen-al-al-a-neen) and aspartic acid are constituents of meat, fish, and grains. Methanol can be poisonous in high doses, but some vegetables and fruit juices contain higher amounts of methanol than does aspartame. Aspartame has the same number of calories as does protein (four per gram), but because of the tiny amount necessary to produce sweetness, it contributes almost no additional calories to the user's diet. Most people find aspartame's taste very like sugar; unlike saccharin, it has no bitter aftertaste. Aspartame seemed as close as scientists were likely to get to a natural low-calorie sweetener.

THE G. D. SEARLE COMPANY

When it stumbled upon aspartame, G. D. Searle had already established itself as a leading innovator of pharmaceutical products. Production of drugs had become a major industry in the 1920s, when the discovery of sulfa drugs in Germany superseded the age-old tradition of herbal and "patent" medicines. G. D. Searle invested early and well in research and development of organic pharmaceuticals. The company introduced Dramamine, the most common anti-nausea drug; Probanthine, the first truly effective anti-ulcer treatment; Lomotil, a powerful anti-diuretic; and a variety of medications for hypertension.

Due to the success of these products, G. D. Searle had an abundance of cash by the late sixties. The company embarked on a campaign to acquire a wide range of businesses in the human and animal health-care fields.

WINNING APPROVAL OF ASPARTAME

In 1970, G. D. Searle applied for FDA approval of aspartame. Over the next few years it submitted about 90 tests, an unusually high number, in support of its petition. These tests indicated that aspartame could be consumed safely in amounts far exceeding any likely human use. In July of 1974, the FDA approved aspartame for use as a sweetener in dried foods.

At this point, however, the heretofore straightforward approval process for aspartame went off track. Consumer attorney James Turner, a former member of Ralph Nader's Raiders, and Dr. John

Olney, professor of neuropathology and psychiatry at Washington University in St. Louis, petitioned the FDA to reverse its approval on the grounds that aspartame might cause brain tumors or brain damage, especially in children. Their concern centered on the effect that heightened levels of phenylalanine and aspartic acid might have over time on brain chemistry. In 1975, the FDA put the approval on hold and appointed a Public Board of Inquiry on aspartame, a common procedure when a new product is challenged.

Before the Board could be convened, however, an FDA scientist announced he had found irregularities in tests G. D. Searle had submitted on another product, Flagyl, which was a treatment for certain venereal diseases. FDA Commissioner Alexander Schmidt appointed a special task force to review twenty-five G. D. Searle tests on several products including Flagyl and aspartame. In March 1976, the task force reported that "we have found instances of irrelevant or unproductive animal research where experiments have been poorly conceived, carelessly executed or inaccurately analyzed or reported." G. D. Searle responded that the task force's findings were "incomplete, inaccurate in some instances" and drew premature and misleading conclusions. The Public Board of Inquiry was disbanded.

With the approval of aspartame at an impasse, G. D. Searle faced other problems as well. With the exception of the tiny Pearle Vision Centers, G. D. Searle's new acquisitions were not doing well. Moreover, prospects for the pharmaceutical industry as a whole appeared depressed due to a widespread expectation, later proved false, that the Federal Government was about to impose price controls.

In the spring of 1977 G. D. Searle hired the former Congressman and Secretary of Defense Donald Rumsfeld as President. Rumsfeld defined pharmaceuticals and Pearle Vision as G. D. Searle's core businesses, and began to sell off the less successful acquisitions.

Meanwhile, new concerns had arisen about saccharin. Canadian tests had confirmed that saccharin caused bladder cancer in laboratory rats. The FDA recommended an immediate ban on saccharin, but Congress rejected this suggestion after receiving 1,000,000 letters that supported keeping saccharin on the market.

Still, the FDA was interested in a safer alternative to saccharin, and in 1978, it agreed to convene another task force to reexamine three pivotal tests on aspartame. The panel reported some problems with the tests, such as whether the rats had consumed the required amounts of the aspartame components being tested. The FDA then asked a group of pathologists from the Universities Associated for Research and Education in Pathology (UAREP) to review twelve tests. The UAREP board reported that the results of the G. D. Searle tests had been accurately represented to the FDA. Aspartame's critics, however, continued to raise further questions.

In an attempt to resolve the aspartame issue, the FDA appointed a second Public Board of Inquiry on aspartame in 1980. G. D. Searle, the FDA, and aspartame's critics Turner and Olney each appointed one member of the Board. It determined that aspartame couldn't cause brain damage or neuroendocrine regulatory dysfunction, but recommended another long-term test on brain tumors before aspartame was approved. Both Searle and the FDA Bureau of Foods disagreed that another study was needed. At this point, Searle had conducted or sponsored 110 tests on aspartame, and while the methodology of two or three of these had been called into question, no responsible parties had disproved the fundamental finding that aspartame posed no risk to public health. Repeating all the tests would cost G. D. Searle \$30–40 million and take as long as four years.

In April of 1981 President Ronald Reagan appointed Arthur Hull Hayes as FDA Commissioner. In July, Hayes, relying partly on a newly released Japanese study that "appears to be negative in terms of brain tumors," approved the use of aspartame in dry foods. Commissioner Hayes stated, "Few compounds have withstood such detailed testing and repeated close scrutiny, and the process through which aspartame has gone should provide the public with additional confidence of its safety." Two of the three members of the 1980 Public Board of Inquiry subsequently endorsed this position. James Turner, now representing the

Community Nutrition Institute, a public interest group, charged that Hayes had "picked his way through a mass of scientific mismanagement, improper procedures, wrong conclusions, and general scientific inexactness."

A cautionary note was sounded in a *Science* magazine article entitled "Aspartame Approved Despite Risks" (August 1981). It quoted John Olney as saying that his interpretation of the aspartame studies "is not that aspartame is a proven neuro-oncogen (cause of brain tumors), but that currently available evidence on the issue is contradictory, inconclusive, and of dubious reliability." However, the article gave equal prominence to Commissioner Hayes' view of his regulatory role: "I do not think most people expect zero risk. I'm not prepared to say there is no risk from aspartame—I'd say that for very few things. But I thought it had been demonstrated that there was no significant risk." The article suggested that the criticism of aspartame "stemmed in part from [the] belief that it was only of psychological, not physiological, benefit to the public. Hayes says that psychological benefits can be just as important."

MARKETING NUTRASWEET

Suddenly, after many years of scientific and regulatory dispute over aspartame, G. D. Searle was confronted with a different set of challenges. How should it be marketed? Was this even the sort of business that Searle, a pharmaceutical company, should be in, or should it license out aspartame? On the one hand, Searle had encountered serious difficulties moving into newproduct areas in the 1970s. On the other, the company had cash to invest.

In late 1981, Donald Rumsfeld committed G. D. Searle to marketing aspartame, and he set up a team headed by Robert Shapiro, G. D. Searle's General Counsel, to manage the effort. They faced the traditional problems of any new business: developing manufacturing capabilities, defining their markets, and setting up an effective management structure. But they confronted a more unusual challenge as well: defining the product itself. Rumsfeld had told the team, "We're going to sell this, but we don't know what it is."Was aspartame a relatively exotic product for hard-core dieters? Should it be marketed like saccharin, or did it have the potential to expand into new areas for low-calorie sweeteners? Should it be sold independently or included anonymously in already-existing diet products?

Shapiro initiated some market tests to address these questions. In association with companies such as Borden, Lipton, and Heinz, aspartame was tried on representative groups of consumers as a sweetener in dried foods. Although the results were good, Shapiro said, "They didn't go through the roof, as we had expected." Further examination of these preliminary test results convinced the team that the problem was not the taste of aspartame, which most users found very close to sugar, but rather the clouded reputation of artificial sweeteners in general. Consumers felt that the products being tested must be sweetened either with saccharin, which had been explicitly associated by prominent authorities with health risks, or with an anonymous new sweetener whose properties were unknown.

The solution, Shapiro decided, was to give aspartame a clear identity and to distinguish it decisively in the public mind from the reputation of previous artificial sweeteners. By late 1982 G. D. Searle had committed to the strategy of marketing an ingredient. It chose the name "NutraSweet" to emphasize that aspartame contained only nutritive protein present in many natural foods. Once the fact was established in consumers'minds that there was a safe new sweetener, product labels could simply advertise "contains NutraSweet." NutraSweet's actual customers, companies such as General Foods,would be relieved of the burden of educating consumers in the complex sweetener debate. G. D. Searle considered the argument that publicizing the new sweetener might attract critics who would not be drawn to an anonymous ingredient listed on a side label. But in the end, the high-profile approach was adopted, Shapiro said, "because we were absolutely convinced there was nothing bad you could say about this product."

Shapiro's six-person team, now named "The NutraSweet Group," found itself in a unique position for marketers of a new product: because of the drawn-out approval process it had a large supply of aspartame ready to go. In 1974, anticipating imminent FDA approval, G. D. Searle had ordered a large batch of aspartame from the Japanese firm Ajinomoto, the world's largest amino-acid manufacturer. In 1980, G. D. Searle had written off this investment. But because aspartame had an extremely long shelf-life, the NutraSweet Group inherited, at no cost, a substantial supply of aspartame which it could begin selling at a profit immediately.

The NutraSweet Group hired the Chicago advertising firm of Ogilvey & Mather to help organize a promotional campaign in advance of the product's national launch. Print advertisements began in March 1983, featuring bold headings and extensive text discussing the NutraSweet breakthrough. A campaign offering free NutraSweet gumballs to anyone who returned a coupon was particularly successful: over three million people responded. Shapiro, who had originally budgeted only a small percentage of his time for communication tasks, found himself serving as the spearhead of a massive promotional effort, visiting shopping centers to oversee consumer try-outs, criss-crossing the country to speak personally with reporters and food editors, and appearing on local and national talk-shows. Four million dollars were originally allocated for this effort, but by mid-1983 the group had spent nearly nine million.

The results of this initial advertising blitz convinced the NutraSweet Group that huge numbers of consumers were deeply dissatisfied with the choice between sugar and saccharin. The response from specialists in the food industry and the press was equally enthusiastic.

With demand for the product exploding, the tiny NutraSweet Group confronted an enormous production challenge. Market studies predicted huge growth in demand for NutraSweet, and Shapiro committed to a rapid expansion of production. Twenty-five million dollars were allocated to expand Ajinomoto's aspartame facilities, and an additional thirty million were committed to producing phenylalanine and aspartic acid in newly acquired plants in Michigan and Illinois. Even these facilities proved insufficient, and in 1983 the Group commissioned yet another production plant in Georgia. By the time of NutraSweet's national launch in 1983, Searle had invested $200 million in the product.

In April of 1983, Kool Aid with NutraSweet and Equal, NutraSweet's table-top competitor to Sweet 'n Low, hit the shelves. The consumer response was extremely enthusiastic. "I felt," Shapiro said, "like a kid who had asked for a pony and been put on top of Secretariat." From late 1982 to late 1983, The NutraSweet Group expanded from the original 6 to over 300 people. Shapiro was later to say, "The NutraSweet Group was given the mission of creating a major business in a year. The marketing achievement is visible, but I'm even prouder of the manufacturing achievement."

Another tough issue was pricing. G. D. Searle's patent on aspartame had been running during the regulatory delays, but in 1982 Congress extended it until 1992. This gave the company some breathing space to profit from its investment in NutraSweet. But how should the NutraSweet Group price the product? Traditional yardsticks such as cost and return seemed inadequate for several reasons. For one, the history of artificial sweeteners was clouded with safety controversies, new product introductions, and reversals of the FDA's position. For another, it could be argued that Nutra Sweet was a unique product with no direct competitors, since its taste was so decisively superior to saccharin. It was possible that Nutra Sweet would find itself with a virtual monopoly of the artificial sweetener market; at the same time it was possible that a new competitor would suddenly appear on the scene. Should NutraSweet develop a pricing policy based on the presumption of long, slow growth or should it attempt to charge whatever the traffic would bear?

This decision was further complicated by the fact that NutraSweet had, potentially, very different values to different customers. This value was largely determined by how much NutraSweet could lower the calorie count of a given product. As a table-top sugar substitute, for example, NutraSweet could virtually eliminate caloric intake, and consequently had a sales value of about $400 per pound. Its value was equally high in areas where it essentially created a new product such as sugar-free Kool Aid—children would not drink anything flavored with saccharin. At the other end, for example as a sweetener in dairy products such as ice cream, NutraSweet could only reduce calories by about one-third. In such products, the value to a food manufacturer of NutraSweet might be as low as $30 per pound.

The pricing decision grew even more significant as it became clear in early 1983 that the FDA was about to approve use of NutraSweet in soft drinks, which would enormously expand its market. Based on these considerations, the NutraSweet Group made a virtually unprecedented decision: different customers would be charged different prices for NutraSweet, depending on the end use and the value of the product to them. Shapiro later called this "a billion-dollar decision."

MANAGING SUCCESS

By late 1983, the NutraSweet Group was relishing its success. Aspartame had survived a grueling series of regulatory challenges and had been approved for use in many countries around the world. Its patent had been extended, consumers and nutritional experts alike had responded with unprecedented enthusiasm, and the business itself was running smoothly. The only clouds on the horizon seemed extremely small. A University of Arizona Professor, Woodrow Monte, had raised some concerns about the breakdown products produced when diet soda sweetened with aspartame was stored for long periods at high temperatures, and *Forbes* magazine had recently reviewed Turner's and Olney's questions about aspartame's safety. Dr. Richard Wurtman of MIT had also expressed concern that large amounts of aspartame might affect brain chemistry over time.

It was at this point that Shapiro received the request for the interview with the local CBS affiliate. As the interview progressed, it became clear that CBS had carefully combed the FDA records for any information or allegations that would call NutraSweet's safety into question.

In anticipation of unfavorable media attention, John Robson, NutraSweet's Executive Vice President and CEO, prepared a memorandum recommending, among other steps:

1. Quickly analyzing viewer reaction survey results after the Rather series,
2. Contacting major national newspapers and newsmagazines,
3. Developing a concentrated response to Monte in Arizona, including broad press contacts, approaches to major political figures, and discussions with the Arizona Health Department,
4. Calling a major press conference,
5. Writing immediately after the series to CBS News to point out any inaccuracies in the series,
6. Developing a "seeding blitz" of expert teams to visit food writers and editors around the country to generate positive stories, and
7. Considering a major media advertising offensive.

NutraSweet's public relations firm, Burson Marsteller, prepared a crisis communication plan which presumed a "worst case" scenario in which the upcoming broadcasts were shown to have seriously damaged consumer attitudes towards NutraSweet. The recommendations included preparing:

1. A pre-produced video newsclip for television,
2. A pre-produced radio newsclip,
3. An all-purpose news release,
4. A telegram to be sent to medical audiences,
5. A white paper covering all safety issues, and
6. A question-and-answer brochure aimed at the general public.

The firm also recommended a twenty-city media tour by top NutraSweet executives, and special approaches to national medical and health associations, financial analysts, trade publications, customer headquarters and sales forces, international product regulators, and Searle employees.

Shapiro feared that NutraSweet would fall victim to "fill-in-the-blank" reporting. He was particularly concerned about the upcoming CBS News series. Reporters had a limited number of prefabricated stories, he contended, and they squeezed the facts to fit their alarmist formulas. In this case, they were determined to report: "company foists unsafe product on consumers to reap huge profits." In view of consumers' experience with the safety claims for products such as cigarettes, the public was probably predisposed to accept such reporting as fact.

In Shapiro's view, all the questions raised about NutraSweet's safety were both false and old news. The problems with certain tests G. D. Searle had conducted or commissioned, he believed, had been thoroughly explored and resolved during the exhaustive FDA review. Monte's expressed concerns about methanol boiled down to "asserting the world was flat." Although methanol could be poisonous at high doses, it had been clearly demonstrated that no conceivable diet could contain enough aspartame to raise methanol to dangerous levels. Wurtman's concerns about the subtle, long-term effects of phenylalanine on neurotransmission were virtually impossible to test, and no evidence existed to support them. The introduction of any new product routinely provoked a rash of unverified consumer complaints.

Shapiro was absolutely convinced that no scientific case could be made against NutraSweet. But he wondered how this point could be made convincingly to the public within the framework of a television news story.

Study Questions

1. How should a manager factor public relations considerations into product planning, service development, or policy changes that are likely to become public?
2. Who should be involved in developing an organization's public relations campaign?
3. How can you best utilize any resource or individual who has developed a track record of credibility with the press and public?
4. How should the personal qualities of executives determine who should be put in front of the press?
5. How should a manager or a managerial team prepare for an interview or a press conference?
6. How credible are NutraSweet's critics, and how should Shapiro and company respond to them?
7. If a similar situation occured today, how would you utilize electronic communications such as E-mail and Web sites?

CHAPTER 13

Diversity and Intercultural Communicaton

Organizations that operate entirely within the United States deal, consciously and unconsciously, with intercultural issues all the time. Advertisers don't run the same sorts of product campaigns in New York or Miami that they would in Kansas. Government agencies and nonprofit institutions seek to include the full range of racial, ethnic, and linguistic spectra of the communities they serve. Marketers of entertainment or style often seek to establish a niche first in gay communities because these consumers are perceived as "fashion-forward," that is, trendsetters. The melting pot is not entirely melted. All these considerations need to be factored into how an organization is perceived or a product marketed.

DIVERSITY

As issues of race, gender, ethnicity, language, and sexual orientation become hotter and hotter in national politics, they equally affect the workplace. Should an African-American boss discuss the outcome of a recent interracial trial with his white secretary? Should an otherwise fine Hispanic employee be told her English language skills aren't up to snuff? Should she be offered help? Should people avoid language that could be perceived as sexist, even if they're joking? Is it appropriate for a Gentile to use a Yiddish expression when speaking to a Jewish coworker? Should you routinely ask about the partner of a gay colleague? Generally, the best answer to these questions is yes, but it always depends on the personal as well as the business aspects of your relationship. One good rule of thumb: When the other person gives you an opening, pursue it, and build on your mutual experience.

This issue comes up even more in international communication. As companies from manufacturers to media conglomerates become increasingly global, managers need to understand the norms of other cultures. Although English is on the verge of becoming *the* international language, standards of behavior and social interaction vary greatly between the United States and England, let alone between, say, France and Japan. In one country an invitation to dinner may be considered an expected politeness, while in another, it may be an invasion of a colleague's private time. Asking about someone's family may be absolutely required in one culture and offensively intrusive in another.

No textbook can cover all such contingencies; one good rule if you're not sure may be the trial lawyer's: Don't ask a question to which you don't already know the answer. Another, and sometimes contradictory, rule is: Be frank about your cultural confusion. Your colleague likely will have been in the same situation himself and will be happy to help out. Finally, do your research; you're likely to have a friend or coworker who knows the terrain better than you do. Our purpose here is to sensitize managers to their increasing need to understand the norms of cultures other than their own. (For a case addressing the special features of international communication, see *International Oil* later in this chapter.)

The opportunities for cultural confusion—personal, commercial, ethical, and linguistic—are almost endless. Imagine marketing a Chevy Nova in Hispanic countries, where "no va" means "it doesn't run." Many products that are perfectly safe to market in first-world countries raise ethical problems when sold in developing countries—infant baby formula, for example, which if mixed with contaminated water can cause death. Working in other cultures means understanding your hosts' conceptions of greetings, timing, hygiene, negotiation, agreement, politeness, personal space, gesture, meal etiquette, and closure.

INTERCULTURAL COMMUNICATION

In an increasingly global market, managers often find themselves communicating with bosses and employees in cultures radically different from their own. American executives may report to superiors in Japan or England; German companies may have their main markets in Africa; businesses in any number of countries may be farming out their manufacturing to China; U.S. or European oil executives may spend much of their careers working in the Arab world or Indonesia. Communicating across cultural divides poses special challenges. The rise of the Internet has created a situation where anyone can talk to almost anyone else instantaneously. This situation has its advantages, but it also poses special risks of misunderstanding.

While English has essentially become the international language, it's important to remember that *there are many Englishes*. A joke in one form of English can be a deadly insult in another. Although it may seem too obvious to emphasize, you must understand the cultural norms and language use of people from other cultures before you can communicate effectively with them. This is true even if they are, say, the South American employees of your Canadian company. A bribe in one culture can be a thoughtful gift in another.

A recent article by Sydel Sokuvitz (*Business Communication Quarterly*, New York, March, 2002) suggests some principles for conducting successful intercultural business communication. Sokuvitz first describes the special challenges global managers face, including:

Coping with a range of tensions that arise out of internationally dispersed activities,

The challenges of maintaining coordinated activities across time-zones, cultural boundaries, and different countries' laws, and

The difficulties posed when the right medium for your message in one culture may be wrong in another.

Drawing on a range of research in the field, Sokuvitz comes up with several provocative conclusions:

Excessive dependence on technological communication such as E-mail can result in problems for both communication and productivity.

Face-to-face meetings with colleagues from other cultures are critical to achieving effective communication.

Studying with students from other cultures is critical to preparing a manager for working in the increasingly globalized economy.

Sokuvitz cites the following example from an article by Fernandez-Aroaz ("Hiring without Firing," *Harvard Business Review*, 1999):

> A U.S.-based telecommunications company was seeking a CEO for its new division in Latin America. An international search was conducted, and a veteran was hired, someone known as an effective manager and marketing expert. "But his run lasted less than a year and was nothing short of a disaster. The simple reason was that he lacked the two skills that the job really required: negotiation and cross-cultural sensitivity."
>
> Eventually the company was saved from near-bankruptcy by bringing in a new CEO who was a native Latin American with work experience in the U.S. His ability to bridge cultural differences is credited with saving the company.

Communications between headquarters and subsidiaries is only one example of the challenges posed by globalization. Companies in one country are under increasing social pressure to take responsibility for the behavior of their subcontractors in other countries. Recently, for example, Nike suffered adverse publicity because of the work practices of shoe manufacturers it employs in Asia.

The successful manager of the future increasingly will be required to be a citizen of the world. While electronic communication may work fine for conveying information or directions, there is no substitute for "speaking the language" of the people with whom you're trying to communicate.

Reed-Watkins Pharmaceuticals

Kirk Lewis had just returned from the first quarter regional kick-off meeting. The past year had been a most challenging yet rewarding year for Kirk. He was appointed General Manager for the Southwest Region for Reed-Watkins Pharmaceuticals. Faced with opening a new office in Phoenix, Kirk had to focus most of his efforts on getting the Southwest office up and running while dealing with the challenges of the recent merger. Kirk was caught off guard when he was approached by one of his managers at the regional office.

Leslie Wilson was the youngest member of the management team. She had been promoted to district manager and moved to the southwest following the merger a year ago. Although less tenured than other managers, she had progressed rapidly in her position and had earned the respect of her peers as well as Kirk for her management skills. When Leslie asked Kirk to speak privately about a "sensitive" issue, he was puzzled and worried. He could tell from her facial expression that she had a serious concern. Leslie sat down with Kirk and related a conversation she had last evening with her sales representative at the regional dinner.

During the regional meeting that week, Will Roberts, Leslie's top representative and recipient of the President's Cup Award, expressed his concern about his future at Reed-Watkins. He told Leslie that he no longer felt comfortable in an organization that employed so few African Americans. To prove his point he asked Leslie to look around the room of 250 people. Leslie was surprised when she counted only seven individuals of color. Now she understood his point of view.

Kirk wasn't sure how to respond to Leslie or to Will. He had always supported diversity with his employees. He remembered that he sent a communication to the region last year promising to bring the issue to prominence in the organization. He had even contacted human resources to find out about the status of the former Reed diversity initiative. At that time he was told that while this was an important issue, the main priority for the organization was to ensure the successful completion of the merger while maintaining sales and profits. Until further notice, all previous corporate initiatives were placed on hold and would be reviewed sometime in the future.

BACKGROUND

Reed-Watkins Pharmaceuticals was formed in 2000 as a result of the merger of two British drug companies that were each founded over 200 years ago. Both Reed and Watkins maintained broad product portfolios although few of their products directly competed. Reed and Watkins had roughly 50,000 employees each worldwide. Although both corporations were based in England, their corporate cultures and management styles were quite different.

For most of its history, Reed incorporated a paternalistic management style. Employees joined the corporation for life and enjoyed long careers. Upper management valued experience and fostered a family atmosphere. The home office maintained a hands-off attitude toward the U.S. division since it was the corporation's largest and most profitable division.

The U.S. division of Reed in turn managed its employees in much the same way. They believed that decision making and accountability should be brought to the lowest level possible. Decisions did not have to go up and down the chain of command. They believed in empowering their management team and implemented training programs to ensure employees had the skills and tools to support this philosophy. In addition, they believed that diverse work teams were the most effective. In the 1990s Reed formally implemented many of the contemporary management approaches such as "empowerment," "cross functional teams," and "diversity."

Watkins Pharmaceuticals also had British roots, but its management style and corporate culture evolved quite differently than Reed's. All divisions of Watkins were managed by corporate. The U.K. had to be consulted for most decisions. Like Reed, the U.S. division of Watkins was the largest and most profitable for the company. However, the Watkins corporate management kept close tabs on operations in the U.S. since its success or failure would affect the entire organization's performance. In turn, the U.S. division's management used the same hands-on style with its employees. Empowerment, cross-functional teams, and diversity initiatives were non-existent at Watkins.

THE MERGER

The pharmaceutical industry enjoyed large profits until the early 1990s. After that, however, governmental cost controls and the increase in managed care forced the industry to maintain prices while their research and development costs continued to skyrocket. Mergers between drug giants were necessary in order to remain competitive and to gain critical mass in research and development dollars. In 2000, Reed and Watkins merged to form the second largest pharmaceutical company in worldwide sales and fourth in the United States. Stockholders were pleased with the result. With complementary portfolios, the newly created Reed-Watkins organization could maintain all products while reducing overhead and administrative costs. The merger would enable the new entity to compete globally. Total combined sales would be over $30 billion. Following the merger, the top management position went to the CEO of Watkins while the CEO of Reed was named second in command. It was clear from the onset that Watkins management would be in control of the new organization.

WILL ROBERTS

Will Roberts, an African American, joined Reed Pharmaceuticals in 1980. For most of his career, Will had an above average performance. Prior to the merger, Will was contemplating a move into management or to another position with greater responsibility. He was assigned to serve on Reed's regional diversity task force in 1998 and was actively involved in the "Career Development" and "Mentoring" subcommittees. After the merger, Will continued to maintain an informal network with other African Americans who were involved in the diversity initiative.

KIRK LEWIS

Based in England, Kirk Lewis began his career with Reed Pharmaceuticals in 1983 as a sales representative and worked his way through the management ranks. In 1990, he landed a position in the marketing department with the U.S. division. His career continued upward, and in 1996 Kirk was promoted to Business Director for the Southwest Region located in Dallas. In the early 1990s, Kirk was one of the initial supporters of Reed's corporate diversity initiative. He was convinced of the value of a diverse organization and implemented programs in his region to support this belief. Kirk

EXHIBIT 1

Reed-Watkins Pharmaceuticals Kirk Lewis, General Manager

Date: March 5, 2000
To: Southwest Region
From: Kirk Lewis

Subject: Diversity and Sensitivity

Over the past two years Reed had been involved in a "Diversity Initiative," its primary goal being to highlight the differences that exist among customers and ourselves, and the *benefit* differences can bring to an organization. "Differences" can be defined as experience, educational background, race, gender, position, age, religion, etc. As an example, many of our customers are becoming much more diverse in their ethnicity, gender, and age and if we are to be successful we need to recognize this, be sensitive to it, and involve diverse groups from our own organization to better help our customers.

While I don't anticipate this brief memo to fully clarify and explain to you the benefits of diversity, I do hope it will at least begin to raise your level of awareness to the importance of *involving everyone in decision-making* and the importance of being *sensitive and respectful of others who may be different from you.* Remember, even though appearances may be similar, we are all different in our own way and we need to be aware of this when dealing with each other and our customers.

Over time, I hope to bring this vital issue to greater prominence throughout the Southwest region and the Reed-Watkins organization. In the meantime, please play a leadership role in respecting and being sensitive to others. Also, please feel free to speak to your manager and/or myself regarding your thoughts and recommendations to promote diversity and respect.

Best Regards,

Kirk Lewis

always maintained an open management style and solicited input and feedback from his employees on key decisions affecting the business. Following the announcement of the merger with Watkins, Kirk was promoted to General Manager of the Southwest for the new organization.

Kirk was excited about the opportunity afforded to him to develop an expansion region in the Southwest. Neither Reed nor Watkins had an existing office in Phoenix, so Kirk needed to secure an office location, move his family, and successfully merge a new team of 24 managers and 250 sales representatives. The merger was truly a logistical challenge as headquarters mandated a balance of former Reed and former Watkins employees in all positions. Kirk carefully formed his team to comply with this decree and for the first few months all seemed to be going relatively smoothly.

Although Kirk understood that the former Watkins management style was the expected norm, he was uncomfortable with the top-down management approach. Kirk continued to operate as he had under the old organization. Most employees were pleased to see Kirk maintain an empowering team approach. There were some employees, however, who looked for more direction and felt uncomfortable making their own decisions. Kirk hoped that he could convince upper management of the value of empowerment and the Reed style of management. He knew that this would take time, and he needed to learn the politics of the new organization before he challenged upper management.

On March 1, 2000, Kirk held his first management meeting. It was the first interaction between managers following the merger. A few days after the meeting, several former Reed employees contacted Kirk complaining about the lack of sensitivity that they experienced from several of the former Watkins employees. One manager said that he overheard racial jokes at dinner, and another was surprised with the "my-way or the highway" attitude of the former Watkins managers. They knew that under the old organization this was unacceptable, but they wanted to know if this behavior would now be tolerated in the new organization. Several managers also inquired about the diversity initiative that had been ongoing at Reed. Would this initiative continue with the merged organization? Kirk's response came in a memo of March 5, 2000 (*Exhibit 1*). The memo was received positively by most former Reed employees as they felt that Kirk would surely move forward to address the issue in the organization. Many of the Watkins employees were confused and were unclear about the purpose of the memo. Everyone in the region seemed to be maintaining a wait-and-see attitude.

When Will Roberts received Kirk's memo in March of 2000, he was hopeful that the diversity initiative would be resurrected with the new organization. Will had worked hard to raise the awareness of the diversity issue with the former Reed employees. However, since the merger, Will had seen a rapid decline in the hiring of African Americans and many of his colleagues left the company. Although this past year was the best of his 20-year career, Will began to question his "fit" with the new organization. He was also wondering what happened to Kirk's pledge to bring the diversity issue to more prominence in the region and the organization.

Study Questions

1. Evaluate Kirk's letter of 5 March 2000. See Exhibit 1. What message does it send? How well has he considered the different segments of his audience? What expectations did he raise?
2. What message did Kirk's lack of communication about diversity after March 2000 send to his various audiences? How should he address the issue of follow-up if he wishes to make up for lost time?
3. If Kirk wishes to retain Will Roberts as an employee, how should he respond to the information provided by Leslie Wilson?
4. How (if at all) should Kirk address the issue of insensitive remarks made by former Watkins employees?
5. Outline the steps Kirk might take to re-invigorate the diversity initiative he announced in March 2000. To whom should he speak or write? In what order? What should he say? What pitfalls should he strive to avoid? Does he have an obligation to push this initiative beyond his own territory? Why or why not?

CASE 13.2

International Oil

Claus Schwaneger, head of field operations for International Oil, was receiving an increasing chorus of questions and complaints from his regional and country directors, who managed explorations and sales over a wide region that stretched from central Africa to east Asia. Although the concerns he found expressed in telephone calls, E-mail messages, memos, and meetings varied, they had a central theme: Various company policies were putting International Oil at a competitive disadvantage, especially in developing countries.

BACKGROUND

Schwaneger figured that some of these problems were growing pains. International Oil was a fairly new conglomerate that had grown out of the European Economic Community (EEC). Its purpose: to provide a united European competitive front against other major international producers and distributors, especially those from the United States and the Arabian peninsula. International Oil didn't drill or sell; its job was to identify opportunities and distribute them fairly among the major European oil companies including British Petroleum and Dutch Shell so that EEC members weren't directly competing against one another. The idea was that International Oil could often put together an attractive bid on a new project by combining the resources and strengths of various European companies. Some companies were stronger on exploration, others on drilling, still others on marketing. A package drawing on all these strengths could often beat bids by the major U.S. and Saudi oil giants in developing fields and markets. But Schwaneger knew the company was stretched thin; it had cast a wide net and often had to send inexperienced managers into relatively uncharted territories. Many of the far-flung managers, who often needed to coordinate their activities, knew each other primarily via E-mail, and the company was considering annual vacation/business conferences so people could put faces together with names.

International Oil also faced some fierce internal competition. Most of its staff had been drawn from major existing European giants, especially Britain, Holland, Germany, and France. With reluctance on the part of some employees, English had become the company's internal language of choice. While this was fine with executives from Germany, Holland, and the Nordic countries, it created some friction with those from France and southern Europe. More important, various nationals tended to push the interests, and retain the practices, of their own respective countries. Top executives had adopted an informal policy of assigning managers

This case was prepared by Michael E. Hattersley © 2003.

to areas outside their own country's national interests; for example, an Englishman was in charge of operations in Indonesia, traditionally a Dutch preserve, while a German woman ran the division that covered the former British colonies in Africa. This often produced strong objections from the member oil companies, which had entered the consortium reluctantly and under political pressure.

International Oil employed about 5000 workers. Many of these, especially the headquarters staff in Brussels, Belgium, were "on loan" from major European government agencies and oil companies. In the field, the leadership tended to be European, while the support staff tended to be employees recruited locally.

POLITICAL AND SOCIAL PRESSURES ON INTERNATIONAL OIL

In the wake of the joint U.S.-British invasion of Iraq, new opportunities for contracts had opened up for International Oil in the Middle East. British troops now controlled the enormous southern Iraqi oil fields. But other major EEC members, especially France and Germany, had opposed the invasion. France, in particular, had maintained lucrative economic and trade relations with Saddam Hussein's regime, which had been deeply in debt to both France and Russia. Both countries wanted their debts honored by Iraq. Meanwhile, the U.S. government seemed determined to block access to Iraq's oil reserves to countries that had opposed the invasion.

Moreover, many constituencies and activist groups who had the ear of the European parliament were demanding that European companies who did business overseas enforce the same environmental, employment, and even animal rights standards followed in Europe.

FIELD MANAGERS' CONCERNS

Schwaneger cleared his desk and took a day to sort out the range of complaints he had received. They fell into a few basic categories:

1. Sometimes I feel members of my own staff from different countries are working against themselves and one another.
2. Our ethical policies, especially those against offering gifts or bribes to local decision makers, are hurting our competitive position.
3. Members of our staff refuse to master the local language or adapt themselves to cultural norms.
4. Often, by the time headquarters has cut a deal with the European oil companies, some competitor has already won the bid.

Schwaneger thought about these issues overnight, and then decided to organize a satellite conference to get these managers talking to one another. He asked each to take five or ten minutes to outline her or his concerns and share experiences. Some typical results:

Jose Aldamar, south Asia:

People at home don't recognize that wining, dining, and gift-giving isn't considered bribery or corruption in my region. In fact it's the essence of politeness. In some areas, the decision-making bureaucrats are supporting whole clans, and get high government jobs with the expectation that they will care responsibly for their own people. It's almost a form of state welfare. If we refuse to play, we'll continue to lose out to competitors who understand this better than we do. The word here is "baksheesh." It really means a sort of consideration, a gesture of respect. They are giving us something, and deserve something in return to preserve their honor and status. We're going to lose out if we continue to insist on imposing European values. It's perceived as arrogance.

Michael Carl, Middle East:

Oil contracting here is in a state of chaos. Nobody in power from Saudi Arabia knows whether they'll be in a position a year from now to enforce existing contracts, let alone sign new ones. Many would rather strike deals with Europe, but they are afraid of what America might do next. We can't even count on the reliability of existing pipeline routes.

Lily Kleinholtz, Africa:

In my region, generally one person has the power to sign the contract: usually the President, sometimes the Interior or Defense minister. While they don't object to personal favors, generally they're more concerned with political considerations: how will this deal affect their future foreign policy, alliances, and future Western support for the current regime? These aren't questions you've prepared me to answer. Perhaps we need greater governmental-political cooperation in Europe. They're looking at bigger issues than the price of oil.

Jeremy Bent, Indonesia:

The decision makers simply don't tell you what they really mean or what they're thinking here. They've always dealt with Dutch Shell, and don't understand quite how we fit in. They'll agree to anything, but somehow the final meeting doesn't take place or the contract is rarely actually signed. My greatest frustration is not knowing where I stand, what I could offer to close the deal. Usually, I don't know the results of a negotiation until I hear them from a friend or read about them in the newspapers. Meanwhile, anti-Western sentiment is rising in the general population.

Jacques Villon, east Asia:

I'd say I face two major cultural communication problems here. The first is my staff: they don't understand the local notions of courtesy. Most speak the language, but they don't understand the role of nuance, gesture, ceremony. They're not comfortable with the East Asian businessman's idea of a night on the town. The second problem is how the government makes decisions; it's impenetrable. You can't really get through to the people who have the power to decide, because you're never exactly sure who they are. Often, it's a secret group, well-protected by a vigilant bureaucracy. I'd call it collusion to keep out competition, except, of course, that's something like what we're trying to do ourselves.

Schwaneger heard another half-dozen similar comments, and then sat down to draft his recommendations.

Study Questions

1. What internal multicultural communication issues does International Oil face?
2. To what degree should International Oil adapt its business and ethical practices to the realities on the ground?
3. What communications challenges does Schwaneger face both inside and outside the organization?
4. What extra support could Schwaneger provide to his field managers?
5. What, if anything, should Schwaneger recommend to top management?
6. What political pressures within the EEC should be taken into consideration in International Oil's decision-making?
7. How should the company balance the convenience of electronic communications with the benefits of personal contact?

CHAPTER 14

Personal and Corporate Ethics

The discussions in previous chapters have been permeated with ethical considerations. As an individual, nothing will be more precious to you than your credibility. That is, do you have a track record of acting in good faith and keeping your word? Have you appealed to the principles as well as the interests of your audiences? As a corporation, over the long term, nothing will be more precious than the reputation of having contributed to the public good by providing reliable products and services at a reasonable cost. In the most general terms, ethics means that the individual has a responsibility to the larger community that makes his or her life possible, productive, and filled with opportunity.

The history of politics and business is rife with examples of empires that have been built by ruthless founders who conquered territories or cornered markets and saw their children or grandchildren become statesmen or philanthropists. But in a global marketplace under constant government and media scrutiny, managers generally don't have a generation to steal or monopolize without getting caught. The revolutions in communication over the past centuries have themselves imposed higher standards on individuals and businesses.

If one believes in the values of a free, competitive market, one will also recognize that quality, fairness, and integrity are marketable commodities not simply because they serve one's self-interest, but also because the public and its institutions, through government, will be judging an institution's products, practices, and personnel.

In an important sense, institutions have become corporate public citizens, and they must share the responsibility of citizenship. If they don't, these responsibilities will be forced on them by their local, national, or global communities. A manager unaware of this will rapidly find herself isolated and unsupported by crucial allies and audiences. A company unaware of this will rapidly find itself regulated, boycotted, or denounced.

We are no longer in a world where Henry Ford could hire thugs to beat up his workers, strikers at steel mills could be shot down in the streets, or families could bribe the government to buy up every railroad or oil well. Today, such events would lead the evening news the following night. This evolution of democratic public opinion has not prevented a Steve Jobs, a Paul McCartney, or a Bill Gates from parlaying personal genius, inventiveness, or foresight into a vast fortune. Individuals are citizens in their companies, companies are citizens in their community, and few managers currently out of jail would argue this is not to the good.

Ethical citizenship—individual or corporate—is no stumbling block to successful managers. Indeed, understanding its responsibilities can be a business, as well as a personal, advantage. Ethics can—and indeed often should—be the subject of vigorous debate; most business people have long since learned that there's no moral ideology that can be applied to every problem. What can help is a grammar of ethics—a language to frame discussions about ethical issues.

ADDRESSING ETHICAL ISSUES

Milton Friedman, the Nobel Laureate conservative economist, wrote an article in the early 1970s called "The Social Responsibility of Business Is to Increase Its Profits." To condense: Friedman argues that individuals, not businesses, have responsibilities. A business's responsibility is solely to increase the earnings of its stockholders. Friedman puts this trenchantly: "What does it mean to say that a corporate executive has a 'social responsibility' in his capacity as a businessman? If this statement is not pure rhetoric, it must mean that he is to act in some way that is not in the interests of his employer." Friedman argues that excessive regulation or public pressure only diverts business from its true social responsibility: generating jobs and producing high-quality, low-cost products. A measure of Friedman's influence is that the general views he propounded are much more popular now than they were 25 years ago; they drove much deregulation during recent U.S. administrations and now drive much government policy in the former Soviet Union and even in communist China.

At the same time, Friedman's rigorous views have not entirely carried the day, especially among business people. "Acting in the interests of his employer," broadly interpreted, can mean giving bribes or burying toxic wastes that may destroy future generations. One important response that business theorists have developed to Friedman's article is that corporations have a number of constituencies: not only stockholders, but also employees, and public interest groups such as environmentalists, consumers, and the general public. Of course, ethical businesses also have to function within the law, which often sets a certain standard of ethical behavior on issues such as monopolies, product quality, and truth in advertising. Even if it isn't breaking the law, the wise corporation usually doesn't want to watch picketers circling its headquarters on the evening news.

In the late 1980s, under the leadership of Prof. Thomas Piper, Harvard Business School developed an ethics module. Its cornerstone is an article by Kenneth E. Goodpaster called "Some Avenues for Ethical Analysis in General Management."[1] Goodpaster, working with Mary Gentile, offers a counterpoint to Friedman's view.

[1]Available through Harvard Business School Press, case 383-007.

He doesn't list the 10 commandments for ethical business behavior; instead, he offers several frameworks for ethical analysis of a business situation. Goodpaster suggests the following simple grid to define ethical situations in a corporate environment:

	Corporation as Moral Agent	**Corporation as Moral Environment**
Business Policy Formulation		
Business Policy Implementation		

This grid makes two key points: (1) Both individuals and corporations are—morally and legally—*persons,* and (2) consciously or unconsciously, ethical decisions are made in at least four ways: during policy formulation and policy implementation, and in the creation of both an internal climate and an external public relations policy.

Goodpaster goes on:

> Insofar as the corporation resembles an individual "person" in the community, ethical issues arise that are analogous to classical issues of personal responsibility: duties and obligations to avoid harm (to self or others), to respect the law, to further justice and the common good, and to provide for the least advantaged.

Goodpaster outlines the three major ethical frameworks that have dominated ethical discussion since the time of the ancient Greeks.

Utilitarianism

This suggests, in essence, that it's in the individual's long-term interest to act ethically (and to develop a reputation for doing so). "In the context of general management, utilitarian reasoning frequently manifests itself as a commitment to the social virtues of the market system, both inside the organization and outside. The greatest good for the greatest number comes from competitive decision making, it is argued, and market forces can be relied upon to minimize social harm." This view implies that ethical and self-interested behavior are the same, and that competition brings out the best in everyone.

Contractarianism

"Moral common sense is to be governed not only by utility maximization, but by fairness. And fairness is explained as a condition that prevails when all individuals are accorded equal respect as participants in a social arrangement. This idea of a social contract has appeal in this view because it emphasizes the *rights* of individuals to veto in a way utilitarianism does not." This view suggests, among other things, that a generally successful system that seriously violates the rights of a minority will eventually collapse—slavery in the United States is a good example. A more contemporary example might be a new drug with great benefits that can be harmful or fatal to some recipients.

Pluralism

"The governing ethical idea in this view is *duty*. For the pluralist, critical thinking about first-level duties suggested by our moral common sense leads not to some single outside umpire (such as utility or fairness) but to a more reflective examination of duty itself. One must try to economize on one's basic list of duties, subordinating some to others, relying on one's faculty of moral perception (or intuition or conscience) for the resolution of hard cases." This comes closest to a religious view—that ethical standards have been received from a higher authority and are trained or ingrained into the healthy human personality.

In the end, Goodpaster does come up with his list of ethical imperatives:

1. Avoid harming others (through your own actions).
2. Respect the rights of others.
3. Do not lie or cheat.
4. Keep promises and contracts.
5. Obey the law.
6. Prevent harm to others (from sources other than your own actions).
7. Help those in need.
8. Be fair.
9. Reinforce these imperatives in others.

Perhaps intentionally, Goodpaster keeps his commandments to nine.

The contrasts between Friedman's and Goodpaster's views of corporate responsibility provide a useful spectrum of debate for both corporate decision-making in general and corporate communication in particular.

Ultimately, business arguments for ethical behavior fall into two categories:

1. You'll get in trouble if you're caught, and
2. Irrespective of consequences, you'll be a better and happier person if you behave according to generally accepted standards of ethical behavior.

In the real world, of course, the first argument isn't always true. As recent corporate history has demonstrated, executives frequently get away with lying, cheating, or stealing. Often, of course, unethical actions catch up with people years or decades later. It's fair to say, however, that managers who *perceive themselves* to be acting unethically or manipulate their values to fit a particular situation find their character, their self-image, and their reputation eroded. In this light, we invite you to revisit the discussion of *authority* in Chapter 1 of this text.

Ultimately, ethics are infused into people by their families, their schools, their experience, their religion, their business environment, and/or their intrinsic sense of justice. Aristotle emphasized 2400 years ago that personal ethics can only exist within the context of a community in which every individual has a stake. Applied to an organization, this means that managers who are responsible for creating an ethical environment must make sure that all members of their "community" feel valued, enfranchised, and fairly treated.

Jared Diamond, an ornithologist and environmental scientist has provided some of the most interesting—and sometimes arguable—analyses of how interactions between humans and nature cause civilizations to rise or fall. In his most recent book, *Collapse* (New York, Penguin Group, 2005), he examines two oil-drilling projects on the relatively pristine island of New Guinea: one managed exploitatively by the Indonesian government, and another managed with environmental sensitivity by the Chevron Corporation. His comments on the motives for Chevron's ecologically-sound practices provide a minicase in corporate ethics. Diamond discovers that the Chevron drilling site constitutes perhaps the most healthy, well-forested, and species-friendly part of the island, and speculates on why:

> (T)he Kutubu oil field functions are by far the most rigorously controlled national park in New Guinea.
>
> For months I was greatly puzzled by these conditions . . . After all, Chevron is neither a non-profit environmental organization, nor a National Park Service. Instead, it is a for-profit oil company, owned by its shareholders. If Chevron were to spend money on environmental policies that ultimately decreased its profits from its oil operations, its shareholders would and should sue it. The company evidently decided that those policies would ultimately help it make more money from its oil operations. How do they help?
>
> Chevron company publications refer to concern for the environment itself as a motivating factor. That is undoubtedly true. However, in conversations over the last six years with dozens of lower-level as well as senior employees of other oil companies, and people outside the oil industry, I have come to realize that many other factors as well have contributed to these environmental policies.

Diamond cites the following causes for Chevron's environmental concern:

1. Avoiding very expensive environmental disasters.
2. Maintaining long-term assets (typical oil wells produce for 20–50 years).
3. Preserving good relations with the surrounding community; widespread dissatisfaction can provoke increased government regulation or plant shutdowns.
4. Gaining future contracts in areas of the world that enforce strong pro-environmental policies.
5. New technologies that make less intrusive extraction methods economically feasible.

On the face of it, the situation Diamond describes is another superficial win-win business ethics case: Do the right thing because it will be more profitable in the long run. But the key phrase here is *in the long run*. Just as a reputation for probity can help an individual over a lifetime, a reputation for social responsibility can enable a company to benefit generation after generation of shareholders. Diamond contrasts Chevron with the behavior of most mining companies which have a history of wreaking drastic and permanent damage on the environment. Frequently, when disaster catches up with them, mining executives have stripped the profits out of the company and gone bankrupt, leaving governments to clean up the mess (or not). As a result, mining is a vanishing industry in the United States. In fairness to mining companies, extracting metals or coal and the resulting damage to the landscape and watershed is much more destructive environmentally than pumping oil. The surviving mining companies are increasingly taking a long-term view of their relationships with the environment and the surrounding communities.

Personal and corporate business ethics could largely be summarized by the motto: Do what's in the best long-term interests of your shareholders—even if that won't please Wall Street this quarter. You'll probably be doing the best thing for yourself and for your organization.

The next two cases invite students to apply these principles to practical ethical dilemmas.

CASE 14.1

Hal of Erhardt & Company: One Audit Senior's Dilemma

There are many personal qualities an auditor is expected to have. Of these, perhaps the most important is integrity. Integrity has been defined by the American Institute of Certified Public Accountants (AICPA) in this way: "A member shall not knowingly misrepresent facts and . . . shall not subordinate his judgment to others." This applies to all auditors, whether they are internal auditors and employees of a company, or external auditors (sometimes called independent accountants), to whom this case especially refers. These auditors, members of often very large public accounting firms, are increasingly rewarded for their ability to find new clients and retain old ones, as well as for traditional technical skills. But society continues to evaluate the auditors by how effectively and conscientiously they serve the public interest. According to William D. Hall (1988), "Without integrity, the auditors' opinion is nothing more than sounding brass or a tinkling cymbal."

A young auditor named Hal was assigned to lead a team of accountants in performing an audit of a company with which they were not familiar. He was to report on the progress of the audit to a seasoned partner-in-charge. As he discovered, even an accountant with relative inexperience is not exempt from reviewing the overall conduct of an audit and the due care that all team members (including the partner) must exercise.

BACKGROUND

An audit team usually consists of a partner-in-charge, a manager, an in-charge senior, and other staff members assigned to the engagement as necessary under the circumstances. The *partner-in-charge* is the person ultimately responsible for the overall engagement. He/she must assure that sufficient evidence has been gathered to support the firm's opinion on the financial statements. In addition, he/she must be satisfied that the audit procedures performed are in accordance with generally accepted auditing standards approved by the AICPA. The *manager* has significant responsibility for the engagement which is delegated to him/her by the partner-in-charge. He/she typically supervises the planning, staffing, and the completion of the engagement. The *in-charge senior* primarily carries out the audit plan in the field in an orderly and timely fashion. He/she is responsible for the daily fieldwork including supervision of staff. He/she makes an initial determination of whether the engagement objectives are being met and gives progress reports to the manager and partner-in-charge regarding any new developments. The other *staff members* assigned to the audit typically perform the tasks which the in-charge senior specifically assigns to them.

THE AUDIT ASSIGNMENT

To this point in his life, Hal's professional experience paralleled that of many other young accountants. He had completed a graduate business program with a major in accounting. He had also worked on external audits in a national public accounting firm for three years, during which he performed specific audit duties and had limited supervisory responsibilities. He was still single and was the sole financial support for his elderly parents.

Hal was hired by the local office of Erhardt & Company, another national public accounting firm, last November 15. Within two weeks, he was called by Frank, the partner-in-charge, to discuss his first assignment. Hal was told he would be one of four seniors assigned to the audit of FBA Group Ltd. (FBA). Frank explained that four seniors were being assigned instead of the usual one, due to the additional risk involved in this engagement. FBA was a wholly-owned real estate subsidiary of a publicly-held company in the financial industry, and Erhardt was auditing FBA for the first time. Frank had already promised FBA management that the audit report would be issued by January 15. Because FBA operated on a calendar-year basis, there was a need to perform the audit without delay.

As the fieldwork commenced, two of the other seniors, Ricardo and Anna, enlightened Hal as to the specific risks entailed in the audit. Ricardo, who had been named the in-charge senior, explained first that FBA had recently merged with another company which was under investigation by the federal Securities and Exchange Commission. Second, the previous external auditors of FBA, who belonged to another national firm, halted their examination after nine months of fieldwork and disassociated themselves from the engagement without issuing an opinion on the company's financial statements. Anna was previously employed by the auditors who disassociated themselves from that audit. As a member of Erhardt's FBA audit team, she refused to assume any responsibility beyond the tasks assigned to her. None of the three seniors was aware of any communication between Erhardt and the previous auditors.

Several days into the fieldwork Ricardo resigned from the firm, and Hal was assigned to replace him. As the new in-charge senior, Hal would be supervising and signing off on all fieldwork during the entire engagement. His previous training led him to feel responsible for gathering sufficient corroborating evidence to allow a reasoned formulation of opinion on the financial statements. Although he had not participated in planning the engagement, he now had to plan the necessary audit procedures for each area in the field.

As January 15 neared, much fieldwork remained to be done. Hal began encountering resistance from his superiors, Brad (the audit manager) and Frank, regarding the audit procedures Hal had determined were necessary under the circumstances. These were more extensive than the procedures they wanted him to perform. In addition, the management of FBA was hostile, threatening not to cooperate with the team over several standard audit procedures Hal insisted on performing. Three accounts for which he felt inadequate procedures were being planned and performed included residual interest, real estate inventory, and notes receivable.

RESIDUAL INTEREST

As a result of the merger reported above, FBA inherited many partnerships, of which the merged company was the general partner. It was previously established that the values of these partnerships (the difference between assets and liabilities) exceeded the value on the merged company's books. Accountants call this excess value "residual interest," and it had been recorded as such on FBA's balance sheet. Hal's superiors asked him to write a detailed list of the audit procedures to perform (that is, an audit program) for the residual interest account. The assignment made him uncomfortable because he was unfamiliar with the area and because he was also going to audit the same account himself. Writing an audit program is normally done by another member of the audit team who is experienced in the area.

When Hal submitted his written program to Brad and Frank for their review, they returned it to him without a single comment or correction (review point) and told him to go ahead. From experience, he expected at least twenty review points on any work submitted for review and even more for an area with which he was unfamiliar. Because the inherent nature of the account makes the recorded amounts open to manipulation by management, auditors typically examine this area more carefully. Hal suggested to Frank that audit procedures should also be applied to the partnerships in question, since their books and records were maintained at FBA's corporate headquarters and FBA could not provide them with the partnerships' audited financial statements. Frank's response was: "We were not engaged to audit the partnerships."

REAL ESTATE INVENTORY

Real estate inventory was typically the largest account balance which Hal had previously audited. He was now asked to write the audit program itself as well as audit FBA's inventory. More assured because of that previous experience, Hal proceeded to write the program. Then he submitted his work for review; once again he received no review points on either the audit program or the procedures performed. When receiving the overall audit plan he noticed there was no intent to do an on-site check of the inventory of property under development. When he brought this to Frank's attention, the response was that it wasn't cost-beneficial to do such observation.

NOTES RECEIVABLE

An audit of notes receivable involves both the notes receivable balance itself and the provision for "uncollectible" receivables. The notes are typically inspected by the auditors and confirmed with the borrowers, but alternate procedures may also be performed. This portion of the job had been planned before Hal joined the firm; he felt the planned procedures were inadequate. The plan stated that the individual note balances at year end should be traced from the audit workpaper to the detailed general ledger and checked against that. Hal insisted that the general ledger was what was actually being audited; as an alternate procedure he wanted a staff person to trace subsequent cash receipts on these notes to validated deposit slips. Brad and Frank felt there wasn't enough time for this extra procedure.

The other vital aspect of notes receivable involves the estimated reserve for uncollectible notes. Linda, the fourth senior, was assigned to this engagement from another Erhardt & Company office. Her task was to determine which notes were severely delinquent and to propose an appropriate reserve amount. Since estimating a reserve is subjective in nature, the issue can lend itself to negotiation between the auditors and the management. When Linda spoke to FBA's management about her reserve figure, their chief financial officer (CFO) became extremely upset and refused to record that amount.

When Frank learned of the incident he sided with the CFO and recorded a substantially lower reserve amount. He justified this by stating that the receivables in question would be collected or that they were backed by collateral. As part of the audit procedures to test for the value of the collateral, Linda approached Hal with a long overdue note of substantial value which was backed by a certain piece of property. Hal telephoned a real estate broker in the city where the property was held to obtain a reasonable quote on the value of the property. The broker's oral response indicated that the property was worth less than one-half of the amount of the note balance.

ADDITIONAL ITEMS

Linda also felt dissatisfied with the adequacy of the audit procedures being performed, given the hostility expressed by FBA's management. She and Hal encountered some additional unusual items besides the three cited accounts. First, none of the client prepared workpapers agreed with the unadjusted general ledger. The workpapers were an inadequate analysis of the accounts in question. Second, important documents appeared and disappeared at different points. For example, a very large note receivable outstanding had been on FBA's books for two years and Linda proposed to reserve the full amount. The same day that the matter was brought to management's attention, a check was produced for the full amount of the delinquency. The check was postdated one year subsequent to Erhardt's target audit date, which also happened to be the maturity date of the note. Frank, siding with an adamant FBA management, saw no need to reserve the note balance.

A further item surfaced when Hal performed a routine analysis of the real estate's net realizable value. He had been relying on a written appraisal of a piece of property as a source document when he examined the cost of the appraisal fee charged to that property. When Hal began performing the net realizable value analysis, he asked to see the appraisal document again, but FBA insisted there was no such document.

WEIGHING THE EVIDENCE

Throughout the audit, Hal and Linda compared their assessments of the evidence. They extended audit procedures as much as possible in an attempt to uncover all errors or irregularities. As January 15 approached, their daily meetings became longer and more intense than ever. By the night of January 14 they realized they had found no obviously material errors or irregularities, but they were still convinced that the audit evidence they gathered was insufficient to support an opinion on FBA's financial statements.

Hal pondered the possible motivations of the partner-in-charge of the audit. Frank might have especially wanted to please FBA because it was a wholly owned subsidiary, which would have given him a chance to seek the parent company as his audit client, too. In today's public accounting environment, a very effective way to advance one's career is to bring in new business. In fact, the audit partners are expected to bring in such business. The FBA audit apparently offered an excellent opportunity to land a substantial client. Such a client could also prove too hot to handle. Hal spent a long sleepless night thinking of what he would say to Frank in the morning about the team's audit findings.

Study Questions

1. What should Hal say to Frank (and to others at the office)?
2. What are the reasons for saying it? How should he say it?
3. What would the consequences of any given course of action be for Hal and for others at Erhardt & Company?

CASE 14.2

McArthur Place

Sitting at her desk at 5:00 P.M. on a cold October afternoon, Emily Stevens, the Controller for McArthur Place, wondered what she should do. She was beginning to feel that any decision she made was bound to lead to trouble. Earlier that day, her friend Carolyn Johnson, the Operations Manager, had come to her with a special request. Now she needed to make a decision that would affect both her standing in the organization and her friendship with Carolyn.

BACKGROUND—MCARTHUR PLACE

The McArthur Place (MP), a $6 million not-for-profit organization in the Chicago area, was founded in the early 1930's and has a long-standing history of providing services to at-risk adult and elderly populations. Over the past twenty years, the services have expanded to include: Housing for homeless seniors; education and employment services, including job retraining and computer instruction; healthcare services; and, home delivered meals. As with most non-profit organizations, MP consistently ran with a very tight operating budget. Given its funding base, sixty percent of which came from federal and state contracts, there was never much, if any, profit to absorb extra expenses (see *Exhibit 1* for income statement). This meant that even small unnecessary expenses were important to the overall performance of the organization.

As the Controller, it was Emily's job to oversee all of the financial operations of the organization and ensure that its assets were properly controlled. This meant that, among other things, all incoming cash receipts and outgoing payments required Emily's review. Generally, the payments coming into the organization were straightforward and simply needed to be allocated according to type. The cash outflows, on the other hand, would often require additional research. For the purpose of researching most payments and processing all deposits, Emily relied on Carrie Fiske, Fiscal Officer. There were, however, several invoices which were overseen by Carolyn, and for which her department would conduct any additional research. These included all utility bills, telephone charges, cell phone and beeper expenses, and organizational supply purchases.

EVENTS LEADING UP TO OCTOBER 15, 1998

Both Emily and Carolyn began at MP in 1993, and they had worked particularly closely over the past two years. During this time, a friendship grew between them, as well as a sense of trust.

EXHIBIT 1 Statement of Operating Revenue and Expenses for Fiscal Year 1998

Revenue	
Public Contracts	$2,944,397
Fee for Service	2,154,287
Contributions/Gifts	555,546
Corporate/Foundation Grants	425,919
Investment Income	92,591
Total Revenue	**$6,172,740**
Expenses	
Education & Job Training	$1,159,067
Housing	1,886,559
Health Services	1,300,862
Corporate/Foundation Grants	1,350,184
Investment Income	468,557
Total Revenue	**$6,165,229**
Net Income (Loss)	**$7,511**

They would often consult with each other as issues arose to either vent frustration or seek feedback on the best way to handle a difficult situation. Both sides felt confident that any requests for maintaining confidentiality would be upheld. In addition to this relationship, Emily worked closely with the Director of Human Resources, Samantha Green, and because of her position as the Controller, Emily was often privy to confidential personnel information.

In July of 1998, Carolyn's son John began working as a driver for MP's nutrition programs. He worked under the direction of the Nutrition Coordinator, Kelly Oaks, and was responsible for delivering meals to homebound elderly throughout the Chicago region. From the very beginning, Kelly and John had a personality conflict. As a new supervisor, Kelly was intimidated by John's relationship to Carolyn. In addition, Carolyn and Kelly had a history of run-ins and miscommunications. While Carolyn attempted to remain neutral during John's first two months at the organization, as she watched her son consistently being disciplined, she was unable to control her protective nature. Soon the conflict between John and Kelly had escalated to a point where John was being considered for termination, and Carolyn was right in the middle of the controversy.

OCTOBER 15, 1998

Emily was sitting at her desk signing checks when Carolyn came into her office and shut the door. Not thinking anything of this action, Emily continued to sign checks while Carolyn began talking. Once it became clear that Carolyn was not simply venting frustration, she put her pen down and listened. To her astonishment, Carolyn handed her $300 to cover John's excessive phone bills for calls to his girl friend (see *Exhibit 2* for a summary of this dialogue).

Emily knew that MP had a clear policy about personal use of telephones (see *Exhibit 3*). While she understood that people often needed to make personal calls during work time, she also monitored

EXHIBIT 2

Carolyn:	Emily, do you have a second? I really need to talk to you about something.
Emily:	Sure, what's up?
Carolyn:	I have a favor to ask you, and I am going to have to ask you to keep this just between us. I don't want you to tell anyone, not Kelly, not Samantha, not even your staff.
Emily:	Carolyn, what's the matter?
Carolyn:	Well, I just was reviewing the phone bill, and I don't know if you know, but John has been having a difficult time with Kelly. She is so unfair and picks on him all of the time. Just because he is younger than the other staff members are, she feels she can intimidate him.
Emily:	Yeah, I had heard that he was having some difficulties.
Carolyn:	Anyway, I was looking at the CellOne bill and noticed that there were a bunch of calls to Sudbury. I mean a lot of calls, like $300 worth. I thought that was strange, so I looked at the number, and I recognized it as John's girlfriend's house. I just about died. I have spoken to John, and I have $300 cash right here which I am making him pay back to MP (handing a wad of dollar bills to Emily). I want to teach him a lesson. But, the problem is, Emily, I don't want him to get fired. I know that Kelly is just looking for an opportunity to get him out of here, and I don't want to give her any ammunition to use against him . . . especially since if I hadn't been John's mother, I never would have known whose calls those were.
Emily:	So, what are you asking me to do?
Carolyn:	I just want you to keep this between us. John has paid back the calls, and I don't see any reason why this needs to go further. He is already so far behind the eightball, and I have asked him to start looking for another job. He's just a young kid, and I don't think it's fair to punish him for this. I just don't want him to get fired. He has promised me that he won't do it again, and besides, all of the drivers make personal calls. He is just the poor kid whose mother happens to work here, so he is being held responsible! So, can we keep this just between us?
Emily:	Let me think about it and get back to you this afternoon. . . .

phone usage to ensure that people were not incurring excessive long distance phone expenses. To facilitate this process and keep management informed, each month Program Supervisors received phone reports for each extension, which listed total calls, length of call, and cost to the organization. In addition, employees were required to pay for any personal call that cost the organization more than $3. Unfortunately, however, these reporting mechanisms were not in place for the cellular phones. Carolyn monitored cellular phones through a process of monthly review. She would look at the cost and inform the supervisor if any phone appeared to be incurring an inordinate amount of charges.

To complicate the situation, Emily also knew of concerns about John's performance based on several conversations with Samantha. Under normal circumstances, when she received the cellular phone bill from Carolyn, Emily would also briefly review it to assess whether it was in the "normal" range. Finding that there were excessive calls, she would follow up with Carolyn and the supervisor to ensure that the personal calls

EXHIBIT 3 Excerpt from the McArthur Place Personnel Policies Manual

Telecommunications

While it is understood that there may be times when organizational phones must be used for personal matters, these calls must be limited and should in no way interfere with business. The organization's telephones are not to be used for personal long distance calls. McArthur Place reserves the right to monitor the use of its various systems to ensure that they are being used properly and for business purposes. Employees who violate this policy will be subject to disciplinary action up to and including termination.

stop and the organization was reimbursed. By handing her the $300 and asking her to cover up the calls, however, Carolyn placed Emily in a very difficult situation.

Now Emily sat at her desk and pondered what she should do. If she went along with Carolyn and remained quiet, would she be ignoring one of the basic requirements of her position—to be objective and fair while protecting the organization? If she decided not to keep quiet, what would that mean for the important alliance between her and Carolyn? Emily knew that she needed to make a decision today, but which was the correct one to make?

Study Questions

1. Is Carolyn's request to cover John's phone bills quietly unethical?
2. Does the case suggest that John has in fact been treated unfairly?
3. Should Emily's friendship with Carolyn have any effect on her decision?
4. Should Emily consult with others before taking action? Who?

CHAPTER 15

Electronic Communication

Much business communication now occurs electronically, and this trend is certain to increase. The ability to transfer a document almost instantaneously from your computer throughout your company or around the world is altering not only styles of communication, but also the nature of the workplace itself. For better and worse, a manager can leave the office early, go home, put on dinner, and then compose a report or instructions that will be on the boss' or subordinates's electronic desks the next morning. Deciding how to use electronic communication most effectively means considering important issues we've addressed in other contexts: *time* and *urgency*.

TIME

Different types of communication require different amounts of time from both the sender and the receiver and, perhaps equally important, different modes of *timing*. A face-to-face visit almost always requires that other things be set aside and that certain social amenities be observed. This takes time and may also interrupt other important activities on the parts of all parties.

URGENCY

Different modes of communication convey different levels of urgency. A beeper message to a doctor on his private line will carry much greater urgency than an advertising brochure received in the mail. Make sure you've calibrated your selection of a medium to the urgency of your message. This also means considering *priority;* a top priority to you may be fifth or tenth on your boss's list.

Electronic mail gives the savvy manager increasingly greater opportunities to use—or misuse—her audience's time. Rules that apply to good communication on paper or in person don't always apply to the evolving conventions of electronic communication. This chapter invites you to consider the following differences.

TELEPHONING

Consider this form of electronic communication, which has been around for a century. Whether we're talking to a close friend or a complete stranger, we don't converse in the same way that we would face to face. Facial expressions and body language count for nothing. Participants can't talk simultaneously, or over each other, as they often do in person. Identity, rapport, purpose, and the nature of the relationship have to be established entirely by word choice and tone. As we dial a number, we make many half-conscious judgments: Will this person recognize my voice or should I introduce myself? Is my call expected or unexpected, welcome, surprising, unwelcome, or even unwanted?Am I calling at the right time? Or, as the receiver, do I have to take this call now, can I return it later, or do I not want to speak to this person at all? Do I reinforce our previous relationship by social conversation or get right to the point of the call? Do I modify my goal or message depending on the reaction of my audience?

At the same time, telephoning shares many of the characteristics of dropping into a colleague's office. You're likely to ask how the person is doing, inquire after his family, or discuss your last meeting or contact. Again, this takes time, and a telephone call can be interruptive—"Sorry, I'm in the middle of a meeting"—or inefficient—"I'll get back to you when I can."

Generally, business phone calls require a caller to quickly establish identity and purpose. These can range from "Hi, old friend, I'm just getting in touch" to "I represent Acme Company and have a product you need." Anywhere across this range, a caller needs to think ahead about how to establish an immediate bond of relationship and/or interest. The caller or receiver also needs to be extremely sensitive to the audience's signals on timing: Should I chat or get right to the point? Should I arrange to get back at a more convenient time?

These points apply to a lesser extent when you are leaving messages on answering machines or voice mail. Here, a vivid image or clear statement of purpose is much more likely to provoke a response than is a rambling monologue. Voice mail messages are less interruptive—the respondent can call back at a time convenient to *his* schedule rather than yours. Unlike less personal forms of electronic communication, they can convey tonal qualities such as friendship or urgency.

Many of the lessons we've learned by making and receiving telephone calls all our lives can be applied to more recent forms of electronic communication.

Finally, businesses are increasingly dependent on automatic telephone responses that offer a menu of choices. This reduces employment costs, but be careful not to misuse technology. Callers should be able to get through to an actual human being who can help them. Sometimes callers are confused by the choices on a menu, and often their questions are too complex to be answered by a machine. A purely mechanized response or long waiting periods punctuated by advertisements and bad music can alienate customers and drive them away.

NETWORKING

The various computer networks have made a vast amount of information that previously would have required a visit to the library available at home or at the desk. They also enable a user to contact a large, otherwise unidentified audience with similar interests or needs. Networking, as a tool for information gathering, research, advertising, and opinion making, is just coming into its own. But the wise manager will be online and able to access sources of information that can contribute to her education or planning. Networking can establish electronic relationships that may well pay off over the long run, both personally and professionally. You need not be connected to a network through your organization to profit from its use; a number of commercial online services are available, often for a base cost of $10 per month for several hours of access. *America Online* and many other services provide access to the Internet.

FAXES

While faxes (facsimiles) are convenient timewise and will preserve some importance in legal or official communication, they may soon be outdated by E-mail. They play an important part in transmitting a document rapidly, but they tend to be messy and hard to read, which limits their distribution potential. Often they require repeated visits to the mail room to receive. Their limited purposes are often as well served by the overnight mail services.

TELECONFERENCING AND SATELLITE VIDEOCONFERENCING

These are similar to meetings or speech giving, and the principles governing these have been covered in previous chapters. They can be much more efficient than flying across the country, and they do allow more nuanced communication than do documents or E-mail. Still, their uses are fairly specialized. A CEO may wish to address employees in a far-flung organization on an urgent issue, for example, or several members of a team making an upcoming presentation may want to compare notes and iron out differences in approach. These modes of communication, especially videoconferencing, are subject to significant time constraints due to both expense and availability. Participants are generally well advised to share materials and a clear agenda ahead of time.

CELLULAR PHONES AND BEEPERS

There may be few more depressing sights than someone in a bathing suit on the beach conducting business over a cellular phone, until you reflect that without it, he might not be on the beach at all. Still, almost every person needs some time when he can't be reached. Most managers hand out their cellular or beeper phone numbers sparingly so that they can be contacted only on matters of importance; the chief exception here is salespeople.

Cell phones can also encourage impulsive calling, often when you're not totally focused on the issue at hand. Before using your cell phone for a business call, be sure you're up-to-speed on the topic, that you know what you want the call to achieve, and that this is the right time for the recipient to hear from you. Also, remember that recipients can be annoyed by low-quality reception on cell phone calls. If your call is unsolicited, or worse, unwanted, recipients may transfer that annoyance to you.

WEBSITES

Websites are an increasingly crucial tool in business communication, but like every medium, they must be used selectively. They're a terrific way to provide regularly updated information to a dedicated audience. But keep the needs of that audience in mind as you design or maintain your website.

Generally, managers outsource website development to professionals, but be careful. Often they'll design websites that are only fully accessible to other website development professionals. Don't be taken in by the fact that they're pushing the fanciest (i.e., most expensive) graphics and technologies. What's most important is whether the website delivers your message effectively to the intended audience. It's usually wise to have your website tested regularly by the least computer-literate person you know.

The three most important qualities your website should posses are:

Clear directions. Make sure any reasonable users can proceed down the decision tree via clear directions to access the information they need.

Responsiveness. Have a hot button on the front page allowing the user to E-mail you directly if they get frustrated and can't find what they need.

Timeliness. If your website is important to your organization, visit and update it regularly. It may have gone down without your knowledge or contain outdated information.

E-MAIL

Often, E-mail is simply a quick way to distribute a memo or send a letter, and in such situations, the principles of good writing covered in Part One of this text apply. But E-mail also provides its own conventions, opportunities, and risks.

John Seabrook, writing an article for *The New Yorker*[1] on Microsoft's struggles with the Justice Department, realized he could E-mail the company's chairman and guru, Bill Gates. He sent the following message:

[1]January 10, 1994, p. 48.

> Dear Bill,
>
> I am the guy who's writing an article about you for *The NewYorker.* It occurs to me that we ought to be able to do some of the work through E-mail. Which raises this fascinating question—what kinds of understanding of another person can E-mail give you? . . .
>
> You could begin by telling me what you think is unique about E-mail as a form of communication.

Within 18 minutes, Seabrook received the following response from Gates:

> E-mail is a unique communication vehicle for a lot of reasons. However E-mail is not a substitute for direct interaction. . . .
>
> There are people who I have corresponded with for months before actually meeting them—people at work and otherwise. If someone isn't saying something of interest it's easier to not respond to their mail than it is not to answer the phone. In fact I give out my home phone number to almost no one but my E-mail address is known very broadly. I am the only person who reads my E-mail so no one has to worry about embarrassing themselves or going around people when they send a message. Our E-mail is completely secure. . . .
>
> E-mail helps out with other types of communication. It allows you to exchange a lot of information in advance of a meeting and make the meeting far more valuable . . .
>
> Email is not a good way to get mad at someone since you can't interact. You can send friendly messages very easily since they are harder to misinterpret.

Since Bill Gates may be the world's most famous and successful user of E-mail, it's worth noting how this response differs from normal written communication. The style falls halfway between writing and conversation: The dots suggest conversational pauses rather than completed thoughts, *E-mail* migrates into *Email,* punctuation is minimal, and there's no formal salutation or conclusion. As Seabrook deduces, "Social niceties are not what Bill Gates is about. . . . Good spelling is not what Bill Gates is about either. He never signed his messages to me, but sometimes he put an '&' at the end, which, I learned, means: 'Write back' in E-mail language."

More interestingly, Gates's interaction with Seabrook suggests what makes E-mail communication distinctive. It can be used as a nonpersonal communication that allows the recipient to judge timing and urgency according to her own situation and needs. E-mail conventions allow brief, efficient exchanges of information or instruction that don't require the time used up by social amenities. Exchanges can be briefer and more idiomatic and depend less on paragraph building and persuasive argument than on concise information sharing. Two people in different parts of a building or different parts of a country can almost instantly alert each other to new facts and situations, needed textual changes, or new job instructions. While a memo or document creates a record and goes into a file somewhere, and therefore needs to provide argument and context, an E-mail message can presume on all previous communication among the parties and get quickly to the point. E-mail improves information access, whether to an individual or to a large audience.

An important, if unintended, consequence of E-mail technology has been its use in relationships, from personal to international. Partners whose work schedules make it impractical to reach each other by phone can, over the business day, discuss and resolve an argument they've had the night before. Friends can receive, and distribute with a few computer strokes, a list of jokes they've found on their network that morning.

During the overthrow of Communism in Russia, much important information on the developing situation got out not through the press but over the computer lines.

At first glance, unintended uses of E-mail may seem to interfere with its business purpose. But like meetings or phone calls, such uses of E-mail can contribute to crucial relationship building. Customers may be more likely to take a phone call from a marketer who has sent an amusing E-mail. Couples may be able to spend more time actually doing their work if they have a new means by which to let each other know when they'll be home or who has to pick up the kids from school.

Another advantage of E-mail is that, unlike a phone call, E-mail allows some time for reflection before response. This can result in more productive and efficient communication in both business and personal situations. E-mail may also play an increasing role in democratizing the workplace. A top executive may be more likely to notice and respond to a brief E-mail nugget than to a memo that has worked its way up the chain of command. Subordinates can be better and more immediately informed of changes in policy or procedures. It's also true, however, that people will often put things in E-mails that they would never communicate in person or in writing. This is probably because they know the receiver will have a chance to reflect on the message and can respond relatively informally, but this characteristic of E-mail also entails risk. Some companies believe there should be a cost to or monitoring of E-mail use or access to the Internet because such privileges can be abused easily. Issues of confidentiality and security also have arisen around the use of E-mail and the Internet. Depending upon your particular system, E-mail may not be the place to conduct highly confidential discussions. All these considerations mean you have to manage your E-mail diet, applying the sorts of prioritizing that Robyn Gilcrist faced in *Yellowtail Marine.*

While E-mail messages may differ from older forms of communication, such as memos or letters, some of the same conventions still apply. When you are composing an E-mail message, remember that if it is successful, it may be passed on to a wide variety of audiences either electronically or in hard copy. It may represent all someone else knows about you. Consider these potential primary and secondary audiences while you're writing; what may be immediately obvious or amusing to your initial recipient may be gibberish to his boss or other colleagues around the world.

The *Portsmouth Herald* (February 18, 2006) warns: "An E-mail can be like a boomerang. What flutters off harmlessly into cyberspace can dart across the world and come rushing back with a vengeance." According to the article, a seif-described "trust-fund baby" who decided she "couldn't keep living off daddy forever" applied for a legal job but upon receiving an offer, wrote back, "The pay you would offer would neither fulfill me nor support the lifestyle I am living." The employer fired back that her behavior "smacks of immaturity and is quite unprofessional. . . . Do you really want," he asked, "to start (angering) more experienced lawyers at this point in your career?" She responded, "bla bla bla. . . . " The potential employer forwarded the exchange to a colleague who posted it on the Internet, and within days it became a featured story in *The Boston Globe*. This illustrates not only the dangers of inappropriate E-mail communications, but also how important it is to make sure your messages don't reach unintended audiences. Commenting in the article, Michael Hoffman of the center for Business Ethics at Bentley College said: "A lot of times we put something in an E-mail that we wouldn't put in a letter or say to someone face-to-face. I think it can get us into trouble when we don't realize how permanent and public it can become."

Effective use of both voice mail and E-mail, while they have the advantage of respecting the audience's time, requires the source to make judgments about *urgency*. How often does my boss check his E-mail? Is this situation so important that I should burst into a meeting if necessary? Conversely, will an E-mail message be less interruptive and more efficient than a meeting or a telephone call?

The E-mail user, like the writer or speaker, needs to ask some basic questions: Am I using E-mail to address a confrontation that, in the long run, is better handled in person? Am I putting something in writing that should be communicated—or modified—in direct conversation? Am I providing my seniors with important information or just grousing? Is this the right medium for my message?

Consider an extreme situation: firing a direct subordinate by E-mail. As the previous discussion has suggested, the evidence shows that people will E-mail comments that they would never—or don't wish to—say face to face. This may mean the comment should never be made or that it should only be made personally and in private; making this judgment can be an important communication decision. Nothing, including E-mail, can serve as a substitute for personal contacts with your subordinates, colleagues, or superiors. New technologies don't really change the basic principles of communication.

Of all the forms of communication, E-mails are probably the most prone to reach unintended audiences. It's terribly easy for the recipient to hit a few keys and copy your message to dozens of people you didn't intend to receive it. You may even inadvertently do this yourself. In a recent *New Yorker* article (June 30, 2003) Ben McGrath tells the tale of a law firm associate who wrote to a friend that he was having a blast, working very little, and spending most of his time sending "E-mails and bullshiting with people." He concluded: "So yeah, Corporate love hasn't worn off yet. . . . But give it time."

As McGrath suggests, the time involved was two minutes:

> That was about how long it took for the hiring department at Skadden to page Jonas (Duke undergraduate, Harvard Law) and put him to work correcting his mistake. Jonas had sent his life-is-good note not to Melissa, but to the firm's entire underwriting group. His task was to write an apology to the forty or so attorneys who had already opened the E-mail and decided that Jackass might be a better name for him. (p. 36)

E-mail carries other risks. As more and more executives conduct increasing amounts of their work through E-mail, they should be aware of other pitfalls, including:

1. *Impulsiveness.* E-mail is so easy to answer it can leave little time for reflection, unlike writing a letter, or a telephone call, where you can assess your interlocutor's response to what you're saying. A mistakenly brusque E-mail response can take a lot of communication to repair. Think before responding.
2. *Tone.* It's often hard to convey tone in E-mail. If a situation or relationship is sensitive, you're probably better off making a phone call.
3. *Thoroughness.* If you're responding to a letter, you'll probably take the time to answer every point raised by your correspondent. Turning on your computer and finding 50 E-mails including a lot of annoying ads may tempt you to rush through them. People tend to glance at the text and answer only the main point in an E-mail. This may create the need for much more E-mail later on.

4. *Passive aggressiveness.* E-mail makes it easy for those who are shy—which, one way or another, includes most of us—to hide behind it. It can make it too easy to hit the ball back into the other person's court rather than address the issues at hand. If you can't solve the E-mailer's problem immediately, tell them when you can.

Misusing E-mail can also damage your reputation as an effective communicator because it can facilitate inappropriate or unwanted communication that the sender would probably be reluctant to deliver in person. It also provides the opportunity to communicate at the wrong time or out of context. What you might tell a friend at a social gathering might be inappropriate to share with a professional colleague, subordinate, or superior at one in the morning. A *New York Times* story (February 21, 2006) reported on E-mail run amok in academia:

> One student skipped class and then sent the professor an E-mail message asking for copies of her teaching notes. Another did not like her grade, and wrote a petulant message to the professor. Another explained she was late for a Monday class because she was recovering from drinking too much at a wild weekend party.
>
> Jennifer Shultens, an associate professor of mathematics at the University of California, received this E-mail from a student in her calculus course: "Should I buy a binder or a subject notebook? Since I'm a freshman, I'm not sure how to shop for school supplies. Would you let me know your recommendations? Thank you."
>
> At colleges and universities nationwide, E-mail has made professors more approachable. But many say it has erased boundaries that traditionally keep students at a healthy distance. These days, they say, students seem to view them as approachable around the clock, sending a steady stream of E-mail messages—from 10 a week to 10 after every class—that are too informal or downright inappropriate.
>
> "The tone they would take in E-mail messages was pretty astounding," said Michael J. Kessler, an assistant dean and a lecturer in theology at Georgetown University. "'I need to know this and you need to tell me right now,' with a familiarity that can sometimes border on imperative."

In an educational setting, it's a teacher's job to let the student know that this sort of behavior marks them as selfish and immature and then, if necessary, simply not respond to future such messages. In the business world, however, recipients may just conclude you're a jerk and write you off. Instant messaging can make one even more prone to these abuses.

The Blogosphere

Blogs currently are primarily an outlet for would-be journalists and people who share the same political opinions. As John Hiler writes in *Microcontent*:

> Were Bloggers parasites feeding off their journalistic hosts? Or were Bloggers creating a new form of grassroots journalism, one that threatened the existence of Journalism as we know it?
>
> Then one day it hit me: parasites and hosts, grassroots and extinction . . . they were all biological metaphors.
>
> All of a sudden it made sense! The truth is Bloggers and Journalists are both parasitic organisms. In biology, we have a term for the relationship that seems mutually parasitic: symbiosis, when both organisms benefit from together. In many ways, bloggers and journalists are in a mutually symbiotic relationship, working together to report, filter, and break the news . . . Something about the blogosphere gives it the feeling of a living, breathing ecosystem.

Ecosystems tend to generate a Darwinian world where species evolve, fail, or succeed, and it's true that as of this writing they're primarily used to create opinionated affinity groups or often dubiously sourced "news." But given the exponential growth of electronic communication, blogs may already be providing a communication opportunity for organizations trying to reach customers, supporters, or a more general audience.

All forms of electronic communication, used effectively, give both the employer and the employee much more flexibility in their use of time, their access to information, their choice of media, and their message design. Still, no electronic medium can ever contain the full range of communication options and techniques available in a face-to-face meeting. E-mail can often offer a tempting but ineffective way out of a difficult communication situation. It's important to maintain consistency between your electronic and your personal communications.

Even more important, a large volume of medical research demonstrates that a reasonable amount of person-to-person contact is essential to one's overall well-being. Edward M. Hallowell, a psychiatrist and senior lecturer at Harvard Medical School, has emphasized that, in the age of the Internet, people benefit greatly from more "human moments" at work. He defines these as "an authentic psychological encounter that can only happen when two people inhabit the same physical space. It has two prerequisites: peoples' physical presence, and their emotional and intellectual attention" (*Boston Globe*, p. G1, 4/13/06). The Internet provides endless opportunities to get your job done without interacting with others, but personal interactions provide essential opportunities for reality-checking and emotional sustenance.

Study Questions

1. If you use E-mail, do you find yourself communicating differently than you would in speaking or writing?
2. Analyze your E-mail. How much is business, how much personal?
3. Have you ever used E-mail for a communication that would have been more effective in another form?
4. How important is it to write correctly when you send an E-mail message? How does the answer to this question depend on your audience?
5. How should organizations take advantage of websites, blogs, and other communication opportunities on the Internet?

Consider these questions when reading the following case.

CASE 15.1

The E-Mail Encounter

After four years with Brown & Smith LLP (the "firm"), Susan Sullivan, a senior accountant hoped to be recognized for her skills and accomplishments. She worked hard to build a reputation within the firm as an exemplary employee. However, in an unfortunate situation, Susan found herself positioned as the scapegoat for a series of management blunders, made by someone other than herself. Although Susan was leaving the firm, she hoped for an opportunity to proclaim her innocence from the managerial mishaps and redeem her reputation.

BACKGROUND

Brown & Smith LLP was one of the largest public accounting firms with offices around the world. Like the firm, some of its largest audit clients had international operations. In order to provide service to these international clients, the firm prepared an international strategic plan. The strategic plan was designed to encompass a description of the services, as well as the offices that performed these services, for the particular client. Therefore the development and implementation of the strategic plan depended on a high level of communication between the engagement personnel.

A typical audit engagement team had several layers of personnel including (in order of seniority) a partner, manager, senior and several staff. An international client with several locations had an audit team assigned to the corporate headquarters and each subsidiary location.

The audit teams at the subsidiary locations reported the results of their work to the corporate audit team upon its completion. The corporate audit manager was responsible for coordinating all communication with the subsidiary audit teams.

E-mail allowed for efficient, timely delivery of business information, regardless of the physical boundaries. Due to the nature and extent of the international engagements performed by the firm, the use of E-mail expanded from an intra-office to inter-office communication medium. Members of the firm around the world used E-mail to communicate with each other on a daily basis.

THE ENCOUNTER

Susan began her career in the Audit Department of the firm in NewYork City immediately upon her graduation from a well-known business school in Boston, Massachusetts. During her third year with the firm, Susan was assigned to Hamstead Inc., a large international audit client. Hamstead was headquartered in NewYork City, and had subsidiary locations in many countries around the world. Susan began her career on the Hamstead engagement as a staff accountant and was quickly promoted to senior accountant.

In March of 1997, the Hamstead corporate audit team conducted a meeting to plan for the upcoming audit. The meeting was focused on the preparation of the international strategic plan as well as a review of each member's responsibility for the engagement. The following personnel, who were all members of the New York City office, attended the meeting:

Partner	Mark Davin
Manager	John Blackwood
Manager in training	Paul Savona
Senior	Susan Sullivan
Staff	Grace Hudson, Jeff Martinelli, and Gregory Miko

After the meeting John approached Susan and asked her for help with the strategic plan. Although she was aware that this was John's area of responsibility, she agreed.

At the meeting held on March 10, it was decided that E-mail would be the most timely and efficient way to communicate with members of the international engagement team. To help John with the planning process, Susan gathered names and E-mail addresses of the appropriate international partners and drafted a copy of the first E-mail message that was to be sent out to them.

Susan worked with John on several occasions and therefore was familiar with his management style. He was known to be very disorganized. In fact, he often misplaced important documents. Considering this, Susan drafted the first E-mail message stating that all correspondence should be sent to the attention of John's administrative assistant. This way the documents could be properly accounted for and filed in a central location, accessible to all corporate team members. However, John refused this suggestion, claiming that he was perfectly capable of handling all of the international correspondence.

April 13, 1997

Susan and John worked on the strategic plan for a few weeks. Finally on April 13, John sent an E-mail message to all of the international engagement partners detailing the reporting requirements and respective deadlines for the Hamstead audit (*Exhibit 1*).

May 17, 1997

Weeks passed and on May 17, Susan realized that the corporate audit team had not received the reporting requirements from the Hamstead engagement teams, which were due on May 15. Susan called John to discuss the delinquency. John verified that he had not received any international correspondence and stated, "I will watch my mail for the next few weeks and then send out an E-mail message by the end of the month to the engagement partners."

May 30, 1997

On May 30, Susan entered John's office. In between the stacks of paper piled on top of his desk, Susan spotted John and said, "John, have you received any correspondence from the Hamstead subsidiaries?" "You know Susan," John gritted "I am really starting to question the competency of the international partners on this account. They don't seem to be living up to their end of the bargain." With that, John sent an E-mail message to the engagement partners (*Exhibit 2*).

Over the next week Susan received several E-mail messages from some of the international partners. All of the messages claimed that their reports were sent to John's attention, according to the deadline presented in his 4/13/97 E-mail message (*Exhibits 3 and 4*).

June 1, 1997

The corporate partner, Mark Davin, was extremely disappointed with the nature of the messages received from the international partners. On June 1, he confronted John, in front of Susan, and asked for an explanation. "I have no idea what the problem could be," John claimed. "I have been watching my

EXHIBIT 1

John_Blackwood@Brown&Smith-US
04/13/97 9:08 A.M.

To: Phillip_Williams@Brown&Smith-London, Jose_Martinez@Brown&Smith-Mexico, Frank_Hausle@Brown&Smith-Italy, Jorge_Corone@Brown&Smith-Venezuela, Vanessa_Gorton@Brown&Smith-Australia, Rainer_Lengle@Brown&Smith-Germany, Hung_Su@Brown&Smith-China, Brenda_DuBois@Brown&Smith-France, Elizabeth_Harding@Brown&Smith-Netherlands, Matthew_Riley@Brown&Smith-Ireland
cc: Mark_Davin@Brown&Smith-US, Paul_Savona@Brown&Smith-US, Susan_Sullivan@Brown&Smith-US
Subject: Request for information

In accordance with the International Audit Instructions for our audit of Hamstead Inc. for the year ended August 31, 1997, we have determined the due dates for audit reporting requirements to be as follows:

Reporting Requirement	Due Date
Planning Memorandum (for each individual Hamstead Inc. company)	May 15, 1997
Early Warning Questionnaire	August 15, 1997
Internal Control Memorandum	September 15, 1997
Year-End Memorandum on Examination	September 15, 1997
Year-End Statutory Financial Statements	October 30, 1997
Fee and Budget Analysis	November 15, 1997

All correspondence should be sent to my attention at the following address or fax number:

Brown & Smith LLP
100 Congress Avenue
New York, NY 10002

Fax: (230) 385-1050

If you should have any questions regarding this timetable, please call me at (230) 385-1000.

Thank you for your continued cooperation on the Hamstead Inc. engagement.

John Blackwood
Manager—Hamstead Inc.
Brown & Smith—U.S.

mail like a hawk and have not received any of the correspondence." After a few minutes of discussion, Susan and Mark left John's office so that he could compile his responses to the international partners.

June 2, 1997

Susan arrived at work on June 2 expecting to find that an E-mail message was sent from John to the international partners. What she didn't expect was that John had blamed her for the entire mishap (*Exhibits 5 and 6*). Susan was furious, although not completely surprised. John had a reputation as being one to only watch out for himself. She decided to call John and ask him about the E-mail messages. Much to her dismay, John was less than apologetic, and told Susan to put the issue to rest (*Exhibit 7*). The insult and injury did not stop after this incident.

June 10, 1997

On June 10, John sent an E-mail message to all the international partners apologizing for the improper handling of the correspondence (*Exhibit 8*).

At this point Susan was faced with a very difficult decision. If she sought an apology and

EXHIBIT 2

John_Blackwood@Brown&Smith-US
05/30/97 10:10 A.M.

To: Phillip_Williams@Brown&Smith-London, Jose_Martinez@Brown&Smith-Mexico, Frank_Hausle@Brown&Smith-Italy, Jorge_Corone@Brown&Smith-Venezuela, Vanessa_Gorton@Brown&Smith-Australia, Rainer_Lengle@Brown&Smith-Germany, Hung_Su@Brown&Smith-China, Brenda_DuBois@Brown&Smith-France, Elizabeth_Harding@Brown&Smith-Netherlands, Matthew_Riley@Brown&Smith-Ireland
cc: Mark_Davin@Brown&Smith-US, Paul_Savona@Brown&Smith-US, Susan_Sullivan@Brown&Smith-US
Subject: Request for information

This note is to serve as a reminder that the Hamstead Inc. corporate audit team has not received the following audit reporting requirements from any of the reporting subsidiaries:

Audit Reporting Requirement	Due Date
Planning Memorandum (for each individual Hamstead Inc. subsidiary company)	May 15, 1997

Please forward the audit reporting requirement noted above as soon as possible as the due date has passed. All correspondence should be sent to my attention at the following address or fax number:

Brown & Smith LLP
100 Congress Avenue
New York, NY 10002

Fax: (230) 385-1050

If you should have any questions, please call me at (230) 385-1000.

Thank you for your continued cooperation on the Hamstead Inc. engagement.

John Blackwood
Manager—Hamstead Inc.
Brown & Smith—U.S.

EXHIBIT 3

Phillip_Williams@Brown&Smith-London
05/31/97 9:00 A.M.

To: John_Blackwood@Brown&Smith-US
cc: Mark_Davin@Brown&Smith-US, Paul_Savona@Brown&Smith-US, Susan_Sullivan@Brown&Smith-US
Subject: Request for information

I apologize for the inconvenience. We sent the information on 5/16/97 via DHL, next day delivery. I can't imagine why you have not received it. We will send out a fax of the document today to the fax number indicated on the 4/13/97 e-mail message.

Regards.

EXHIBIT 4

Vanessa_Gorton@Brown&Smith-Australia
05/31/97 7:30 P.M.

To: John_Blackwood@Brown&Smith-US
cc: Mark_Davin@Brown&Smith-US, Paul_Savona@Brown&Smith-US, Susan_Sullivan@Brown&Smith-US
Subject: Request for information

We sent the information. It went to the attention of John Blackwood. Courier records indicate that it was delivered on 5/16/97.

Please advise.

EXHIBIT 5

John_Blackwood@Brown&Smith-US
06/02/97 9:17 A.M.

To: Phillip_Williams@Brown&Smith-London
cc: Mark_Davin@Brown&Smith-US, Paul_Savona@Brown&Smith-US, Susan_Sullivan@Brown&Smith-US
Subject: Request for information

I am grateful for your offer to send a fax version of the planning memorandum. It seems as though the Hamstead Inc. corporate senior, Susan Sullivan, misplaced the original copy.

Regards.

demanded a retraction of the E-mail message, she would risk conflict among the audit team. On the other hand, if she did not address the issue she would accept blame for the mishaps and damage her reputation with the international partners and other members of the firm.

July 1, 1997

Susan struggled with the situation for weeks. She decided that she needed to take action. She hoped for an opportunity to remove her name from the mishap and restore her reputation within the firm. But no such opportunity appeared. She considered speaking personally with the members of the U.S. audit team. However, this would not redeem her reputation with the international partners. She considered calling all of the partners to explain the situation. However, this was not the most efficient way to communicate her message. After considering all of the options available to her, she decided to send out an E-mail message to all of the Hamstead engagement partners (*Exhibit 9*).

The first few hours after Susan sent the E-mail messages were stressful as she anxiously waited to hear from the recipients. She wondered how the partners would receive her message and whether or not E-mail was the appropriate way to send it.

Days after Susan's E-mail was sent, John approached Susan and asked her to join him in his office. John expressed his extreme disappointment with Susan's actions, as well as his desire to put an end to the situation. Susan agreed. Susan never heard anything from anyone else on the Hamstead audit team.

On Susan's last day with the firm, a member of the human resource department shared some interesting information with her. Evidently, there were

EXHIBIT 6

John_Blackwood@Brown&Smith-US
06/02/97 9:23 A.M.

To: Vanessa_Gorton@Brown&Smith-Australia
cc: Mark_Davin@Brown&Smith-US, Paul_Savona@Brown&Smith-US, Susan_Sullivan@Brown&Smith-US
Subject: Request for information

It seems as though the Hamstead Inc. corporate senior, Susan Sullivan, misplaced the original document that you sent. Be assured that we are in the process of addressing the situation. In the meantime, can you please send another copy of the planning memorandum via fax or express mail to my attention, as indicated on the previous message.

Thank you for your cooperation in this matter.

EXHIBIT 7

Summary of a phone conversation:
06/02/97 2:37 P.M.

John: Brown & Smith, John Blackwood speaking.
Susan: Hi, John. It's Susan. I was wondering if you had a minute to discuss the Hamstead Inc. account.
John: Sure, Susan. What's going on?
Susan: Well, with regard to the mishaps with the reporting requirements from the subsidiaries . . .
John: Yes, what about it?
Susan: I noticed that you sent out some messages regarding the handling of these documents.
John: Yes, I felt that they deserved an explanation. After all these so-called mishaps affected over half of the subsidiaries.
Susan: Yes, John, I agree. But I am a little concerned about the explanation that was given. I mean we did find the originals buried on your desk. They were not lost. And I was not happy with my name being pinned to the crime when, in fact, I had nothing to do with it.
John: Well, Susan, you know that sometimes you have to make sacrifices for the good of the team. In this case the corporate team. Besides, whom else could we blame?
Susan: It is not about blaming anyone. It is just a matter of explaining the unfortunate situation.
John: You certainly are not suggesting that I tell 12 international partners that I lost their reports on my desk. Are you forgetting that I am up for partner this year?
Susan: Of course not, John, but . . .
John: Well, I hope that this conversation has cleared up any concerns you might have had about the way the matter was handled. I assume that this is the last we will hear of this. Is that correct, Susan?
Susan: Yes John. Good-bye.

several other senior accountants who were subject to the same treatment from John Blackwood. Disclosure of the Hamstead situation encouraged the other senior accountants to defend their accomplishments. And although the firm was not pleased with Susan's approach to the situation, in terms of the content and medium of the message, they were impressed that she had the courage to stand up for her reputation.

EXHIBIT 8

John_Blackwood@Brown&Smith-US
06/10/97 10:07 A.M.

To: Phillip_Williams@Brown&Smith-London, Jose_Martinez@Brown&Smith-Mexico, Frank_Hausle@Brown&Smith-Italy, Jorge_Corone@Brown&Smith-Venezuela, Vanessa_Gorton@Brown&Smith-Australia, Rainer_Lengle@Brown&Smith-Germany, Hung_Su@Brown&Smith-China, Brenda_DuBois@Brown&Smith-France, Elizabeth_Harding@Brown&Smith-Netherlands, Matthew_Riley@Brown&Smith-Ireland
cc: Mark_Davin@Brown&Smith-US, Paul_Savona@Brown&Smith-US, Susan_Sullivan@Brown&Smith-US
Subject: Request for information

As many of you are aware, there has been some confusion among the corporate audit team regarding proper handling of the reporting requirements received in our office from all of the subsidiaries. I am writing to apologize on behalf of myself and the U.S. Hamstead Inc. partners for this confusion. I can assure you that the matter has been taken care of and you can expect a more efficient handling of reporting requirements in the future.

Again, all correspondence should be sent to my attention at the following address or fax number:

Brown & Smith LLP
100 Congress Avenue
New York, NY 10002

Fax: (230) 385-1050

If you should have any further concerns regarding the reporting requirement process, please call me at (230) 385-1000.

Thank you for your continued cooperation on the Hamstead Inc. engagement.

John Blackwood
Manager—Hamstead Inc.
Brown & Smith—U.S.

EXHIBIT 9

Susan_Sullivan@Brown&Smith-US
07/01/97 9:54 A.M.

To: Phillip_Williams@Brown&Smith-London, Jose_Martinez@Brown&Smith-Mexico, Frank_Hausle@Brown&Smith-Italy, Jorge_Corone@Brown&Smith-Venezuela, Vanessa_Gorton@Brown&Smith-Australia, Rainer_Lengle@Brown&Smith-Germany, Hung_Su@Brown&Smith-China, Brenda_DuBois@Brown&Smith-France, Elizabeth_Harding@Brown&Smith-Netherlands, Matthew_Riley@Brown&Smith-Ireland
cc: Mark_Davin@Brown&Smith-US, Paul_Savona@Brown&Smith-US, Susan_Sullivan@Brown&Smith-US
Subject: Request for information

I am the senior accountant on the Hamstead Inc. audit engagement. I am writing this message in response to the e-mail messages sent out by John Blackwood, corporate manager of Hamstead.

As John's messages accurately point out, there has been some confusion among the corporate audit team regarding proper handling of international correspondence. However, contrary to John's message, I was not the cause of this confusion. As with all international engagements at Brown & Smith, responsibility for international correspondence lies with the corporate manager. My involvement with the matter was limited.

This message was not intended to be a counterattack on a colleague. Rather, the intent of this message was to present my firm disagreement with John's message and to uphold my reputation as an employee of Brown & Smith.

Regards.

Study Questions

1. How does communicating by E-mail vary from telephone conversations or talking personally?
2. Was the tone of the E-mails Susan sent and received inappropriate? If so, how?
3. What steps should Susan take next?
4. Evaluate John Blackwood's and Susan Sullivan's communications from an ethical standpoint. Was either guilty of unethical behavior. Why or why not?

Unifone Communications

The room was divided: on one side of the table were the senior executives of WorldNet Incorporated, and on the other side was Unifone Communications, a global telecommunications company. You could feel the hostility between the two corporations. As Leonard Snipes sat there in the conference room listening to Tom Marshall, the Executive Vice President of Product Operations & Chief Operating Officer, explain Unifone Communication's position on the current contract, he could just see the anger building with the executives of WorldNet. It took four months of proposals and counter proposals before the two corporations could agree on a rate structure. Now a month and a half later, the foundation of the contract was being criticized.

Tom talked of how the industry was rapidly changing, and how the WorldNet contract was restricting the company from using alternate telecommunication carriers, thus preventing Unifone from taking advantage of the deregulated market. Tom went on to explain how the contract provided no flexibility to operate the business properly, and that surely if the contract was adhered to, then Unifone Communications would fail.

The meeting ended with very hostile feelings. Unifone's management saw no effort on WorldNet's part to help resolve the issue; the overall feeling was that WorldNet was only concerned with whether Unifone would meet the $500,000 monthly commitment. WorldNet's position infuriated Tom to the point where he was determined to disconnect all WorldNet service by the end of the current year. Working in Product Operations for the past two years, Leonard knew that this would be next to impossible, seeing that WorldNet represented approximately 90% of the Unifone Communications U.S. and International Direct Dial termination (the link between the Unifone network and the end customer) service. As Carrier Relations Manager, it was Leonard's responsibility to deal with WorldNet on a daily basis; ultimately he would be the one most affected by Tom's outburst. Leonard knew that if these two corporations were going to have a successful relationship, the bridge had to be repaired ASAP.

HISTORY OF UNIFONE COMMUNICATIONS

Unifone Communications was founded in 1992 to take advantage of the deregulation of the telecommunications market through the use of a dedicated private network designed by Unifone engineers. This network is made up of dedicated circuits, frame relays, satellite links, and other forms of telephone circuits, which connect 20 countries. Customers within these countries can access the

EXHIBIT 1 The Theory Behind the Unifone Network

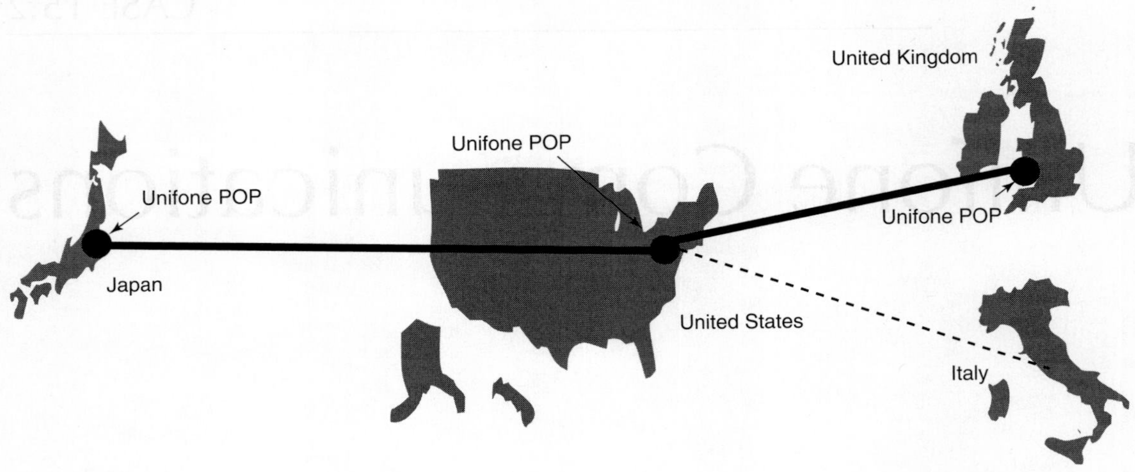

Example #1: A customer dials into the Unifone Communications network in Japan; this customer wants to send a fax to the United Kingdom. The minute of traffic enters the Unifone network in Japan and flows all the way through the international circuits to the Unifone Point of Presence (POP) in the U.K., where it is then sent to the customer via a local carrier in the U.K.

Example #2: That same customer wants to send a fax to Italy. Unifone does not have a POP in Italy, but 99.9% of the time it is going to be cheaper to dial directly from the U.S. than from Japan. So that minute of traffic will travel the Unifone network to the U.S., where it will be handed off to WorldNet, who dials internationally for Unifone.

Unifone network and deliver fax traffic around the world (see *Exhibit 1*).

As Unifone Communications' growth began to accelerate, the need to bring on a new and innovative telecommunications carrier to help deliver traffic became more urgent. In the beginning it made sense to use AT&T to help establish Unifone as a quality telecommunications provider, but with growth comes the cost-cutting efforts to help increase margins. By switching service to WorldNet, Unifone Communications would save approximately 50% to 75% on its local and international delivery traffic. One Unifone executive commented:

> In the beginning, the relationship worked well. If Unifone needed additional circuits installed, within a week they were available. The rate structure WorldNet offered was fantastic, as they were willing to negotiate on routes that we needed, while we gave them traffic to routes that they needed. The relationship worked so well, that Unifone added additional services with them: 1-800 dial in, PBX (office phones), co-location (Unifone housed equipment with them), Wholesale Voice, and Resale Voice. The WorldNet representatives were very happy as Unifone Communications grew to a $750,000 + per month account.

THE CURRENT CONTRACT

About four months before the expiration of the previous contract, prior management started to build a new contract with WorldNet. It was a very painstaking process, as WorldNet insisted on a certain rate structure, and was not very flexible in its negotiations. WorldNet realized that much of the Unifone network had been built with WorldNet circuitry, leaving management Unifone with little leverage.

From September to December, Unifone and WorldNet continued to negotiate, basing the contract on potential growth projections and past performance. During the final month of the contract, it was announced that, John Smith, Senior Manager in charge of the negotiations, would be leaving Unifone. John's final act as a Unifone employee would be to complete the WorldNet contract. At this point, the bickering seemed irrelevant to John; he just wanted to finish and get on to his new job. He assured Tom that Unifone would have no problem meeting the minimum commitment of $500,000, and he chose to ignore the new zero growth projections being released from finance, because that would mean starting the negotiating process all over again. Given John's status with the company, Tom took John's word and signed the contract without question.

On December 31, 1997, Leonard Snipes accepted a new role as Carrier Relations Manager for Product Operations, taking over for John. His main responsibility would be to negotiate and hedge carrier rates against one another to achieve a least-cost routing structure for company traffic. Upon arriving at his desk the first day after the New Year, a folder appeared containing the current contracts for all Unifone's U.S. international carriers. At the top of the file was the newly signed WorldNet contract, which took effect on January 1, 1998.

There were many similar and overlapping responsibilities between Leonard's old position and his new position, allowing him to jump right into the routing and negotiating function. Over the next two weeks, Leonard started to experience some barriers that prevented him from sending company traffic to the lowest cost carrier. This barrier was the minimum commitment clause stating that Unifone Communications must spend $500,000 on a monthly basis or pay the difference between the minimum and the invoiced amount. Leonard came to find out quickly that WorldNet was not the lowest cost carrier for much of their service, but because of the commitment, he was forced to keep the traffic on WorldNet's circuits. When Leonard informed Tom of the problem, Tom immediately asked to have a meeting set up with WorldNet.

CURRENT STATUS

The relationship between Unifone Communications and WorldNet continued to deteriorate after the meeting, and Leonard was stuck dead in the middle of it. WorldNet refused to negotiate or pass any new savings on to Unifone. They imposed an unexplained Federal Communications Commission fee of 5% on the overall invoice. Unifone's in-house customer service representative was removed.

One of the biggest issues dealt with the need for additional WorldNet capacity. Unifone's new product is a fast growing broadcast fax service. This type of service uses a lot of capacity, and unfortunately it is not high margin. WorldNet was not pleased when the order for 21 new circuits was placed. The order meant decreased margins for WorldNet, because more U.S. terminated traffic would be flowing through their circuits, and international traffic is what gives them the largest margin. Unifone's engineers immediately started to see errors in the WorldNet orders. The circuits would be going to the wrong location, the channels in the circuit would be blocked, or some other unexplained reason would hold up the service. What used to take WorldNet 5 day to install was now taking 45 business days.

At this point the relationship had completely broken down, and an emergency planning session had been called between Unifone's upper management to help brainstorm how to attack this issue. Present at the meeting were Leonard, Geoff Canyon, Senior Manager of Capacity Planning, and Kimberly Malone (Leonard and Geoff's Manager), Director of Projects and Infrastructure Expansion. The following is the minutes of the meeting.

WORLDNET: ISSUE, CONCERNS, AND POTENTIAL STRATEGIES

Issue: 1 year, $500,000 Monthly Commitment for voice traffic out of the United States

Concerns:

1. Achieving the Financial Commitment on a monthly basis while using Least Cost Routing.
2. Restrictive wording and application of contract.
3. Inflexibility of WorldNet's management that was displayed during the initial meeting.
4. Renegotiating of rates and contract term and commitment.

5. Product Operations strategy had changed since contract was signed.
6. Shift in UNIFONE's growth (International to Domestic).
7. Allocation of Federal Communications Commission (FCC) charge.
8. Lack of customer support from WC (installation of circuits).

Potential Strategies:

1. Struggle through the contract until it expires and work to replace WorldNet.
2. Work with WorldNet to extend contract on a long term/matching rate theory.
3. Petition for the corporate attorney's time to look at a potential WorldNet breach of contract due to excessively long circuit install time and lack of customer support. Unifone wants to meet its commitment but can't because WorldNet is not providing local capacity.
4. Have a senior level management meeting to rebuild relationship and address administrative concerns.
5. Tie multiple products together to meet minimum commitment.
6. Walk away from contract and incur penalties.
7. Order DS3 circuit (28x the normal T1 circuit size) for the LA site and fill with approximately 3.4 million minutes/month = $190K.
8. Convert existing T1 circuits to an additional DS3 circuit into Marlborough.
9. Begin to install new carriers into the Unifone network.
10. Work with WorldNet, hoping to reduce the monetary commitment, offsetting it by increasing the contractual cost per minutes.
11. Negotiate on the Wide Area Network piece of the business. WorldNet currently contains no piece of the network. Use this to help supplement part of the minimum commitment.

As Carrier Relations Manager, it was agreed upon that it was Leonard's responsibility to build Unifone's strategy for repairing the WorldNet relationship. This strategy was to be written in the form of a memo to Tom, where it would be agreed on and signed off by management.

Study Questions

1. Should Leonard's goal be to repair the relationship with WorldNet?
2. To what extent is it his responsibility to decide corporate strategy?
3. What should he say in the memo?
4. How do points of view collide between individuals? Between corporate cultures?

PART THREE

Technique

CHAPTER 16

Effective Writing: A Brief Manual of Style

INTRODUCTION

This manual is designed as a resource that you can use throughout the course and afterward. In focusing on the basic elements of good writing, it supplements the discussion of accuracy, clarity, brevity, and vigor in Chap. 1 and the treatment of the psychological and persuasive aspects of style and tone in Chap. 8. It has five main sections: sentence structure; word choice; punctuation and mechanics; paragraph unity and coherence; and text formatting.

Effective writing results from rewriting. Once you have outlined your chosen structure (see Chap. 6), generate a first draft quickly without worrying too much about the finer points of style. This will allow your thoughts to flow freely. Because writing is a form of thinking, in the process of drafting, you'll usually discover new arguments for your position, new information you need, and new objections you must answer. Nothing crystallizes thought as much as the exercise of translating it to prose. Then and only then should you turn to this manual to tighten and improve your style.

The baseline on good writing is correct use of the language. If you have fundamental problems with grammar, usage, or sentence structure, your instructor will suggest other resources and exercises to help correct these deficiencies. As we all know, however, distracting errors often creep into the prose of educated and conscientious writers. Collectively, these errors result in fuzziness and imprecision. Even if your readers are not consciously confused or irritated by the lack of clarity, they will certainly find it more difficult to read attentively and respond positively. Thus, good writers must also be good editors. A survey of the most distracting lapses in business writing included comma errors, run-on sentences, missing apostrophes, faulty word choice, and spelling errors.[1] Discussions of these issues and others follow.

[1]Donald J. Leonard and Jeanette W. Gilsdorf, "Language in Change," *Journal of Business Communication,* vol. 27, no. 2 (Spring 1990), p. 46.

Once your style is "correct," however, there may still be room for improvement. Many grammatically correct sentences still lack clarity, power, and vigor. This manual is designed for all those who generally write correct English but could use help with the finer points of grammar and with turning correct writing into effective writing.

I. SENTENCE STRUCTURE

A. Correctness

1. Learn to Recognize the Main Subject and Verb of the Sentence

A sentence expresses a complete thought. Every sentence contains a subject and a predicate or verb:

> (subject) (verb)
> The *company declared* a profit.

Either subject or verb may be expanded with modifiers of various sorts:

> The *company,* which only last year suffered a loss of $270 million, *declared* a profit in the last quarter of the year.

But the main subject and the main verb still contain the essential meaning. As you edit, be aware of the main subjects and verbs of your statements. Revising a wordy or tangled sentence requires you to identify or strengthen its grammatical heart—the main subject and main verb.

2. Make Subject and Verb Agree in Number

A singular subject takes a singular verb; plural subjects take plural verbs. When you edit, be sure that the subject of the verb, and not a noun that just happens to be close to the verb, determines whether the verb is singular or plural. This is easy when sentences are short and simple. But errors can be made when the subject is some distance from the verb or when the subject follows the verb:

> *The chief financial officer,* as well as many other top managers, *is* (not *are*) on vacation.
> *These new software products,* unlike the one introduced last December, *have* (not *has*) been popular.
> There *is* (not *are*) *a shortage* of highly skilled workers. (Here *shortage* is the subject.)

Note that nouns in modifying or parenthetical phrases ("as well as many other top managers") and nouns that serve as the object of prepositions ("of highly skilled workers") cannot serve as the main subject of a verb.

Collective nouns, such as *company, team, committee,* and *department* are treated as grammatically singular. They refer to a group as a unified whole:

> The new product *team deserves* a bonus.
> The ethics *committee is* still in session.

Compound subjects are plural:

> *Maria and Sam are* both in the running for the promotion.

Occasionally a compound of two closely related items may be construed as singular:

> The *hiring and firing* of subordinates *is* an important managerial task.

3. Avoid Run-on Sentences

Run-on sentences fail to respect sentence boundaries. They attempt to join two complete thoughts with insufficiently strong punctuation or connective words:

> The *company,* which only last year suffered a loss of $270 million, *declared a profit* and the chief executive *officer was congratulated* by the board of directors.

In this example, there are two main subjects and two main verbs; they need a clear boundary between them. The boundary can be provided by inserting a comma before *and:*

> The *company,* which only last year suffered a loss of $270 million, *declared a profit,* and the chief executive *officer was congratulated* by the board of directors.

by a semicolon alone:

> The *company,* which only last year suffered a loss of $270 million, *declared a profit;* the chief executive *officer was congratulated* by the board of directors.

by a semicolon plus a so-called conjunctive adverb plus a comma:

> The *company,* which only last year suffered a loss of $270 million, *declared a profit; consequently,* the chief executive *officer was congratulated* by the board of directors.

or by splitting the passage into two separate sentences:

> The *company,* which only last year suffered a loss of $270 million, *declared a profit.* The chief executive *officer was congratulated* by the board of directors.

Finally, to avoid the passive construction:

> The company, which only last year lost $270 million, declared a profit. The board of directors congratulated the chief executive officer.

(For more on the different ways to punctuate compound sentences, see "Punctuation and Mechanics.")

4. Avoid Unintentional Sentence Fragments

Sentence fragments are incomplete thoughts punctuated as sentences. Unintentional sentence fragments confuse a reader, and they suggest carelessness or immaturity on the part of the writer. To correct inadvertent fragments, turn them into complete sentences, or combine them with the neighboring sentence to which they logically belong:

Fragment Staff members objected to the introduction of yet another word processing program. *The reason being that they had already learned three new programs in two years.*
Staff members welcomed the new word processing program. *Even though they had already learned three new programs in two years.*

Corrected *Having already learned three new programs in the last two years,* staff members objected to the introduction of yet another word processing program.
Even though they had already learned three new programs in the last two years, staff members welcomed the new word processing program.

Some writers use sentence fragments deliberately for emphasis and expressiveness; but in most business documents, fragments should be used sparingly, if at all. They may seem melodramatic or sarcastic:

The task force tried to turn the situation around. *But in vain.*
The committee regretted not having notified the sales force earlier. *As if that would have made a difference.*

5. Avoid Dangling Modifiers

Introductory modifying phrases, whether participles or noun phrases, must logically apply to the noun that immediately follows them. Otherwise, your sentence will be illogical, like the following:

As *executives and buyers* of McGregor's Ltd., I am seeking your input regarding the new Employee Discount Program.

As written, the introductory phrase illogically equates *executives and buyers* with *I*. Revised, the sentence might read:

As *executives and buyers* of McGregor's Ltd., *you* will have a role in shaping the new Employee Discount Program.

Or the problem can be eliminated by turning the phrase into a clause with its own subject and verb, thus removing the implied equation:

Since the support of the executives and buyers is essential to any policy change, I am seeking your input regarding the new Employee Discount Program.

Introductory participles (verb forms typically ending in *-ed* or *-ing*) must also logically relate to the noun immediately following. The closest noun must be capable of performing the action implied in the participle. Be sure your sentence does not change horses midstream, as in the following examples:

Dangling *Realizing* Mr. McGregor seldom compromised, *the structure* of the memo would play a vital role in its success.
Revised *Realizing* that Mr. McGregor seldom compromised, *we* felt the structure of the memo would play a vital role in its success.
Dangling By *stating* that tradition can stand in the way of progress, *the employees* will understand that some changes are needed.
Revised By *stating* that tradition can stand in the way of progress, *the memo* seeks [or *I seek*] to persuade the employees that we need to make some changes.

Removing dangling constructions clarifies your meaning and eliminates fuzziness in your writing.

6. Maintain Parallel Structure Where Required

Parallel structure means expressing logically equivalent ideas in a grammatically equivalent form. Faulty parallelism occurs most often because items in a pair (x and y) or series (x, y, and z) don't appear in the same grammatical form:

Faulty In selecting trainees, Ms. Ladenburg looked for *good references* (noun phrase), *experience in sales* (noun phrase), and *the applicant had to demonstrate good oral communication skills* (independent clause).

Parallel In selecting trainees, Ms. Ladenburg looked for *good references, experience in sales,* and *good oral communication skills* (three noun phrases).

Faulty parallel construction is one of the most common causes of bad business writing. While readers or listeners may not say to themselves, "She just violated a grammatical rule," they will notice the inaccuracy and will instinctively think less of the communicator. Respecting parallel structure is another powerful tool for avoiding fuzzy writing.

B. Vigor and Emphasis

Your sentences may be free of grammatical errors, but do they convey confidence and energy, or do they put the reader to sleep? Consider the following techniques for making your style vigorous and emphatic, and thus holding the reader's attention.

1. Use the Active Voice

Most managers have heard that they should avoid excessive use of the passive voice:

Active Bob told Bill.
The company decided. . . .

Passive Bill was told by Bob.
It has been decided that. . . .

The first sentence of each pair is stylistically superior for two reasons: It conveys action and energy, and it has fewer words. Passive constructions rob your sentences of vigor and brevity. Since a passive sentence subordinates or hides the actor ("It has been decided that. . . . "), it often sounds cowardly or evasive. Yet studies have shown that passive constructions occur in 75 percent of business prose. Why?

Sometimes a business writer needs to convey information without assuming responsibility for it. Or to maintain an objective tone, a manager may prefer the impersonality of the passive voice. For example:

Due to market conditions, a number of workers *must be laid off.*

But this does not mean that every sentence needs to be passive. Use passive constructions sparingly. You'll portray yourself as a doer rather than as a victim, and your prose will come alive.

2. Exploit the Power of the Main Subject and Main Verb

In an emphatic sentence, important words occupy prominent positions. Don't waste the power of the main subject and the main verb on "filler," as in the following sentence:

Weak By definition, *the practice* (main subject) of redlining *is* (main verb) an instance of arbitrary discrimination against individuals.

The heart of this rambling sentence is wasted on an empty, abstract statement (*the practice . . . is*). To locate the *real subject* and the *real action* in such a sentence, follow Richard Lanham's advice.[2] Ask yourself, Who's doing what to whom? or Who's kicking whom? Then express that action in a simple, active verb. *Redlining* is the real subject. What does it do? It *discriminates.* So revise accordingly:

Emphatic By definition, *redlining* (main subject) *discriminates* (main verb) against individuals.

3. Use Parallel Structure to Organize Rambling Sentences

The following sentence, while grammatically correct, is rambling and hard to grasp:

Rambling The goal of the new planning process is to provide headquarters with more accurate information about the long-range needs of each division so that they can be reviewed and coordinated at the corporate level to ensure that capital is allocated fairly in accordance with coherent overall strategy.

This sentence, also typical of bad business writing, binds several ideas together with weak connectives such as *about, so that, to ensure that,* and *in accordance with.* Rather than link the ideas end to end, consider making them three parallel "goals" expressed in parallel form (to . . . , to . . . , and to . . . .). Compare:

Parallel The goals of the new planning process are *to gather* accurate information about the needs of each division, *to review* these needs at the corporate level, and *to allocate* capital fairly according to an overall strategy.

Parallel structure saves words and throws your main points into relief. The reader can now see the connections: gathering information and reviewing needs will lead to fairer allocation of capital.

4. Divide Rambling Sentences in Two

You can also increase emphasis by breaking one rambling sentence into two short ones, using a period, colon, or semicolon:

Weak The proponent's claim is very weak as studies show that parents make the final decision to purchase and serve advertised cereals.

Emphatic The proponent's claim is weak; studies show that parents make the decision to purchase and serve advertised cereals.

[2] *Revising Business Prose* (New York: Scribner's, 1981).

Dropping *very* and *final* also contribute to making this sentence more emphatic.

5. Avoid Oversubordination

Good writing uses subordinate phrases and clauses with care. A sentence with excessive subordinate subjects and verbs spreads itself too thin. Reduce unnecessary subordination by putting key words into the key grammatical positions—the main subject and main verb:

Weak	*Because the proposal provides a framework for more frequent consultation* with local leaders *than has previously been the case,* an improvement in communication and flow of information should be effected *if it is adopted.* (three subordinate clauses)
Emphatic	*Because the proposal provides for more consultation with local leaders,* adopting it should improve communication. (one subordinate clause)

6. Put the Most Important Idea at the End of the Sentence

The end of any utterance carries the most weight; the next most emphatic position is the beginning. Thus, key words should appear at either the beginning or the end. In particular, don't let a sentence trail off into insignificance:

Weak	The company declared a profit in the last quarter as a result of software innovations that proved extremely popular with many customers.
Emphatic	As a result of software innovations that proved extremely popular, the company declared a profit.
Weak	The advertising campaign was canceled, although the initial results were encouraging up to a point.
Emphatic	Although the initial results were encouraging, we canceled the advertising campaign. (emphasizes the cancellation) *or* We canceled the advertising campaign despite encouraging initial results. (emphasizes "despite the initial results")

As these examples demonstrate, you can advocate a point of view or plant the impression you wish by making your sentences emphatic.

Vigorous writing gives you far more control over your content and its impact, and it's also more economical. Each of these revisions is several words shorter than its weak equivalent. Saving a few words per sentence may not seem like much, but this practice can reduce the length of a document or a speech by 10 to 20 percent. Your reader or listener will be grateful.

A final note on sentences (this is a correctly used sentence fragment). As you review your draft, you will notice that most of your sentences are declarative; that is, they make a statement: "Bob told Bill." The alternative sentence structures are interrogative ("Did Bob tell Bill?") or imperative ("Bob, tell Bill."). Interrogative and imperative sentences strike the reader more forcefully than declarative ones because instead of merely conveying information, they demand a response: answer me, do something. Some business writers are fond of the interrogative form called the *rhetorical question* (that is, a question to which the writer already has an answer), such as "Should we respond to these attacks, or should we crawl into a hole?" Beware; the reader may cringe at the obvious. Frequent use of interrogative or imperative sentences can make your prose seem overheated. Use them only occasionally, when you're looking for maximum impact.

II. WORD CHOICE

Once you've developed your draft and edited it with an eye to paragraph and sentence structure, a few key tests will ensure that your language is as clear, concise, and forceful as possible.

A. Double-Check Words Commonly Confused or Misused

To be sure you have chosen the word you need, be aware of the following commonly confused words:

Word	Meaning
accept	to receive, come to terms with
except	other than, but
advice	noun: counsel
advise	verb: to counsel
affect	verb: to have an effect on
effect	verb: to bring about
effect	noun: influence
among	shared by three or more
between	shared by two
as	used to introduce phrases or clauses
like	used to convey similarity between nouns and pronouns
assure	to give confidence to
ensure	to make sure of
insure	to cover by insurance
attend	to go to
intend	to plan
compose	to make up, constitute
comprise	to include
continual	repeated
continuous	uninterrupted, ongoing
e.g.	for example
i.e.	that is
eminent	distinguished
imminent	about to happen
its	possessive pronoun: belonging to it
it's	contraction of *it is*
farther	more distant
further	over more time or in a greater amount

precede	to go before
proceed	to move ahead
principal	adjective: most important
	noun: chief officer of a school
	noun: amount of a loan
principle	noun: a basic truth
there	adverb: as opposed to here
their	possessive pronoun: belonging to them

B. Where Possible, Use Simple, Familiar Verbs

Novice writers tend to think that the longer the word, the more impressive it will be, but the reverse is usually true. We do not recommend offering your reader a steady diet of monosyllables; but most business prose is so heavy with polysyllabic, Latinate words that a dose of simple Anglo-Saxon words is bracing.

In particular, consider simplifying polysyllabic verbs, such as *accomplish (do)*. Many overworked verbs ending in *-ate* have simpler equivalents: *facilitate (help, aid)*. Simple verbs are also better than controversial coinages ending in *-ize,* such as *finalize (finish, complete)*. Ironically, readers soon tire of words newly added to the language. New coinages that are not yet widely accepted should also be avoided:

Fancy word	Familiar equivalent
access	use
construct	build, make
encounter	meet
impact (verb)	affect, influence
incent	move, motivate
initiate	start, begin
iterate	repeat
liaise	meet, talk
motivate	move, inspire
optimize	improve, maximize
orientate (when meaning 'familiarize")	orient
prioritize	rank
replicate	repeat, reproduce
suboptimal	less desirable
terminate	end, finish; fire (an employee)

Generally, business communicators should also avoid verbs likely to be used in the tabloids: *skyrocket, devastate, plummet,* or *thrill,* for example. Leave melodrama to the ad writers.

C. Resist the Noun Plague

The *noun plague* refers to the common overuse of attributive nouns (nouns used as adjectives) and nouns that contain an idea better expressed as an active verb. Consider:

> Three classifications of nominalizations are processed by this office and finalized for payroll name entry action by the controller's office.

Classifications is an inflation of *classes,* and *nominalizations* apparently means *names* or *workers. Payroll entry name action* illustrates the logjam created by three attributive nouns and can be expressed more clearly and forcefully by using a verb. A revision of the sentence might read:

> This office handles three classes of workers and sends their names to the controller, who enters them on the payroll.

Technical language in many fields relies on attributive nouns. If the communicator is not careful, the nouns may pile up beyond the point of comprehensibility, as in the following example:

> Minimum rear wheel touchdown or moment of takeoff conditions require the use of high-speed landing and takeoff procedures.

Inserting a series of hyphens to clarify how the nouns relate to one another might help:

> Minimum rear-wheel-touchdown or moment-of-takeoff conditions. . . .

But so many nouns are piled together here that even hyphens can't restore the momentum. The real problem is that the attributive nouns contain all the meaning of the sentence, and the nouns that carry the grammatical weight are empty (conditions, procedures). Hyphens or commas may help in less extreme instances, however.

On inspection, some attributive nouns prove to be redundant. Eliminating the unnecessary ones and inserting a preposition often solves the problem: *proposed capital allocation requests* means *requests for capital.* Another symptom of the noun plague is superfluous "tag nouns." Each of the nouns in italic type is redundant:

Hiring *process*
High-*level* position
Increased production *volume*
Risk *factor*

D. Eliminate Extra Words

Almost all the stylistic devices mentioned so far—using emphatic sentences, parallel structure, active verbs, and cutting back attributive nouns—suggest condensing your draft rather than adding to it. But the point is worth stressing again here. Avoid the following wordy phrases:

Wordy	**Concise**
the course of action that we recommend	our recommendation
in view of the fact that	because, since
owing to the fact that	
regardless of the fact that	although
the question as to whether	whether

in the event that	if
in the process of	during, while
during the course of	
regarding the matter of	about
concerning the matter of	
advance planning	planning
at this point in time	now, at this point, at this time
circle around	circle
connect up	connect
consensus of opinion	consensus
disappear from sight	disappear
end result	result
enclosed herein	enclosed
in close proximity	near, close, proximate
joint cooperation	cooperation
main essentials	essentials
necessary requisite	requisite
potential opportunity	opportunity
refer back, report back	refer, report
surrounding circumstances	circumstances
as well as	and

These are other ways of tightening your style by eliminating unnecessarywords:

- *Cut back modifiers.* Generally, adjectives (which modify nouns, such as *distinguished* colleague, *important* problem) and adverbs (which modify verbs, such as *slowly* moved, *easily* decided) should be used sparingly in business writing. When you edit your draft, test every modifier to see if its presence really contributes to your meaning.
- *Turn clauses into phrases.* "The task that we are going to accomplish today" can be expressed just as clearly by "today's task."
- *Eliminate repetition.* If you've used the same word twice in a sentence or in adjacent sentences, take one out. You'll usually discover that the repeated word either is redundant or can be replaced by a shorter pronoun.
- *Seek a more economical organization.* Often, in editing your draft, you'll discover you've repeated information or arguments. Make these points once and move on. If you find yourself using phrases such as "as I said before," this almost always signals an opportunity for tighter organization. Bring the material you're about to discuss back into the original treatment of this topic.

Clarity, brevity, and vigor are improved if you can spot wordiness and remove it from your prose. This takes discipline and courage. Without the underbrush, your main idea becomes more visible; it may be exposed as weak or banal. Without the reassuring cadences of "It has come to my attention" or "There is considerable evidence," you may fear sounding simpleminded or blunt. This is precisely where good writing itself can help your analysis and your strategy. Once your main idea stands forth clearly—to you as well as to your audience—you can judge its merits and revise it if appropriate.

E. Minimize Jargon

Jargon means language familiar to a tight subgroup, but strange in meaning or usage to the general public. Examples come easily from the computer world, where people are always interfacing, downloading, or thinking outside the box. As long as hackers are talking to each other, these are normal terms of discourse. When addressed to a larger audience, they can sound esoteric or affected. What is clear to one group may be mysterious to another. In short, whether a given buzzword is jargon depends heavily on your audience.

There are really two sorts of jargon. Legitimate jargon consists of specialized words or usages that serve as efficient shorthand in a particular profession, industry, or circle. Managers talking among themselves naturally use the technical terms of finance, marketing, and accounting for this purpose. They are not abusing jargon when they mention *debt, equity, breakeven point, push/pull strategies,* or *selling short,* though the person on the street might be a little hazy as to what most of these terms mean. Sometimes, "vogue words" from currently fashionable fields pass into the public vocabulary. MBA students in recent years talked of *logging face time* with instructors to gain their favor and called empty class comments *chip shots.* Both of these terms have recently showed up in the press. More familiar examples include talking about the *short circuit* in a relationship, the *half-life* of an idea, or the prospect of receiving *feedback* from a boss.

Technical terms become illegitimate jargon when they are pressed beyond their original meanings and substituted for perfectly good words available in the general vocabulary: "I interfaced with the marketing department." Here, the writer is using a technical or official-sounding word that contributes nothing to meaning, and sounds silly. Consider the following passage from a book on management:[3]

> The Golden Rule is another codification of considerations which should govern our choice of actions lest we end by sub-optimizing in terms of our interpersonal objectives.

The business buzzwords in this passage are *interpersonal objectives,* from organizational behavior, and *optimizing,* which seems to come from the applied mathematics of decision trees and forecasting. *Codification of considerations* and *in terms of* are similar to jargon in that they attempt to sound important while meaning nothing. Even a technical audience intent on being amused would probably prefer to hear:

> Obeying the Golden Rule helps people get along with each other.

As Martin and Ohmann have pointed out, the thoughtless use of illegitimate jargon "is more than an irritant to the reader. It is an insidious friend to the writer, for it gives him a sense of power and facility that he has not earned by thought. He can compose in jargon without reflection and with almost no reference to reality."[4] Like other bad writing practices, use of jargon adds unnecessary words.

[3]Quoted in Harold C. Martin and Richard M. Ohmann. *The Logic and Rhetoric of Exposition,* rev. ed. (New York: Holt, Rinehart, and Winston, 1964), p. 243.
[4]Ibid, p. 244.

This section does not purport to cover all the minute points of punctuation and mechanics. For complete coverage consult a handbook or professional reference, such as *The Chicago Manual of Style* (from the University of Chicago Press and available in any library). What follows is a quick survey of the most common rules.

A. A Comma Separates Introductory Words, Phrases, or Clauses from the Body of the Sentence

Nonetheless, the policy must be changed.
To this end, we should consider expanding our product line.
As this policy is open to debate, I thought a two-sided approach was best.

B. A Comma Sets Off Parenthetical Words, Phrases, or Clauses

The committee, *however,* refused to comment to the press.
The treasurer, *always concerned about the bottom line,* objected to the bonuses.

The use of a comma is required to distinguish essential from nonessential information. When set off by commas, the information is nonessential (a *nonrestrictive* element):

The products, *which were heavily advertised,* sold briskly. (This implies that all the products in question were heavily advertised.)

Compare a *restrictive* or essential phrase or clause that is *not* set off by commas:

The products *that were heavily advertised* sold briskly. (This implies that there were other products that were not so heavily advertised.)

Some writers and editors also preserve the distinction by using *which* for nonrestrictive clauses and *that* for restrictive ones (as we did above).

C. A Comma Punctuates Compound Sentences Joined by *and, but, or, not, for, so,* and *yet*

When used to join two complete thoughts, these familiar coordinating conjunctions require a preceding comma:

The company defended its record on worker safety, *and* several union leaders supported its statements.

Omitting the comma results in a run-on sentence (see Section I). Note, however, that linking these two thoughts with only a comma (with no coordinating conjunction) constitutes a *comma splice,* a common error. If you wish to omit the conjunction, you must use a semicolon:

The company defended its record on worker safety; several union leaders supported its statements.

D. Generally, a Semicolon Separates Two Halves of a Sentence, Either of Which Could Stand as a Sentence on its Own

Use of the semicolon prevents short, choppy sentences and suggests that the two ideas are intimately connected, whereas a period would divide them.

As in the last example in Section III C, two complete but related thoughts can be joined by a semicolon. The two thoughts in a compound sentence can also be joined by *conjunctive adverbs* such as *however, therefore, consequently,* and *thus.* When used in this way, these words take a semicolon before them and a comma after them:

> The company defended its record on worker safety; *however,* several union leaders disputed its statements.
>
> The company defended its record on worker safety; *therefore,* OSHA retracted its complaint.

Using a comma instead of a semicolon before these linking words results in a comma splice (see Section III B).

E. A Comma Separates All Elements in a Series

Some writers omit the next-to-last comma (the one after *deadlines* in the example below), but it is always clearer to insert a comma between all items in a series:

> The R&D managers complained about working conditions, unrealistic deadlines, and staff support.

Without the second comma, this sentence would imply that *unrealistic* describes both the deadlines and the staff support.

F. A Single Comma Should Not Separate a Subject from its Verb or Verbs

A single comma should not separate a subject from its verb or verbs. Such commas mislead the reader into thinking a new main thought is beginning:

Incorrect The marketing *campaign* designed by the consultant, *brought* impressive results.

Correct The marketing *campaign* designed by the consultant *brought* impressive results.

Incorrect The marketing *campaign* designed by the consultant *brought* impressive results, *and opened up* several new territories.

Correct The marketing *campaign* designed by the consultant *brought* impressive results *and opened up* several new territories.

A parenthetical element, set off by two commas, may occur between the subject and its verb:

Correct The marketing campaign, which was designed by the consultant, brought. . . .

G. Use Apostrophes to Indicate Possession

The singular possessive can always be correctly formed by adding *'s* to the singular form of the noun (even if the singular already ends in *s*):

> The *department's* vacation schedule was set up by Carl.
> The memo was addressed to *Jonas's* boss. (*Jonas'* is also acceptable.)

The plural possessive is formed by adding an apostrophe to plural nouns ending in *s* and by adding *'s* to plural nouns that do not end in *s:*

> The *three new products'* sales were disappointing.
> The *children's* programming was sponsored chiefly by cereal companies.

Be careful not to confuse the plural form of a noun (*companies*) with the singular possessive (*company's*) or the plural possessive (*companies'*). The words are used correctly below:

> Both *companies* were bankrupt (plural).
> The larger *company's* workers attempted to buy out the stockholders (singular possessive), but both *companies'* futures looked bleak (plural possessive).

IV. PARAGRAPH UNITY AND COHERENCE

Writing effective paragraphs requires sensitivity to both logical coherence and pleasing visual layout. Section IV A considers ways to ensure coherence within and among paragraphs. Section IV B describes effective transition strategies.

A. Paragraph Unity

Your outline—the order in which you make the points that support your thesis—serves as the scaffolding for your document (see Chap. 6). Is your organization likely to involve the audience and commit them to the course of action you desire? If so, you're ready to move to the next step: building your written or spoken paragraphs. Novice writers tend to break off one paragraph and start a new paragraph when the previous one looks too long on the page. Professional writers realize that a successful paragraph is a complete unit of thought that advances the argument.

Only after you've filled in your outline can you make the final paragraph divisions. You may find that you've buried a crucial point in the middle of raw data. Or one paragraph may go on for a page or more. If so, the paragraph probably covers several topics that need to be sorted out. Proper paragraph length is crucial to good writing, because the breaks give the reader or listener a chance to check his understanding of the argument before moving on. Generally, paragraphs that run more than one-third of a page look intimidating and may invite the attention to drift. Conversely, one-sentence paragraphs, while occasionally useful for emphasis, lend themselves to assertion rather than to argument and persuasion.

Generally, the first sentence of your paragraph should state the main point that you will develop in the following sentences. Once you've written your document or developed your speech, test it. One good exercise is to list the first sentence of each paragraph, read them in order, and see whether they build a coherent and compelling case for your conclusion. If so, you've established the basis for a concise and persuasive argument. Sometimes, the thesis sentence should fall toward the middle or end of the paragraph, but a writer needs to master the basic principles of organization described here before making variations on them. Another good exercise is to review your text to make sure that the last sentence of each paragraph leads naturally into the first sentence of the next. If there are gaps, consider using one of the following transitional devices to link the units of thought.

B. Coherence: Using Transitions

Transitional words and phrases signal relationships between ideas. They can signal identity (continuation of an established topic or argument), contrast (clashes within a given set of ideas), concession (acknowledgment of valid opposition), change (a shift to a new topic or argument), or closure. Commonly used transitional expressions include:

Identity	for example; in addition; moreover; also; the following; first, second
Contrast	although; while; however, nevertheless; on one hand, on the other hand
Concession	of course; granted; admittedly; to be sure
Change	on another note; to move on; turning to
Closure	in conclusion; to sum up; in short

Generally, transitions from one paragraph to the next should be clearly signaled, while transitions from one sentence to the next should be unobtrusive.

Transitions within and between paragraphs should signal the progress of the argument and show how each part fits into the whole. Generally, they should correspond to the headings and subheadings of the outline. Effective paragraph transitions demonstrate in a sentence how the next point follows from the previous point and how the topic fits into the thesis. They cite points you've already said you'll cover, or they explain how the next major area you intend to address develops your argument. For example:

> When addressing our production problems, we need to look closely at *the following three areas.* (identity)

This defines the purpose of a section of your report and dictates the thesis sentences of the next three paragraphs.
Or:

> While we have recommended several major changes in our practices in this report, *others have suggested even more radical solutions.* (contrast)

This signals a turn in the direction of your argument.
Or:

> Now that we've identified solutions to our problems, *let's look at how we can implement them.* (change)

This lets the audience know that you're moving from one major topic to the next.

Sentence transitions should make your ideas flow seamlessly. Because paragraphs are units of thought, they need to define the major areas of the argument. Because sentences build that unit of argument, they need to exhibit shared purpose. Each should demonstrate the importance and relevance of the paragraph's thesis. For example:

> While we have recommended several changes in our practices in this report, others have suggested even more radical solutions. Some have said we should close down certain stores. Others have recommended that we abandon certain product lines. Still others even have suggested that we put our business up for sale. Such solutions are self-destructive and unnecessary.

Here the sentences cooperate to demonstrate the thesis and prepare for the conclusion. Or:

> Now that we've identified solutions to our problems, let's look at how we can implement them. We should increase our advertising budget, change some of our purchasing practices, and inspect stores more frequently to ensure they are meeting our standards for cleanliness. Taken together, these steps will increase our profitability.

Other transitional strategies include the following:

1. *Enumeration:* While related to parallelism, enumeration signals to the audience how many points they have to pay attention to. This can be indicated either by numbering the points or by listing them (first, second, third . . .).
2. *Repeating key words.* If you've identified important topics you want to address (markets, distribution, production), citing the word itself as you begin a new paragraph will signal a new unit of thought.
3. *Demonstrative adjective plus noun.* This device works particularly well when you're drawing a conclusion from a previously developed body of information: "This decline in sales. . . ." It can draw audience attention back to the main thesis.

All these transitional devices demonstrate relationships, pulling your ideas or evidence together into an argument. As with every rule in communication, there are exceptions. Sometimes, you want to drive your point home by being surprising and/or blunt.

V. TEXT FORMATTING

The careful use of titles, headings, numbered or indented lists, and white space can help communicate your structure and tone clearly and accurately. You want to highlight main ideas, indicate subordination, and make the progress of your argument stand out.

Accurate *headings* and *subheadings* make a text attractive and accessible. Purely formal headings (*Introduction, Recommendation, Rationale, Implementation, Conclusion*) label these structural divisions and help a reader find the parts of greatest interest easily. Equally helpful are *topical* headings (*Best Advertising Techniques; Why We Need to Respond to This Crisis Now*). Finally, you can use headings or italic type to drive home your main points *(Direct Mail Advertising Brings a 10% Increase in Sales; If We Don't Respond to These Accusations, the Results Will Be Disastrous).*

Often, these techniques can be used in combination, so that a reader who may not have time to follow your argument word for word can skim the document and still retain your key points.

Listing important items or facts can throw them into relief and emphasize clear support for your general point, examples, or facts that result in a key conclusion. Precede them with numbers or bullets, and set them off from the main text, as we have done here:

1. Number or bullet the items.
2. Keep them brief.
3. Don't overuse listing; it will blunt the impact.
4. Keep all points in parallel construction.

The above four points are parallel because they are all imperative sentences, but the same points could be made in clauses or phrases. For example:

We need to remember:

1. To number or bullet all points,
2. To keep them brief,
3. To avoid overusing lists, and
4. To keep all points in parallel construction.

Unlike in the first example, all the numbered items here are parts of a single sentence (We . . . construction.), requiring the *and* at the end of the third point. Finally, keep numbered or bulleted items brief. If you find each requires a paragraph, use headings or subheadings instead.

One common form of listing in business is the *agenda*. Keep it brief, even if it is accompanied by supporting materials, and make sure the points are in an order that will aid your meeting goals.

White space (such as spaces between the numbered items above) gives the reader visual relief and helps make your message stand out.

Effective formatting can convey information about the tone and meaning of your document. Consider *letters*. A business letter in which every paragraph begins flush left (not indented) with extra space between paragraphs conveys a sense of seriousness to the reader. Indented paragraphs seem more friendly and informal. As a general rule of thumb, in letters paragraphs should be indented (because they're personal communications); in memos paragraphs should begin flush left (because they're statements of policy and/or intended for wide distribution).

VI. A QUICK NOTE ON STRUCTURING JOB APPLICATION LETTERS

An exception to the above guidelines may be a *job application cover letter,* which you want to look forceful. Here, blocking of paragraphs may serve you well. But how such a letter should look depends heavily upon your relationship to the interviewer or decision-maker. If you know the person well or even have established a relationship by telephone or electronic communication, you may want to send a friendly, indented, even colloquial letter. (For more on cover letters, see Chap. 6.)

If you're applying cold to a position for which you're reasonably qualified, you may send a letter with blocked paragraphs covering the following points:

Paragraph 1: State your interest in the position and a brief summary of your qualifications.

Paragraph 2: Show you know something about the organization and emphasize why you're interested in working for it.

Paragraph 3: Show how your skills fit the organization's needs.

This model for a cover letter could be described as the *I, you, we* approach. The first paragraph should briefly highlight the most attractive aspects of your resume (*I*). The second should show that you know something about the organization's needs (*you*), whether through experience or research. The third should show that the two of you can work well together (*we*). Avoid the most common fault of job application cover letters: the overuse of *I*. Except in the most extraordinary circumstances (such as a request from the organization for detailed information), keep the letter to under a page.

There are three basic types of cases you can make to demonstrate you're the right candidate for a job:

1. *Experience:* My skills fit your needs.
2. *Analogy:* Skills I've developed are transferable to this position.
3. *Interest:* I've always wanted to do this, and my record demonstrates success at taking on new challenges.

Most application letters will combine these approaches, geared to your level of qualification for the job. On rare occasions, you may decide to use a *broadcast letter,* sent to dozens of firms in your field on the chance that one will respond. Such a letter should be extremely brief and cite your main achievements in a bulleted list to attract maximum attention at a glance.

CONCLUSION

All these principles of good writing return to the fundamental premise of successful communication: Understand and respect your audience. Make your points clearly, pitch your argument at a level the audience can understand, don't condescend or fawn, use the language well, and don't waste anyone's time. Accuracy, clarity, brevity, vigor, and appropriateness will ensure that your document is read and your message received.

OTHER RESOURCES

Lanham, Richard. *Revising Business Prose.* New York: Scribner's, 1981. This text demonstrates very effectively how to move from first draft to the final product.

Munter, Mary. *Guide to Managerial Communication.* Englewood Cliffs, NJ: Prentice-Hall, 1992. This standard business communication text offers many useful examples of effective business communication and graphics.

Piotrowski, Maryann V. *Effective Business Writing: Strategies and Suggestions.* New York: HarperCollins, 1989. This text concentrates on examples of how to write effectively in a variety of typical business situations.

Strunk, William Jr., and E. B. White. *Elements of Style.* New York: Macmillan, 1979. This brief book concentrates brilliantly on the essentials of clear, powerful writing.

Zinsser, William. *On Writing Well: An Informal Guide to Writing Nonfiction.* New York: HarperCollins, 1985. This text provides concise advice on effective writing in both business and personal matters.

CHAPTER 17

Effective Speaking: A Brief Manual of Style

Effective oral communication requires that a manager use all the communication skills covered in Part One of this book. The following discussion suggests some ways that they can be adapted to the special situation of a speaker facing an audience. Generally, strong oral presentations require preparation, clear structure, and effective delivery. Managers exercise their skills in oral communication when they pick up the telephone or talk one on one. Although this chapter can help you improve such relatively informal interactions, it focuses on more formal oral communication.

PREPARATION

Managers make speeches for many reasons: to pass information upward or downward to motivate subordinates, to entertain at a social occasion, to rally allegiance to a new policy, to convince others to support and carry out a particular course of action. The first step in speech preparation, as in any communication, is to define your goal and test it against the context. Usually, your goal seems self-evident; often, it's not. Many times, a problem arises between means and ends. If you want to improve the profitability of your department, you can be led far astray by defining your goal as *selling more product*. While increased sales may be an appropriate, even necessary, means to your end, increasing margins or lowering overhead may be a better strategy to achieve your real goal. Don't fall into the means/ends trap.

Once you've defined a clear business goal, *test it against the context by asking some key questions:*

- Is it ethically sound?
- Are adequate resources available to achieve it?
- Will it get the support of those whose cooperation you need?

- Does it conflict with other business goals of equal or greater importance?
- Does it stand a reasonable chance, given the internal and external competitive environments?

A manager has only so much credibility, energy, and goodwill to spend. All these assets are at greater risk in speaking than in writing, because a document can be revised, while a speech conveys the full force of your position and personality, often once and for all. A significant speech may be the most important opportunity you have to influence, or catch the attention of, key members of your audience. When you test your goal against the organizational context, ask yourself whether these assets will be increased or depleted by the time you've achieved your goal.

Next, *define and analyze your audience*. The techniques of audience analysis summarized in Chap. 3 apply as much to speaking as to other business communication situations. But additional factors apply to oral presentation. Who are the real decision-makers, and is a speech the best way to reach them? Is your audience likely to be supportive, neutral, or hostile? Is the audience's attitude uniform, or are you facing a group that contains radically divergent points of view? How does this audience expect to be addressed? Do you appear before audience members as a suppliant asking for their help, a colleague reasoning with equals, or an acknowledged authority sharing information and advice?

The answers to these questions have important implications when you're planning your argument, style, and tone. Perhaps persuading decision-makers one on one is more likely to build consensus in favor of your position than risking opposition in a public forum. Some decision-makers may be likely to agree with you in private but will be unwilling to go along in public for political reasons or owing to concerns about status. A colleague who agrees your plan is the best solution to an evident problem, for example, may feel obligated to oppose it in public because her subordinates or allies oppose it. Consider ways to give such an opponent a graceful way out of the conflict.

Perhaps your audience is supportive and merely needs to be motivated. If you're preaching to the converted, your task is relatively simple: Give audience members the information they need to do their job well, and provide them with arguments they can use to persuade others. Perhaps your audience is neutral. In this case, you must explain why action is necessary and why your approach is superior to reasonable alternatives. Perhaps your audience is hostile. In this case, you must demonstrate that you understand their point of view before they can be brought to consider the merits of your argument.

Usually, your audience's likely attitude toward your proposal will be mixed. Often, divergent views among audience members are sufficiently strong to threaten a stalemate. In business, as elsewhere in life, it's frequently easier to do nothing than to do something that may alienate significant constituencies. In designing your message, make sure that you've acknowledged and responded to all the influential interests represented in the audience. The exercise of identifying these interests will suggest commonalities that underlie apparently conflicting positions: "While we disagree about what to do about it, all of us recognize that we face a common problem." This strategy can remind people that they are all on the same team and may suggest a solution that can command majority support. Even those who continue to disagree with you will be more willing to listen if they feel you've taken their position into consideration.

How does your audience expect to be addressed? Is it a small group or a large crowd? Does it convene regularly, or are all these people in the same room together for the first time? Are there certain shared conventions that you should acknowledge to be heard? Meetings likely will be put off by a florid oratorical address, while large groups may be bored by important but esoteric details. What approach will convince this audience that you're all on the same side? Speakers often violate their audiences' expectations of timing. Few business audiences ever wish the speaker had talked longer. Take this into account in your planning. Many presenters prepare a speech of reasonable length, start out anxious, then realize they have the audience with them and begin to embellish or ramble. It's usually wise to prepare a shortened version of your planned speech; you may find that your time has been cut or that your audience is less attentive than you'd hoped.

Finally, *how do audience members perceive you?* Partly, this will depend on how well they know you. If the answer is "not at all," your first task is to establish your right to their time. Has someone they respect brought you to their attention? Cite the connection. Have you sought them out yourself? Tell them what you can do for them. Most often, your audience will know you either in person or by reputation. But *what* do they know? Is it correct? If not, it is better to confront the misunderstanding directly than to avoid it. Is what you're about to propose consistent with your past record? If not, explain the disparity. Does the audience have a reason to distrust you? If so, explain why things have changed. The single most important asset of a speaker is credibility. It's a fine art to mention your credentials without sounding as if you're boasting. Often, providing audience members with materials in advance can bolster the respect and attention they accord you.

STRUCTURE

You've analyzed your audience and decided on your basic line of argument. Now ask, How much do they need to know about my topic in order to agree with me? Usually the answer is: Less than you know yourself. A manager thoroughly convinced of the wisdom of his or her proposal feels an understandable pressure to tell all. Don't try. When reading a memo, people have the opportunity to pause, reflect, or look back at the previous page. But during a presentation, an audience can absorb only a few key points. Make sure that these points are the ones you want them to remember and that they stand out clearly.

High school speech teachers are fond of saying, "Tell them what you're going to tell them, tell them, and then tell them what you've told them." Up to a point, this is good advice. By the end of your first few sentences, your audience should understand exactly what you're proposing. Nothing loses an audience faster than a rambling **introduction.** Only if audience members know where you're going will they be able to follow you and judge your argument on its merits. Then, as you progress, signal clearly how each key point fits into your overall argument. Although no successful communicator should be bound by rigid formulas, a good rule of thumb suggests that audiences can absorb your main proposal and three supporting arguments.

The **body** of an effective presentation accomplishes two key purposes: It sells the benefits of your proposal, and it acknowledges and neutralizes reasonable opposition. The order in which you achieve these goals depends upon the attitude of your audience. If you face a generally hostile audience, you need to confront their objections immediately. The most powerful arguments will have no impact if you haven't won your audience's undistracted attention. Until a hostile audience knows you understand, and to some extent share, its concerns, it will be hard to move. If your audience's objections are subtle (maybe there's a better alternative) or are liable to arise later (on reflection, or while speaking to others), then address those objections only *after* you've explained the merits of your own case. Often, the best way to disarm opposition is to present alternative positions as reasonable, but slightly less preferable than your own proposal. This conveys objectivity on your part, enables you to point out the downsides of other possible actions, and suggests maturity of judgment. Such an approach is especially appropriate when your audience holds a wide range of attitudes toward your subject: Whether audience members agree with you or not, all feel included in the discussion.

An adequate **conclusion** "tells them what you've told them." An excellent conclusion looks to the future by emphasizing the benefits to the audience of adopting your proposal. It also outlines next steps. This demonstrates not only that you know where you want to go, but also that you have a credible plan for getting there. Another important point: Clearly signal the fact that you're concluding. Audiences will usually pay a lot of attention to your beginning, less to the middle, and a lot to the end. Letting them know you're almost finished gives you the opportunity to drive your main point home when attention is at its highest.

As you develop the **structure** of your speech, first double-check to make sure you've set reasonable goals and shown respect for your audience's time. While we'll address each of these points in upcoming materials and examples, it's worth emphasizing them here. Don't set yourself an impossibly high threshold. While even the most brilliant speech may be admired as a work of art, it is unlikely to completely transform your audience's viewpoints on the issue at hand. They have usually had other inputs and have invested too much effort in forming their own judgments on the subject to adopt your view wholesale. Often, moving even a minority of your audience a few degrees in your direction is enough to achieve your goal. Second, don't speak a moment longer than necessary to accomplish your purpose. Audience expectations and external constraints count heavily here: A presentation at a professional seminar or academic conference may be expected to fill an interesting hour, while a new idea thrown out at a business meeting may require only a few sentences. Remember that a successful speech is often only the beginning of a communication process.

One theme runs through all these suggestions on constructing an effective presentation: *You're most likely to win over your audience by convincing them that you all share common ground.* The most rigorously logical argument, backed with exactly the right amount of irrefutable evidence, will fail to persuade audience members if it violates their deeply held beliefs or cuts against their vital interests. Most successful business presentations emphasize something important that the speaker and audience share: a goal, a problem, a value, or an interest. Convincing audience members that you're on their side is at least half the persuasive battle. See Chap. 5 for a more detailed discussion of structure and argument.

Effective presentations work because they embody a style and a tone that maintain a rapport with the audience. The best analysis and the clearest and most convincing structure can be wasted if your language or gestures haven't connected with the audience. Again, achieving maximum rapport depends largely on how well you've judged the context. Consider the following situations: You're reporting to superiors at a decision-making session, informing colleagues of a decision from on high which they may not like, firing up a sales force, presenting disappointing news to stockholders, assigning tasks to subordinates, introducing a company project to an interest group or community whose support you need, running a weekly staff meeting, or explaining your product, service, or policy to a skeptical press. In each of these situations you need to deliver your message memorably, with empathy and force.

Unless you're delivering a research report or a carefully worded policy statement, it's important to adopt a natural, conversational tone and to pitch your language to the high-middle intelligence level of your audience. This means that while everyone can follow you, your most perceptive auditors—who are likely to be the opinion makers—will find constant value in what you're saying. This approach means observing some important basic principles:

1. Plan your speech carefully, but don't write it out word for word. Practice it aloud, so the oral rhythms become fixed in your mind, but don't memorize a text. If you do, you'll probably sound overrehearsed, and if you miss one key connection, you're likely to go blank. It's usually best to practice from a list of key topics that you have before you for reference as you speak.
2. Try to condense key points or arguments in vivid images that will stick in your audience's mind.
3. Speak to audience members as if they're a collection of individuals rather than an undefined mass. Especially when you begin a speech, your audience is likely to appear to you as a blur. Pick out three or four members from different sections of the audience and direct your remarks to them. This has several advantages: It can make *you* connect, convincing you that you are really speaking to people rather than throwing your words into a void. You'll get responses that can energize you. As you shift your eyes from one audience member to another, those in between will feel included.
4. Use the resources of body language. Business people typically deliver presentations in one of three situations: sitting around a table, standing behind a lectern, or working an audience from an open space. The conventions for each of these situations vary, but certain rules apply to all of them. Employ gestures sparingly, and make sure they correspond to, or enact, your meaning. The larger your audience, the broader your gestures must be to reach everyone. Find a way to look relaxed when you're still. When you do use your arms and hands, keep them away from your torso, without waving them in the air. Otherwise, you'll look defensive, insecure, or deceptive.
5. Constantly seek out the eyes of trusted auditors, which will indicate to you how you're coming across. We almost never see ourselves as others see us. Videotaped practice can be very helpful here.

6. While every business presenter can improve his or her performance, don't imagine there's a formula that can always guarantee success. Ultimately, audiences will always realize if you're not being you.

A final thought: The goal in practicing speaking is to improve, not to achieve perfection or do a good imitation of a role model. Robert Kent, when he taught at Harvard Business School, advised students: "If you improve your delivery by 10 percent, you may actually improve your effectiveness by a factor of 2."

GRAPHICS

Using Traditional Graphics. Many business presentations can be enhanced by the use of graphics, and the conventions of some all but require them. Graphics include flip charts, handouts, props, slides, videotapes, PowerPoint, and use of a chalkboard. All of these, used appropriately, can enliven a presentation and make it more memorable. Equally, all can be abused—and usually are. Some general rules of thumb:

1. *Keep it simple.* Most effective graphics can be grasped at a glance. In certain specialized situations it's appropriate to put long lists of numbers on the screen or into a handout—when you're leading experts through the details of a budgeting proposal, for example. But for the most part, *use graphics only when a picture will be more vivid and economical than words.* A bar chart may be a great way to demonstrate how sales will rise if your proposal is adopted. A pie chart may quickly acquaint your audience with your suggestions for allocating resources for the coming year. Passing out a new product for people to examine may explain it far more clearly than several paragraphs of text. Try to make sure that your picture is "worth a thousand words."
2. *Don't hide behind your graphics.* Many business presenters use graphics as a way of avoiding direct interaction with their audience. It's relatively easy to read a presentation from an outline on a screen or available in a handout. In some situations, this is the expected approach, for example, when consultants are reporting results to clients, or when a presenter conducts a training session containing a good deal of technical information. In these cases, detailed outlines can help an audience follow a complex argument or ask for clarification of an important point. Too often, however, business presenters use outlines of their speeches to avoid facing the audience. It can feel more comfortable to speak to a screen than to address real people. Ask: Am I selling my information or selling myself? Detailed duplicates of your remarks risk making you sound redundant or convince audience members they'd be better off in their office reading a memo. Often audiences will read ahead and stop paying attention to what you're actually saying. If you're using graphics, leave them on the screen only for the length of time you want your audience to pay attention to them. Nothing is more distracting than a speaker covering one topic while the graphics display another. Except in specialized situations such as the ones described above, outlines work best to introduce key points, emphasize them, or conclude.
3. *Ask yourself what graphics are right for which situations.* A chalkboard or flip chart may be best for a training situation where your relationship to the audience

is interactive, and they can see their remarks being valued as you write them down. Pictures, samples, or models may be the best way to convince an audience of the value of a new product line or design. Key quotations may provide a useful focus for discussion. Handouts—pamphlets that combine text and graphics—may serve as a useful takeaway that provokes audience members to reflect further on your remarks. But you should consider whether they should be handed out *before* the presentation—when they might either help the auditor follow or distract from the speaker—or after—when they might be either useful takeaways or throwaways.

4. *Use the minimum number of graphics necessary* to enliven the presentation and drive home key points. Audiences can absorb only a certain amount of information. They'll develop a subconscious resistance to a speaker who overloads them or provides them with more information than they feel they need. In most business presentations, graphics should serve as interesting punctuation, not the substance of your speech. The purpose of a business presentation is to send off your audience members as enthusiastic advocates of your idea. They'll be more likely to be so if you've left them with a few powerful images they can pass on, rather than a mass of details they're likely to forget.
5. *Don't use visual aids that you aren't sure you can manage well.* Nothing throws a presentation off track faster than a technical gaffe. If the wrong slide comes up, or if there are typographical errors in your graphics, the audience will start making judgments about your competence rather than about the quality of your information and arguments. A related and obvious, but often neglected, point: Make sure your graphics are clearly visible to all members of your audience. Often, this involves pretesting the presentation setting.

As a general rule, make sure your graphics contribute to, rather than detract from, your credibility as a speaker. In the end, this is your most important asset. Whether or not you're likely to speak to this particular group again, your reputation, among both your colleagues and future audiences, will precede you. Don't be remembered as the presenter who was hostage to the screen, or who repeated her visuals verbatim. This will convey doubts about both you and your proposal, since you haven't added value to material the audience members could read for themselves. One useful guide to effective graphics is by Gene Zelazny, *Say It with Charts* (Homewood, IL: Business One Irwin, 1991).

Using PowerPoint. Plenty of information is easily accessible on the Internet about how to design PowerPoint graphics, and we won't repeat it here, but we will suggest some tips on how to employ it effectively. PowerPoint is currently the most-used graphics generator, and it has led to an explosion of displays in business presentations. But, as we've suggested elsewhere, while vivid graphics, however dazzling, are useful to drive your central points home, they won't carry your argument alone. There's an increasing resistance to business presentations based primarily on PowerPoint graphics for several reasons:

1. They invite a naturally shy or ill-prepared presenter to hide behind them.
2. Presenters can become entranced with designing elaborate graphics that are perfectly clear to themselves but take more time to explain than could be accomplished in a few words.

3. Interpreting one graphic after another gets boring.
4. Overuse of elaborate graphics deadens your capacity to establish a dynamic relationship with your audience.
5. Overuse of PowerPoint can make the audience feel bullied into submission rather than persuaded.

PowerPoint, like all graphics, should be used to present information succinctly, not to make an argument. It works best in a Tell format, less well in Sell, Consult, or Join formats, where it should be used sparingly or not at all (see Mary Munter's graph [currently on page 41]. Often a one page handout that the audience-member can take away and reflect on after will prove more effective than a series of slides that flash by.

As Edward Tufte wrote somewhat melodramatically in *Wired* magazine ("PowerPoint Is Evil," September 2003, wired.com):

> Imagine a widely used and expensive prescription drug that promised to make us beautiful but didn't. Instead the drug had frequent, serious side effects: It induced stupidity, turned everyone into bores, wasted time, and degraded the quality and credibility of communication. These side-effects would rightly lead to a worldwide product recall.
>
> Yet slideware—computer programs for presentations—is everywhere: in corporate America, in government bureaucracies, even in our schools. Several hundred million copies of Microsoft PowerPoint are churning out trillions of slides each year. Slideware may help speakers outline their talks, but convenience for the speaker can be punishing to both content and audience. The standard PowerPoint presentation elevates format over content, betraying an attitude of commercialism that turns everything into a sales pitch.

For more of Tufte's thoughtful and sometimes hilarious reflections on PowerPoint abuse, see "The Cognitive Style of PowerPoint: Pitching out Corrupts Within," (Graphics Press, Cheshire, Connecticut, 2006).

In most presentations, connecting with your audience depends upon maintaining credibility and interest. That involves engaging them with your personality and convincing them that they are following your honest thoughts in real time. Don't let an infatuation with, or an addiction to, graphics get in the way of that. Keep the audience engaged.

GROUP PRESENTATIONS

Most of the principles covered earlier in this chapter apply to all types of business presentations. But there are special challenges involved in presenting as a group. Some members of a team are determined to be stars, while others would prefer to avoid the limelight. To achieve success, groups must project consistency, an overarching message, and members' willingness to reinforce each other rather than compete.

Accomplishing these crucial objectives means presentation teams must allocate tasks fairly, plan well, and support each other once they're in front of an audience. The following suggestions apply whether a group is providing recommendations to a client, trying to interest investors in a new business opportunity, reporting results to superiors, briefing stockholders, or giving a press conference.

1. Think of the presentation as a whole, rather than as a collection of parts. While each speaker's individual contribution must stand on its own, make sure a coherent argument runs through the whole. Naturally, there will be a division of labor; different speakers will address the topics in which they're most experienced: strategy, production, marketing, personnel, operations, finances, organization. Make sure these are ordered in a way that will make sense to the audience and will take into account its level of familiarity with all topics.
2. Frame the presentation so that it comes across as coherent. One effective way to do this is to have one speaker serve as the moderator, offering an introductory overview, then returning at the end to conclude and field questions. Let the audience members know what you're proposing, and what it means for them, off the top. Also, let them know how long you're going to speak, so that they can adjust their expectations appropriately.
3. Make sure you've covered all the key concerns of your audience. It's easy to create a presentation in which each speaker has done a good job while some crucial point has fallen through the cracks.
4. Create a "house style." Usually, audiences will be judging your teamwork as much as they're judging your proposal. Try to achieve consistency in your imagery, level of intensity, use of detail, common themes, and graphics.
5. Give every speaker a chance to shine, whether this is by virtue of excellence as a presenter or command of a given area.
6. Make the transitions from one speaker to the next seamless. On the most basic level, this means each speaker should be introduced, either by his predecessor or by the emcee. Emphasize each team member's credentials by providing a brief summary of why he or she is qualified to speak on the topic—this can be done in the introduction, by the moderator, or by the previous speaker. Equally important, make the transitions from one speaker to the next contribute to building your argument: "Now that I've explained the need for our product, X will tell you how we can market it successfully."
7. Support each other. Cross-reference other speakers to validate their remarks, and explain how previous topics fit into the big picture.
8. Conclude by emphasizing benefits to the audience and next steps.

HANDLING QUESTIONS AND ANSWERS

Most presentation situations involve fielding questions from the audience. Many are composed largely or entirely of this art. There are a few situations in which a businessperson should avoid a question-and-answer (Q&A) session. For example, when you're delivering bad news to a large audience and it would be wiser to let them reflect on it, address their concerns afterward one on one or in small groups. Sometimes you don't have the answers or can't make them public yet. In these cases, if audience members expect or demand a response from you, tell them why you can't answer now and when you'll be able to. In most business situations, however, taking questions and handling them well is an essential part of the communication process.

Some ground rules for managing a Q&A session:

1. *Set a time limit, and stick to it, within reason.* This enables you to keep things moving and avoid wearing out your audience. But don't stop fielding questions

until the interaction has convinced you that major concerns have been answered as best they can. Find ways to broaden your answers so that they address concerns of groups rather than of individuals.

2. *Know what questions you'll be asked ahead of time.* A good presenter has done enough audience analysis to identify major concerns. Your introductory remarks should have answered major objections to your information, proposal, or course of action. Still, your audience will include individuals with different information, or decision-makers with different agendas, and you must be adroit and informed enough to demonstrate your understanding of their views or interests. When you don't know the answer, be willing to say so and tell the questioner when you'll get back to him.
3. *Make sure you get across or reinforce your main points.* Use your audience analysis to generate an agenda for the Q&A session, then emphasize these at every opportunity. Avoid repeating canned answers, but find ways to tie specific questions to your general points.
4. *Don't put yourself or your team on the defensive.* Except in the most unusual situations, don't call opponents' motives into question or react with hostility. This strategy can work only when the majority of your audience seriously disagrees with a vocal minority. For the most part, your audience will appreciate gestures of generosity to hostile or misinformed questioners.

EXTEMPORANEOUS SPEAKING

While this chapter concentrates on prepared presentations, most of your speaking—and perhaps most of your communication—will take place in less formal situations: meetings, one-on-one discussions, and informal conversations. It is in these situations that most business really gets done. Be aware that a casual encounter with a colleague in a hallway can be as consequential as a major presentation to a large audience.

This insight suggests the following points you should consider about your personal conversational style.

1. *How do you sound to other people?* Is your speaking tone harsh or pleasant? Do you use the language correctly and succinctly? Some people can benefit from voice training that helps them achieve a more modulated tone, better grammar, or a less pronounced accent. Others can learn from feedback that they come across less attractively than they think.
2. *Are you more interested in yourself or your interlocutor?* As we've said before, nothing will make others feel like you're a great conversationalist as surely as showing interest in their situation or point of view.
3. *Have you thought through your agenda in the conversation?* Obviously, there are times when conversations with colleagues are simply part of an ongoing relationship and have nothing to do with the business at hand: discussions about your family, your partner, your lack of a partner, or the joys and frustrations of daily life. But very often people conversing in a business situation have legitimate mutual interests or disagreements that can best be discussed informally. Casual one-on-one or small group encounters may be the best place to iron out a misunderstanding or float a new idea.

Think through how the principles we've outlined on effective public speaking may also apply to your personal business conversations as well.

JOB INTERVIEWS

In Chap. 12 we address interviews with the press; here we offer a few suggestions on a more personal topic: job interviews. No guidelines can cover every situation, but most of the principles of effective speaking we've covered so far apply. You can take several steps before and during a job interview that may help you to be taken seriously:

1. Make sure your cover letter follows the guidelines listed at the end of Chap. 6.
2. Include a clean resume that highlights, rather than exhausts, your accomplishments.
3. Have your *own* agenda for the interview, and prepare sensible questions that suggest you're negotiating for the job, not pleading for it.
4. Follow up the interview with a letter that expresses gratitude, enthusiasm, and any reinforcing points that occurred to you afterward.

Appendix

Case 16: Dotsworth Press
Case 17: "Fair Is Fair," Isn't It?

Dotsworth Press

Dick Garanti was vexed. The morning mail had just arrived, and on his desk was a letter from Betty Friedman, Head of the Affirmative Action Office, and an Employee Performance Appraisal form from the Personnel Office for his editorial assistant, Mary Wilson. The letter from Ms. Friedman concerned the charges Mary had made that he and Bob Collins, Director of Personnel, had engaged in "male collusion" in an effort to keep Mary's position from being upgraded from clerical to editorial. The letter began:

> Following an extensive investigation into the possibility of having Mary Wilson's position as Editorial Assistant upgraded, it was determined that, because the secretarial duties exceeded 30 percent of her total responsibilities, the position could not be classified higher than Clerical, Grade 3. We discussed the frustration Mary experienced around this issue, as well as the ways in which it obviously impacted on your relationship.

Dick winced and automatically circled "impacted on." The letter continued:

> Mary would have liked you to increase her responsibilities in order for her to continue her professional growth, but, if I understand things correctly, there are no resources to fund another kind of position.
>
> Your past appraisals of her performance suggest that Mary is very well qualified for an Assistant Editor position. We are encouraging her to apply for other such positions that may open at Dotsworth in the future.
>
> Thank you for your cooperation.

"Betty, you have overstepped your bounds," Dick said to no one in particular. He was pleased that the Affirmative Action Office had found in his favor. In his view, however, Affirmative Action had no authority in the matter of job ratings; that was entirely the province of the Personnel Office.

Then he turned to the Employee Performance Appraisal form from Bob Collins (see *Exhibit 1*). The form, a part of the annual performance check on all employees, had to be completed, read and signed by Mary, and returned to the Personnel Office by the middle of next week. Dick began to review the sequence of events that had led to his dissatisfaction with Mary Wilson.

BACKGROUND

Dick Garanti was an editor of *Dotsworth Magazine,* a specialized magazine published by Dotsworth Press, a division of the ITT Publishing group. This magazine was a three-year-old venture for the

EXHIBIT 1 Employee Performance Appraisal Form

Please complete the following appraisal of the employee's performance over the past year:

Quality of performance:

Unsatisfactory Conditional Satisfactory Superior

Productivity:

Unsatisfactory Conditional Satisfactory Superior

Attitude:

Unsatisfactory Conditional Satisfactory Superior

Initiative:

Unsatisfactory Conditional Satisfactory Superior

Please attach a one-page assessment of the performance of this employee during the past year. Please note areas that need improvement, specific accomplishments, other outstanding items of interest.

Employee Comments

If you choose, you may express your comments about your supervisor's evaluation. Your signature indicates that you have read the above appraisal of your performance; it implies neither approval nor disapproval of the evaluation.

Employee Signature Date

company. Dick used the services of the press's production staff, but he had one editorial assistant, Mary Wilson, who reported directly to him and who worked exclusively on the magazine. Mary had been hired three years before as an editorial assistant, which in the ITT Publishing group had a Clerical, Grade 3, rating. Editorial assistants were required to perform a variety of editorial and secretarial duties, to participate in the publishing process from the time a manuscript was received through its return to the author or its publication. The minimum requirements were a college degree (with background preferably in English) and excellent word processing skills.

Mary came to the job from a secretarial position in a bank. She had a B.A. in English and wanted, she had stated in the job interview, to get into publishing. For the first year and a half she performed her duties very well. Her general attitude was excellent—she and Dick worked well together, and Dick had consistently rated her work "superior" on the Employee Performance Appraisal forms. He had also given her generous salary increases.

Soon after she began working at Dotsworth, Mary enrolled in a master's degree program in English at a local university. All of her courses were in the evening, so they did not interfere with her job. Some months later Mary had a frank discussion with Dick about her ambitions to move into an editorial position at Dotsworth or some other publishing house. Her decision to earn a master's degree was inspired in part, she said, by her desire eventually to obtain a professional position in publishing. Dick told her at this time that the position of editorial assistant would, for the next two years at least, be a clerical one. He indicated, however, that he would support her candidacy in any entry-level editorial position that became open at Dotsworth or elsewhere. Mary said she understood that the editorial assistant position would probably always be a dead-end job, but she wanted to be given more challenging work, for she was bored by many of the routine clerical tasks she was asked to perform. They then agreed that Dick would assign her some publishing tasks that might prepare her for her next job.

Mary flourished under the new assignments. She had, for example, taken on some professional duties and had done exceptionally well at them. At the same time she continued to perform all of the clerical duties she had been hired to do. Things in the office were going well. Dick felt he had a good working relationship with Mary, though he knew she would probably soon move on to another position. At about this time Mary began to date one of Dick's colleagues and friends, David Smith, the editor in the Reference Division of Dotsworth Press. On occasion Dick and his wife would see David and Mary socially. Infrequently Mary would ask special favors for time off, usually to mesh with David's schedule. Dick was generally happy to comply with her requests when they did not interfere with the work of the office. Mary also willingly worked overtime without pay after an illness had put them behind schedule in meeting production deadlines.

THE PROBLEMS OF THE LAST TWO MONTHS

For several months before she earned her master's, Mary looked for an editorial position. Dick gave her time off for job interviews, and he wrote supportive recommendations for her. But the job market in publishing was extremely tight and Mary, though she had several interviews over the course of three or four months, was unable to find another job. She was discouraged, but she set her hopes on her master's degree.

But that didn't help, either. She launched a job search immediately after she earned her degree, but she came up with nothing. Then, two months ago, without warning, Mary placed on Dick's desk a letter she had written requesting that her editorial assistant position be changed to assistant editor (*Exhibit 2*). In the letter she stated that she wanted her job level changed to a Grade 4. Dick was a little surprised at the substance of the letter, but even more surprised that Mary had chosen not to speak to him personally about the matter. Instead, she had set the letter on his desk

EXHIBIT 2 Mary's Letter

RG:

It has been almost three years since I began as an editorial assistant for *Dotsworth Magazine,* and during that time my job description has not been updated. I have, however, been asked to perform duties of an editorial nature in the last two years. With this in mind, I would like to have my official job description revised to reflect the editorial nature of my position and my title changed to assistant editor. Some of these nonsecretarial duties that I have been performing include:

1. Reviewing manuscripts submitted to *Dotsworth Magazine.*
2. Composing correspondence with authors, outside reviewers, and advertisers.
3. Ensuring standards of style and content in articles published in *DM.*
4. Monitoring budget for *DM.*
5. Overseeing manuscript evaluation process.
6. Substantive editing, copyediting, and proofreading.
7. Managing office.

Mary

while he was out of the office, just before she left for a long weekend.

The following Monday morning Dick called Mary into his office. Mary repeated the substance of the letter, underscoring that she had taken on new duties and responsibilities and that she now felt entitled to be upgraded to a Grade 4. She reminded him of her new degree and pointed out that the work she had taken on for him was consistent with that performed by other assistant editors in the company. She said she felt underemployed and spoke of her growing boredom with her clerical duties.

Dick listened sympathetically, but he finally told her that he was in a bind. What he needed in the office was someone to perform clerical duties. He simply could not change her job level to a Grade 4, for in the company's structure anyone rated Grade 4 or above was prohibited from performing clerical duties. And, until the magazine was more profitable, he would not have the budget to hire both clerical and editorial personnel.

Mary left his office visibly upset. From that day on, Dick felt an undercurrent of tension in their relationship. Mary continued to do her work, but she appeared to be unhappy and seemed reluctant when Dick asked her to do any routine tasks. She seemed eager to take on more tasks that involved greater responsibility. For example, she answered professional mail herself and authorized publication of some promotional materials with his approval. Dick felt she exceeded her authority, however, when she approved the printing of the summer issue of the magazine without his final review. This action represented a break with established office procedure and resulted in the publication of an issue in which the page numbers in the table of contents were incorrect. During this period his friendship with David Smith cooled considerably, and though this saddened and disappointed him, Dick tried to put it out of his mind.

Things deteriorated rapidly. About a month ago Mary went on her own accord to Bob Collins in Personnel to ask his office to review the situation. Dick was angry and astonished when he received a letter from Bob apprising him of Mary's formal request to have her position upgraded. He called Bob immediately on receiving the letter and told him that Mary had acted independently and without authority in presenting Personnel with a new job description. They set up an appointment for the next day for the three of them to discuss the situation.

At that meeting Mary sketched her side of the story. When it came time for Dick to speak, he indicated that though Mary had indeed been performing some editorial duties, and performing them well, he could not support the changes she had written into the job description. He needed a clerical person, and if Mary's job description were officially to include the editorial duties she had listed, her level would automatically be changed to Grade 4, a level that by definition did not permit her to perform routine clerical duties. Dick handed Bob a copy of the official job description for the position (*Exhibit 3*) and the meeting ended.

The tension between Dick and Mary persisted. They rarely spoke to one another, and Mary left the office for long, unexplained periods. She spent what to Dick was an inordinate amount of time with Dave Smith and his staff during working hours.

A week later Bob wrote a letter to Mary, a copy of which he sent to Dick, stating that he and his office had investigated the situation and found that her position was appropriately classified at its present level, Grade 3. The nature and level of the responsibilities of her position, Bob wrote, were similar to those of other editorial assistants at Dotsworth Press and in the Publishing Division of ITT.

After Mary received this letter, her performance degenerated. Though she continued to keep up with the paper flow, she made it clear she resented being given typing and other clerical tasks. She became sullen, and on a couple of occasions she was openly insulting and abusive. She seemed to be generally unwilling to take direction at all. Dick regretted it, but felt he could no longer work with her under these conditions.

Finally, two weeks ago, Mary lodged a complaint against both Dick and Bob Collins with the Affirmative Action Office. She charged the two of them with "male collusion" in keeping her position from being upgraded. During the brief investigation that followed, Betty Friedman never once

EXHIBIT 3 Job Description

Date: March 6

To: Bob Collins, Director of Personnel

From: Dick Garanti, Editor

Subject: Job Description for Editorial Assistant

- Participate in the many functions of the editorial office of *Dotsworth Magazine,* from the time a new manuscript is received through its return to the author or its publication. Record new manuscripts and correspondence with authors, reviewers, editors, and printers. Prepare correspondence; respond to routine inquiries about the magazine or the status of manuscripts. Maintain necessary files and records. Process a variety of manuscript-related correspondence with authors (acknowledgments, acceptances, rejections). Receive, screen, and route incoming telephone calls; schedule appointments for the editor. Open, sort, and deliver incoming mail; prepare and process outgoing mail.
- Perform coordination and editorial duties to ensure accurate publication of *Dotsworth Magazine.* Transmit manuscript to production; receive typeset materials and galley/page proofs and make necessary corrections.
- Perform other related duties as required or directed.

contacted Dick. As far as he knew, she talked only to Mary. But he kept his own counsel as he waited for the Affirmative Action Office to respond to Mary's charge.

Now Dick sat with the two pieces of mail before him, the summary from Betty Friedman and the Employee Performance Appraisal form that he was being asked to fill out for Mary Wilson.

Study Questions

1. How would you define the problem that has arisen between Dick Garanti and Mary Wilson? What aspects of the scene have particular bearing on the problem? For example, is Mary's relationship to David Smith incidental or does it significantly complicate the situation?
2. Evaluate Dick's formal and informal appraisals of Mary so far. Has he provided clear and effective feedback? Has Mary responded appropriately to his comments and direction?
3. What action should Dick take regarding Mary's recent performance? Should he talk to her and try to repair their relationship? Should he request that she be transferred to another editor? Should he consider firing her? Should he simply fill out the performance appraisal and await further developments?
4. If you were Dick, how would you evaluate Mary's performance? In filling out the appraisal form, what would be your primary and secondary objectives?
5. As Dick Garanti, fill out Mary Wilson's performance appraisal form and provide the one-page (300–500 words) assessment requested.
6. As Dick Garanti or Mary Wilson, prepare to role-play an interview in which Wilson's performance appraisal and any actions Garanti proposes to take will be discussed.

CASE 17

"Fair Is Fair," Isn't It?

Sitting at his desk on the afternoon of August 10, Dean Bob Frederick was perplexed by the recent turn of events involving the university central administration, his administrative secretary, and himself. The dean reread the memorandum from the personnel director which specified "remedial action" to be taken in disciplining Laura Adams, his administrative secretary. He knew he had contributed to the problem by writing the memo defending Laura and even more so by initially allowing her to take a class during working hours, a violation of university regulations. But if the university permitted minority employees to enroll in courses during working hours, why shouldn't Laura be allowed to do so? He knew that Laura was very unhappy about the present circumstances. She was worried about keeping her job and maintaining her reputation at the university. He also knew Laura felt the decision was not fair, since she had secured her supervisor's permission to take the class and now was being punished. As Dean Frederick pondered his next action, he wondered how the incident involving Laura had gotten so out of hand. With all his other job pressures, he certainly could do without this additional burden.

Reprinted by permission from the *Case Research Journal*.

BACKGROUND

Dr. Bob Frederick was Dean of the College of Business at Southmont State University, a university of about 20,000 students located in a medium-sized city in the Southeast. Dr. Frederick, in his fourth year as dean, supervised over 100 faculty members and 20 administrative staff members in the college. In the dean's office, there were four employees: Laura Adams, his administrative secretary, a secretary, and two clerks.

Laura, the most senior employee, had worked in the college for almost 10 years and was regarded by the dean and others as an excellent employee. She knew the job well, had fine skills, and was a valuable asset to the dean's staff. For almost 7 years she had been working on a Bachelor of Business Administration degree, taking two courses per semester, including summers, in addition to her full-time position in the dean's office. Although her progress had been slow, Laura had maintained almost continuous enrollment at considerable personal sacrifice. She was now approaching the end of her program. The degree program requirements that had been in place when Laura entered the university were "expiring" at the end of the summer term, and a calculus course was being added to the list of required courses. Consequently, Laura was determined to complete her last two courses in the summer term and graduate at the August commencement.

Southmont State had a long-established policy of supporting the continuing education of university employees. This policy included inservice training programs as well as college credit courses for employees seeking undergraduate degrees. For those pursuing college credit through formal university classes, the institution had adopted detailed regulations under its Employee Education Program, which specified:

1. Classes must be taken outside normal university working hours (normal working hours include meal breaks).
2. Exceptions will be considered only if the employee is within six credit hours of graduation and a required course is not available outside normal working hours.
3. Exceptions must be approved by the president of the university or the vice president of Business and Finance.
4. If an exception is approved for the employee to attend class during working hours, class time will be charged against the employee's annual leave at 150 percent of the length of the class period. For example, an employee will be charged 90 minutes of leave for attending a 60-minute class.
5. Enrolling in or attending of classes during normal working hours without an approved exception will be considered sufficient grounds for termination of university employment.

It was well known that exceptions were rarely approved.

Also, the university offered limited financial support to full-time employees with at least six months of service for enrollment in job-related college courses. Under the Staff Scholarship Program, the university paid the tuition for a maximum of 6 semester hours of course work upon proper application, recommendation by their supervisors, and approval of the president. Explicit in the program guidelines was the statement that supervisors, in recommending staff scholarships, must give employee job performance and university goals highest priority.

Laura Adams had participated in the Staff Scholarship Program since enrolling at Southmont and had always received the support of her supervisors. For this summer, Laura had received $330 from the scholarship fund for two three-credit courses costing $165 per course.

The two summer courses in which she was enrolled were Industrial Marketing (offered at night) and International Marketing (offered from 10:50 A.M. to 12:30 P.M. on Monday through Friday). Laura was aware of the prohibition against course attendance during working hours; however, the day course was necessary for her graduation and was not offered at an alternate time. Also, when she discussed the situation with Dean Frederick, he told her that, under the circumstances, it was all right for her to take this course during the day, provided she would make up the lost time resulting from class attendance ($8^1/_3$ hours per week). He was also aware of Laura's desire to complete the degree in the summer term to avoid taking additional courses to satisfy the new degree requirements which would take effect in the fall semester.

Laura was not completely comfortable with being absent from the office from 10:50 until 12:30 during the 5-week term of the International Marketing course even though she did have Dean Frederick's approval. However, since she forfeited her 1-hour lunch period each day, she was losing only about 40 minutes of work time per day, and she was making up that time after hours. Also, she was aware that at least one other employee in the college was taking a course during working hours under the scholarship program. In fact, Laura had read a piece in a university publication, *Southmont Insights,* about black employees who were completing their degrees under a program permitting them to enroll in courses during the work day. She reasoned that if it was fair for one person to be off during the normal work period, it ought to be fair for another.

THE STAFF ENROLLMENT AUDIT

A routine audit of staff course enrollment by the Personnel Department at Southmont State revealed Laura's name on the roll of the International Marketing class. Laura was called over to the Personnel Department to meet with Agnes Johnson, benefits manager, on August 1.

Laura told Ms. Johnson that she was familiar with the Staff Scholarship Program and was aware that it did not normally permit class enrollment during regular working hours. When asked if she had been granted an exception, Laura replied that she had Dean Frederick's permission to take this course, although she did not have it in writing. When Laura mentioned the article in *Southmont Insights* and inquired if the formal exceptions requirement applied to all employees, Ms. Johnson replied that the student in question was entitled to take courses during working hours under the provisions of the university's Black Staff Scholarship Program. That program was part of the university's mandated desegregation agreement established under the terms of the settlement of the 1968 civil rights suit *Powell v. Morgan* (see *Appendix A*).

In view of the circumstances, Ms. Johnson suggested that Ms. Adams secure a statement from Dean Frederick explaining what had happened.

On August 2, Laura delivered to Ms. Johnson a memorandum from Dean Frederick which included the following points:

1. Ms. Adams had obtained his permission to enroll in the International Marketing course in the 10:50 to 12:30 period.
2. She was making up the time lost because of class attendance by using her lunch hour plus extra time after work.
3. This course was the only available course that would fit in her degree program.
4. The two courses she was taking would complete her degree requirement. If she did not complete the courses this summer, she would have to take an additional course under new program requirements that would take effect in the fall.
5. She would comply with the university requirement that she be charged 150 percent of the class period time against her annual leave.

Ms. Johnson forwarded Dean Frederick's memo to Mr. Alex Farrell, Director of Personnel, to whom the apparent violation had been directed for action.

THE CENTRAL ADMINISTRATION'S RESPONSE

Alex Farrell reviewed the information he had received on the infraction, including the copy of Ms. Adams's staff scholarship application, the notes from Agnes Johnson's meeting with Laura, the memo from Dean Frederick, and telephone conversations with the dean. After considerable thought, Farrell wrote a memo to the vice president for Business and Finance, Lawrence Sheffield, outlining the issue and his recommendation for action:

1. Ms. Adams was a long-term and valued employee who had been working on a degree for about 7 years.
2. A clear violation of a university procedure had occurred, but he did not feel the termination of Ms. Adams was warranted.
3. Her annual leave should be charged at the 150 percent rate for lost time. Dean Frederick's office would need to submit corrected time and leave records for this period.
4. Ms. Adams was to repay the $165 for the daytime course to the staff scholarship fund.
5. Since Ms. Adams was aware that she had violated a university procedure, she should receive a written reprimand from Jerry Forrest, the academic vice president (Dean Frederick's superior).

On August 8, Lawrence Sheffield replied to Alex Farrell that he concurred with his recommendation and that Mr. Farrell should notify Dean Frederick of the appropriate remedial actions to be implemented.

THE DEAN'S DILEMMA

When Dean Frederick received the August 10 memorandum from Alex Farrell outlining the actions to be taken in the Laura Adams case, he was disturbed. He knew the importance of having established personnel procedures, and recognized the problems that could result in a large organization if central administration did not make sure that those procedures were observed. However, he believed the punishment in this case was unduly harsh. Were they trying to make an example of her? Perhaps more importantly, was it right for her to be disciplined so harshly for this violation of the staff scholarship procedure while other employees on campus, because of their race, were allowed to attend classes during normal working hours? He picked up the copy of *Southmont Insights* that Laura had showed him and scanned the reference to the Black Staff Scholarship Program:

> The Black Staff Scholarship Program, which permits black employees with at least two years of college to attend classes during regular working hours so degrees may be completed in a more timely manner, has produced two graduates with three more due to graduate this December.

Although he was well aware that Southmont had a strong commitment to affirmative action, the current situation troubled him. After all, "fair is fair," he thought. Laura was upset about the action taken against her and did not feel it was just. She had even talked about seeing a lawyer to file a reverse discrimination charge against the university, especially if the university tried to terminate her. Dean Frederick knew that Laura wasn't going to be terminated, but he didn't think the actions that were going to be taken were fair, either. He knew that he had contributed to Laura's "delinquency," and he felt some responsibility for this. She had relied on his approval of her enrollment. He certainly had to consider his obligation to her, and her work as a valued staff member. Shouldn't he be willing to take some of the heat for the problem he had helped create?

Should he appeal the action recommended by the personnel director and approved by the vice president of Business and Finance? Possibly he could get a concession on the formal reprimand, since Laura seemed especially hurt by the potential damage to her fine record. The dean did not want to lose the support of a highly valued employee, but he also was reluctant to challenge Lawrence Sheffield, a powerful campus administrator, or his own boss, Jerry Forrest. Even though he wasn't comfortable with Sheffield's decision, Dean Frederick wasn't sure he could change anything if he tried. With the economy weakening and the state budget tightening, he knew that he would have some tough budgetary battles to fight in the near future. He would need the support of both Sheffield and Forrest in these negotiations. Maybe this was a fight he should not pick.

Dean Frederick also understood the need for Southmont's affirmative action program, brought about by the long history of underrepresentation of minority employment in state institutions of higher education. But should the remedies that address past discrimination result in inequitable treatment of present employees? He had wrestled with this issue many times himself. He was also aware that the courts themselves were having difficulty resolving the legality of preferential selection in support of affirmative action programs (see *Appendix B*).

It seemed to him that this situation had gotten completely out of hand. Certainly he had underestimated the consequences of approving Laura's request to take the class, a decision which he had made without a great deal of thought. Although it was true that a rule had been broken, this had now become a "federal case." As he pondered what to do, he hoped to find a solution that would satisfactorily address the merits of both sides of the issue. Or was this seeking the impossible?

APPENDIX A

A Note on the Court-Ordered Desegregation Settlement Affecting Southmont State University

In ruling on a 1968 civil rights lawsuit (called "*Powell v. Morgan*" here) filed initially against another public university in the state, the federal judge rendered a decision which ordered desegregation at all public higher education institutions in the state. In 1984, following the court's determination that inadequate progress had been made in dismantling the racially dual system of higher education, plaintiffs and defendants proposed a "stipulation of settlement" to the court. The negotiated stipulation of settlement had the concurrence of plaintiffs, defendant state officials, and the NAACP Legal Defense Fund. It was not, however, accepted by the Civil Rights Division of the Department of Justice, which objected to the proposal's use of numerical goals and quotas and the absence of a "victim specificity" standard. (A "victim specificity" standard requires that evidence of racial discrimination against an individual be established before a remedy can be provided to that person.)

After reviewing the proposal and hearing oral arguments, the judge signed the agreement over the objections of the Justice Department. In explaining the justification for the remedies of the settlement, the judge stated:

> The ultimate goal is *not* an ideal ratio or mix of black and white students or faculty. The goal is a state system of higher education in tax supported colleges and universities in which race is irrelevant and in which equal protection and equal application of the law is a reality. On the road to achieving this state of color-blindness, there must be color-consciousness to overcome the residual effects of past color-based desegregation. The proposed settlement decree is not illegal, and it offers promise of more effective remedies in attacking a seemingly Gordian problem. . . .

The lengthy stipulation of settlement contained thirteen sections, one of which provided the foundation for the Black Staff Scholarship Program at Southmont State University:

> Public higher education institutions will, within 120 days, request adequate funding through the budgetary process to institute a staff development program to enable black staff members to obtain advanced degrees and become eligible for positions of higher salary and higher rank within all institutions of higher education in the state.

As implemented by state institutions, the Black Staff Scholarship Program provided special funding for staff development which included release time from work, conference attendance, course enrollment opportunities, training seminar participation, internships, etc.

To administer all actions specified in the stipulation of settlement, the court identified a Desegregation Monitoring Committee which would establish procedures for monitoring and reporting progress on the desegregation of public institutions under the court order. The committee had reviewed and approved Southmont's specific program.

APPENDIX B

A Note on Preferential Selection and U.S. Supreme Court Decisions

Title VII, Section 703A, of the 1964 Civil Rights Act states:

> It shall be unlawful employment practice for an employer (1) to fail or refuse to hire or to discharge any individual or otherwise to discriminate against any individual with respect to his compensation, terms, conditions, or privileges of employment because of such individual's race, color, religion, sex, or national origin.

Although this section of the Civil Rights Act, known as the equal employment opportunity (EEO) law, provided a legal foundation for addressing discriminatory practices of employers, the rather general language of the act resulted in varying interpretations by employers, employees, unions, federal enforcement agencies, and even the courts.

To implement Title VII many employers have developed affirmative action plans in which they establish goals and implement policies and procedures to assure employment opportunities for protected groups underrepresented in the workforce. In some cases, in the attempt to fulfill EEO obligations and commitments, employers have initiated programs that provide preferential treatment for underrepresented, protected groups.

The legality of preferential selection in support of affirmative action programs is highly controversial. The courts have not provided broad, clear guidelines on this issue, having tended to rule, instead, on relatively narrow grounds.

The U.S. Supreme Court has upheld preferential treatment of minorities when a union and company have voluntarily agreed to an affirmative action plan giving preference for admission to a training program to blacks (*Kaiser Aluminum v. Weber, 1979*). However, in a case involving the layoff of white teachers with more seniority than black faculty (to achieve a specified racial composition), the Supreme Court ruled that the affirmative action layoff plan of the school board and the teachers' union unlawfully violated the rights of white teachers *(Wygart v. Jackson Board of Education, 1986*). In a more recent case, the City of Birmingham and some black firefighters agreed to a consent decree which specified an affirmative action program to hire and promote firefighters. A group of white firefighters filed a racial discrimination suit charging reverse discrimination. In a 5 to 4 vote, the Supreme Court ruled that the white firefighters could raise a court challenge to the affirmative action decree (*Martin v. Wilks, 1989*). However, the 1991 Civil Rights Act revised the court's decision by greatly restricting legal challenges to consent decrees. The 1991 Civil Rights Act prevented challenges from parties to the suit who could have objected before the consent decree is entered or from those whose interests were represented by parties to the suit.

In ruling on cases brought before them, the courts have considered a number of factors: evidence of a history of discrimination by the employer, whether a voluntary affirmative action program had been agreed to by the union or employees and the employer, whether the challenged practice was the result of a court-ordered action, the severity of the impact of a preferential treatment on a nonminority party, and other issues. Observers expected the changing composition of the U.S. Supreme Court and forthcoming decisions on related cases to further define public policy in this evolving area of civil rights law.

REFERENCES

Mathis, Robert, and John Jackson. "Equal Employment." In *Personnel/Human Resource Management*. St. Paul, Minn.:West, 1991.

Twomey, David. "Title VII Court Ordered Remedies"; "Consent Decrees and Voluntary Affirmative Action Plans"; "Reverse Discrimination." In *Equal Employment Opportunity Law*, 2nd ed. Silver Spring, Md.: South-Western, 1990.

Study Questions

1. How did the problem in this case arise? Who is responsible for the current situation? What might he or she have done differently? What should Dean Frederick do now? What should Laura Adams do now?
2. What arguments can be made in favor of the university policies regarding employee enrollment in courses during working hours?
3. What recommendations, if any, would you make to university administrators regarding explanation of the appropriateness of the existing policies?
4. What arguments might be made opposing these policies and their implications for Laura Adams?
5. What recommendations, if any, would you make to university administrators to modify the existing policies?

Index

A

O

P

Q

R

S

Y

Z